The Socio___
Social Se___

Edited by
Michael Adler, Colin Bell,
Jochen Clasen and Adrian Sinfield

EDINBURGH
EDUCATION AND SOCIETY
SERIES

General Editor: Colin Bell

EDINBURGH UNIVERSITY PRESS

© The Contributors 1991
Edinburgh University Press
22 George Square, Edinburgh

Set in Linotron Palatino
by Koinonia Ltd, Bury, and
printed in Great Britain by
Page Bros Ltd, Norwich

British Library Cataloguing
 in Publication Data
The sociology of social security.
 – (Edinburgh education and
 society series
I. Adler, Michael II. Series
362.0941

ISBN 0 7486 0258 5 (cased)

CONTENTS

List of Contributors	v
1 Towards a sociology of social security MICHAEL ADLER, COLIN BELL, JOCHEN CLASEN AND ADRIAN SINFIELD	1
2 Expanding the concept of social justice: implications for social security BETTINA CASS	16
3 What is enough? New evidence on poverty allowing the definition of a minimum benefit PETER TOWNSEND AND DAVID GORDON	35
4 Alternative futures for social security ABRAHAM DORON	70
5 Lessons from the recession in Scandinavia 1975-1985 STAFFAN MARKLUND	80
6 Salami tactics and the Australian welfare state PETER TRAVERS	95
7 Irregular employment patterns and the loose net of social security: some findings on the West German development KARL HINRICHS	110
8 Pull-down effects, unemployment and interests in the welfare state HEINER GANSSMANN	128
9 Gender, class and the welfare state: the case of income security in Australia SHEILA SHAVER	145
10 The particularism of West German welfare capitalism: the case of women's social security STEPHAN LEIBFRIED AND ILONA OSTNER	164

11 Means-testing in Europe: a growing concern
   WIM VAN OORSCHOT AND JOHN SCHELL   187
12 The paradox of managing discretionary workers in social
   welfare policy
   MICHAEL LIPSKY   212
13 The social shaping of information technology: computerisation
   and the administration of social security
   MICHAEL ADLER AND ROY SAINSBURY   229
14 Interorganisational relations in the pursuit of social security
   BJØRN HVINDEN   249
15 Social injustice: the differential enforcement of tax and
   social security regulations
   DEE COOK   265

Bibliography 278
Index 306

CONTRIBUTORS

Michael Adler is a Senior Lecturer of Social Policy in the Department of Social Policy and Social Work, University of Edinburgh (United Kingdom)

Colin Bell is Professor of Sociology in the Department of Sociology, University of Edinburgh (United Kingdom)

Bettina Cass is Professor of Social Policy in the Department of Social Work and Social Policy, University of Sydney (Australia)

Jochen Clasen is a Postgraduate Research Student in the Department of Social Policy and Social Work and the Department of Sociology, University of Edinburgh (United Kingdom)

Dee Cook is a Lecturer in Criminology at the Centre for Criminology, University of Keele (United Kingdom)

Abraham Doron is Professor of Social Policy at the Paul Baerwald School of Social Work, Hebrew University of Jerusalem (Israel)

Heiner Ganssmann is Professor of Sociology at the Institute for Sociology, Free University of Berlin (Germany)

David Gordon is a Research Associate in the Department of Social Policy and Social Planning, University of Bristol (United Kingdom)

Karl Hinrichs is a Research Associate at the Centre of Social Policy, University of Bremen (Germany)

Bjørn Hvinden is a Research Fellow at the Institute of Applied Social Research (INAS), Oslo (Norway)

Stephan Leibfried is Professor of Social Policy and Social Law at the Centre for Social Policy, University of Bremen (Germany)

Michael Lipsky is Professor of Political Science in the Department of Political Science, Massachussets Institute of Technology, Cambridge, Massachussets (United States of America)

Staffan Marklund is Professor of Sociology and Social Policy, University of Umeå (Sweden)

Wim van Oorschot is a Lecturer in the Sociology of Social Security in the Department of Social Security Studies, Catholic University of Brabant, Tilburg (The Netherlands)

Ilona Ostner is Professor of Sociology at the Centre for Social Policy, University of Bremen (Germany)

Roy Sainsbury is a Research Fellow in the Social Policy Research Unit, University of York (United Kingdom)

John Schell is a Lecturer in Social Security Law in the Department of Social Security Studies, Catholic University of Brabant, Tilburg (The Netherlands)

Sheila Shaver is Deputy Director of the Social Policy Research Centre, University of New South Wales (Australia)

Adrian Sinfield is Professor of Social Policy in the Department of Social Policy and Social Work, University of Edinburgh (United Kingdom)

Peter Townsend is Professor of Social Policy in the Department of Social Policy and Social Planning, University of Bristol (United Kingdom)

Peter Travers is Senior Lecturer in Social Administation at the School of Social Sciences, Flinders University (Australia)

1
TOWARDS A SOCIOLOGY OF SOCIAL SECURITY[1]
MICHAEL ADLER, COLIN BELL, JOCHEN CLASEN AND ADRIAN SINFIELD

INTRODUCTION

A book entitled *The Sociology of Social Security* constitutes a challenge to those in both the sociological community and the social security industry who contend that sociology has contributed very little and has little to contribute to our understanding of social security. Although social security has attracted a certain amount of attention from lawyers and economists, it is true that social security has not, at least until recently, attracted much attention from sociologists. This is in spite of the centrality of social security for what has become known as the 'welfare state', its enormous significance for those who depend on it for their livelihood, its institutional and ideological salience, and the vigorous claims which are frequently made about its insidious effects on family life, work incentives, social cohesion and the moral order of society (for examples of such claims, see Herder-Dorneich, 1982; and Murray, 1984 and 1990).

Given the relative neglect of social security by sociologists, the decision to publish a book with this title calls for an explanation. This is in three parts. The first, which is a normative judgement, is that the failure of sociologists to take social security seriously is a matter of considerable regret since the manifest importance of social security as a social institution makes it a very rewarding subject for sociological inquiry. We believe that sociological analysis has a major contribution to make not only to an understanding of social security but also to attempts to formulate alternative scenarios for social security and to modify and reform existing social security provisions. The second, which is a statement of fact, is that there are encouraging signs that a sociology of social security is now beginning to emerge. The chapters which follow, all of which were originally presented at the Second International Seminar on the Sociology of Social Security which was held at the University of Edinburgh in July 1989, are testimony to this. The third, which may be no more than an aspiration on our part, is that the publication of this book may provide some further impetus to the development of a sociology of social security.

The First International Seminar on the Sociology of Social Security took place at the University of Bergen in June 1984. It was held under the joint auspices of the Research Committee on Poverty, Social Welfare and Social Policy of the International Sociological Association (ISA) and the International Social Security Association (ISSA). Several of the papers presented were subsequently published (see, for example, Sigg, 1985; *International Sociology*, 1986; and Sinfield, 1989) but efforts to publish a book based on the proceedings of the seminar proved unsuccessful. In introducing the five papers which were published as a group in *International Sociology*, Else Øyen, the organiser of the Bergen Seminar, referred to the very limited interest shown in the subject by the sociology profession generally, a view which had been expressed by many of the participants at the seminar (Øyen, 1986a). Nevertheless, the Bergen seminar was a very lively one and marked an important stage in the development of a sociology of social security.

The Second International Seminar, which was likewise held under the auspices of the ISA and ISSA, was financed by grants from the Department of Social Security (DSS), the Economic and Social Research Council (ESRC), the Social Policy Association (SPA) and the Faculty of Social Sciences at the University of Edinburgh. It was attended by some seventy participants from fifteen countries and the twenty-eight papers were organised into five streams dealing with the Objectives of Social Security, Social Security and the Labour Market, Social Security and Gender, the Administration of Social Security and the State of Social Security Research. It was a considerable success and the quality of the papers reflected the growing emergence of a distinctive sociology of social security in the intervening five years. As editors, we were faced with a difficult task as there were enough papers of sufficient quality and interest to fill more than one volume. Some papers could not be included because they were destined for publication elsewhere (for example, Hakim, 1989; Hennessy, 1990; Craig, 1991; and Korpi, 1991). Subject to this constraint, our selection of papers was guided both by the salience of the sociological analysis they embodied and by the general appeal of the issues they raised. The result is an unashamedly international collection of papers, reflecting the emergence of the sociology of social security on an international stage, rather than in any particular country. Most of the papers included in the book have been revised, some of them quite extensively, for publication.

The remainder of this introductory chapter is devoted to a discussion of three inter-related issues. First, we attempt to explain why it is that a sociology of social security has taken so long to develop, compared with the more rapid development of other fields of applied sociology and other orientations to social security. Secondly, we set out a possible agenda for the sociology of social security which seeks to identify the particular contribution which sociology can make to our understanding of social security. Finally, we indicate how the papers included in this book contribute to the sociology of social security.

THE NON-EMERGENCE OF THE SOCIOLOGY OF SOCIAL SECURITY

The fact that social security has attracted so little attention from sociologists calls for an explanation. This situation clearly applies to the United Kingdom but also applies, to a lesser or greater degree, elsewhere. A full explanation would have to account for the extent to which the sociology of social security has developed in different countries and would call for a comparative analysis of factors which have contributed to this situation. Unfortunately, we are not in a position to provide such an analysis, and focus instead on the absence of a developed sociology of social security in the United Kingdom. However, our account does have implications for other countries and it will be interesting to know how applicable it is to the position elsewhere.

Given the long history of research into the workings of the social security system in the United Kingdom, many overseas observers have expressed particular surprise that the sociology of social security is not more firmly established in this country. However, as Pinker (1971) and others have pointed out, there was an early bifurcation between the concerns of sociological theory and those of empirical social investigation. In the period leading up to the Second World War, social anthropology was the leading social science and, by comparison, sociology was very slow to gain a foothold in British universities. Moreover, the evolutionary concerns of major sociological figures, in particular Hobhouse and Ginsberg, did not embrace the empirical study of social institutions while the ameliorative concerns of the major figures in the tradtion of empirical social investigation, in particular Rowntree, Bowley and the Webbs, eschewed any serious interest in sociological theory. After the war, one figure (T H Marshall) did, for a while, succeed in straddling these two traditions but this did not prevent the establishment, first at the London School of Economics and then at Manchester, Birmingham and elsewhere, of separate Departments of Sociology and Social Administration (as Departments of Social Policy were then called). Associated with this departmental bifurcation was a division of academic labour. Subject areas associated with the major institutions of the welfare state, in particular housing, social work and, of course, social security, tended to be left by sociologists to social administration, and, with the specific exception of health, ceased to be the subject of much sociological research. While sociology developed middle-range theories which led to a spate of theoretically informed empirical studies, the primary influences on social administration were moral and political rather than theoretical. Thus, for more than 20 years, various strands of Fabian Socialism rather than any form of sociological theorising were the major formative influences on social administration and thus, it followed, on the study of social security.

Sociology and social administration were both given a considerable boost by the expansion of higher education in the 1960s and 1970s. Numerous professorial chairs were established, a large number of new departments were created and there was a substantial expansion in both undergraduate and postgraduate studies. Although Sociology Departments were able to fill most of their posts from applicants who had undertaken postgraduate research in the subject, the slower development of postgraduate research in social administration meant that Social Administration Departments were less likely to be able to do so. As a result, the establishment and growth of social administration resulted in the recruitment of a larger proportion of staff who had received their postgraduate training in other social science disciplines. They included a large number of staff who had trained as sociologists. Unfortunately, however, the problem-focussed character of social administration meant that this did not result in the development of a distinctively sociological orientation to the subject matter of social administration.

The growth of sociology in the 1970s and the 1980s led, on the one hand, to a diversification of theoretical and methodological concerns and, on the other, to the establishment of a large number of sociological specialisms (for an account of the recent development of British sociology, see Eldridge, 1980; and Abrams *et al.*, 1981). Likewise, the growth of social administration resulted not only in the decline of Fabian hegemony and its replacement by a substantial degree of ideological pluralism but also in the adoption of a more explicitly multi-disciplinary approach to policy and the development of a number of policy specialisms.

The development of sociological specialisms, like that of specialisms in other disciplines, can be explained in terms of a combination of internal and external factors. Internal factors include the theoretical predispositions and personal preferences of academic sociologists while among the external factors are the opportunities generated by professional training and research funding. In the United Kingdom, neither of these factors has played a facilitating role in the development of the sociology of social security. The professional training requirements for teachers, town planners, housing managers, health service administrators and community physicians, social workers and, latterly, business managers have encouraged, and in some cases been largely responsible for, the development of sociologies of education, planning, housing, medicine and health care, social work and organisations. By contrast, the fact that social security in the UK is administered by generalist civil servants whose only training is provided by their employers (the Department of Social Security) has meant that the first of the external factors has not been operative. At the same time, in stark contrast with the plurality of funding sources in most other fields of policy, the dominant role of the Department of Social Security (DSS) in funding and facilitating research on social security has resulted in an emphasis on research designed to meet the short-term needs of policy-makers rather than basic research. This point was made very clearly by the Head of the Social Security Research Branch in the DSS at the Edinburgh Seminar:

> The priorities of the DSS research programme, as with that of any government department, are set by Ministers' needs for policy development and policy evaluation rather than by the insights of the social sciences. It is very much a programme of applied research, directed to establishing the impact of particular policies, both in terms of measuring whether intended effects are being achieved, and in terms of identifying any unintended effects. The research programme of the DSS is not, therefore, organised according to social scientific concepts or theories about the relationship between social security programmes and other social and economic behaviour. (Hennessy, 1990, p. 125)

In consequence, the focus has been on contemporary, problem-related research rather than historical or comparative research, and on multi-disciplinary research rather than research from the perspective of a single discipline. Research on the economics of social security has been more actively promoted, but this is an exception which reflects the special role which economists play within government. Because of what is seen to be their intrinsically critical orientation, sociologists have not succeeded in gaining a comparable foothold in government. Thus, the second of the external factors has not been operative either.

It should now be clear why the sociology of social security has not developed as a distinct sociological specialism within the United Kingdom. A division of academic labour within higher education between Departments of Sociology and Departments of Social Policy in which social security was, in effect, assigned to the latter provided little or no internal encouragement. At the same time, the absence of any profession closely associated with the administration of social security or of any courses of professional education and training in which sociology could have been expected to play a part, together with the dominant role played by the DSS in funding and facilitating research and its marked preference for short-term, problem-orientated research from a multi-disciplinary perspective provided little or no external encouragement.

However, we must be careful not to overstate our case. As we have already pointed out, there are some encouraging signs that a sociology of social security is now beginning to emerge. In the United Kingdom one institution (the Department of Sociology at the University of Essex) has played a particularly important role in this development and the fact that Essex is one of the very few universities in the UK in which there is no departmental barrier between sociology and social policy and no rigid division of labour between the two disciplines which are taught in the same Department lends considerable support to our argument. Many of those who have contributed most to the development of a sociology of social security in the United Kingdom, including Townsend, Marsden,

Sinfield, Veit-Wilson, Land and Walker (for references to their work, see below) worked in the Essex Department on the major sociological study of poverty and the distribution of resources in the United Kingdom (Townsend, 1979) which began at the London School of Economics but was completed at Essex.

Our argument is also supported by the fact that elements of the sociology of social security appear to be more strongly developed in those countries, like Sweden and (West) Germany, where social policy is not a rival discipline to sociology and the subject matter of social policy is of fundamental concern to sociologists. In (West) Germany, for example, the 'Sektion Sozialpolitik' was founded in 1976 as a subgroup of the 'Deutsche Gesellschaft fur Soziologie' (German Sociological Association). The group has managed to increase its membership to around 350 individuals and institutions. Of course, not all of them have been working on problems relating to social security but interest in social security has grown considerably and appears to be quite strong. Increased sociological research on social security has been influenced by economic and social developments since the 1970s which affected the current and future income-security of a large part of the population. A growing number of one-parent families, the impact of demographic change especially with regard to the increasing number of retired people, high levels and long spells of unemployment and an increasing tendency towards a polarisation of the labour force into 'core' and 'periphery' sectors are some of the factors which seem to have induced more empirical and theoretical studies by sociologists on (West) German social security arrangements (see, for example, Leibfried and Tennstedt, 1985a; Bauer and Leibfried, 1986; and Opielka and Ostner, 1987). Other contributory factors appear to have been a growing awareness of criticism of the bureaucratic and often very unresponsive structure of the social security system and the ways in which it functioned, for example, to maintain the privileged position of male 'clients'. Furthermore, attempts were made to continue the debate on state theory which flourished in the 1970s and to transform it into a debate on welfare state theory (see Vobruba, 1983).

Additional elements of a sociology of social security appear to be developing rapidly in those countries like the Netherlands, where courses of professional training for social security staff have been established. It is here, in particular, that we see some signs for optimism. The professionalisation of areas of specialised occupational activity is likely, in time, to lead to the professionalisation of social security and to the introduction of courses of professional training for social security staff analogous to those which have been developed for other welfare professionals such as teachers, housing managers, health administrators and social workers.

The recent establishment in the United Kingdom of a set of agencies which are to assume responsibility for different facets of social security administration is likely to open up a wider debate about staff training. This could well lead to the introduction of externally taught and validated courses for social security staff. Sociological analysis could, and we believe should, make a major contribution to the professional training of social security staff. There is the danger that training could be reduced to a very limited service function 'detached from the mainstream of sociology' as happened in the early years of the sociology of education (Banks, 1971, p. 1) but given the strength of the sociology profession today, we believe that the establishment of such courses could provide an important external stimulus to the development of the sociology of social security as a sociological specialism in its own right.

A SOCIOLOGICAL PERSPECTIVE ON SOCIAL SECURITY

We have already asserted that sociological analysis has a major contribution to make to our understanding of social security. In assessing the particular contribution it could make, it is important to recognise that contemporary sociology is characterised by some quite fundamental disagreements of a theoretical and methodological nature. Depending on their conception of the discipline, different sociologists would undoubtedly express very different opinions.

In our view, the practice of sociology calls for the exercise of what C. Wright Mills (1959) has called a 'sociological imagination'. According to Giddens (1986) this entails three related forms of sensibility and involves the exercise of an historical, an anthropological and a critical imagination. An historical imagination is needed to grasp just how differently people live today compared with the way they lived in the relatively recent past while an anthropological imagination allows us to appreciate the diversity of modes of human existence which are experienced by people of different societies. Combining these two forms of imagination makes it possible to break free from what Giddens calls 'the straitjacket of thinking only in terms of the society we know in the here and now' (ibid., p. 28) and it is in this sense that the sociological imagination contributes to the critique of existing social institutions. However, it does not follow from this that sociologists are only interested in muckraking or the seamier side of life. On the contrary, sociologists are just as interested in the more mundane and everyday forms of behaviour. What it does mean is that sociology takes nothing for granted and that, while it is concerned to explain why things are as they are, it is also bound to point out how, and in what circumstances, they could be otherwise.

The conception of sociology we have just outlined carries with it a set of methodological prescriptions. Since sociology is concerned with the study of social institutions, which Giddens defines as 'socially reproduced modes of belief and behaviour' (ibid., p. 8), sociological analysis is likely to be historical and comparative and to adopt a critical stance even where these institutions are contemporary.

Having characterised sociology in this way, we are now in a position to identify the contributions which sociology could make to our understanding of social security. We do so under six headings:

1. A sociological definition of social security

Most studies of social security take for granted the definition of social security which appears in the relevant social legislation but one serious problem with this approach is that there are substantial national variations in the ways in which social security is defined. This creates problems for comparisons of any kind, whether these are historical or between different social security systems, and is, in any case, profoundly unsociological. A sociology of social security cannot be undertaken without an examination of alternative meanings of the concept of social security (George, 1968; and see also Berghman, 1991), both as an end-state or goal and as a means to achieving that end. Using the International Labour Office's definition of social security in terms of providing social protection for the population (International Labour Office, 1984), sociologists have analysed the social division of the means to social security into its public, fiscal and occupational components (see, for example, Sinfield, 1989). Such an approach provides a challenge to conventional administrative categories and allows the characterisation and comparison of public social security provisions and their functional alternatives, both historically and between different countries. There is also a need for closer study from a sociological perspective of the many terms employed in social security policy and practice – see, for example, the work on the social construction of poverty and benefit adequacy which are independent of administrative formulations (Townsend, 1979; and Veit-Wilson, 1987).

2. A sociological characterisation of social security systems

However it is defined, an adequate understanding of social security calls for an appropriate characterisation of its salient features. This may be in terms of the conventional administrative categories e.g. social insurance and social assistance, flat-rate and earnings related, contributory and non-contributory, means-tested and non-means-tested, but may also involve more sophisticated sociological characterisations such as those employed by Esping-Andersen (1990), who distinguishes three 'welfare-state regimes' in terms of their social security arrangements, and Leibfried (1990), who identifies four types of European welfare states in terms of the relationship between societal poverty, employment policy and social security. An appropriate characterisation is an essential prerequisite to sociological studies of the conditions which give rise to the emergence of different forms of social security and of the past, present and possible future development of social security provisions.

3. Comparative studies of the origins and development of social security systems

In a pioneering paper, Rys (1964) argued that sociologists had a particular contribution to make in identifying and examining the factors which led to the establishment and development of social security schemes. Recent developments, in the non-industrialised countries of the third world (Midgley, 1984) as well as in advanced industrialised societies, have led to a questioning of Rys' evolutionary model in which social assistance and other non-public forms of social security provision are seen as the precursors of social insurance. Valuable comparative research has been conducted, ranging from more qualitative studies involving a small number of countries and specific sections of social security provision (e.g. Heclo, 1974) to more quantitative methods including a large number of countries and the whole range of social insurance programmes (e.g. Alber, 1987). A more recent comparative study of the origins and development of social security systems is by Esping-Andersen (1990) although it is by no means clear that he has provided a definitive account (for a critique, see Castles and Mitchell, 1990). Studies of this type can be prospective as well as retrospective in that they can also contemplate alternative scenarios for social security (e.g. basic income proposals) and seek to identify the social preconditions for their emergence. A useful overview of comparative research on the origins and development of social policy, including social security, can be found in Wilensky et al., 1987.

4. Macro-sociological studies of the impact of social security on social stratification

Social security provisions are often introduced in response to socially constructed states of need and dependency but their impact on the conditions they are intended to ameliorate is often a great deal more complex. Sociological studies (e.g. Townsend, 1979), have shown that means testing can actually add further dimensions of deprivation to those already experienced by people with low incomes or no incomes at all. Similarly, Land (1976 and 1983) in the United Kingdom, Riedmüller and Kickbusch (1982) in (West) Germany and Pateman (1988a) in Australia have shown how social security provisions can replicate and magnify gender dependencies within the household, while Walker (1980) has demonstrated how social security provisions for the elderly replicate and magnify inequalities in the labour market. Studies of this kind can be particularly insightful if they involve comparisons between different types of social security provisions or between social security and other redistributive mechanisms such as income tax (e.g. Krätke, 1987). In this way, sociological studies can explore the effects of social security on the changing nature of social stratification and on various forms of socially reproduced inequalities in society. This, in turn, can shed new light on theoretical debates on sociologically constructed concepts of class (e.g. Lepsius, 1979; Krätke, 1985) and gender in relation to the (welfare) state.

5. *Micro-sociological studies of the experience of social security*

Macro-sociological assessments of the impact of social security on social stratification call for, and indeed need to be based on, micro-sociological studies of what it means to be a recipient of social security and of what effects this has on how people see themselves, on their attitudes and on their behaviour (good examples are Marsden, 1973; and Townsend, 1979). It is not necessarily easy to distinguish people's responses to their own needs and circumstances – e.g. to the fact that they may be poor, unemployed, disabled or in debt – from their experience of claiming social security, but the attempt should not be abandoned for this reason. Different forms of social security may be variously experienced as status-demeaning or status-enhancing and the experience of social security may or may not have an effect on attitudes and behaviour. Thus, it may or may not affect attitudes to work, to financial support and care within the household, to other recipients of social security in similar circumstances and, more generally, towards society and the state. Sociological studies have an important role to play in elucidating these meanings and assessing their significance.

6. *Sociological studies of the administration of social security*

At the Bergen Seminar, Adler (1985) referred to the paucity of sociological research on the administration of social security. In the United Kingdom this can be explained in terms of the interplay between several of the internal and external factors referred to above. As a result, there has probably been less sociological research on the administration of social security in the United Kingdom than on the administration of potentially much more contentious areas of public administration, such as the police or prisons. Moreover, it is significant that one of the most widely cited sources (Hill, 1969) did not result from a piece of empirical research but drew instead on the author's own experience as a social security officer.

With one or two exceptions (such as Catrice-Lorey, 1980 in France and Mashaw, 1983 in the United States of America), there appears to have been very little research on the administration of social security in other countries. However, the enormous importance of social security to the lives and livelihoods of those who depend on it, the vast scale of its activities and the considerable power which is vested in its officials calls for a large and ambitious programme of sociological research into routine (and not so routine) forms of administrative decision-making, and into the relationships between the Department, its clientele and other organisations with which it is in contact. In this area, as in others, theoretically informed studies, such as Mashaw's innovative study of routine administrative decision-making in the United States Disability Insurance scheme, which brought together the normative concerns of administrative law with the more positive concerns of organisational sociology (Mashaw, 1983), would be particularly useful. The value of historical research is demonstrated by

Cates' (1983) study of the part played by the administrative leadership in promoting a particular ideology and normative structure during the first twenty years of the United States Social Security programme.

AN OUTLINE OF THE BOOK

In the final part of this introduction, we consider the contribution of the chapters which follow to the development of the sociology of social security. We are very conscious that there are some obvious gaps in the coverage which we hope can be remedied in future volumes. In particular, the countries considered are confined to western market economies – all are members of the Organisation of Economic Co-operation and Development (OECD) with no countries from the Third World or from the currently changing societies of Eastern Europe and the USSR.

The first five papers examine conceptual and analytical issues which have often been neglected in the examination of specific social security systems. In developing a theory of social justice for the assessment of proposals for social security reform, Bettina Cass engages with philosophical studies of justice, drawing particularly on the work of John Rawls and subsequent developments and critiques of his approach. She then applies the theory of distributive justice to examining three very distinct models of social security reform. Her chapter demonstrates the value of establishing an explicit normative framework against which both the objectives (or ends) and the means of social security can be evaluated. It also indicates the importance of locating any model for reform and any assessment of it in a social, political and economic context. Her analysis reveals the strength, from both a theoretical and a policy perspective, of examining any social security proposal as part of a broader policy package particularly including labour market strategies.

The need to establish explicit independent and scientific criteria against which the workings of any elements of a social security system can be judged is also demonstrated by Peter Townsend and David Gordon in their examination of alternative measures of the adequacy of the benefit level required to keep people out of poverty. They consider both research attempts to define and measure poverty and views from a cross-section of the population of what is thought to be minimally adequate. Exploiting new evidence from a large London study, they put forward a 'threshold' of income necessary to escape poverty which is significantly above current rates of benefit. In consequence, particular attention is given to the implications of employing more or less restrictive conceptualisations and operational definitions of poverty and need for the setting and assessing of benefit levels.

The importance of the societal context in understanding and attempting to predict the long term changing structure and priorities of social security systems is a central element of Chapter 4. Three possible alternative futures for the public service welfare state are considered by

Abraham Doron: the basic maintenance of the existing structure of public provision, a shift towards market dominance in the provision of services and benefits with a consequential transfer from the state to both family and market, and a greater reliance on the growth of employment-based private welfare states on either the American or Japanese model. In his analysis of these three scenarios, he examines both the preconditions for significant shifts in these different directions and discusses the implications for individuals and the wider society of such changes.

In the following chapter, Staffan Marklund examines the different ways in which the social security systems of the four Nordic countries have responded to economic stagnation and recession since the early 1970s. There is a tendency for analysts – particularly outside Scandinavia – to treat the separate countries as some social-democratic welfare state entity. By contrast, Marklund demonstrates that there is much to be learnt about the flexibility and robustness of social security systems from a detailed study of the differing impact of political and economic changes upon them in four relatively similar countries. Systems with wider coverage and higher benefits seemed more resistant to short-term crises and financial pressures for change. His examination reveals the salience of differences in both the class structure and the political environment. The significance of individuals' labour market value and the weakness and vulnerability of those outside the labour market emerge particularly clearly.

Peter Travers, in Chapter 6, uses a historical and political analysis of the development of social security in Australia to assess the thesis of 'creeping universalism' in the selective structure of the Australian welfare state put forward by Robert Goodin and Julian Le Grand in their analysis of 'middle class capture' (1987). In tracing the frequently shifting directions of policy changes in relation to income support for older people, he raises significant questions about the adequacy of conventional classifications of countries by the characteristics of their benefit systems – in this case the non-contributory structure of the Australian system.

The relationship between inequalities in the labour market and the impact of social security systems, mitigating, replicating or magnifying them are examined in Chapters 7 and 8. Karl Hinrichs continues a debate which questions the 'wage-labour centered' (Vobruba, 1990) structure of (West) German social policy where social security provisions are predominantly granted to those in 'standard employment relationships', i.e. to full-time workers with regulated and relatively stable career patterns. Hinrichs examines in detail whether and how far an erosion of the standard employment relationship has become an empirical reality. He concludes that, while the number of people employed on a 'traditional' basis has been stable, almost all increase in employment since the 1970s has been in the area of irregular jobs. The author remains doubtful whether a guaranteed minimum income could overcome the polarisation in the labour force, and instead proposes to extend existing social security regulations to areas beyond the traditional standard employment relationship in order to allow the increase of 'deviations from a linear full-time career' in a positive way.

Heiner Ganssmann looks at social security programmes and asks whether they can contribute to halting the trend towards a growing social marginalisation of the unemployed. He attempts to locate possible 'pull-down' effects in the welfare state which could give currently employed workers reasons for solidarity with their unemployed counterparts on 'rational grounds'. Unemployment insurance provisions, for example, can be perceived as a kind of 'side contract' between the employed and the unemployed, where the former pay the latter for not offering their labour power for lower than the going rate and thus preventing a downward spiral which would worsen the position of the whole labour force. Applying a rational choice, or game theoretical, framework, the author points out that a (re)construction of interests, although theoretically problematic, can be a 'useful step of analysis', if extended to the subsequent attempt to explain discrepancies between observable actions carried out by agents and 'rational' interests as assumed by social scientists.

In Chapters 9 and 10, two particular social security systems are examined with regard to their impact on and implications for the situation of women. Sheila Shaver takes a fresh look at theoretical concepts concerning the relationship between gender, class and the welfare state. She stresses that the working, function and impact of social security systems, as key institutions of welfare states, cannot sufficiently be understood as either 'patriarchal' or 'straightforwardly capitalist'. While social security arrangements in most countries assume and reinforce a sexual division of labour, the historical developments and national differences have to be taken into account in order to go beyond a purely functional account of the welfare state, which can demonstrate the limits of state intervention but fails to explain the determination of specific institutional arrangements. Shaver's contribution to this volume is an attempt to 'rework the conceptual triangle of gender, class and the state' by examining the Australian social security system.

Stephan Leibfried and Ilona Ostner also stress the need to analyse the impact and function of social security arrangements in relation to national traditions, historical developments and political struggles. All these contribute to specific national types of 'welfare mix', i.e. mix of benefits and services provided by the state, the market and the family. In discussing the particular welfare mix in (West) Germany, Leibfried and Ostner demonstrate the comparatively strong traditional orientation to services provided by women within families at the same time as the access to, and levels of, social security benefits are largely determined by contribution criteria and individual earnings from employment – and there is no reason to believe that this will be different in a unified Germany. The authors conclude that categorisation of different welfare state 'types' or 'regimes' has to take account of gender imbalances which themselves are affected by national social security arrangements and the combination of the welfare mix in different countries.

The last five papers all deal with aspects of administration. Chapter 11 focuses on mean-testing. Van Oorschot and Schell argue that the central concerns of the sociology of social security are to assess the ways in which social security institutions balance individual and collective interests, and the extent to which they contribute to social integration or give rise to social exclusion. Although they concede that means-testing has many attractions, they draw attention to its dysfunctional consequences for society and conclude that, as an administrative mechanism, means-testing is seriously deficient in that it ruptures the bond between the individual and society and thereby undermines social integration. They also identify the social and political factors which have led to an increase in mean-testing in five of the six European countries they studied (the single exception is Belgium) and speculate on the implications of this development, which runs counter to the trend identified by Rys (1964) away from means-tested social assistance to non-means-tested social insurance.

Chapter 12 focuses on discretion. Michael Lipsky argues that front-line staff in social welfare institutions, who interact with and make decisions about individual members of the public, need to exercise a certain amount of discretion and that the problem for higher-level officials therefore becomes that of influencing their behaviour without directly challenging their discretion. He uses the comparative method to compare two instances in which higher-level officials sought to restrict the discretionary behaviour of front-line staff – Aid to Families with Dependent Children (AFDC) and the Social Security Disability Insurance (SSDI) scheme – with one instance in which they sought to expand it – the Employment Training (ET) Choices programme run by the Massachusetts Department of Public Welfare. Although the cases are not strictly comparable, Lipsky identifies their common features and draws some general conclusions about the circumstances in which attempts to influence the exercise of discretion are most likely to succeed.

In Chapter 13, Michael Adler and Roy Sainsbury analyse the Operational Strategy, the massive programme to computerise the entire social security system in the United Kingdom, by considering the ways in which internal and external forces have contributed to its development,and examine the opportunities for organisational innovation which this has both opened up and foreclosed. Using an analytical framework derived from Jerry Mashaw's study of the SSDI scheme in the United States (Mashaw, 1983), they question the assumption that computerisation has merely led to improvements in administrative efficiency, arguing instead that the Operational Strategy has promoted a particular (bureaucratic) view of what good administration comprises. They also present the results of a consultative exercise which suggests that, although those who were consulted supported improvements in bureaucratic efficiency, they did not want a more bureaucratised service and would have preferred a different balance between bureaucratic, professional and juridical values.

In the following chapter, Chapter 14, Bjørn Hvinden outlines an analytical framework for studying inter-organisational relations which is based on the nature of dependency relations between pairs of organisations in respect of the tasks they carry out. This framework provides a good basis for comparative research and Hvinden uses it to compare the relations between, first, social security and social services departments and, second, between social security and vocational rehabilitation services in Scotland and Norway. In so doing, he provides an explanation for differences in observed relations between organisational units at the local level in terms of divergent institutional arrangements and legal frameworks.

In the final chapter, Dee Cook compares the differential responses to supplementary benefit (social assistance) fraud and tax evasion, which she regards as objectively similar economic crimes. Although tax evasion is on a much larger scale than social security fraud, far more resources are directed towards investigating the latter than the former. Likewise, the enforcement strategies for the latter are stricter and the penalties awarded greater. Cook explains these 'paradoxes' in terms of three inter-related considerations: the historical and ideological construction of taxpayers as 'givers' to the State and welfare claimants as 'takers' from it; the fact that tax payers are seen as 'economic successes' while claimants are seen as 'economic failures'; and the fact that taxpayers are seen to embody the alleged virtues of the 'enterprise culture' while claimants embody the evils of the 'benefits culture'. In so doing, she draws attention to the injustices which result from these practices.

NOTES

1. The editors wish to gratefully acknowledge the assistance they received from Catherine Donovan, Sarah Irwin, Linda Jackson and Zhengwei Wei during the conference and throughout the process of producing this book.

2
EXPANDING THE CONCEPT OF SOCIAL JUSTICE: IMPLICATIONS FOR SOCIAL SECURITY
BETTINA CASS

INTRODUCTION

This chapter has three inter-related objectives: to develop a theory of social justice and consider its usefulness in guiding and evaluating current debates in social security reform; to explore the merits and shortcomings of three major models of social security reform which are currently the subject of advocacy; and finally to contribute to debates about social security reform in Australia and similar Anglophone countries. I begin with John Rawls' conception of social justice as a useful starting point for reconstructing ideas about distributive justice applicable to a wider range of allocative institutions than those envisaged in the original view of 'justice as welfare'.

According to Rawls:

> A set of principles is required for choosing among the various social arrangements which determine the division of advantages and for underwriting an agreement on the proper distributive shares. Those principles are the principles of social justice: they provide ways of assigning rights and duties in the basic institutions of society and they define the appropriate distribution of the benefits and burdens of social co-operation. (Rawls, 1972, p. 4)

Michael Walzer's contribution to the debate claims that there are different spheres of justice which ought to be kept distinct. Justice has to do with the distribution of resources, and different considerations apply according to the type of resource in question; there is no one set of criteria which covers the distribution of very different types of resources and goods. For example, if the principle of *merit* is applied in the labour market to the distribution of rewards, then applying it also in the tax/transfer system leads to the accumulation of disadvantage on the one hand and the accumulation of advantage on the other. This exacerbates inequality and domination by the advantaged. Therefore by using different criteria of distribution in different spheres, a system of redress can be established in certain spheres to mitigate inequalities generated in others (Walzer, 1983).

However, this does not mean that social justice principles should operate only in some spheres and not in others, e.g. in welfare but not in the remuneration for work. According to Campbell (1988) it is essential to bring together the three major areas in which social justice must operate: in remuneration for employment, in welfare and in the administration of law. I would add also in gender relationships in the sphere of private life within household and family, and in public life in market processes and political organisation.

Theories of social justice are developments of social contract models of the legitimation of power and citizenship within the authority of the modern capitalist state. Social contract models had their beginnings in the mid-seventeenth and eighteenth centuries, with the growth of capitalism and of the economic and political power of the centralised state, in the theories of Hobbes, Locke and Rousseau. Such models assume an individualistic view of society, according to which persons are the sources of their own political rights and duties, and embody the liberal view that encroachment on the freedom of such individuals requires justification. Political societies are seen as a form of association whose object is to secure the interests of their members in a way which is consistent with the intrinsic equal autonomy of all.

To expand the concept of social justice beyond its liberal beginnings, while developing the principles of freedom and autonomy, it is useful to outline a set of objectives which denote the intended outcomes of institutions guided by social justice principles.

As a working model, the objectives of social justice principles applied to the project of reforming social security policies and labour market policies would include:

1. *Protection of the vulnerable* by systematically reducing inequalities in the distribution of income and resources (Goodin, 1985)
2. *Provision of the conditions for Autonomy*, i.e. to provide the conditions for full social, economic and political participation (Weale, 1983; Gorz, 1985)
3. *Provision of the conditions for Social as well as Political citizenship to be enforced, protected and legitimated* (Korpi, 1989)

In understanding the principle of 'protecting the vulnerable' it must be remembered that vulnerability is not an inherent condition, but a creation of economic, social, political and gender inequalities. Protection of the vulnerable then requires the provision of a Basic Income Guarantee and the conditions to live in dignity (Jordan, 1988). But the objective must go further to provide the conditions which make people less vulnerable; to provide the opportunities, resources and access to services which structurally reduce the incidence, severity and duration of vulnerability, and the causes of vulnerability.

'Autonomy' is defined as freedom to participate, which requires provision of the opportunities and the resources to participate in economic, social and political life.

'Social citizenship' means the creation of social institutions which treat, value, reward and include individuals not only as political citizens (i.e. in their relationship to state processes of representation, participation and civil rights) and not only as economic actors in their relationship to the market, but also as social participants, engaged in a range of valued activities (e.g. caring work in family, household and community) and rewarded as such in the allocation of resources.

To begin the discussion of institutional arrangements which might bear social justice principles, I start with Rawls' concept of 'justice as fairness' in the distribution of the benefits and burdens of social co-operation, which depends upon the following pre-conditions:
- an effectively regulated public conception of justice in which the rules are known, accepted as reasonable and largely followed; i.e., the conception of justice is accepted as fair and is accorded legitimacy
- citizens are seen as having mutually enforceable, free and equal rights to demand a fair share of the common pool of resources.

A public conception of social justice requires that the rules of social justice be universal, general, public and capable of ordering social claims with finality and comprehensiveness.

Principles of Allocation

According to Rawls there are two basic steps in establishing a just system of distribution:

1. Certain primary goods must be provided as of right and equally to all citizens. These are goods which provide the background conditions and resources necessary for exercising and developing human capacities, skills and talents as autonomous individuals:
- basic liberties (thought, speech, conscience, freedom of movement)
- free choice of occupation
- free capacity to receive fair shares of income and wealth. These are not only material resources to guarantee survival, but the guarantees of freedoms to pursue a human life as a morally autonomous individual.

2. Following the universal provision of basic liberties and basic resources (including income, health care and shelter) certain principles of allocation are set down to guide the further distribution of benefits. In the words of Rawls' 'Difference Principle':

> social and economic inequalities are to be arranged so that they are both (a) to the greatest benefit of the least advantaged and (b) attached to offices and positions open to all under conditions of fair equality of opportunity. (Rawls, 1972, p. 83)

To summarise at this point the Rawlsian prescription for social arrangements based on principles of social justice: the *first step* is to maximise basic liberties and ensure that these resources are distributed equally to all citizens. The *second step* is that the unequal distribution of other goods may be introduced, if this has the effect of maximising the position of the worst off.

JUSTICE AS WELFARE

'Justice as welfare' implies that social justice has inescapable ties to the treatment accorded to those who fare worst in the prevailing social and economic arrangements, legitimising redistribution and alleviating or removing the conditions which create oppression, poverty and exploitation. This does not imply that 'need' must be the prime criterion within this conception of justice, but an approach which does not address adequately the problem of what constitutes fair treatment for the deprived cannot be considered an acceptable conception of social justice. The Rawlsian conception of social justice therefore contains elements of:

1. A *rights based* approach to the distribution of primary goods (freedom, autonomy, satisfaction of basic needs) based on concepts of equality.
2. A *needs-based* approach to the distribution of income, resources, opportunities so as to redress inequalities generated by other social and economic institutions. In this regard the 'Difference Principle' stipulates criteria of redress, justifying unequal treatment to benefit the disadvantaged.

A full statement of such a system of social justice would therefore demand that disadvantaged groups be accorded full and equal political rights and the material assistance necessary to develop their abilities to the same extent as those who are not disadvantaged, i.e. equality of opportunity, equal access to education and provision of a basic income guarantee. The subsequent economic system is then regulated so that the benefits of increased wealth improve the circumstances of the disadvantaged, through a progressive tax system, the provision of an *adequate* basic income and a network of publicly provided services, i.e. through state-organised redistribution of resources.

SOCIAL DEMOCRATIC CRITIQUE OF REDISTRIBUTIVE MODELS OF SOCIAL JUSTICE

A social democratic critique of redistributive models of social justice argues that the Rawlsian conception of social justice depends on an equal distribution of political rights, but is not nearly as vigorous in recommending greater equality of economic resources. In fact, it takes an unequal market as given (Lukes, 1977; Campbell, 1988). Such liberal contract theories do provide strong justifications for welfare state *redistributive justice* (e.g. through income support, an equitable tax system, health and welfare services) but they leave untouched an examination of the principles underlying the primary distribution of resources namely the principles underlying:

- access to paid employment
- security of paid employment
- rewards from paid employment
- access to property and wealth.

In liberal conceptions of social justice the primary allocation of income and wealth is taken as given. Such an assumption enables principles of market efficiency, rather than equity, to be seen as desirable and necessary in the functioning of markets. As Campbell (1988) notes, fundamental conflicts can be established between social justice in redistribution and the unjust workings of markets which promote inequitable outcomes. In such circumstances redistributive justice is essential, but it will be only partially effective in improving the circumstances of the most disadvantaged. In fact, it is unlikely to provide the conditions for full autonomy, i.e. full participation in political, social and economic life.

A social democratic position is summed up in the aphorism 'distribution according to need, contribution according to ability'.

What are the needs to be satisfied?
- the basic material needs of human survival
- the need to participate with autonomy, exercise rationality and develop capacities (which is the liberal conception of human needs)
- the need to express creativity and sociability (a communitarian conception of human needs). This conception emphasises that human needs include not only the capacity to be economically active, but also to participate creatively in the social life of the community in a range of non-market spheres (Gorz, 1985).

A social democratic approach to social justice has a Rawlsian base in concentrating on the meeting of basic needs, but gives much more vigorous support to redistributive allocations which benefit the least advantaged. The concept of what constitutes need is a wider one; not just the need to have basic freedoms and liberties protected and a 'basic income' and services provided, but the provision of resources and conditions to participate fully in all aspects of social and economic life as an autonomous, creative and sociable individual.

A FEMINIST CRITIQUE OF THE RAWLSIAN CONTRACT THEORY OF REDISTRIBUTIVE JUSTICE

A withering critique of the contractarian basis of Rawls' theory of justice is provided in Carol Pateman's general critique of contract theories of social organisation and their underlying moral principles (Pateman, 1988b). She demonstrates convincingly that Rawls' fiction of the 'original position' of individuals behind the 'veil of ignorance' is based on a conception of the representative individual as 'pure reason', without body, or sex. In fact both sexes are subsumed within a form of masculine pure reason, within men who are 'heads of families' representing their wives and children. Indeed, the individual whose vision is obscured behind the veil of ignorance is not permitted to know:

> his place in society, his class position or social status; nor does he know his fortune in the distribution of natural assets and abilities, his intelligence and strength, and the like. Nor, again, does anyone know his conception of the good, the particulars of his rational plan

of life, or even the special features of his psychology, such as his aversion to risk or liability to optimism or pessimism. More than this, I assume that the parties do not know the particular circumstances of their own society. (Rawls, 1972, p. 137)

The overwhelming *silence*, of course, is whether or not the individual is permitted to know 'his' sex, or the gender order of 'his' society, or the patterns and intersections of public and private life, or sex and gender relations and the distribution of resources and power based upon it. It is not my purpose in this chapter to mount a feminist critique of a veil of ignorance so impermeable (or perhaps so incomplete?) that it does not even give us the chance not to know the shape and properties and purposes of our bodies or the gender order of our society. Indeed, what Rawls' 'original position' infers is that sex and gender relations do not even matter in the eventual configuration of institutions and principles which are devised.

But the issue is a crucial one for reconstructing theories of social justice which break with the liberal contractarian conventions and which acknowledge the central position of sex and gender differences for the purpose of constructing allocative institutions which redress inequalities. For redistributive justice has the onerous responsibility of redressing not only the inequalities of income and power generated by the market, but also the inequalities of income and power generated by the gender order.

Accepting the social democratic and the feminist critiques of liberal conceptions of social justice, an expanded conception of *distributive justice* must:

- redefine and reconstruct the principles of justice and apply them in the labour market and in the workplace, e.g. in wage fixation and income distribution, in entry into secure jobs, anti-discrimination and equal opportunity provisions, opportunities for education and training which enhance life-time earnings capacity.
- redefine and reconstruct the principles of justice and apply them to the relationship between men and women in the public sphere (i.e. in employment and in citizen/state relations) and in the private sphere (e.g. in protection from violence, in provision of the conditions to receive an independent income, in dismantling of the conditions of dependency, in making a radical re-appraisal of the value of caring work carried out outside of the market and in reshaping those public policies which perpetuate undemocratic distributions of paid and unpaid work).

To bring these theoretical considerations to bear on the project of social security reform, it is clear that provision of a Basic Income Guarantee alone and a progressive tax system, even a universal health care system and universal access to education, will have very little impact on the *relative position* of the least advantaged, if they remain in low income groups throughout most of their lives; if their earnings capacity and educational qualifications remain low; if they have access only to relatively insecure and low paid jobs; if their access to employment is impeded by discriminatory employment practices; if they carry out unpaid caring work in the household for a significant part of their adult lives in a society where material rewards are distributed according to market activity; if they find their social participation highly constrained and limited by lack of material resources; if they live in a community or locality where distance, diminished labour market opportunities and inadequate services (transport, childcare, education and training) make both social and economic participation very difficult, if not impossible.

APPLYING THE PRINCIPLES OF DISTRIBUTIVE JUSTICE

The concerns of this chapter begin and end with an exploration of the ethical bases and possibilities for social security reform in Australia, but these concerns are relevant also to debates in other advanced industrial anglophone countries (Britain, United States and New Zealand in particular). It has been noted by Leibfried that the so-called 'Anglo-Saxon' type of liberal welfare state (into which category he places Britain and the United States) is characterised by a residual 'welfare regime' in which the welfare state acts as 'compensator of the last resort'. This is contrasted with the social democratic Scandinavian 'welfare regime' characterised by full employment, where the welfare state is 'employer of the first resort' and the right to employment is backed up by an institutionalised concept of social citizenship embedded in social security arrangements (Leibfried, 1990). Australia, whilst not included in the original classification, nevertheless fits well into the Anglo-Saxon category. This discussion of models for reform of both social security and labour market policies has an Australian focus, but wider applicability to similar welfare regimes.

In applying a much-expanded concept of social justice to the project of social security reform, I start from the premise that it is possible to restructure social security, labour market and community service policies and incomes policy so as to reduce inequality and prevent poverty. This is predicated in the first instance on ethical principles concerned with redistribution through the tax/benefit system to protect the vulnerable, i.e. those groups rendered vulnerable by age, gender, ill health, disability, unemployment, and by the obligation to care for other vulnerable people. Essentially these are groups excluded from labour market participation by their stage in life, by the state of their health and employment capacities, by class disadvantages, by the state of the labour market and by discriminatory processes. In another category are those who are excluded from paid work as result of a private obligation to care for others who depend upon them.

However, this project goes further than the arena of redistribution and examines government interventions into labour markets and the organisation of the conditions of employment which provide stronger guarantees of social citizenship that are embedded in welfare regimes characterised predominantly by tax/benefit redistribution. Where the principles of redistribution are residual and conditional on coalitions of political support likely to change as governments change, the project of 'protecting the vulnerable' runs a considerable risk of being conflated with a narrowly defined concept of need, one which can be used to legitimate withdrawal of benefits from those whose needs are officially deemed to be less great or less deserving. This risk has been particularly strong in the anglophone welfare states since the recessionary periods commencing in the mid 1970s, when the growing hegemony of 'market rationality' in economic policy placed considerable emphasis on reducing social expenditure as a proportion of gross domestic product and reducing the sphere of direct government provision of services.

Moving beyond residualism and its inherent risks, the object of protecting the vulnerable requires not only an emphasis on social security arrangements but also on the distribution of resources which promote autonomy. A welfare regime institutionalising autonomy would provide the material conditions for full participation in economic activity as a basis of social citizenship, i.e. enshrine 'full employment' in economic and social policy with the associated education, training and employment programmes (Korpi, 1989). The question remains, however; how would such a regime, predicated on the right to *paid* work, accord value to caring work carried out outside of market arrangements and market systems of remuneration?

REFORMING LABOUR MARKET PROCESSES AND OUTCOMES

Moving to current political processes and the collective political actors who are carrying the debate about welfare state reform, it is clear that to expect the tax/benefit system to be the major bearer of principles of justice is to sit on the margins of a social democratic tradition. The onset of recessionary periods in most of the capitalist welfare states since the mid 1970s, associated with high rates of unemployment and joblessness, high rates of long-term unemployment whose share of all unemployment has not been reduced significantly even as employment growth has increased, has been accompanied by the imposition of tight fiscal restraint by most governments (OECD, 1988b and 1989a). These marked changes from the economic and social policy 'certainties' of the post-war capital/labour 'settlement' with its associated variants of Keynesian welfare regimes in the anglophone countries have precipitated a differently framed welfare debate, promulgating a broader conception of distributive justice in response to what is perceived as the crisis of legitimacy in welfare state provision and effectiveness (Mishra, 1984a; Rowthorn, 1989; Saunders, 1987d).

Analyses of corporatism formulated in relation to those welfare states with developed social democratic institutions, predominantly based on studies of welfare regimes in the Scandinavian countries, identify the importance of vigorous government intervention into the labour market to achieve public and private sector employment growth and to reduce unemployment (Rowthorn, 1989; Korpi, 1989; Esping-Andersen, 1985). These studies emphasise the significance of public policies institutionalising 'full employment', with the associated public investment in education and active labour market programmes as the old industrial structures of capitalism change and skills are made redundant. Also identified is the critical role of trade union activity in reducing high levels of income inequality (for example, through the Swedish 'solidaristic wages policy'), to improve the position of low wage earners and to remove the wage differential between male and female employees (Esping-Andersen, 1985; Borchorst and Siim, 1987). Such labour market interventions are seen as central to social justice principles, even more likely than tax/benefit redistribution to protect social citizenship, to prevent marginality and exclusion and the associated construction of high rates of poverty and social divisiveness (Esping-Andersen, 1985; Korpi, 1989).

Leibfried's characterisation of the Scandinavian welfare regime as one in which the state is 'employer of first resort' and where the right to work underpins social citizenship, stands in marked contrast to those anglophone welfare regimes where neither the right to paid work nor the right to income support are institutionalised, and where the state is 'compensator of last resort'. This categorisation points to the clear dangers of pursuing only the right to social security and income support as the key to reform, as if the market could be left to embody only efficiency principles while the tax/benefit system must bear the full burden of 'compensation'.

As Flora Gill (1989) has shown in the Australian context using the example of wage fixation, the theoretical dichotomy between equity and efficiency in the market is invalid, because efficiency can be defined only with reference to desired ends. The definition of such ends might well include the breaking down of labour market segmentation and reduction of wage inequalities since both rigid segmentation and high wage inequalities contribute to inefficiencies in labour market functioning. Further, Bob Rowthorn (1989) has demonstrated in a cross-national study of the major OECD countries the various ways in which lower wage dispersions (i.e. reduced income inequality), a more generous social security system and in particular high employment rates interact to produce more egalitarian outcomes in the Swedish and Norwegian welfare states. It would appear that a dual strategy is required to pursue justice through both tax/benefit redistribution and through primary distribution from waged work, using public investment and government regulation to increase public and private sector job growth, dismantle the impediments to skills acquisition which confront those who would otherwise enter and remain in the secondary labour market and to improve the relative income position of the low paid. To do otherwise is to mount relatively unwinnable campaigns on the transfer side alone, expecting that social security and welfare will continue to do battle against the inequalities which unregulated markets generate. The clearest example of this would be to mount a campaign to improve the adequacy of benefit payments in a period of high levels of unemployment and joblessness, when a considerably greater proportion of people of workforce age are being forced into dependency on welfare benefits, without also claiming the right to paid work and the provision of those labour market programs and job creation measures required to support such a claim.

Analyses by Mishra (1984a), Esping-Anderen (1985), Korpi (1989) and Cameron (1984) show that such a dual strategy requires the development of egalitarian corporatist institutions, in which a well organised and strong labour movement is prepared to negotiate and has the institutionalised power to negotiate not only about the market wage and industrial conditions, but about training and skills acquisition and responses to unemployment. A further condition is a willingness of government and the unions to integrate incomes policy and social wage provisions; to use public policies to provide net advances in living standards through a concerted effort to reduce unemployment; to provide strong job growth, education and training programmes, childcare provisions, adequate levels of social security payments and other forms of income support and to introduce industrial legislation recognising the parental responsibilities of employees, and labour market reforms which address the discriminations which confront women, ethnic and racial minorities and people with disabilities. The social policy literature identifies the Nordic welfare states and Austria as having some, but certainly not all elements of such corporatist models, which vary considerably in their levels of egalitarianism (Rowthorn, 1989; Mishra, 1984a; Borchorst and Siim, 1987).

However, there are weaknesses and lacunae in the corporatist model and theories, firstly because they look only to the intersections of market and state, formal economy and politics, and secondly, because the key players within the representative structures developed to accommodate those interests, the 'social partners' are identified as capital, labour and government. It is clear that the corporatist theorists, like the social contract theorists, are silent on the subject of sex and gender, on private life and non-market work and their processes of representation or, more accurately, the absence of their processes of representation. This critique is particularly well developed in Borchorst and Siim's account of women's low representation in formal state power structures and the continuing sex segmentation of the labour market and of caring work in the social democratic, corporatist welfare states of Denmark and Sweden (Borchorst and Siim, 1987).

To take an Australian case, since 1983 the social partners to the Accord between the Labor Government and the the trade unions who sit in such advisory bodies as EPAC (The Economic Planning and Advisory Council) and NBEET (National Board of Employment, Education and Training) have included representatives of business, industry, the unions and government and, in Australia as in no other OECD country, representatives of the welfare sector through ACOSS (The Australian Council of Social Service). But there is no representation from the women's movement. Such formally representative bodies are concerned primarily with the intersections of market and state; the relationships between economy, education, training and government.

There is no formal arena of corporatist institutions where caring work and non-market activity in community and household are the subject of representation, debate, advice, negotiation and policy formulation. In an adequate theory, and in adequate policy activity and decision making, market/state/private life and gender order must be brought together.

SOME MODELS FOR CHANGE: THE BASIC INCOME APPROACH, WORK/ WELFARE 'CONTRACTS', INCOME SECURITY/LABOUR MARKET LINKAGES AND THE NECESSITY FOR FULL EMPLOYMENT

At this point I turn to an analysis of three major models of welfare state reform which are the subject of intensive debate in international social policy literature.

These three models, while simplifications, point to three very different conceptions of ways to organise the provision of income support for people of workforce age, and also embody different assumptions and political ideologies. Yet their objectives are similar, namely to link income support arrangements with changing labour market requirements. The essential difference between them is the emphasis placed on the respective obligations of the state and of citizens receiving benefits, the emphasis placed on workforce re-integration as a desirable goal and the means adopted to achieve that goal, in particular the attitude towards compulsion.

THE BASIC INCOME APPROACH

In order to achieve adequacy, uniformity and simplicity of tax/transfer arrangements and to respond to current labour market developments in some advanced industrial countries, there are strong advocates for the introduction of a uniform Basic Income Guarantee (Jordan, 1988; Basic Income Research Group, 1989). The basic income model is the successor to the guaranteed minimum income schemes proposed in the 1970s, and is based on the premise that universal state-guaranteed receipt of a basic income on an individual basis is a right inherent in citizenship. While the basic income would be effectively 'clawed back' through the tax system as non-transfer income rises, no reciprocal obligation would be placed on recipients to seek work, enter education or training, or take suitable employment. The view is expressed strongly by advocates of this approach that compulsion to remain available for work or to take any employment offered is no more than the compulsion of the poor and part of an attempt to drive down wage rates for low paid workers in the United Kingdom and United States. In fact, given the inexorable thrust towards labour market flexibility which has already seen a significant increase in part-time and casual work, the provision of a basic income would provide security to workers with low earnings capacity and therefore better incentives for part-time and insecure work. As an advocate of the basic income approach states:

> it allows poor people to participate on the same terms as better-off ones, rather than relying on coercive methods which would be quite unacceptable for people in the market sector of the economy. (Jordan, 1988, pp. 117-118)

Further, its advocates argue that the basic income approach would enable people – usually women caring for children, elderly or disabled relatives – to receive income, not as 'pay' but as an entitlement based on citizenship. Finally, such an approach, providing a universal basis for citizenship, would promote social cohesion and improve the conditions for more efficient absorption into the emerging flexible labour market.

There are considerable strengths in the basic income model which include the emphasis on:

- adequacy and uniformity of payments
- equitable treatment
- the removal of all notions of desert, i.e. holding no conception of the 'deserving' or 'undeserving'
- simplicity and integration of tax/transfer arrangements
- providing income security during workforce entry for those with low earnings capacity, and effective on-going augmentation of low earnings

However, there are also weaknesses, the major danger being the lack of attention given to the linkages between income support arrangements, education and labour market programmes which might improve labour market chances and earnings capacity. The provision of a basic income without such additional programmes might do little more than entrench an 'underclass' of recipients, including women doing caring work, with little chance to increase their income through full integration into secure employment. It is entirely likely that the basic income model would entrench the position of disadvantaged workers in the secondary labour market, and justify a retreat from efforts to regulate labour markets. Some advocates put forward arguments based on the premise that equity principles can only be pursued through the tax/transfer system, while the functioning of labour markets should embody only efficiency principles. One example is the view expressed by Keith Roberts (1985) in the *Basic Income Research Group Bulletin* that the introduction of a basic income would not only relieve the British government of the need to operate a 'complex, unpopular and increasingly expensive social security system', but the government would no longer be required to 'subsidise ailing industries and regions, or introduce job creation schemes'. This viewpoint holds that the introduction of a basic income would enable the 'labour market to operate freely, as the classical economists assumed and their modern disciples advocate' (Roberts, 1985, pp. 2-3).

Without suggesting that all basic income advocates also support free labour market principles, it is clear that the basic income approach in itself looks only to reform of the tax/transfer system, and has little to say about equity-based reforms of the labour market, e.g. through wage regulation to increase the relative position of low paid workers, through efforts to improve the skill levels and hence the earnings capacity of those who would otherwise inevitably enter and remain in the secondary labour market, or remain marginal to labour market activity.

However, the principles of adequacy, uniformity, equity, simplicity and capacity to augment market earnings are essential features of the basic income model which must be accorded strong credence. So too is the emphasis on the recognition of non-market forms of caring work as one of the major, socially useful activities of adult life. What the basic income model highlights is similarities in class disadvantage and low income, departing from the use of categories of income support to divide recipients on the basis of desert, and to rationalise discriminatory distinctions in rates of payment and income tests. The clearest example in the Australian social security system is the historical legacy of the unequal treatment of pensions and benefits, based on an expectation of long or short term receipt of benefit, a distinction whose legitimacy has been totally eroded by long durations of unemployment.

The fundamental strength of the basic income approach is that it does not give priority only to market work as the key activity legitimating entitlement to income support (e.g. conferring entitlement only on active job seekers or on those who are fully excluded from paid work by illness or disability), and in this way using labour market status as the only benchmark of entitlement. The basic income approach fully recognises caring work, and includes it with market work as the basis for entitlement synonymous with social citizenship. Further, it envisages new combinations of market work and caring work, supported by the security of a basic income.

THE WORK/WELFARE CONTRACT MODEL

At the opposite pole to the basic income approach is the work/welfare contract model which has reached its apogee in some of the States of the United States in relation to sole parents receiving Aid to Families with Dependent Children (Handler,1987). This model replaces the concept of entitlement by the concept of a 'contract' whereby recipients have an obligation to become self-sufficient in return for income support and services. The emphasis is on compulsion, on the enforcement of work requirements in return for benefits, with the possibility of education, training, childcare and health insurance as part of the package. The rhetoric of reform in respect of welfare support for sole parents tends to be 'tough', and deeply infused with rehabilitative overtones. The provision of welfare to the poor under compulsory workfare programmes is imbued with the necessity to undertake market work. Firstly, the incentive structure ensures that rates of income support are kept lower than those of the lowest paid work; secondly it is assumed that the ability to work is purely an individual's responsibility and much less attention is paid to employment expansion, appropriate conditions and adequate wage structures; thirdly, there is almost no credence given to the value of non-market caring work, either in terms of contribution to the welfare of children, or in terms of overall economic welfare.

As a result, adequate income support to protect disadvantaged women and their children has been delegitimised, and considerable emphasis placed in a majority of States on speedy entry to the workforce, because of the alleged undermining effects of welfare on workforce incentives and family stability. Handler, a strong critic of training and workfare programmes as they are applied to sole parents, writing in the Institute for Research on Poverty Journal *Focus* in its special issue on 'Welfare Reform and Poverty' notes that it is the emphasis on *compulsion* which is most disquieting about these programmes. Taking one example, the Californian Programme GAIN (Greater Avenues for Independence) offers a range of labour market assistance towards workforce re-integration as set out in a 'contract' which specifies the reciprocal obligations of the participant and the local administration. Even though the notion of a contract is depicted in terms of 'empowerment', Handler notes that the balance of power lies totally with the administration to enforce the conditions, while the participant cannot hold the county to provide suitable training or suitable job opportunities. In other words, the notion of a free contract between equal partners in terms of reciprocal obligation is an impossible one to sustain where there is no concept of the state 'as employer of last resort'.

The workfare component of the Californian programme does provide one year of employment when all attempts to enter the regular labour market through job search and training have failed. Under this scheme, payment is made at a standard very low rate for employment in public and private non-profit agencies, but the remuneration is not in the form of wages carrying the usual employee conditions of qualifications for unemployment benefits, social security, sickness or vacation leave. Clearly, what is operating here is a reflection of the 'less-eligibility' principles which underpinned social relief programmes in Anglo-American welfare systems in the nineteenth century and the first half of the twentieth century, and which are resurfacing strongly under conditions of libertarian political thought and economic rationalism in the management of social expenditures.

These US workfare arrangements may be contrasted with the conditions of employment in Australian private sector employment experience programmes like JOBSTART and the highly effective and equitable Community Employment Programme (abolished in 1987), where employment conditions include standard award wages and the usual employment benefits. It must be noted that trade union activity and surveillance in Australia ensured that these conditions would be put in place. The contrast between the US workfare arrangements and the Swedish emphasis on the 'employment principle' in their labour market policies is even more stark. The significant difference lies in the fact that the involvement of the union movement in labour market programmes in Sweden has ensured that the jobs created in the public sector and the jobs subsidised in the private sector which have made Swedish employment policies so effective in reducing unemployment, provide payment and conditions commensurate with regular labour market employment (Jagenas, 1985; Wadensjo, 1987). I have introduced the Swedish labour market/income support linkage at this point to emphasise that it is not the focus on work and training which is intrinsically flawed in the USA models under discussion, but the type of work offered, the subjugation of income support, and the lack of protection for participants, precisely because of the emphasis on compulsion and denial of citizenship.

The crucial difference between the United States work/welfare linkages and those which are highly developed under the Swedish model, is the major role of the trade unions in Sweden in protecting wages and work conditions and being fully concerned and formally involved with the organisation of labour market policy and therefore with the re-integration of unemployed people into the labour market.

It should also be noted that because the US model gives almost no recognition to the value of caring work in the States' welfare programmes, the US Senate's *Family Welfare Reform Act* of 1987 which covers income support, training and job placement programmes (among other matters) has lowered the ages of children whose parents are required to participate in the work requirement component of AFDC schemes from six to three. Indeed, what we see here is the very antithesis of the basic income approach to welfare reform, one which asserts the primacy of the market and compels labour force participation.

In Australia there is a strong historical legacy of recognising caring work in the social security system. The sole parents pension enables sole parents to care for their children until the youngest child is sixteen, to combine part income support with part-time employment, and to enter education and training to improve their earnings capacity and employment possibilities. Carers' pension provides an appropriate form of income support for men and women to care for a disabled co-resident or infirm elderly spouse, close relative or close friend. Family allowance supplement provides additional income for low income mothers who, in the great majority of instances in two parent families, are not in the labour force or are employed part-time or, if sole parents, are in low paid work (Landt and Foreman, 1989). These are examples of income support for socially recognised, non-market caring work which *must* continue to confer entitlement in a reformed social security system which protects against vulnerability. It is in these circumstances that the vulnerability of the people cared for is as much an issue as the vulnerability of their carers. This consideration does not mean that carers should not be provided with the conditions to work part-time when circumstances permit and to enter full-time employment. What it does mean is that a one-sided emphasis on the 'market work' principle not only denies the existence of one of the major activities of adult life, but ignores its social and economic contribution.

BASIC INCOME GUARANTEE/LABOUR MARKET LINKAGES

I turn now to the model of basic income guarantee/labour market linkages, which is predicated on the commitment to full employment in public policy arrangements.

To begin within the latter aspect, Adrian Sinfield claims that the basic premise for an alternative social security strategy in Britain is the 'necessity for full employment'. He advocates this firstly because of the impoverishing effects of high levels and long durations of unemployment which are borne by the victims of labour market change and economic restructuring, and the increase in inequality which this causes. Secondly, his advocacy is concerned with the considerable economic costs of unemployment resulting from decreased industrial output, reduced revenue and increased social expenditures. Further, the effectiveness of strategies to increase skill levels, educational and job qualifications, and to remove barriers to the employment of women, racial and ethnic minorities and people with disabilities demands that commensurate attention be paid to the generation of employment growth (Sinfield, 1983).

The objective of a 'full employment' economy was of course recognised by Keynes and Beveridge in the UK, and by Chifley and Coombs in Australia in the immediate post-war period, as the necessary partner of social security to maintain adequate levels of economic security (Coombs, 1982; Macintyre, 1985). It is clear however, that the objective of 'full employment' in the 1990s would need to include full recognition and accommodation of women's employment aspirations, which have increased substantially in the post-war period. Indeed, the 'full employment' objectives of the emergent welfare systems of Britain and Australia were predicated on ideologies of sexual divisions which saw married women predominantly as carers in family and household, and only secondarily as market workers (Baldock and Cass, 1988).

The basis for the third and preferred model of social security reform is the adoption of a newly formulated concept of full employment as the primary goal of economic and social policy. Only within this framework and the commitment to it in social expenditure and investment policy can a fully adequate system of income support be implemented and only within the objective of systematically reduced levels of unemployment can effective and equitable policies be formulated to satisfy the increased job-seeking of women, older jobless people and people with disabilities. Finally, sustained growth in employment is crucial to provide the context for increased emphasis on education and training.

The clearest example of a model of effective income support/labour market linkage is provided by the Swedish 'active labour market policy'. This links adequate income support arrangements with a range of labour market measures which include not only training and retraining but a strong emphasis on subsidised employment in the private sector and jobs created in the public sector. Both income support and labour market programmes are jointly administered through Regional Labour Market Boards, so that individual assessments can be made about the most appropriate combination of training, job search assistance and job creation which is suitable for the participant and relevant to conditions in the local labour market (Wadensjo, 1987; Jagenas,1985: Larsson, 1988). While this highly interventionist, integrated labour market/income support policy has been one of the major factors contributing to Sweden's relatively low rate of unemployment, (in mid-1989 standing at 1.5 per cent), the programme has also contributed substantially to the relatively high labour force participation rate and low unemployment rate of people with disabilities and the high labour force participation rate of women. But this emphasis on the 'employment principle' has not subjugated income support to a residual, stigmatised and inadequate payment so as to preserve the principle of 'less eligibility'. Rather, income support is an equal partner in the comprehensive set of arrangements, with adequacy and equity remaining dominant concerns. Given the much lower dependency ratios prevailing in Sweden compared with most other comparable countries (a product of generally higher employment rates, particularly for women), it is clear that there is a strong revenue base for adequate income support payments and that a considerable proportion of social expenditure is invested in job creation, training and especially childcare programmes which support labour force activity (Cass and Whiteford, 1989).

What are the weaknesses of this model? Firstly the 'employment principle', while far from compelling workforce participation by reducing both benefit payments and the lowest market wage and in fact doing the opposite of both, is nevertheless based on the expectation of economic activity by most able-bodied adults. And indeed, this is exactly what does occur in Sweden, with men and women having almost equal labour force participation rates at 86 per cent and 81 per cent respectively. In Australia the comparable figures are 75 per cent and 50 per cent (OECD, 1989a). To sustain this pattern of economic activity, Swedish laws have intervened considerably into the functioning of labour markets, and into the processes of the gender order, providing paid parental leave which may be shared by both parents and paid leave for parents to care for sick children along with a very high measure of wage equity for male and female employees. In other words, the regulation of paid work also recognises the caring responsibilities of parents, and has attempted to redress gender inequalities (Borchorst and Siim, 1987).

However, as Scandinavian feminist literature shows, the unequal gender order is certainly not superseded, since women are much more likely than men to be employed part-time and to have much less active participation in the formal arenas of political life. In addition, Sweden's high degree of sex segmentation in the labour market militates against women's participation in the industrial and occupational hierarchies of control and decision-making. While state policies have certainly helped to integrate women into economic life through the 'institutionalisation of equality policies', and have substantially improved women's social and economic situation as both mothers and wage-earners, women's dual responsibilities have been maintained and they are significantly underrepresented in the politics of corporatism (Borchorst and Siim, 1987).

CONCLUSIONS

In assessing these three models for social security reform, an analysis based on the criteria of social justice developed earlier suggests that: the *basic income model* would redistribute income through the tax/transfer system with no other basis for legitimacy and entitlement than citizenship; it would most benefit those with the least market power; it would recognise and provide rewards for caring work which is not carried out in the market; it would provide augmentation to those employed in low paid, insecure and irregular employment; it would abolish categories of entitlement based on overt and covert notions of desert; it would encourage simplicity and uniformity of income support arrangements.

The weaknesses, however, are that in paying no attention to the structures and conditions of the labour market, it would be very likely to entrench the position of workers with little labour market power in the secondary labour market or on the margins of the market, and also entrench the gender divisions of caring and market work. While the concept of 'social citizenship' is clearly a communitarian, social democratic one, the policy adopted in the basic income approach is paradoxically a liberal one, since the approach looks only to the tax/transfer system to carry principles of social justice and would leave the workings of the market to concepts of flexibility and efficiency unfettered by regulation.

The *work/welfare contract model* is based on an alleged contract between equals, in which the recipient is held to have contractual obligations to work or train in return for benefit. It is actually based, however, on a negation of citizenship rights, since entitlement to income support is replaced by coercion, either to accept the contract or to seek work in a labour market unregulated by minimum wage legislation or by union protection. The 'market principle' has almost complete hegemony and caring work is given little, if any, recognition. Social institutions are arranged not to protect the vulnerable or to provide the conditions for autonomy, but to demand economic activity without those public investments required for job creation and the union organisations necessary for the protection of waged work or the provision of a guaranteed minimum income for those who cannot derive sufficient income from labour force participation.

The third model, which *links a basic income guarantee with job creation and an active labour market policy*, has the potential to integrate both adequate social security payments and increased labour force activity for those who would otherwise be excluded. While based on an institutionalised commitment to full employment, it also has the capacity to recognise those forms of caring work which take place outside of market arrangements, and which are essential to social life and economic welfare as well as ensuring the well being of those made vulnerable by childhood, old age, illness and disability. Its carriage depends upon the development of more egalitarian structures of representation in which social movements such as the women's movement and welfare organisations have an established place with the trade unions in promoting the interests of those engaged in paid market work, caring work and the interests of those who cannot gain access to a market income.

While this chapter has proceeded at a fairly high level of theoretical analysis, its purpose is to provide a framework for debates about social policies which will institutionalise principles of social justice and contribute to sustainable employment growth. It is clear that the key players have varying and unequal degrees of effective representation under current conditions in the liberal anglophone welfare states. In the Australian context, which provides the impetus for this chapter and to which it hopes to contribute, the key players in the processes of social security reform – trade unions, industry, central government, the women's movements and welfare organisations – have different interests but unequal resources for full participation. The full development of democratic processes of participation is essential if principles of social justice are to be properly debated and institutionalised in welfare regimes, the functioning of labour markets and the relative value given to market activity and caring work.

3
WHAT IS ENOUGH? NEW EVIDENCE ON POVERTY ALLOWING THE DEFINITION OF A MINIMUM BENEFIT*

PETER TOWNSEND AND DAVID GORDON

A reasoned basis for the rates of benefit which are to be paid by any government to the elderly, sick, disabled, unemployed and children is ordinarily expected to be provided in official publications or at least in ministerial statements. That can be illustrated from the histories of the advanced industrial nations and was broadly true of Britain until the social security review of 1985 (DHSS, 1985). The arguments which are put forward politically for the rates of benefit usually draw on scientific attempts to define and measure poverty, and they also draw on the views held by different sections of society about the level of income regarded as minimally adequate to surmount poverty. The two perspectives – scientific and social – often come close together, but sometimes they diverge. This chapter presents new evidence for Britain on these two perspectives.

THE INTERNATIONAL CONTEXT OF MEASUREMENT

The rapid internationalisation of the economy has made comparison between the methodologies or practices of nation-states in defining basic income needs and paying particular rates of benefit to poor people all the more important, and has posed vital questions about the reconciliation of definitions of poverty in the 'first' and the 'third' worlds (Townsend, 1986, pp. 7–12 and 1987a; and George, 1988). That dual process of reconciliation (among rich countries and between rich and poor countries) can be said to have begun only recently; its implications for long-established discriminatory attitudes within nation-states but also for future scientific social enquiry are profound.

Thus, pressure to define both income rights and social rights among the member countries of the European countries is growing fast. A third European anti-poverty programme is about to begin. The signs are that research will be a stronger feature of this programme than of its predecessors. This therefore is the right occasion to review European definitions of a minimally adequate income and to reflect on the implications of that

---

* Previously printed in Social Services Committee, *Minimum Income*, Memoranda laid before the Committee, HC 579, Session 1988-89, November 1989.

review for a wider awareness of international causes of poverty and of the need for better policy relations between countries, as well as for better-grounded policies within countries.

Before examining approaches to the definition of 'adequacy' in relation to new British evidence, this ferment of international enquiry and activity deserves to be illustrated. Thus the European Commission estimates that within the Community the extent of poverty grew from some 30 million in 1981 to 44 million in 1988. In that year the President of the Commission, Jacques Delors, called attention to the paradox of the substantial percentage of GDP being devoted to social welfare and yet the growth of 'so many' poor people. Both the ILO and the OECD have referred repeatedly to 'the persistence' of considerable poverty (ILO, 1984, pp. 5, 29 and 31; OECD, 1985, p. 58-59) and have played an important part in calling attention to its significance (see, for example, OECD, 1976 and 1981, and Sawyer, 1976). A new OECD study concluded that there is a substantial amount of both 'absolute' and 'relative' poverty in eight rich countries, including Britain (OECD, 1989b). Even in Sweden about 5 per cent of the population are considered officially to be poor (Vogel *et al.*, 1988). A large number of European studies are now available (for example, Ferge and Miller, 1987; George, 1988; Room, Lawson and Laczko, 1989; Walker, Lawson and Townsend, 1984). Great efforts are also being made to assemble complex survey data on income and poverty from all the major industrial countries. The most impressive of the cross-national analyses now being undertaken is perhaps the Luxembourg Income Study (for example, Rainwater, 1988; Smeeding, O'Higgins, Rainwater and Atkinson, 1989).

It would be possible to review rapid developments in the study and measurement of poverty in a large number of European countries. Events are moving fast in Denmark, Western Germany, Belgium, France, Italy and Portugal, and a long account could be given of work in the 1980s (for examples for each of these countries see Hansen, 1986; Schütte and Süss, 1986 and 1988; Deleeck, 1989, and Luttgens and Perelman, 1988; Mossé, 1983; Sarpellon, 1983; and Silva and da Costa, 1989).

As in Europe, there is evidence from official data prepared in the United States of an increase in the extent of poverty. Government estimates show a proportionate decline to the mid-1970s, but a sharp rise in the 1980s, to an estimated 33 million, or 14 per cent, in 1987. The increase in the estimated number of children living in poverty has provoked particular concern (see also Smeeding and Torrey, 1988, Danziger, 1989; Reich, 1989).

The United States is not the only country outside Europe where there has been a marked acceleration in public and scientific interest in poverty in the 1980s. For a number of years Australia has been in the forefront of research investment and technical advance (for example, Social Welfare Policy Secretariat, 1981; Cass, 1986; Whiteford, 1981, 1985 and 1987).

Estimates of poverty are made regularly in India on the basis of an annual income and expenditure survey, and there is a growing stream of local and community studies (for a review see Townsend, 1990b). Earlier silence on the subject in the Soviet Union has also now been replaced by an official admission, made by the Prime Minister, Nikolai Ryzhkov, to the Congress of Peoples' Deputies that '40 million people live below the poverty line [apparently reckoned at 75 roubles a month]' (*The Independent*, 8 June 1989).

In this brief outline of international developments it is evident that the phenomenon of poverty is taken very seriously, even if there remain major problems of consistency of definition and measurement.

ECONOMIC PERSPECTIVES ON A POVERTY LINE

Like national governments, international agencies have had problems in defining poverty and distinguishing that phenomenon successfully from inequality. Part of the problem is a familiar one in the post-war history of international organisations – that different governments have different practices and that it is not always easy to decide which one of them should be followed by all nations in the future. But another part of the problem has been the lack of agreement, or perhaps lack of convincing alternative practices, within the social sciences themselves.

To review the experience of almost any of the major international agencies in producing, or commenting upon, operational measures of poverty, is to be introduced to the lack of concerted guidance offered by the social sciences. For example, when embarking on its first programme of pilot schemes and studies to combat poverty the European Commission adopted a broad and relativistic definition of poverty, but when it came to defining the concept in operational terms, the Commission fell back on an income inequality standard developed first by economists like Wilfred Beckerman (1980) and subsequently by the OECD (1981; see also OECD, 1976). By 'an income inequality standard' we mean the arbitrary, or relatively arbitrary, selection of a low level of income as a poverty standard – such as the lowest decile or quintile within the distribution of income from rich to poor, or levels of income below half the median income. This kind of standard is not as unproblematic as it may sometimes seem. There can be very complex questions to be answered, for example in determining alternative definitions of income, deciding the levels of income which are 'equivalent' for households of different size and composition, and measuring income deficits and not just numbers of people who are included in the measure (in Britain such problems have been reviewed recently by Stark, 1988; Jenkins, 1989; and Atkinson, 1989).

This resort to income inequality standards on the part of the international agencies has followed a long line of research papers and books using inequality criteria and not 'subsistence,' 'basic needs' or 'relative deprivation' criteria in defining poverty – or, rather, in selecting an income standard marking the onset of poverty. One obvious reason has been the failure to investigate, and consistently apply, criteria of a kind independent of income itself, to establish what conditions and effects are associated with particular levels of income. Sometimes this seems to arise from hesitation to risk applying criteria, however plausible, used by only a few social scientists and for which there might be insufficient political support, especially from officials representing state governments

In principle international agencies themselves might have done a lot more to remedy the deficiency over the last 10 or 15 years. They are still reproducing those income standards, or something very like them, which were regarded as very rough or interim technical solutions of the problem in the early or mid-1970s. Comparatively little progress on international standards of 'adequacy' or a poverty line seems to have been made. Thus in a thoughtful paper prepared for the OECD in 1988 a specified percentage of median income was still recommended as the most viable approach (OECD, 1988a). Had more advice been given about evidence of material or other forms of deprivation justifying the selection of a particular income standard, perhaps the prospects for international investigation and action would be very different. The best 'official' or 'institutional' attempt to contrast measures of income inequality and poverty in a technically sophisticated form for even one country that we have been able to find is that provided by the Swedish statistical office (Vogel *et al.*, 1988, especially Chapter 5).

From the time of Adam Smith onwards it is economists more than other social scientists who have played a big part in defining and measuring the phenomenon of poverty. As reported above, they have greatly influenced reviews undertaken by international agencies, including the EC, the OECD, the ILO, the World Bank and others. In the 1980s the diversity and ingenuity of technical applications have grown. Good examples of this can be found from the growing literature in Britain (Atkinson, 1985a and 1985b; Desai and Shah, 1988; Clark, Hemming and Ulph, 1981; Foster, 1984; Lewis and Ulph, 1988) and in the Netherlands (Hagenaars, 1985; Van Praag, Hagenaars and van Weeren, 1982; and de Vos and Hagenaars, 1988). In a recent innovative paper Tony Atkinson has formalised different poverty measures and has also pointed out that conclusions may still be reached about trends in poverty even when there is disagreement about the point on the income scale where the poverty line is drawn (Atkinson, 1985b).

Certainly there is much to be said in favour both of formalising poverty statements and establishing the exact upper and lower limits of conclusions which follow from drawing the poverty line at different levels of income. However, this can have the disadvantage of diverting attention from what we believe is the central task – namely to try to settle disagreements about income needs and social needs by investigating the experiences and opinions of people in those situations. Atkinson is well aware of this problem and admits that 'economists have remained wedded to volumes of statistics as a means of presenting results and have not been very creative in seeking alternatives. Indeed, since most of the work on poverty is now secondary analysis, we do not even have the case-studies which increased the impact of the early research' (Atkinson, 1985b, p. 20).

The problem exists, though, not only in producing empirical support in the 1980s and 1990s for alternative measures or definitions but also in trying to conceptualise poverty in the first place. Some economists have done more than to select an arbitrary level of low disposable income. They have found the distinction between 'absolute' and 'relative' poverty useful in classifying different approaches. One long-standing view is that there is 'an irreducible absolutist core in the idea of poverty' (Sen, 1983 and 1985a). This has been criticised on grounds that it imposes a 'minimalist' as well as static view of the extent of human needs in poor as well as rich societies (Townsend, 1985). Nonetheless the distinction between absolute and relative poverty has certain advantages. While the former tends to be restricted largely to physiological needs the latter can open the way to a full consideration of social (including physiological) needs (Townsend, 1979). One recent demonstration of the power of this argument can be found in a response by Donnison (1988a; see also Donnison, 1989b) to an unhistorical and inconsistent paper by Ringen (1988), who claimed that 'there never was such a thing as the absolute concept of poverty and no one has argued that there should be' (p. 353).

Because the distinction between absolute and relative poverty has controversial reverberations some analysts have begun to experiment with different classifications. Atkinson suggests that it is helpful to distinguish between two rather different conceptualisations:

> One is concerned with standards of living and the other with minimum rights to resources. On the standards of living approach, we are concerned that people attain a specified level of consumption, as represented in the US poverty line by its reference to 'consumption requirements' and its origins in the Department of Agriculture economy food plan. On the rights approach, people are entitled, as citizens, to a minimum income, the disposal of which is a matter for them. The reference to citizenship is deliberate. Entitlement to a minimum is seen both as a reward for citizenship and as a prerequisite for participation in society. (Atkinson, 1985b, p. 4)

There are a number of problems about such a distinction. Emphasis on 'consumption' requirements implies the neglect of those aspects of human need which have to do with productive activity, and social roles, customs, obligations and participation. Emphasis on 'rights' invokes ideas of political choice instead of scientific observation and measurement of the objective conditions of social association and participation. However, Atkinson opens up possibilities of reformulating previous approaches to 'adequacy' and the poverty line, both by extending former notions of 'subsistence' into modern ideas of 'standards of living' (bearing in mind the example of approaches in Sweden and not just the United States) and by examining subjective views of minimum needs and entitlements, as established by sample surveys of opinion.

A SUMMARY OF APPROACHES TO MEASUREMENT IN BRITAIN

We will attempt to summarise recent work in Britain of relevance both to the definition of a minimally adequate income and to policies which implement that definition. Both in scientific work on poverty and in the experience of anti-poverty strategies, Britain offers results which may be relevant in other cultural contexts.

The formulation adopted by Lord (then Sir William) Beveridge in the early part of the 1939–45 war as a basis for paying new benefit rates after the war was a formulation which has had a major influence not only in Britain but throughout the world. This was the idea of 'subsistence.' Different governments have used this idea in an operational form both to legitimise benefit scales and measure trends in the extent of poverty. Interestingly enough, countries which had been members of the British Empire, later the British Commonwealth, especially Australia, Canada, South Africa and India, took up and developed that conception (see for example Department of National Health and Welfare, Canada, 1970; Social Welfare Policy Secretariat, Australia, 1981).

The limitations of this idea have to be understood in preparing the way for an alternative formulation. Beveridge's starting point was expressed in the following sentence: 'In considering the minimum income needed by persons of working age for subsistence during interruption of earnings, it is sufficient to take into account food, clothing, fuel, light and household sundries, and rent, though some margin must be allowed for inefficiency in spending' (Beveridge Report, 1942, pp. 84–85). Only about 6 per cent of total estimated requirements was allocated to this 'margin'.

The subsistence approach to the definition of poverty is one which may be said to be dominated by the individual's requirements for physiological efficiency. But this is a very limited conception of human needs, especially when considering the roles men, women and children actually play in society. People are not just physical beings; they are social beings. They have obligations as workers, parents, neighbours, friends and citizens which they are expected to meet and which they themselves want to meet. Scientific observation of people's behaviour after they have experienced a drastic cut in resources shows that they sometimes act in fulfilment of their social obligations before they act to satisfy their physical wants. They require income to fulfil their various roles and participate in the social customs and associations to which they have become habituated, and not only to satisfy their physical wants.

Moreover, their physical wants turn out to be predominantly social in two senses. External social institutions or culture define the form taken by the goods which are consumed, as well as their marketing and distribution, and influence individual perceptions of what goods are 'needed' in everyday life. External social institutions and culture also govern social and individual behaviour and therefore energy, dietary, clothing, fuel and housing needs. Thus, employing institutions govern the kind and amount of work to be done, and hence, the intake of nutrients required physically to perform work tasks. Leisure and lifestyle conventions also influence the quantities as well as kinds of food, fuel, shelter and clothing which are used (for fuller exposition of this argument see Ferge and Miller, 1987, Chapter 2; and Townsend, 1990a).

British evidence shows that the population with incomes which fall below the minimal levels paid by the state has increased to 2.4 million, that those dependent on minimum benefits is now over 7 million and that another 6 million have incomes which are only from 1 per cent to 40 per cent above these levels. The total of 15.4 million. comprises 29 per cent of the total population (see Table 3.1, p. 64, below).

The acceleration in the number in the population dependent on means-tested assistance has coincided with an unprecedented rise in the real income of the richest people, largely attributable to government policies. Since 1975 the share of aggregate incomes after all cash benefits and taxes of the poorest quintile has declined by 22 per cent. The corresponding share of the richest quintile has increased by 16 per cent. Most of this change has taken place in the 1980s. A number of reviews have been undertaken (for example, Stark, 1988 and Jenkins, 1989) which have applied the latest findings and theories in inequality measurement and have reinforced the conclusion that 'income inequality has increased between the mid-seventies and the mid-eighties' (Jenkins, 1989, p. 18). The trend has been the reverse in some other European countries such as the Netherlands which has also experienced severe recession and high rates of unemployment during the 1980s (see, for a precise example, Netherlands Scientific Council for Government Policy, 1985, p. 21).

Using the British case as a good example, we wish to draw attention to the practical implications of more and less restrictive conceptualisations and operational definitions of poverty and hence of levels of benefit which in some sense have to be defended as 'adequate'. If a 'minimalist' approach is taken to the definition of the income needs of the different groups in poverty, there is a grave risk not only of denying those sections of the population ordinary goods and facilities and any chance of honouring social expectations of them but of institutionalising deeper as well as wider inequality, from which envy, resentment, protest and violent crime and disorder can too easily spring. The question is not whether a subsistence income can be defined and guaranteed, but whether poor as well as rich people have an income adequate to contribute positively to society, by having the resources both to meet the obligations which are expected of them and to participate in the customs and activities which contribute to cohesion and productivity in every way. Many problems of social development turn on the answers that are given to this fundamental question.

In Britain social scientists are conscious of a huge impoverished section of the population variously described as a new 'underclass,' the multiply deprived or disadvantaged, and those experiencing mass poverty. The causes and consequences of 'social polarisation' or the 'growing divide' are attracting close examination (for example Pahl, 1988; Walker and Walker, 1987). There are large differences in health and expectations of life between rich and poor areas. While mortality rates among the rich sections of the population are falling rapidly, those among the poor are static or only falling slowly. Material deprivation, including low income as well as bad housing and working and environmental conditions, is the predominant cause of these differences (see, for example, the evidence reviewed in both the Black Report and the 'Health Divide' in Townsend, Davidson and Whitehead, 1988). The demonstrably high correlation between income and mortality deserves more attention (Wilkinson, 1986 and 1990). In practice there is increasing agreement that the concept of 'deprivation' covers the various conditions, independent of income, experienced by people who are poor, while the concept of 'poverty' refers to a lack of income and of other resources which makes those conditions inescapable or at least highly likely.

In the mid-1980s the British Government formally abandoned the subsistence standard which had prevailed in principle since the acceptance of the Beveridge Report of 1942. The two critical texts are the Green Paper on Social Security in 1985 and the DHSS Technical Review of Low Income Statistics of 1988. Although social scientists and others had often argued that the subsistence standard had not been precisely formulated and, moreover, was too meagre, that standard nonetheless gave coherence to social security and historical legitimacy to the formulation of citizens' rights and a basic income sufficient to meet needs. In the war and for many years after the war it represented a national touchstone – something which the great majority of the population could and did enthusiastically support.

The government broke away from this understanding in the 1985 Green Paper (DHSS, 1985). It made no attempt to collect information about the conditions, health and financial problems of people living on social security, or indeed those who failed to qualify for it and had lower incomes.

The Green Paper contains the statement that 'there is now no universally agreed standard of poverty' and that 'many commentators have come to argue in favour of a relative rather than an absolute standard of poverty or deprivation' (*ibid*, p. 12). But there is no intimation of what that standard should be. Different volumes of the report merely proceed to give limited information about the composition of the poorest 20 per cent of the population.

New evidence on poverty

The government cannot pretend that the old standard has been superceded unless it is prepared to define what should be put in its place and is therefore prepared to consider scientific evidence about malnutrition, ill-health and premature death, homelessness, destitution in the inner city and lack of access to educational and social opportunities or jobs that are caused by lack of income. It shrinks from the implications of such an exercise. This destroys any basis there might have been for the changes to social security. There is no minimum, no bottom line, no safety net, no principles or statement of what income for British citizens is minimally adequate to meet today's needs.

The second, revealing, text is the DHSS Technical Review of Low Income Statistics (DHSS, 1988a). For many years DHSS statisticians had reproduced income data collected in the annual Family Expenditure Survey in a form which showed how many in the population had incomes smaller than the basic levels of income support provided by the State, how many actually received benefit, and how many had incomes only marginally above the state's standard. Although the publication of this information was unnecessarily delayed, at least it offered criteria of progress. Table 3.I is based on this information.

The authors of the 1988 DHSS Technical Review of Low Income Statistics, closely following the 1985 Green Paper on Social Security, which had offered no substitute definition of a poverty line, concluded that the long-established statistical series on low incomes should be replaced with a more innocuous series showing the incomes of different tenths of the population ranked according to income, adjusted according to household composition (DHSS, 1988a; and Government Statistical Service, 1988).

There is something to be said for having an additional series of statistics about income distribution, but not without specifying the value assumptions on which that series is constructed or could reasonably be reconstructed, giving alternative results, and not without preserving the valuable former series. Significantly, neither statisticians nor social scientists outside government were involved in this exercise.

Only weeks after the government published the first instalment of the new series a report from Europe punctured one of its major assumptions. Thus, the actual net incomes of households are recalculated by means of an 'equivalence' scale to equate the incomes of different sizes and types of households. The authors of the technical review suggest that equivalence scales 'are broadly similar and give similar results'. The primary reference is to a 1978 study in the DHSS itself (Van Slooten and Coverdale, 1978). However, analyses of the Luxembourg Income Study, which is an elaborate comparative study of income distribution in ten countries, has revealed that choice of scale can have a big effect on who are counted in each country's poorest tenth (for example, whether the majority are elderly widowed people living alone or young families with children). When 34 equivalence scales were reviewed the average amount allowed for each additional person in the household was found to vary from 12 per cent to 84 per cent. Four types of scale, with very different implications for economies of scale and the composition of the population measured to be in poverty, were identified. If these four are applied to income data for the United Kingdom the percentages of poor in households comprising a married couple with two or more children rises respectively from 11.0 to 12.8 to 22.5 and finally to 36.9 (Buhmann, Rainwater, Schmaus and Smeeding, 1989; see also Rainwater, 1988). Such variations have in fact been well known for some years. For example, Whiteford listed 44 estimates from different sources for a single person, taking a married couple as 100 per cent. The estimates varied from 49 per cent to 94 per cent. For a couple with two children the figure varied from 111 per cent to 193 per cent (Whiteford, 1985, Table 5.1).

Long ago statistical advisers to governments elsewhere warned of the problems of equivalence scales. The United States Department of Health, Education and Welfare concluded:

> There are several problems with this technique. The underlying assumption of equivalence is arbitrary. Also it assumes that the degree of satisfaction achieved is independent of the absolute level of expenditure (or consumption). There is no empirical evidence or theoretical basis to support such an assumption. Furthermore, the results are sensitive to the commodity chosen for the index... [Different commodities] lead to quite different equivalence scales. (US Department of Health, Education and Welfare, 1976, p. 26)

Again, the Australian Bureau of Statistics decided to test the method used at the DHSS with Household Expenditure Survey data for that continent. 'The results were disappointing', it was reported, 'being highly sensitive to prior information' (ABS Discussion Paper, reported in Australian Social Welfare Policy Secretariat, 1981,p. 89).

Late in 1988 the House of Commons Social Services Committee expressed doubts about the rigid way in which equivalence scales had been applied (Social Services Committee, 1988). The new Department of Social Security refused to make any concessions. They continued to resist demands for empirical investigation. They also continued to resist calls for representation on technical committees of independent outside advisors. They maintained their argument that choice of equivalence scale was immaterial (DSS, 1988b). However, the critical, unanswered, question is whether the standard of equivalence is 'real'. That is, it could be one based on current practice affecting substantial sections of the population – such as the former supplementary benefit scales or the present income support scales. Or it could be 'objective', in demonstrating when families of different composition do actually have the same standard of living (on selected scientific criteria) despite having different disposable incomes.

Government statisticians have still to explain contrary results produced from different statistical series on low incomes. The contrasting evidence was exposed by the House of Commons Social Services Committee (Social Services Committee, 1988, pp. xxiii–xxvi) but memoranda of evidence submitted by one of the authors of this chapter in August 1988 and, it is believed, by the Department of Employment, have still to be considered (see Townsend, 1988). The new set of figures about low incomes from the former DHSS produce the conclusion that although the richest deciles have gained most in real income in the early eighties, the poorest decile gained by 8 per cent between 1981 and 1985. However, data drawn from the reports of the Family Expenditure Surveys produce a figure of 5 per cent for the lowest decile. This data are reproduced as Table 3.2, see p. 65, below. At no stage has the Director of Statistics of the Department of Employment disavowed the 'bridging' statistics of income distribution published in Hansard, July 27, 1987, for the year 1983, or the interpretation that could be placed on the tables of the distribution of income (by deciles) published in annual reports of the FES. The composition of the lowest decile in the two cases is of course different. But this provides a sharp illustration of the importance of the choice of equivalence scale and the need to submit that choice to independent cross examination.

EVIDENCE FOR A PARTICIPATION STANDARD OF INCOME – SUBJECTIVE: THE AVERAGE OF POPULATION ESTIMATES OF NEED

One form of research on a 'poverty line' which is attracting interest is the elucidation of representative opinion. People can be asked what is the minimum income on which their household can manage or related questions (for example, Deleeck, 1989). They can be asked a variety of questions about their capacity to manage on the incomes which they receive. Or they can be asked to specify the different necessities of life and whether they can afford to obtain them (Mack and Lansley, 1985). By direct and indirect methods the minimum levels of income which in different senses are democratically authorised may be specified.

The study by Mack and Lansley is a sophisticated example. The majority of a national sample of 1174 people classified 26 items from a much longer list as the 'necessities of life'. Poverty was defined as 'an enforced lack of socially perceived necessities'. Among the difficulties of adopting this approach is the selection of the number of necessities the lack of which denotes poverty. A more fundamental problem is that certain needs of a community may not be perceived by any members of that community, or may not be perceived by more than a few, or may be underestimated universally by a population. People's behaviour may reveal what are treated as necessities even when they are not believed to be such. Criteria of need therefore have to be sought externally to social perceptions – whatever might be said about the valuable legitimising functions of mass endorsement of particular standards in a political democracy. Otherwise social scientists will be missing something quite fundamental in the human condition. Social scientists cannot therefore be satisfied with the consensual assessments of the population even when they constitute valuable contributory evidence about needs and standards of living.

NEW EVIDENCE ON ADEQUACY

We can illustrate the possibilities of establishing a subjective 'poverty line' from the 1985-86 London survey. A key question in the survey was whether disposable incomes were 'adequate' for ordinary life and work. Study of the circumstances of individual families with low incomes – revealing their exposure to deprivation, meals foregone, problems of ill-health, and even heating switched off in the depths of winter – could be described in relation to income, and tended to indicate the shortcomings of state benefits. The cumulative force of this varied individual evidence, to which many other studies now contribute (for example, Bradshaw and Holmes, 1989), must not be forgotten. But there is another dimension to that kind of evidence.

The London population as a whole appears to disagree substantially with the government about the minimum income needed by individuals and families to surmount poverty. All sections of the population define the level of income needed by families and individuals much higher than the levels paid in income support, formerly called supplementary benefit. Approximately 2700 adults were interviewed at length throughout London. There was a follow-up study in Bromley and Hackney in which a further 800 adults were interviewed and a related study was carried out by MORI in Islington, sponsored by the council (MORI, 1988).

In the survey each adult was asked a large range of questions covering employment, income and living standards. Towards the end of each interview, questions were also asked about the meaning of poverty, its presumed causes, how the household managed on its income and how much was needed in weekly income to stay out of poverty. Finally interviewees were asked whether actual household income was much above or below this level. Each individual was left in no doubt about the serious purpose of these questions.

We compared the estimated weekly income believed to be needed with the minimum income to which that household would have been entitled in certain circumstances under the supplementary benefit and housing benefit schemes. Readers will appreciate that social security benefits were lower in 1985-8 than they are now but in many cases had approximately the same purchasing power. At the time, the supplementary benefit rate, which excluded housing costs, was £29.50 per week for a single householder, £47.85 for a married couple and £73.05 for a married couple with one child aged 12 and another aged 8. The different scale rates are given in Table 3.3, see p. 66, below (col. 2).

Nearly all the households interviewed put the basic income required to surmount poverty substantially higher than the minimum rate of means-tested support for which their type of household was theoretically eligible. For 10 different types of household the average estimate ranged from 21 per cent to 118 per cent above government figures, with 61 per cent being the average excess (Table 3.3).

The difference between public estimates of a minimum weekly income and the government's minimum was found to be even larger in the 1987 Islington study (MORI, 1988, p. 48). The average household put the minimum income required (excluding housing costs) at a level of disposable income which was 78 per cent above the scale rates of supplementary benefit in that year (see Table 3.4, see p. 67, below). Indeed, in that borough as many as 35 per cent considered that they were living on incomes below the level they had specified in the interview as necessary. Taken together, the two surveys provide strong evidence from representative sources that the public does not consider the government's levels of benefit to be adequate.

For various age-groups and family types the difference between rich and poor in their estimates of weekly income needed to surmount poverty was much smaller than might be expected. The rich tended to estimate income needs at a rather higher level than did poorer people. However, two-thirds of the London population estimated weekly needs in the range 40 per cent to 56 per cent above the minimum benefits payable by government, with only the richest (at 66 per cent above) and the poorest sections (at 32 per cent) falling outside this range. A marked difference was found between the elderly and the young. This was found to be partly a function of the higher levels of benefit to which pensioners are in fact entitled, com-pared with younger, especially unemployed, people. But it was also a function of declining expectations with age and comparisons in practice made with the lower purchasing standards of income experienced at younger ages. A full account of these data will be given in a subsequent report.

There is therefore majority support among Londoners, in terms of weighed assessments, for a 61 per cent increase in the minimum payments of income by the state. For Islington the figure is rather higher, as reported above. The new income support scheme, which came into effect in April 1988, cannot have changed the order of magnitude of this difference between state and people. Although some beneficiaries experienced small increases in the new weekly rates which were introduced in April 1988, others experienced decreases, and substantial numbers no longer receive additional allowances augmenting the basic rates. So-called 'transitional protection' is also being phased out, as the new (lower) rates of benefit overhaul the old (higher) rates by the simple stratagem of denying inflationary increases to the latter. Given the growth of the economy and the differential experience of the effects of inflation and tax reductions, the gap between public perceptions of income needed and the weekly rates paid by government could now be even larger than it was measured to be in the London studies for the period 1985–87 reported here.

One further conclusion can be drawn from the subjective evidence reported from a representative sample survey of Londoners. The great majority testify not only to the inadequacy of minimum state benefits. They also consider that more taxes should be raised to reduce the gap between rich and poor. The basis for this conclusion should be explained. Some 30 per cent of the London population of 6.8 millions is in or near poverty by the state's standards (this figure compares with the government's estimate for Britain in 1985 of 29 per cent having an income below or on the margins of the then basic rates of supplementary benefit). At the other end of the scale one-sixth, or 16 per cent of the population, have an income 400 per cent or more above the state's standard. Even a majority of the people at that high income level say the gap between rich and poor in their living standards is too wide, and, although rather fewer go on to agree that they ought to be taxed more, that proposition is nonetheless supported by a very substantial proportion of them.

EVIDENCE FOR A PARTICIPATION STANDARD OF INCOME – OBJECTIVE: A THRESHOLD OF MULTIPLE DEPRIVATION

The second form of research on a 'poverty line' involves objective assessment. We have not attempted to demonstrate a correlation between deprivation and income. Numerous other studies have identified the nature of the inverse correlation between income and deprivation scores, and this relationship is now well proven (Townsend, 1979; Mack and Lansley 1985; Bradshaw and Holmes, 1989). We have built upon this previous work.

It has been proposed that the best scientific criterion of poverty is objective 'relative deprivation', or the point on a ranked income scale where deprivation grows disproportionately to falling income, and at which people withdraw from fulfilment of some if not all of their social roles and from participation in social customs, and are multiply deprived materially and socially. A national study concluded that the hypothesis was plausible but that, because of a mixture of difficulties of (i) choosing representative indicators of everyday participation in roles and customs, and (ii) reducing cash income, income in kind and the availability of assets to a single quantifiable variable, the provisional evidence was not conclusive (Townsend, 1979).

Others have undertaken more sophisticated statistical analysis of the same evidence and have concluded that the hypothesis can be defended more robustly (Desai, 1986; Desai and Shah, 1988). Desai concluded on the basis of techniques of canonical correlation that the threshold was at the approximate level of 60 per cent above the then scale rates of supplementary benefit. Experimental studies using the same methods have been undertaken, or are being undertaken, in some other countries (for example, Chow, 1981; Bokor, 1984). The graphical representation of income in relation to deprivation was found to compare closely with 'satisfaction' scores for family income in a study carried out in the Office of Research and Statistics in the United States Social Security Administration (Vaughan and Lancaster, 1980). One formal analysis of the similarities and differences between the 'relative deprivation' concept of poverty and previous concepts (Sen, 1981, 1983, 1985a, 1985b and 1985c) has been applied, using Dutch data for 1983 (de Vos and Hagenaars, 1988).

The hypothesis of the existence of a poverty 'threshold' is controversial because of its political as well as substantive implications. It is therefore unsurprising that there is no universally agreed statistical definition of the 'poverty threshold/line', although a number of different 'thresholds' are possible. In order to overcome this problem, we have used discriminant analysis, a technique that does not require a pre-defined 'poverty threshold'. We have assumed that two groups exist, a generally smaller 'multiply deprived' group (poor) and a larger group who suffer from less deprivation (non-poor). Since there is a direct relationship between income and deprivation, the income level (or narrow band of income levels) at which these two groups can best be separated 'objectively' can be considered to be the 'poverty line'. Obviously, there will never be a perfect separation between these two groups (multiply deprived and less deprived), since even when a marked threshold exists there will always be some overlap. For example, people with reasonable incomes may suffer from multiple deprivation due to historic circumstances (e.g. they have only recently got a job or just paid off large debts), or people currently on low incomes may suffer little deprivation due to previously accumulated wealth. However, we would expect a 'good' analysis to correctly classify the majority of cases. Because discriminant analysis does not appear to be widely utilised we have set out some of the constraints in Appendix 1 to this chapter. Our use of cluster analysis, demonstrating a threshold of deprivation, is explained in Appendix 2.

In the 1985–86 London survey an attempt was made to measure deprivation as well as income in detail. A distinction was made between material and social deprivation (Townsend, 1987b). Within these two primary types of deprivation 77 indicators were also developed to cover 13 forms of deprivation – dietary, clothing, housing, home facilities, environment, location, work, rights in employment, family activity, community integration, participation in social institutions, recreation and education. Certain modifications had to be made in the initial formulation and our full list is set out in Appendix 3.

The choice of such indicators is sometimes misunderstood. In principle we were seeking to cover all activities and events in order to establish standard or majority norms, conventions and customs, so that non-participation or marginal participation in those norms, conventions and customs could be identified. The definition and measurement of an entire pattern of individual participation in social events, customs, roles and relationships is plainly a huge exercise in itself. Although we wished to undertake such a comprehensive exercise, the resources to do this were simply not available. Instead we tried to do the next best thing, by examining previous reports of social surveys and evidence about appropriate indicators, before we constructed the 77 indicators and groupings used in the London work. This is very different from making 'subjective' or 'arbitrary' judgments – as dismissively alleged in some official publications (for example, DSS, 1988a).

We produced separate indices of material and social deprivation for each individual and then aggregated the 'scores.' Respondents were ranked in broad bands of income. To avoid the circularity implicit in equivalence scales, people were ranked within the type of household in the sample to which they belonged. In other words, each type of household was treated separately.

We then applied statistical checks to find whether the persons in any income band experienced significantly raised levels of deprivation, relative, that is, to the expectation of there being a linear relationship between falling income and rising deprivation. Different household types suffer from different levels of deprivation. Couples on average suffer from less deprivation than single people. Retired couples suffer on average more deprivation than couples of working age, and retired single people suffer on average from more deprivation than single people of working age. The household types that suffer from the most deprivation are single parent families, large families (couples with four or more children, four adults plus children) and households containing two adults of the same sex and children.

Table 3.5 (see p. 68, below) summarises the discriminant analysis results. We have confined the analyses to some of the principal types of household, uniform in composition. Some household types, usually larger in size, are in fact rather varied in composition, and technical problems of measurement arise. The weekly amounts shown in the first and fourth columns are the income levels at which the two groups (multiply deprived and less deprived) can best be separated. By our previous definition this level of income equates to the 'objective poverty line'. Two qualifications have to be made. First, these results are provisional in the sense that discriminant analyses have been run on only a few of the summary variables (see Appendix 1 and 3). We expect that a much higher percentage of explanation would be achieved if all the variables were used. Second, we will add more household types when we have been able to examine some of the problems of internal variability in composition.

Table 3.6 (see p. 68, below) presents the results as a percentage of the rates of supplementary benefit then payable. The 'threshold' of multiple deprivation is at a level of income for a couple under pensionable age which is 57 per cent above, and for a couple with two children 51 per cent above, government rates of means-tested assistance. These results deserve to be reproduced for much larger sub-groups of the national population. They are preliminary only. However, Table 3.7 (see p. 69, below) shows the comparison of the discriminant analysis 'poverty line' and the self-assessed weekly levels of income required to avoid poverty. With the exception of the results for couples under 60, there is remarkably close agreement between these two methods. This demonstrates the intriguing possibility that by using discriminant analysis it may be possible to 'objectively' calculate a 'poverty line' for most household types that would correspond with the judgements of the majority of the population.

Both the discriminant analysis and self-assessment methods of calculating a 'poverty line' show that government weekly rates of means-tested assistance fall substantially short of meeting the minimum income needs of small households and couples with children.

CONCLUSION

A number of international and national studies of poverty and scientific approaches to the measurement of an 'adequate' income or a 'poverty line' are reviewed in this chapter. The aim has been to focus attention on the central importance of both subjective evidence from representative cross-sections of the population, and the objective measurement of poverty.

New data from a representative sample survey of 5.5 million adults living in Greater London are presented. Two principal findings are reported here. According to the subjective opinions of Londoners, the minimum incomes required for different types of household to surmount poverty averaged 61 per cent above the minimum rates of means-tested benefits payable at the time by the government.

Second, the extent of material and social deprivation, measured by a large number of indicators, was compared with the disposable incomes of this representative sample of Londoners. Using discriminant analysis techniques, a 'threshold' of necessary income required to surmount poverty was established at levels for different types of household considerably in excess of the minimum rates of means-tested benefit payable by government. For the types of household for which we considered we had sufficient numbers the average additional percentage of income required was 66 per cent.

This evidence needs to be reproduced nationally, and explored in studies using larger samples of the population. There is heartening confirmation from a number of other countries that the observed correlation between deprivation and income is now being taken a lot more seriously than hitherto, so that greater priority can be given to the substantive and not only the technical questions of establishing a 'poverty line.' There are studies from Luxembourg (especially Groupe d'Etude pour les Problemes de la Pauvrete, 1982a and b; Dickes, 1987, 1989), France (for example, Villeneuve, 1984) and the United States (Mayer and Jencks, 1989) as well as Britain.

APPENDIX 1: DISCRIMINANT ANALYSIS

Linear Discriminant Analysis is a statistical technique that allows the difference between two or more pre-defined groups to be studied with respect to several variables simultaneously (Klecka,1980). In this preliminary study two groups were defined on the basis of their level of estimated net disposable weekly income and repeat discriminant analyses were run at steps of £5. For example, for single individuals under 60 years old, people were assigned to one group or the other if their income was less than £30, £35, £40, £45, £50 up to £100. Discriminant analyses were run for all these income levels. The material and social deprivation summary variables were used in the analysis of couples with 2 and 3 children and for single individuals under 60. The Discriminant Analysis results for single parents with one child and for couples under 60 were complex so these analyses were re-run using a more detailed data set (e.g. the dietary, clothing, housing, home facilities, environment, location, family activity, social integration, recreational and educational deprivation summary variables – see Appendix 3).

The Discriminant Analysis results showed that for single persons under 60 and for couples with 2 and 3 children the percentage of cases classified correctly and the Eta and Wilks Lamda statistics increased to a single optimal level and then decreased. (The Eta and Wilks Lamda statistics are both measures of the ratio of the between groups sum of squares to the within group sum of squares. A 'good' discriminant function is one which maximises between group variability). In the case of single parents with one child and couples under 60, the percentage of cases correctly classified increased to a small sub-optimal peak before declining slightly and then rising to a single optimum value. This may be due to either 'noise' in the data caused by sampling error or possibly to the presence of a third, extremely deprived group in these household types. The optimal results, where the percentage of cases classified correctly is at a maximum, are shown in Table 3.5 for a number of household types.

The fact that there was a single optimal result suggests that when the sample is divided into two groups there is a single level and/or narrow band of income below which one group can be considered to be multiply deprived compared with the other group. For each of the household types in Table 3.5 (with the exception of single parents with one child) this multiply deprived group was always smaller than the other group. In the case of single parents with one child the multiply deprived group was slightly larger than the less deprived group. This is not surprising considering the high levels of deprivation associated with this household type (see main text).

The use of Discriminant Analysis in this way allows the statistical testing of the hypothesis that there is a level of income below which multiple deprivation can be said to occur. This testing is independent of supplementary benefit levels. There are however a number of assumptions and problems that must be discussed before this conclusion can be accepted.

1. The optimal number of groups.

The number of groups is predefined at the start of the analysis. It is possible that there may well be 3 or more groups actually present which would obviously negate the conclusion that there is a single level and/or narrow band of income below which one group can be said to be multiply deprived. In order to exclude this possibility hierarchical cluster analyses were applied to the data for each household category.

Clustering was done using both Ward's method with a Euclidian distance similarity matrix and Average Linkage using a Pearson's correlation similarity matrix (see Appendix 2). The results were consistent with there being two major groups present for each of the household categories shown in Table 3.5. Since Ward's method clusters on the basis of dissimilarity and Average Linkage is a similarity clustering algorithm, the concordance of these results is probably significant. Both methods have been shown to yield good cluster recovery (Milligan, 1981, Morey et al.,1983; Scheibler and Schneider, 1985)

2. The problem of wealth

There are a number of families with low disposable incomes who are not multiply deprived. These families make up a significant percentage of the incorrectly classified cases. These are often families who have middle incomes but also large mortgages (new home owners) and therefore their disposable income is small. However they often have a degree of wealth in the form of savings and consumer durables. They are also often able to obtain credit on the basis of their wealth. Discriminant analyses deducted from estimated disposable income (Table 3.5). This provides an indirect method of dealing with the large mortgage problem but the problem of wealth in the wider context remains (Townsend, 1979, Chapter 5).

3. The validity of the data.

The results are only valid if the original data from which they are calculated is representative. The problems of the representativeness of the London Survey data have been discussed elsewhere (Townsend et al., 1987), but in general the data can be considered to be valid for the household types used in the analysis.

4. Assumptions of Discriminant Analysis.

In order for the Linear Classification Functions to be correct the data is assumed to have a multivariate normal distribution with equal co-variance structures (Huberty, 1975; 1984). Preliminary analysis has demonstrated this to be so for a number of the household types; however further work needs to be done. The computed probabilities may not therefore be exact but this need not negate the conclusions of this study (Lachenbruch, 1975; Huberty *et al.*, 1987).

APPENDIX 2: CLUSTER ANALYSIS

Cluster Analysis a generic term that encompasses a large range of statistical classification procedures which, since the advent of high speed computers in the 1960s, have rapidly expanded in number. Well over 100 different clustering algorithms have been proposed, yet no adequate statistical theory exists that would allow the different advantages of these algorithms to be distinguished (Blashfield and Aldenderfer, 1978; Blashfield, 1980). Jardine and Sibson (1968) and Hubert (1972; 1974) demonstrated that the 'single linkage' and 'complete linkage' methods of Johnson (1967) would theoretically yield the most perfect cluster solutions. This work resulted in many researchers using these hierarchical methods, although the results were often poor. More recently, a number of empirical evaluation studies by psychologists during the late 1970s and the 1980s have led to a series of recommendations on which methods have the greatest utility.

The results of Monte Carlo studies with continuous data have shown:
1. Hierarchical algorithms generally produce more reliable cluster solutions than non-hierarchical methods.
2. Single linkage and complete linkage algorithms generally fail to resolve cluster structure with real data sets due to their high sensitivity to chaining (cluster overlap). They are however very efficient at clustering ideal or perfect data sets.
3. The efficiency of cluster recovery is dependent both on the nature of the data set, as would be expected, but also on the distance measure used to construct the similarity matrix.
4. Ward's method is the most robust method using a similarity matrix constructed from Euclidean distances. It is particularly good at recovering cluster structure even when considerable cluster overlap is present.
5. Average linkage is the optimal method with correlation coefficient similarity matrices. It is particularly robust to the presence of outliers in the data set.

(Bayne *et al.*, 1980; Blashfield, 1976; 1977; Blashfield and Morey, 1980; Edelbrock, 1979; Edelbrock and McLaughlin, 1980; Milligan, 1980; 1981; Morey *et al.*, 1983; Scheibler and Schneider, 1985).

If the data set to be analysed has not been subjected to multivariate tests for outliers or there is no *a priori* reason to assume that outliers are not present, then it would seem wise to cluster using both Ward's method (with Euclidean distance) and Average Linkage (using correlation). It must be noted that Ward's method is such a robust algorithm that it will even produce a cluster solution with multivariate normally distributed data (i.e. no true clusters) if there is sufficient variation along the first

New evidence on poverty

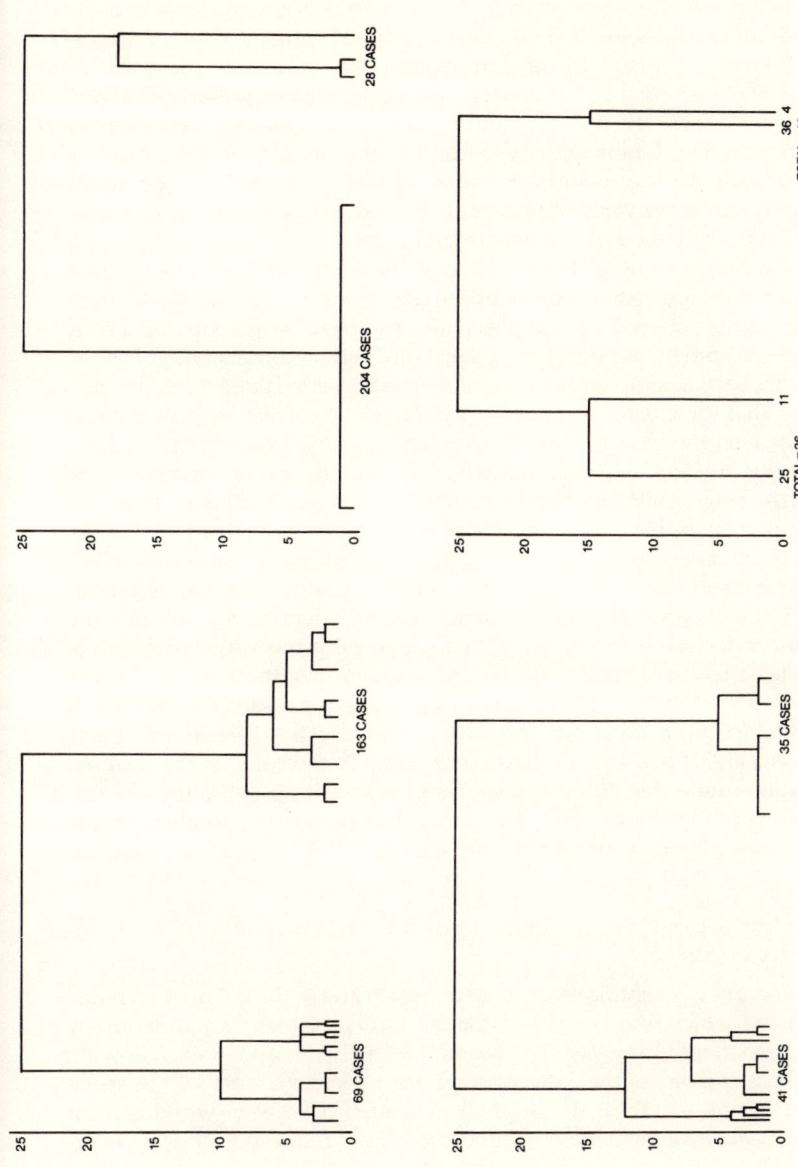

FIGURE 3.1 Cluster analysis results

principal component axis (Morey et al., 1983). This is not necessarily a problem since a partitioning on this basis is often as useful for classification purposes as true clusters (Morey et al., 1983).

In this study, cluster analysis was undertaken on all the household types shown in Table 3.5. Both Ward's Method (using Euclidean distance) and Average Linkage (using correlation) were used since there was no reason to suspect that multivariate outliers were not present. The variables used were the dietary, clothing, housing, home facilities, environment, location, family activity, social integration, recreational and educational deprivation summary variables (see Appendix 3). The family activity summary variable was not used in the cluster analysis of household types that did not contain children.

The results showed that in each case there appeared to be two groups present Figure 3.1 shows the dendrograms from cluster analysis of single individuals under 60 and couples with 3 children. Two groups are clearly visible in both household types, using both methods of clustering. The fact that these two completely different methods yielded similar results indicates that the cluster solutions are likely to be correct. Ward's method clusters on the basis of dissimilarity (i.e. cases are grouped on the basis that they are less dissimilar to each other than the rest of the other cases) and Average Linkage clusters on the basis of similarity (i.e. cases are grouped on the basis that they are more similar to each other than the rest of the other cases).

The identification of two groups as the optimum result has been done by visual examination of the dendrograms. Identifying the optimum number of clusters in any given solution is one of the 'major problems of cluster analysis' (Everitt, 1979). The problem results from the lack of theoretical studies of cluster analysis as there is no agreed definition of what 'optimum solution' means (Aldenderter and Blashfield, 1984). Mojena (1977) has argued that a large jump in the value of the Realised Deviates under his Rule 1 can be used to identify an optimum solution. However this seldom yields definitions that differ from visual inspection of a cluster dendrogram (Dunn and Everitt, 1982).

APPENDIX 3: OPERATIONAL MEASURE OF MATERIAL AND SOCIAL DEPRIVATION

An account of scientific work on deprivation and of the initial operational measure which was developed for the 1985–86 Greater London Survey has been given elsewhere (Townsend, 1987b). In this appendix, following analysis of many of the data collected, the revised measure will be specified. About a sixth of the original indicators have been withdrawn or modified. Reasons include misunderstanding of questions put by interviewers, ambiguity unwittingly introduced in the questions, customs or practices turning out to be shared by fewer than 50 per cent of the population, and difficulty in obtaining reliable information.

The need for a coherent concept is very real. A great deal of scientific and statistical work on deprivation has been carried out in the 1970s and 1980s in Britain, much of it concerned with area deprivation and the justification of the selective allocation of resources under various urban aid programmes (see for example, Department of the Environment, 1975a and 1975b; Holtermann, 1975; Davies, 1984). There is little doubt that much of the work was prompted by the growing volume of interest in the use of social indicators for purposes of information, analysis and planning.

The need for information which is both more comprehensive and more reliably representative of the experience and activity of the entire population is becoming manifest. The government and many other bodies are incurring huge indirect costs at the present time in relying upon the information conveyed by a few restricted indicators. To give a few examples, there is little or no routine information on household living standards, income or wealth, individual states of physical and mental health, the type, range and intensity of immediate social, including family, relationships and the nature and extent of individual work and other activity.

A Measure of Multiple Deprivation

A more elaborate attempt to meet the problems of defining multiple deprivation operationally was developed in the Greater London interviews. Two general points should be explained. First, it was assumed that in principle the items listed in any definition of material and social deprivation should represent all aspects of the material and social conditions of life. For various, mainly practical, reasons it is impossible to apply this principle comprehensively, although it is possible to cover large areas of experience in interviews which are prolonged.

Second, it was assumed that the definition should be 'objective' rather than subjective, the items to be selected were to be indicators of conditions, relationships and behaviour rather than of attitudes or beliefs, important though it may have been to establish independently the nature of those attitudes or beliefs against which conditions and behaviour could be compared. Again, this principle is difficult to fulfil in interview conditions.

The types of deprivation covered by the survey questionnaire were as follows:

MATERIAL DEPRIVATION	SOCIAL DEPRIVATION
Dietary	Rights to employment
Clothing	Family activities
Housing	Integration into community
Home facilities	Formal participation in social
Environment	institutions
Location	Recreation
Work (paid and unpaid)	Education

A list of 77 indicators or groups of indicators was developed to reflect types of deprivation under these headings. The modified outcome is summarised below. The list of 77 indicators or groups of indicators includes a number which are based on international practices (e.g. indicators on safety at work and poor conditions at work recommended by the OECD) and others drawn from previous national surveys by government and non-government investigators, and all appear, from scrutiny of the early questionnaires completed by interviewers, to be valid (in the sense that in every case they reflect the conditions, experience and activities of a statistical majority of the population). Two further points should be emphasised. The sample interviewed in Greater London were invited for many of these indicators to say whether or not they believed them to be 'necessary in today's conditions', that is, necessary to them as individuals. Majority opinion on the elements believed to be necessary to present-day living standards can therefore be compared with majority circumstances and behaviour. Second, the interviews also included a large number of questions about forms of subjective deprivation. The relationship between objective and subjective deprivation can therefore be extensively explored. Examples of the results are given above.

An Illustrative Index of Multiple Deprivation

A distinction was drawn between material and social deprivation and a division was made into 13 specific types of deprivation. A total of 77 indicators or groups of indicators were selected (with a total maximum score of 94). As explained above, a number of these were later withdrawn from the list or modified. The original list with notes about outcome is set out below:

Material Deprivation (figures are percentages)

1. Dietary deprivation

    6.9   i. At least one day in last fortnight with insufficient to eat
    4.4   ii. Short of food on at least one occasion in last 12 months to meet needs of family
   13.2 iii. No fresh meat or fish most days of week (alternative formu-

lation for vegetarians)
- ** 26.0   iv. No special meal or roast most weeks
- ** 32.8   v. No fresh fruit most days

2. *Clothing Deprivation*
- 7.9   i. Inadequate footwear for all weathers
- 14.1   ii. Inadequate protection against heavy rain
- 5.6   iii. Inadequate protection against severe cold
- 3.5   iv. Fewer than three pairs socks/stockings in good repair
- ** 13.4   v. No dressing gown
- ** 20.2   vi. Bought second-hand clothing in last 12 months

3. *Housing Deprivation*
- 3.4   i. No exclusive use of indoor WC and bath
- 0.1   ii. No electricity
- 26.4   iii. Housing not free of damp
- 8.6   iv. Housing not free of infestation
- 12.3   v. Poor access to accommodation
- 9.2   vi. Overcrowded (fewer rooms – excluding kitchen and bathroom – than persons)
- ** 24.3   viii. External structural defects
- ** 12.6   ix. Internal structural defects
- ** 33.5   x. All rooms not heated on winter evenings
- ** 20.4   xi. Poor state of internal and/or external paintwork and decoration
- *   xii. No spare room for visitor to sleep

4. *Deprivation of Home Facilities*
- 37.7   i. No car
- 2.5   ii. No television
- 3.6   iii. No radio
- 24.4   iv. No washing machine
- 1.3   v. No refrigerator
- 32.3   vi. No freezer
- 2.5   vii. No electric iron
- 0.8   viii. No gas or electric cooker
- 6.3   ix. No vacuum cleaner
- 32.1   x. No central heating
- 11.7   xi. No telephone
- 6.2   xii. Lack of carpeting in main rooms

5. *Deprivation of Environment*
- 39.1   i. Nowhere for children under five to play safely outside
- 37.2   ii. Nowhere for children aged five to ten to play safely nearby
- 32.0   iii. Risk of road accidents around home
- ** 22.0   iv. No garden
- ** 6.7   v. Industrial air pollution
- ** 11.6   vi. Other forms of air pollution
- ** 13.8   vii. Problem of noise from traffic, aircraft, building works

6. Deprivation of Location
- 11.0   i.   No open space (like park or heath) within easy walking distance
- 4.1   ii.   No shops for ordinary household goods within 10 minutes journey
- 36.6   iii.   Problem of litter in local streets
- 8.5   iv.   Doctor's surgery or hospital outpatients department not within 10 minutes journey
- ** 27.0   vi.   No recreational facilities for young people or older adults nearby

7. Deprivation at Work
- 24.9   i.   Poor working environment (polluted air, dust, noise, vibration and high or low temperature – maximum score of 9)
- 38.6   ii.   Stands or walks about more than three-quarters of the working day
- *   iii.   Works 'unsocial hours'
- (to follow) iv.   Either poor outdoor amenities of work or poor indoor amenities at work (maximum score of 10)

7a. Alternative Series on Deprivation at Work
(for people not answering questions applying to paid employment and who have shown they undertake at least 20 hours unpaid work altogether caring for children, sick or disabled or elderly persons in the household or elsewhere)
- i.   Repeat the total score for housing deprivation (item 3 above – maximum score of 11)
- ii.   No central heating (4 x. above: repeat score if necessary)
- iii.   No telephone (4 xi. above: repeat score if necessary)
- iv.   Worked 50 or more hours in last week (Unpaid work but also including any paid work)
- v.   Air pollution (items 5 iv. and 5 v. above)
- vi.   Repeat the total score for locational deprivation (item 6 above – max. score 5)

Social Deprivation (figures are percentages)

8. Lack of Rights in Employment
- 5.5   i.   Unemployed for two weeks or more during previous 12 months
- 26.7   ii.   Subject to one week's termination of employment or less
- 17.4   iii.   No paid holiday
- *   iv.   No meals paid or subsidised by employer
- 48.6   v.   No entitlement to occupational pension
- 28.8   vi.   Not entitled to full pay in first six months of sickness
- 14.1   vii.   Worked 50 or more hours previous week

      8.3 viii. Experiences discrimination at work on grounds of race, sex, age, disability or sexual orientation
9. *Deprivation of Family Activity*
    39.5 i. Difficulties indoors for child to play
    36.5 ii. If has children, child has not had holiday away from home in the last 12 months
    26.1 iii. If has children, child has not had outing during the last 12 months
    * iv. No days staying with family or friends in previous 12 months
    43.3 v. Problem of the health of someone in family
    12.9 vi. Has care of disabled or elderly relative
10. *Lack of integration into Community*
    9.4 i. Being alone and isolated from people
    9.7 ii. Relatively unsafe in surrounding streets
    3.6 iii. Racial harassment
    * iv. In illness no expected source of help
    * v. Not a source of care or help to others inside or outside the home
  ** 25.0 vi. Moved house three or more times in last five years
11. *Lack of Formal Participation in Social Institutions*
    31.1 i. Did not vote at last election
    * ii. No participation in trade union or staff association, educational courses, sport clubs or associations, or political parties
    * iii. No participation in voluntary service activities
12. *Recreational Deprivation*
    29.8 i. No holiday away from home in last 12 months
  ** 21.8 ii. Fewer than three hours a week of specified range of leisure activities
13. *Educational Deprivation*
    19.7 i. Fewer than 10 years education (people under 60 years of age)
    31.9 ii. No formal qualifications from school or subsequent educational courses or apprenticeships

Material and Social Deprivation: Total indicators or groups of indicators is 70 from an initial list of 77 (with a maximum total score of 87).
Please note: * More than 50 per cent and thus excluded from the overall index.
              **Excluded from Discriminant Analysis in the present series.

APPENDIX 4: 1985-86 LONDON SURVEY – METHODS

The survey of 'Londoners' Living Standards' was conducted in some 1700 households across London, using stratified random sampling. First, 30 wards were selected at regular intervals from a total of 755 London wards, ranked by four indicators of material deprivation: percentage of economically active adults who were unemployed, percentage of households overcrowded, and percentage of households not owning a car and neither owning, nor buying, their own home. The last two indicators are surrogates for income and wealth respectively. All four indicators were drawn from 1981 Census data. Unlike censuses in some other countries, data about income and wealth are not collected in the United Kingdom census. This procedure at the first stage was designed to ensure representation of prosperous and deprived populations in the city.

Second, within each of the 30 wards approximately 120 addresses were selected at random from the Postcode Address File. This file has the advantage of being up-to-date but the disadvantage of including a high percentage of ineligible addresses – many being non-residential and others being buildings which are either vacant or even demolished. Interviews were completed with 56 per cent of households expected to be eligible for the survey. Within households, 73 per cent of the individual adults who were members of those households were interviewed. Exceptional efforts were made to secure a larger response, although it was known at the time that government as well as independent survey organisations, including the OPCS, were concerned about the fall in response rates in the London region and, often within the range 50-60 per cent, tended to be lower than that in any other region. An unusually large number of recall visits were arranged by the body carrying out the interviews, the Research and Intelligence Unit's Survey Services Group of the Greater London Council, to try to find individuals at addresses where no contact had been established. After the Greater London Council was abolished in April 1986 the survey organisation MORI generously undertook a programme of recall visits and interviews. In the event, most of the interviews were carried out between September 1985 and May 1986 and the recall programme produced a further 200 interviews in the summer and early autumn of 1986.

The basis of the survey lay first in a household questionnaire covering housing, locational and household information and, second, an individual questionnaire. Each member of the household over 16 was invited to answer questions about employment/unemployment, income and savings, unpaid work, health experience and attitudes towards deprivation.

The final response yielded data from 1716 households and 2703 individuals within those households. A detailed account of the fieldwork will be found in Owen (1987).

By the normal criteria of representativeness which are applied to sample data we found that the 1985–86 survey conformed closely with

Census information about the Greater London population, by age, sex, economic activity, occupational class and ethnic status. This is described in detail in the full report.

With the winding-up of the Greater London Council the Poverty Research (London) Trust (whose Trustees are Professors Adrian Sinfield, Hilary Rose and Alan Walker) took over the financial management of the survey. A follow-up survey which had all along been planned in the most and least prosperous boroughs of London (Bromley and Hackney) to unravel further aspects of the relationship between poverty and the labour market, was now undertaken by MORI. A representative sample survey in three of the wards in each of the boroughs was completed in 1987. Altogether, interviews were completed with 407 individuals in Bromley and 381 in Hackney.

The administration of the final stages of the research programme, and the development of computer disks and files, took place at the Polytechnic of North London during 1986–1988. Access to the data is encouraged, at modest cost, and is available at PNL and the Department of Social Policy and Planning in the University of Bristol. A copy of the files will also be lodged shortly at the ESRC Archive Data at the University of Essex.

ACKNOWLEDGMENTS

Many people have been associated with the London survey of 1985–86 and we owe a debt of gratitude to all those Londoners who patiently submitted to interviews, as well as the interviewers themselves under the direction of Jenny Owen. The Greater London Council, and especially its Industry and Employment Branch under the chairmanship of Michael Ward, found time in the final year of their existence to discuss and finance such a project and give it their blessing. Robin Murray and Irene Brueghel greatly contributed to the conception and fulfilment of the programme. As the principal staff during the fieldwork and analysis of the data in the earliest stages, Ute Kowarzik and Paul Corrigan laid the groundwork for a number of reports and for this paper. During a series of research workshops at the LSE, Meghnad Desai in particular provided a sense of confidence and direction. Adrian Sinfield, Hilary Rose and Alan Walker gave unfailing support as the Trustees of the Poverty Research (London) Trust through good and bad times, as did Brian Gosschalk and his organisation MORI. Full acknowledgments will be given in the forthcoming major report on the survey. Critics of intellectual positions are not always credited with the stimulus they provide: since *Poverty in the United Kingdom* was published in 1979 the development of the definition and measurement of poverty in a series of reports and papers, culminating in this chapter would have been a lot less complete without the criticisms of Amartya Sen, David Piachaud, Aleida Hagenaars and others. More specifically, we have gained from comments upon an earlier draft of this chapter by Bruce Bradbury, Paul Dickes, Gaston Schaber, Denton Vaughan, Stephan Leibfried, Paddy Hillyard and Lee Rainwater.

TABLE 3.1 Changes in extent of poverty 1960-1985 (Britain) (according to the State's Standard of Low Income)

Income in relation to supplementary benefit standard	1960a	1975	1979	1981	1983	1985
			Number in thousands			
Below SB standard	1260	1840	2090	2610	2700	2420
Receiving SB[b]	2670	3710	3980	4840	6130	6960
At or up to 40 per cent above SB standard	3510	6990	5500	7210	7550	6040
Total	7440	12540	11570	14660	16380	15420
			Percentage			
Below SB standard	2.3	3.5	4.0	4.9	5.0	4.5
Receiving SB[b]	4.9	7.0	7.6	9.1	11.4	12.9
At or up to 40 per cent above SB standard	6.4	13.2	10.4	13.5	14.1	11.2
Total	13.6	23.7	22.0	27.5	30.5	28.6

Notes: (a) The 1960 data are for the UK and are on a household rather than an income unit basis. It should be noted that the estimates are based on national assistance scales, not supplementary benefit scales. (b) Drawn separately from supplementary benefit sample enquiry with people drawing benefit for less than 3 months excluded. Thus people unemployed or sick or disabled for less than 3 months are counted as having the incomes they last had in employment.
Sources: For 1960, Abel-Smith and Townsend (1965, pages 40 and 44). The data are drawn from the FES of that year. For subsequent years, the DHSS has published analyses of the FES. The most recent of these, covering 1985, was published in 1988.

TABLE 3.2 Changes in Disposable Household Income of relatively rich and poor at constant (1985) prices (£s per week)

Year	Lowest decile	Lower quartile	Median	Upper quartile	Highest decile
1979	47.38	83.71	154.07	221.13	298.39
1980	47.67	86.62	158.62	224.29	306.61
1981	51.04	87.37	154.89	228.21	305.65
1982	50.11	84.04	150.43	222.68	295.87
1983	51.25	84.58	148.37	220.82	302.79
1984	49.75	83.80	150.44	226.57	307.72
1985	48.44	83.45	152.73	232.74	322.59
1981–85					
Loss or gain in £s	-2.60	-3.92	-2.16	+4.53	+16.94
Percentage change	-5.1	-4.5	-1.4	+2.0	+5.5
1979–85					
Loss or gain in £s	+1.06	-0.26	-1.34	+11.61	+24.20
Percentage change	+2.2	-0.3	-0.9	+5.3	+8.4

Source: Written answer to Parliamentary question, Hansard, 22 July, 1987; Department of Employment (1980-1986), Annual Reports of the Family Expenditure Survey, London: HMSO.

TABLE 3.3 Subjective assessments of Weekly Disposable Income required* to keep household out of poverty (Greater London region, 1985–86) compared with basic scale rates of supplementary benefit

Household type	(1) Estimated weekly income needed (£)	(2) Basic income payable under S.B. (Nov. 85–Jul. 86)	(3) Per cent (1) ÷ (2)
Single person 60+	52.35	37.50a	140
Single person <60	64.26	29.50b	218
Couple 60+	73.05	60.00a	122
Couple <60	104.49	47.85b	218
Couple with 1 child	100.62	57.95c	174
Couple with 2 children	109.12	73.05d	149
Couple with 3 children	118.36	83.15e	142
Couple with 4+ children	143.15	i	–
2 adults, no children	73.85	61.00j	121
3 adults	103.66	71.45f	145
3 adults with children	138.61	81.55g	170
Single parent family	80.80	47.50h	170
Single parent family + adults	–	i	–
4 or more adults	117.46	i	–
4 or more adults plus children	147.35	i	–

Notes: (a) long term rate assumed (b) ordinary rate assumed (c) child assumed to be under 11 years (d) one child assumed to be 11-15, one under 11 (e) two children assumed to be under 11 and one 11-15 (f) assumed to be couple on ordinary rate plus non-householder aged over 18 (g) same as (f) plus child under 11 (h) one child assumed, under 11 (i) too many possible combinations to give an approximate yardstick (j) assumed to be parent, on single long-term householder rate, and adult son or daughter over 18 on ordinary non-householder rate.

*In interviews the question was formulated as follows: 'How many pounds a week do you think are necessary to keep a household such as yours out of poverty?' Interviewers were instructed to stress that the income to be estimated must be total *disposable* income. From each individual estimate actual expenditure on housing per week by that household was deducted, and the first column of the table gives the resulting average according to household type. These averages provide a useful comparison with the minimum weekly benefits paid by the government, as listed in the second column.

TABLE 3.4 Subjective assessments of Weekly Disposable Income required* to keep household out of poverty, (Islington, 1987), compared with basic scale rates of supplementary benefit

Household type	(1) Islington 1987 (£)	(2) Basic income payable under S.B. (Apr.87–Apr.88)	(3) Per cent (1) ÷ (2)
Single person 60+	61	38.65a	158
Single person <60	75	30.40b	247
Couple 60+	80	61.85a	129
Couple <60	107	49.35b	217
Couple with 1 child	121	59.75c	203
Couple with 2 children	132	75.35d	175
Couple with 3 children	121	90.95e	133
2 adults, no children	92	63.00j	146
3 adults	134	73.70f	182
3 adults with children	149	84.10g	177
Single parent family	93	49.05h	190
Single parent family and adults	167	i	–
4 or more adults	105	i	–
4 or more adults plus children	–	i	–

Notes: (a) long term rate assumed (b) ordinary rate assumed (c) child assumed to be under 11 years (d) one child assumed to be 11-15, one under 11 (e) two children assumed to be under 11 and one 11-15 (f) assumed to be couple on ordinary rate plus non-householder aged over 18 (g) same as (f) plus child under 11 (h) one child assumed, under 11 (i) too many possible combinations to give an approximate yardstick (j) assumed to be parent on single long-term householder rate, and adult son or daughter over 18 on ordinary non-householder rate.
* In interviews the question was formulated as follows: 'How many pounds a week, after tax, and after payment for your accommodation, do you think are necessary to keep a household like yours out of poverty?'
Interviews were carried out between 16 July and 10 December 1987. The table is based on 3046 successful interviews (see MORI, 1988, for an account of the research methodology).

TABLE 3.5 A measure of weekly disposable income required to surmount multiple deprivation

Household type	Disposable weekly income before paying housing costs			after paying housing costs		
	(1)	% correctly classified	number in sample	(2)	% correctly classified	number in sample
Single person >60	£65	76	198	£60	73	189
Couple >60	£85	82	176	£75	81	162
Couple plus 2 children	£150	65	143	£110	75	102
Couple plus 3 children	£165-175	77	34	£125	79	28
Single parent plus 1 child	£85	82	54	£80	80	49

Notes: (1) and (2) These two sets of figures represent the weekly amounts which optimise the percentage of deprived and non-deprived people who are correctly classified. See Appendix 1 for an account of the methodology. Some households in the sample had to be excluded from these analyses because insufficient information was provided about one or more of the following: disposable income; housing costs; and the two sets of indicators of deprivation.

TABLE 3.6 Weekly income required to surmount deprivation as a percentage of basic means-tested assistance scales

Household type	Weekly income required, after deduction of housing costs, as a percentage of basic means-tested assistance scales
Single person >60	203
Couple >60	157
Couple with two children	151
Couple with three children	150
Single parent with one child	168

Note: As in Table 3, assumptions have had to be made about the ages of children so that basic rates could be estimated.

TABLE 3.7 Weekly income required to surmount multiple deprivation: Self Assessment and Discriminant Analysis methods compared

Household type	(1) Self-assessment		(3) Discriminant Analysis
	Greater London 1985–86 £	Islington 1987 £	Greater London 1985–86 £
Single person >60	64	75	60
Couple under 60	104	107	75
Couple plus 2 children	109	132	110
Couple plus 3 children	118	121	125
Single parent plus 1 child	81	93	80

Note: For methods see Tables 3.6 above and Appendix 1.

4
ALTERNATIVE FUTURES FOR SOCIAL SECURITY
ABRAHAM DORON

There is an old Jewish tradition which says that, after the destruction of the Temple in Jerusalem, prophecy, or predicting the future, became an occupation of fools alone. In accepting the task of discussing the future of our social security systems I am very much aware of the dangerous position in which I put myself. I can only hope that what I write will not put me entirely in this category.

The very fact that we are prepared to discuss possible futures for our social security systems is built on the assumption that it is within our capacity, as human beings and part of human societies, to influence the future that awaits us. We believe, as the British sociologist Anthony Giddens argues, that we are not condemned to be swept along by forces that have the inevitability of laws of nature over which we have no control, but rather by forces that to a large degree we can harness and thus achieve our objectives with their help (Giddens, 1982, p. 26). This means that we must be aware of the alternative futures for our social security systems that are potentially open to us. In using our sociological imagination we can therefore attempt to explore such possible futures.

It is also important to emphasise that any attempt to explore the future of social security cannot be undertaken in a political vacuum. It is by necessity strongly connected with the highly politicised and emotionally charged debates currently going on in most of our societies about the future of national social policies. The fact is that we are in the midst of a period of upheaval in which most advanced industrial countries are in the process of trying to reshuffle the social security arrangements which became an integral part of the postwar social and political consensus. It is believed that basic changes are underway, and that we are at the edge of a decisive historical moment as Heclo maintained (1981). Rein and Rainwater discuss the 'reframing of the intellectual discourse about the future developments of social policy' (1987, p. 143). And Mishra notes the break-up of what he calls the de-facto political consensus around the mixed economy and welfare and the end of the golden age of the Western welfare State (1984b, p. 163).

Alternative futures for social security

No matter what the facts are, the widespread feeling is that the social democratic (or liberal in American terms) welfare state with its vision of social justice and equality is on the brink of collapse. What has happened is that the intellectual and moral base of the welfare state has weakened considerably and its traditional supporters from within the labour movement, the trade unions, middle class liberals and groups within academia are in retreat. There is no doubt that the welfare state is under intense political attack. Although there are serious economic pressures and fiscal strains involved in these developments, the attack does not simply reflect economic limits. With renewed strength conservative forces hostile to the welfare state are the spearhead of these attacks (Weir, Orloff and Skocpol, 1988).

The three primary objectives of the contemporary welfare state – social protection, equality and integration (Flora, 1985) – are all embodied in social security. Moreover, social security is the critical mechanism of the welfare state for the realisation of the aims of social protection. A threat to the welfare state inevitably involves a negation of its core institution. Attempts to dismantle social security, or to disable it seriously, carry with them the danger of undermining the individual sense of social and economic security which was the major political achievement of the post-war mixed social systems which can pass as both social democratic and largely capitalist industrial societies. The question is to what extent are the basic solidaristic and redistributive premises of social security being threatened in the existing circumstances and what are the alternative prospectives offered.

The intention in this chapter is to discern and outline three such possible alternatives and discuss their implications for the well being of individuals and families and for the future of capitalist industrial societies. They are as follows:

1. *Maintaining the Existing Institutional Arrangements.* In this scenario the present social security systems are conceived as a central and vital institution of advanced modern industrial societies and therefore their continuous maintenance should be taken as an 'irreversible' fact (Therborn and Roebroek, 1986). In spite of much talk about the crisis of social security, under this scenario, it will continue to function for the foreseeable future without any major dramatic changes, or only with some modest incremental modifications.

2. *The Realisation of the 'Neo-Conservative Dream'* (see Glennerster, Power and Travers, 1989). The main premise of this scenario is the dismantling of the edifice of social security to which we have become accustomed, and the transfer of the functions it has performed to individuals and the private market. This scenario is being described by some as a dream but, if we look carefully into what is actually happening in some of our societies, it has a good chance of becoming reality where political conditions are hospitable to such changes.

3. *The Creation of Private Welfare States in the Field of Social Security.* Under this scenario, the gradual promotion and widening of occupational social security arrangements at individual places of work, or for particular social groups, will either replace the existing universal social security systems or effectively marginalise them. Social security will thus be transformed into a system of provision only for the residual population of the poor.

MAINTAINING THE EXISTING INSTITUTIONAL ARRANGEMENTS

The main premise of this scenario is that the social security system, being the core of the welfare state in advanced industrial societies, cannot be dismantled in the democratic societies in which we live (Therborn and Roebroek, 1986). Maintaining the system does not necessarily mean the preservation of the current status quo, but rather, the continued maintenance of the dynamics of the present system with its constant flow of adjustments and adaptation to the changing circumstances of economic growth, fiscal constraints and redistributive imperatives. Its essential features, such as the universalistic approach based on the social rights of citizenship, will, however, be preserved.

This premise bases itself on the fact that there are a number of sets of political and economic factors which operate in modern capitalist-democratic societies that are strongly in favour of maintaining the existing social security arrangements.

First, the fact that large parts of the population are actually dependent for their livelihood on the existing social security arrangements ensures that, as long as the regimes remain democratic in their nature, social security will remain intact. The electoral power and the ability to decide who will rule that rests with the majority of the population, makes it impossible for those in power, even when they so desire, to make significant reductions in the existing social security systems.

Second, there are a number of demographic and economic trends which operate in the same direction:

1. *The Ageing of the Population.* In most welfare States the aged constitute nearly 15 per cent of the total population. This increase in the proportion of older people means that it is imperative that we have a comprehensive and adequate income maintenance system for them and also that we provide properly for their increased health care needs. Only a public social security system can assume responsibility for those needs. One can add here that the growing electoral power of the aged population, and their children and other relatives, which could potentially serve as a powerful political lever, could be used by the elderly to force governments in democratic societies to continue and maintain social security systems advantageous to them.

2. *The Growth of Unemployment.* Since the economic crisis of the mid-1970s most industrial societies have not succeeded in maintaining full employment. Rates of unemployment have increased steeply and have reached the level of 8, 10 and even 12 per cent or more of the labour force.

It is estimated that the level of unemployment will continue to remain high and most industrial societies are faced with the reality of having to cope with a large and permanent pool of unemployed people. The need to assure the unemployed and their families an adequate income makes maintaining social security a practical necessity.

3. *The Demographic Scare.* Most advanced industrial welfare states suffer from low fertility rates which are not sufficient to reproduce the existing populations. The fear that the population is declining, which is perceived as a decline in national strength and vitality, serves as a powerful incentive for those countries to continue to maintain and even improve the social security programmes for families with children. These trends and policies seem to be visible in Sweden and other Scandinavian countries, Germany and elsewhere (Kamerman and Kahn, 1981).

4. *The Growth of Single Parent Families.* In most countries there is a significant rise in the number of single parent families, mainly single women with young children. These families are unable to maintain themselves without considerable social security benefits. Again, the assumption is that the number of these families will continue to rise. Social security systems are, therefore, needed to deal with the problems of these families.

Third, there is a strong political base which favours this scenario. In fact, we have a broad-based political coalition in support of social security which can be seen as guaranteeing the continuing maintenance of the established system. In most countries, in addition to the solid base of electoral support, the coalition in support of social security encompasses broad support in the national legislative bodies which in many cases transcend party and class lines, and the support of the strong public bureaucratic organisations administering the social security programmes. This combination of an almost universal coalition of citizens and major political and bureaucratic institutions, which all have a common stake in the preservation of the system, seem to make a wholesale dismantling of it improbable. (Weir, Orloff and Skocpol, 1988, pp. 422–445)

All the factors mentioned in this scenario make social security systems a political and functional necessity. The support for the social security systems stems, however, not only from functional necessity. There are two additional factors involved in the resilience of the existing arrangements; their entrenched institutional base and their apparent effectiveness.

While the existing social security systems were mostly created as a response to a particular historical situation, i.e. the post-Second World War political settlement, during the past four decades they have become an integral part of the institutional structure of modern industrial societies. It is difficult to envisage the removal of these. Moreover, it has become evident that only publicly maintained, compulsory, tax-backed social security systems are capable of covering the main risks of income loss in modern industrial societies, securing long-term inflation-proof benefits, attaining albeit modest but important redistributional goals, and sparing low-income workers from the need to apply for means- or income tested assistance (Aaron, Bosworth and Burtless, 1989, pp. 117-118).

It is these factors which provide the necessary support for the existing social security arrangements to survive in the foreseeable future. The strength of these variables, which may vary from country to country, will make this possible in spite of the various economic constraints and the strengthening of political forces committed to dismantling, or at least to reducing, the extent of social security protection.

REALISING THE CONSERVATIVE DREAM

This scenario foresees the dismantling of the present social security systems and their eventual privatisation. Its prescription for the future has strong support among political forces which describe themselves as Neo-Conservatives or 'the New Right'. It also has considerable support from other powerful groups across the entire political spectrum, and among the public at large, who are disappointed and dissatisfied with the existing service systems for one reason or another.

Three sets of variables are operating in our societies towards the realisation of this scenario. These are ideological motivation, economic and other interests and the creeping privatisation that is already taking place in parts of our social security systems.

1. *Ideological Motivation.* It is well known that the drive for privatisation in general, and within the social services in particular, is highly motivated by ideology. Ideological beliefs are always a powerful force capable of mobilising people to action. The belief in the superiority of the market economy, which has gained increasing support in the last decade as confidence in collective action has declined, has also become a strong factor in the demands for privatisation in the field of social security. This belief in privatisation is particularly prominent among certain schools of conservative economic thinking which are feeding this process by supplying arguments, presented as scientific, to strengthen their ideologically-motivated demands.

The essential ideological premise here is based on classic laissez-faire and the competitive private market (Ruggles and O'Higgins, 1987). It emphasises the values of individualism which are institutionally, underpinned by the free market (Mishra, 1984b, p. 162). The future which is envisaged is a major structural rollback and remarketisation of social security provisions in order to reinforce the market discipline among the populace, depress labour mobilisation, increase workers' dependence on the market, redress the balance of class power and redefine class boundaries (Esping-Andersen, 1989). And it is set on reducing total Government spending, especially in resources allocated to social programmes (Ruggles and O'Higgins, 1987).

2. *Economic Interests.* The forces acting for privatisation are not only ideological. Behind them are strong economic interests, including those of

Alternative futures for social security

the business community, various service providers and even professional groups. All of these are liable to reap considerable financial gains from the privatisation of social security and other social service systems (LeGrand and Robinson, 1985) (for example, the introduction of private medicine into the public hospitals in Israel). It is obvious that the profit motive is a driving force behind the demand for privatisation within these circles. The wish to make profits is a legitimate motive in our societies, and at a time when the assumption of the superiority of markets has gained dominance, the profit motive has become a particularly important factor in promoting this conservative scenario.

In simple terms the desire here is to return to an earlier form of unrestrained capitalism. This will certainly promote the economic interests of the business, managerial and professional classes but at the price of allowing the cost of economic change to fall on the weaker parts of the population (Mishra, 1984b, p. 165).

3. *Other Interests.* The drive for privatisation of social security and health care is also promoted by the interests of the well-to-do, elite population groups, who want to assure for themselves the considerable advantages of the private provision of services in these vital areas. The creation and expansion of pockets of private provision in the fields of pensions and health care enables the strong and wealthy elite groups to maintain the preferred status that private provision assures them in contrast to the less desirable or even low status of the general and universal provision system. Private provision is designed not only to maintain the status differentials but also to assure a higher quality of service to the elite groups (Papadakis and Taylor-Gooby, 1987; Walinsky, 1965). The support of privatisation in this case expresses a clear desire to preserve and possibly strengthen the existing patterns of class division.

4. *Creeping Privatisation.* While no clear policy decision may have been made in favour of the privatisation of social security or health care which would thus change radically the prevailing mixed economy of welfare, we are confronted with the fact that privatisation of these systems is actually taking place and even being accelerated by the use of many hidden or indirect strategies.

The most widely used hidden strategy of privatisation is the strategy of *attrition* (Starr, 1985). This is actually a strategy of privatisation under duress. It is carried out by preventing the allocation of adequate resources to the existing public social security programmes and thus making them less attractive, less efficient and less able to meet the needs of the recipient population. The result is that the public service becomes increasingly handicapped in its capacity to fulfil its tasks. Inevitably, under these circumstances, the middle classes and the higher paid groups among the working class who can afford it move to private services that are ready and willing to meet the needs of these better-off population groups. Its occurrence has an important cumulative effect. What is happening is that the inferior quality of public provision becomes a condition which tends to reinforce itself. As the quality of the service offered by the public programme declines, more people tend to leave it and meet their needs by means of private provision. As more people leave it, the pressure to maintain the quality of its provision declines.

The facts are that only the better off population groups have the ability to articulate their dissatisfaction with the erosion of a public service programme. It is primarily these groups that have the political power to act against the erosion in the quality of the service. When these groups lose interest in a public service, what inevitably follows is its further decline. This is happening because the same groups that earlier abandoned the public service now oppose the allocation of the additional resources required to improve the quality of the service which is no longer serving them. What follows is that the weak population groups that are stuck with a low quality service develop a disparaging attitude towards it and they too seek to leave it. In the end privatisation takes over and the public service becomes marginalised serving only the poor.

Another hidden strategy in the process of privatisation is to impose *user charges*. This strategy is intended to raise additional revenue for the service and control the demand for it (Parker, 1976; Judge, 1980). In practice however, it becomes another channel leading to privatisation (Birch, 1986).

The introduction of charges always begins with small payments supposed to be largely symbolic. What usually happens is that the so-called 'symbolic' charges become quite high and approach the level of prices in the free market, or even exceed them. As a result, the public service loses its rationale since what it offers can be obtained at a lower cost on the free market. Such a situation is clearly a prescription for privatisation.

An additional indirect strategy for privatisation is the granting of *tax relief*, tax credits or tax deductions to the users of privately provided services (Starr, 1985). A person enroling in a private pension plan or a private health insurance plan becomes entitled to tax benefits that reimburse him for a large part of the costs of the private service. The declared rationales for the use of this strategy are to diminish the pressure on the public services, to give more choice to the users and to reduce the cost of the public services. Interestingly the tax expenditure this strategy requires is not considered by its proponents as a public expenditure. The outcome of this strategy is a *de facto* privatisation as it enables the use of private services at a heavily subsidised price.

This indirect privatisation strategy was actually adopted by the present British Government. In its White Paper on the Health Service published at the end of January 1989, the Government proposed encouraging people 60 years old and over to take out private medical insurance. Those who pay for it, whether the elderly person or a member of the family, will be entitled to income tax relief for these payments (Working for Patients, 1989).

All three types of variables described here are in an open or hidden manner leading to privatisation and are strengthening these societal forces interested in realising the Neo-Conservative Dream.

PRIVATE WELFARE STATES

This scenario is not based on a dismantling of the existing public social security or health care systems but, rather, on their marginalisation. The intention is to transform them into institutions catering to the needs of only small, residual poor population groups. Under this scenario, the occupational welfare system will become the main channel of social security provisions (Titmuss, 1958; Sinfield, 1978; Root, 1981).

What is distinctive in the social security systems, as they are known at present, is that they are basically public, universal and provide benefits to the population as a whole, mostly as a right of citizenship. The occupational welfare system is, on the other hand, essentially private and provides its benefits only to select groups of the working population on the basis of merit, work performance and productivity (Abel-Smith and Titmuss, 1974, p. 31). The scenario thus provides legitimisation for maintaining two parallel social security systems; a more deserving system on the basis of work performance at particular workplaces, and a less deserving one on the basis of need for those on the margins of the labour force. In this sense it creates 'private welfare states' for selected, stronger and better off groups of the working population. Japan may well be a good example of such a dual system.

In political terms, this scenario means a shift of attention from public social security policies to the individual workplace as the main source of income security. The effect of such an evolving trend, i.e. the growth of private welfare states, will lead to an increase in the centripetal forces in our societies and augment the divisions within the working population at the expense of the solidarity and mutual support function of society as a whole (Root, 1981).

The primary characteristic of the private welfare states are not only the coverage of the strongest and most affluent groups of the working population, but also the extensive range of social security benefits with which they provide their members. The weaker and less organised groups of workers earning lower wages receive fewer, if any, occupational welfare benefits. But the weaker groups are in greater need of such benefits and of protection against hardship during critical times in their lives.

The private welfare states thus become distinctive status-preserving systems which define the social and economic conditions of particular working groups. Moreover, they also define their status on the stratification ladder (Esping-Andersen, 1985, p. 149). The effect in terms of working conditions, living standards, social status and prestige has been one of the chief factors in the consolidation of the new class division which is emerging in advanced industrial societies. The societal implication of this phenomenon is an emerging refeudalisation of modern society in which the workplace is replacing the feudal structure of the medieval world.

This scenario of promoting and nurturing private welfare states has strong backing among a wide spectrum of ideological, political and interest group supporters.

First, the labour movement and the trade unions support the extension of workplace-related social security and other health and welfare benefits as part of their traditional struggle to improve wages and working conditions. Any extension of these benefits is considered an important expression and achievement of labour union power.

Second, groups of workers which have succeeded in obtaining for themselves generous occupational welfare benefits are, of course, interested in keeping them and, if possible increasing them further. Other groups of workers which have not yet attained these benefits are naturally interested in obtaining them as well and in creating their own private welfare state.

Third, some forces located on the right wing of the political spectrum tend to support the evolution of the private welfare state. Their support is linked to the wish to strengthen the hierarchical elements and the work discipline among the working population by making the whole range of welfare benefits conditional on merit and achievement at the individual workplace. In an indirect way there is in this approach support for the neo-Conservative dream of dismantling the universal welfare state.

Fourth, employers and governments are seeking to realise some of their aims by promoting this scenario. To many employers who oppose government intervention, the provision of occupational fringe benefits to their workforce is important as a backdoor avoidance strategy against encroachment by the state and a defence against public social security (Rein and Rainwater, 1987, p. 151). For governments it can serve as a useful strategy for shifting the burden of public provision to the private occupational sector. For both Governments and employers, it can extend the effective range of control of management over labour (Sinfield, 1989).

It seems that the broad political support this scenario has gives it a good chance for eventual realisation. In addition, the fact that private welfare states are already an accepted feature of the existing social and economic arrangements certainly operates in its favour.

In the event that social security and other social services are allowed to follow this kind of occupational demarcation, this will have an enormous social and political effect on our societies. A new and modern version of feudalism will become the order of the day. The effects, vividly described by Esping-Andersen, will be that broader group loyalties will become sacrificed at the expense of narrower corporate loyalties. Collective loyalty to public social security schemes will thus easily evaporate and increase the risks of class fragmentation, divided loyalties and eventually welfare backlash (1985).

SUMMARY

In any assessment of the significance of the three scenarios outlined in this paper, it is obvious that only the first scenario reflects the trend wishing to maintain the continuity, stability and effectiveness of the universal social security arrangements created as an integral part of the post-Second World War political settlement. The other two scenarios are clearly designed to break this continuity and bring about radical changes in the social security systems currently operating.

Both of these scenarios offer a rather different vision of the future relationships between the working population, the state and the market, and each has far reaching implications for the re-shaping of society and politics. In both there is a clear intent to reduce government responsibility for the provision of social security benefits to the population as a whole. Both seek to change the existing distributional patterns to the disadvantage of the more deprived and marginal population groups (Øyen, 1986). In spite of these seemingly undesirable effects, the two scenarios draw considerable support and it would be unwise to underestimate the appeal they have within broad population groups.

In terms of promoting the primary objectives of contemporary welfare states – social protection, equality and integration – the first scenario seems certainly to be preferable. It reflects the remarkable consensus and legitimacy of the universalistic idea permeating the existing social security arrangements which prevailed for most of the post-Second World War period. It is also in accord with the long-term democratic-egalitarian aspirations which have marked the evolutionary historical process of modern industrial societies for the last two centuries.

In emphasising this preference one should, however, bear in mind that the political and social organisation of social security expressed in the first scenario does not necessarily reflect the end of evolution of social thought, in the Fukuyama meaning of 'endism' (Fukuyama, 1989), about these organising principles. The intention here is not to overrate the permanence of a certain institutional form of social organisation, but rather to point out that at this historical junction the first scenario seems to be more desirable than the others outlined in this chapter.

Apart from stating one's preference, it is difficult, of course, to speculate whether or not one or another of these scenarios will eventually become reality. Moreover, since the three scenarios are not mutually exclusive, it may well be that something from each will find its way into future arrangements and create a new and different equilibrium between them. As projectors and not prophets, we will however, have to wait and see what the future holds.

5
LESSONS FROM THE RECESSION IN SCANDINAVIA 1975–1985

STAFFAN MARKLUND

INTRODUCTION

The western world was heavily influenced by the so-called oil price shocks that occurred in the autumns of 1973 and 1974. Energy prices went up and unemployment increased. A number of nations experienced problems with their trade balances and large public deficits. The trend of continuous growth in welfare spending since World War II was increasingly seen as a major problem. The scientific debate about the crisis of the welfare state predated the actual economic crisis that followed the oil price shocks (Drucker, 1969; Habermas, 1975; O'Connor, l974; King, 1975; Brittan, 1975). To the extent that welfare was in focus in these early writings, it was seen not only as too costly but also as unpopular and ineffective to produce welfare. In the main the definition of the welfare state was synonymous with any modern society. From the late 1970s up till the present day this so-called crisis debate produced a vast literature concerned with the general economic, political and social problems of modern society (Offe, 1984; Hall, 1979; Birch, l984; King, 1983; King, 1987; Lash and Urry, 1987; Keane, 1984; Keane and Owens, 1986). The perspective was critical of extended public welfare programmes on the grounds of their assumed effect on 'civil society', 'public life' and the functioning of the economic and political markets. Few writers specifically analysed welfare structures or compared nations to allow for variations in this respect.

The more specific literature dealing with the effects of the economic recession on welfare can be divided into two major categories. First, those who argue that the welfare state is extremely stable or irreversible (Habermas, l975; Offe, 1984; Therborn and Roebroek, 1986; Brittan, 1975). Second, studies that show that public welfare is in danger of being undermined partly or totally (OECD, 1981; Piven and Cloward, 1982; Block et al., 1987; Munday (ed), 1989; Schmidt, 1983). A realist position somewhere in between shows that some parts of the welfare system are under more serious threat than others. Thus, a German study shows that pensioners are safer than the unemployed and people on means-tested programmes (Alber, 1985).

This chapter is concerned with the robustness of social security during economic stagnation. To what extent is the welfare system irreversible? What factors can explain differences in social security stability? The strategy is to present some indicators of how public welfare was affected by the recession in each of the four Nordic nations and after that to look at plausible explanations for the variation between nations in this respect.

STABILITY AND CHANGE IN DENMARK, FINLAND, NORWAY AND SWEDEN

The four Nordic nations constitute a set of countries similar enough to allow meaningful comparison and yet different with respect to the effects of the economic crisis on public welfare. The four nations all fit into the category 'social democratic welfare state regime', as Esping-Andersen has defined it (Esping-Andersen, 1990). They all have extensive state welfare programmes of the universalistic kind covering the majority of the population. The room for private welfare is limited. None of the nations were seriously damaged by cuts or reductions in spending levels. Nor did any of them experience dramatic changes in the profile of public welfare expenditure.

The growth rate of social spending decreased in the 1980s in Denmark, Norway and Sweden, but Denmark and Sweden are still world leaders in welfare spending per person. In Finland, social spending continued to grow throughout the period. The fact that Norway shows such a slow growth in social security spending as a share of its GDP is due to the fast growth in its GDP caused by the oil exploitation. Between 1975 and 1985 the growth in stable prices was almost as high in Norway as in Finland, see Figure 5.1 (Statistical Report of the Nordic Countries, 1989, Table 2.1.1).

When 1980 is used as the basis for comparing social security spending per capita, Norway and Denmark lag behind Finland and Sweden more obviously in the later year (see Figure 5.2). In all four nations, however, social security and social assistance has kept its share of total public spending during the period. With differences between the nations concerning the level of these costs the variation over time has been extremely small (Marklund, 1988, p. 28). This means that social welfare was not a favoured area in the attempts towards limitation of public economy growth.

The picture of relative stability in overall spending does not fully capture the fact that the social policy climate in all four countries became more grim in the 1980s. A number of cost reducing activities that affected social programmes were introduced by governments in each nation, in particular after 1980. Many different strategies came into use. More restricted indexation rules, increased charging for services, freezing of benefit levels and income tests were frequently used measures. More resolute retrenchments occurred in some of the smaller programmes such as help for the handicapped or unemployment compensation.

As these strategies of welfare reduction differ with respect to their

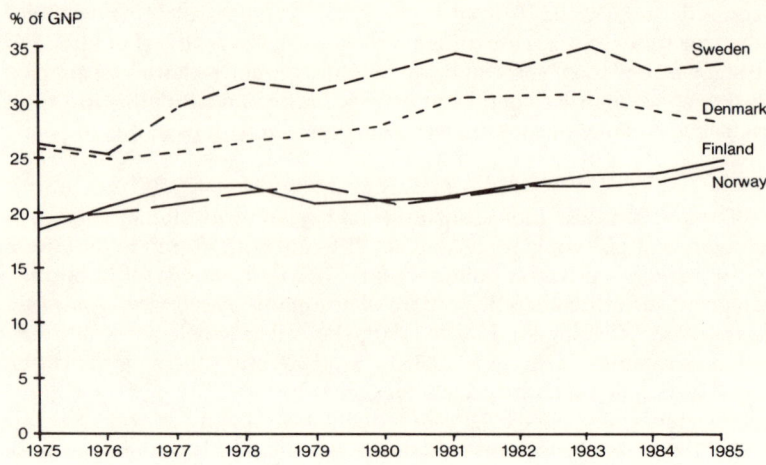

FIGURE 5.1 Social security expenditure as a percentage of GDP

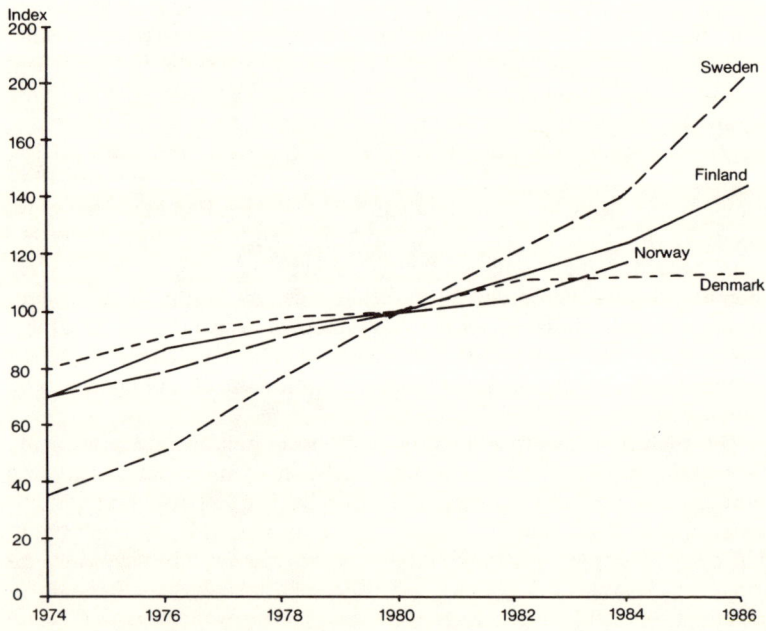

FIGURE 5.2 Social security expenditure per capita aged 15–64 in 1980 prices

distributional effects and their implications for individual families, it is necessary to distinguish between welfare cutbacks that affect large parts of the population to a small degree and selective measures that hit small groups more seriously. The re-introduction of income tests and increased charges for users of public services are both selective measures with important negative effects on small groups. Slower indexation and the freezing of benefit levels will also affect welfare users and cause more damage to those completely dependent on welfare, but the number of people concerned is much larger and the effects on individual families are more limited.

To study the details of welfare changes in these qualitative aspects is complicated. All four nations experienced positive reforms as well as cutbacks and restrictions in their welfare programmes. Adjustments of welfare programmes that are inefficient or inappropriate are not necessarily a part of a welfare cutback strategy.

Throughout the 1970s all four nations continued to carry out social policy reforms that included substantial increases in social security benefits and extended coverage. In Finland the expansion lasted even longer with a major pension reform being introduced in 1983. The reaction to the oil price increases of 1873 and 1974 was in all four nations delayed for at least five years. It took until around 1980 for governments to perceive the situation as a major economic crisis and to implement systematic restrictions in welfare spending (see Figure 5.3).

In terms of welfare cutbacks there is no doubt that Denmark has been the leading Nordic nation, followed by Norway and Sweden. But even Finland was hit by restrictions in the 1980s. Denmark was in all respects most seriously hit by both general and selective measures of welfare reduction. De-indexation of social security benefits, freezing of benefits, the reintroduction of income tests on pensions and other social security programmes and the introduction of service charges have all been frequently used in Denmark since the late 1970s. This massive attempt to reduce welfare spending was defended by reference to Denmark's extremely costly welfare sector and the severe situation of the Danish economy.

The fact that Norway partly followed a similar selective strategy of welfare cutbacks and in addition used general cost reduction measures is more surprising. Norway was the only nation that gained from the oil price increases as it had started to exploit its North Sea oil. Furthermore, Norway was, from the Nordic perspective, a welfare laggard with an underdeveloped and inexpensive public welfare system and had programmes waiting to be enforced. A major improvement was planned in the 1975 pension reform that aimed to raise basic pensions considerably, but it was abandoned in 1980 and never came into operation. It should also be noted that Norway had a lower level of unemployment and a lower share of the population on means-tested social assistance compared to the other three nations (Marklund, 1988, p. 53 and 58). Thus, it did not have to spend large

FIGURE 5.3 Welfare restrictions 1975–79 and 1980–85 in Denmark, Finland, Norway and Sweden

1975–79	1980–85
Denmark	
Means-tested child benefits lowered and abolished for 15-17 year olds in 1975.	Income test on pensions re-introduced.
Income test on all child benefits introduced in 1976.	Income test on child benefits sharpened.
Lower subsidies on medicine and pharmaceuticals.	Invalidity insurance made income related.
Restrictions in unemployment benefits introduced in 1975.	Decreased subsidies for medicine.
	Introduction of one waiting day in health insurance.
	'Freeze' on sickness compensation.
	Restrictions in labour offer law.
	Stricter control of unemployment benefits.
	Restrictions in unemployment compensation for school leavers and long term unemployed.
	'Freeze' on unemployment compensation.
	General modification of social security index.
Finland	
Changed indexation reduces compensation for most pensioners.	Lower pensions due to decreased compensation for own or spouse's income.
Decreased compensation on pension system.	De-indexation of pensions.
Tightened eligibility for invalidity pensions.	Reduced maternity compensation after 100 days.
Decreased compensation level in sickness insurance.	
Norway	
Restrictions on post-payments of pensions.	'Freeze' on minimum pensions.
Increased fees for hospital services.	General de-indexation.
Restrictions in subsidies for medicine and pharmaceuticals.	Pension supplements made dependent on the income of spouse.
	Increased fees for paramedical treatment.
	Restrictions in car subsidies for the handicapped.
	Restricted rules for self-claimed sickness.
	Lowered housing allowances for families with children and for old age pensioners.
Sweden	
Increased fees for hospital services.	Modification in social security index.
Restrictions on subsidies for medicine and pharmaceuticals.	Lowered compensation in part-time pensions.
	Income related fees for hospital services for the elderly.

shares of its social budget on unemployment compensation and needs-based services.

Sweden was hit by general reductions, in particular by de-indexation. Selective measures were used only to a limited degree in increasing service fees in particular programmes. A lack of new reforms and serious attempts to reduce expectations were the major demands of the Swedish welfare crisis. It cannot be demonstrated that the Swedish welfare system became markedly more selective.

Finland experienced limitations in some marginal welfare programmes in the early 1980s but at the same time it was engaged in introducing major welfare reforms in the health services and pension systems. The net effect was an improved welfare standard and a growth in spending.

Before accepting this as a true picture of what went on in the four nations, a few remarks should be made. The information presented here was mainly gathered at the central government level. In all four nations, regional and local governments play a crucial financial and administrative role. Limitations as well as expansions in welfare services may well have taken place at these levels. Another important area of welfare is located within the labour market and individual firms. There are variations between the nations in private and occupational welfare and there seems also to have been some growth over time in these areas. It should also be emphasised that decreased social security spending and dismantling welfare programmes may have to do with changed needs and demographic changes in the populations.

With these remarks in mind, however, the development of the four Nordic nations show different degrees of stability and change in their social welfare structures between 1975 and 1985. The Danish public welfare system suffered most from both general and selective cutbacks. Norway followed the same route of using both selective and universal reductions, but to a much weaker extent. Sweden was affected by cost reducing general measures but less selective ones and should be placed third in terms of cutbacks. Finland expanded its welfare programmes throughout the decade and was only affected by negative reforms to a limited extent.

THE POLITICAL ECONOMY OF THE WELFARE CRISIS

It is reasonable to believe that the economic situation will affect the need to reduce welfare spending. Decreasing growth rates and increasing public deficits are both linked to social policies. Generous welfare conditions are thought to affect work incentives negatively and social welfare is a large part of the public budget. It is also reasonable to assume that political conditions will affect both how this need is interpreted and the strategy of welfare cuts. Large parts of welfare reform in Scandinavia are connected with Social Democratic governments although major reforms have often been supported by one or the other opposition party and often in political harmony. Since the late 1970s the neo-liberal critique of the welfare state has become stronger in the public debate and, with the exception of Finland, non-socialist, so-called bourgeois, governments have taken office.

There is no doubt that the economic recession affected the nations differently (see Figure 5.4). For various reasons, not least historical ones, Denmark was in severe economic trouble. Denmark had in the late 1970s huge public deficits and consequently large foreign debts. It also had large deficits in its foreign trade balance and balance of payments. The growth rate was for most of the years negative or close to zero. These problems in the general economy and in the public economy could be and were used to justify welfare reductions in Denmark.

However, when we compare the economic situation of Denmark and Sweden, it is evident that the Swedish economy showed all the same signs of disease. Sweden had large public deficits and foreign debts. For the whole decade Sweden's public deficits were in fact larger than Denmark's. Its growth rates were negative or low, its trade and payment imbalances also negative for most of the period. After 1983 Sweden regained a positive trade balance but its public deficits remained large.

Finland was to a lesser degree affected by the international recession, partly due to its trade with the eastern bloc and partly due to the more favourable composition of its export sector. The Finnish budget deficits were sizeable (Figure 5.5) and it is surprising how little these influenced the fulfilment of welfare reforms which had been decided in the pre-recession years.

The situation of social policy in Norway is not easy to explain by macroeconomic factors. After 1978 Norway had an extremely favourable trade balance and balance of payments. The central government budget reported a large surplus after the early 1980s. Very little of the prosperity went into social reforms. On the contrary Norway managed to replace Finland as the least developed welfare state and the share of the GDP that was allocated to welfare stagnated during the 1980s. Even if one takes into account that some of the profits from the oil exploitation could not be transferred to public spending in a simple manner but were invested in industrial development, welfare reductions and the restrictive Norwegian welfare policy cannot be understood in economic terms.

Economics can also be seen in terms of economic policies and economic perspectives. In a study of economic policies in the 1970s and early 1980s, Mjöset (1986) found that all four Nordic nations had gradually deserted traditional anti-cyclical economic views in favour of more restrictive monetary policies. This change is more related to economic ideologies than to economic realities as Denmark, Norway and Sweden had very different economic situations. Finland kept a more varied economic policy and adopted restrictive policies during the economic recovery after 1983.

The stagnation that followed the first oil price increase in 1973 was met

Lessons from the recession in Scandinavia

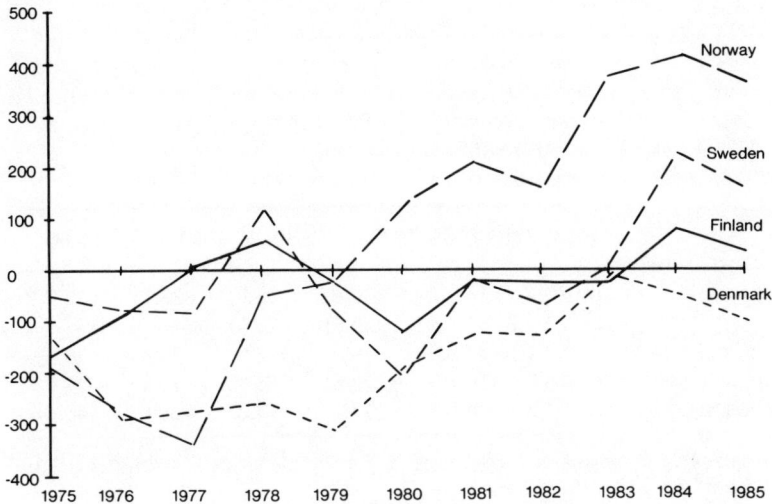

FIGURE 5.4 Trade balance (millions of US dollars)

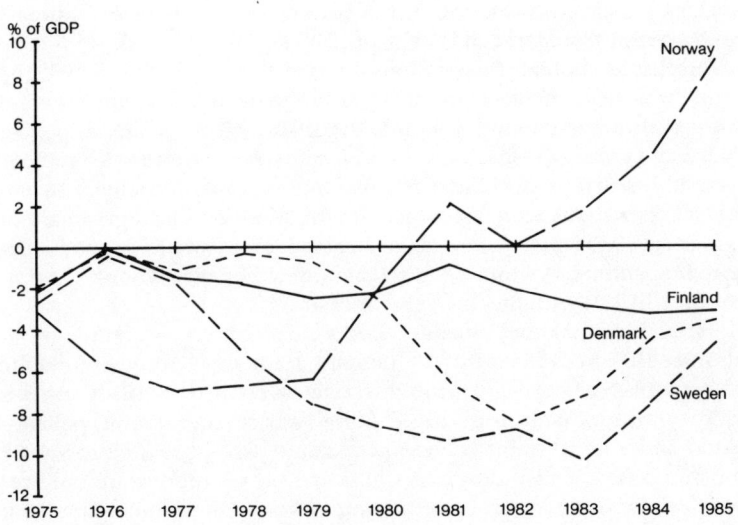

FIGURE 5.5 Central government deficit or surplus

TABLE 5.1 Indices of government strength and electoral support 1973–86

	Number of years of Social Democratic governments (minority) or coalition		Average Conservative Party share of the electorate[1]		Average Social Democratic share of the electorate	
	1975–79	1980–85	1973–79	1980–86	1973–79	1980–86
Denmark	min 3.7 coal 1.15	min 2.7	10.4 (23.0)	15.9 (24.0)	33.1	31.7
Finland	coal 4.4	coal 6.0	19.3	22.0	26.8	28.5
Norway	min 5.0	min 1.9	22.6	33.6	44.5	43.9
Sweden	min 1.8	min 3.2	17.1	23.2	44.1	46.1

[1] Figures in brackets for Denmark refer to the added strength of the Conservative and Progress parties

with the conventional Keynesian response of expanding public spending. In the weak recovery between 1977 and 1979, however, the first signs of a reorientation of economic policies could be seen. The situation was regarded as a structural crisis and it was met by restrictive financial and monetary policies, revaluation of the currencies and increased interest rates (Mjöset, 1986; Marklund, 1988, pp. 71-74).

When the second major recession occurred between 1979 and 1982 the reaction was more diverse, but mostly restrictive monetary policies were instituted although Finland went into the crisis with an expansive policy. In Norway a series of restrictive economic measures were adopted including credit restrictions and increased real interest rates. Extremely strong financial restrictions were introduced in the so-called May agreement in Denmark in 1980 which meant tax decreases for industry and drastic cuts in public spending. A similar policy was adopted by the Swedish government in 1979, but with much weaker measures.

In sum, Denmark and Sweden were seriously hit by economic problems after 1975 as defined by productivity, trade imbalances and public deficits, while Norway went through a business boom due to its North Sea Oil. They all gradually introduced more restrictive economic policies. Finland had a more stable economic situation as well as a more varied economic policy. Thus, differences in economic conditions are only remotely related to differences in economic policies. On the other hand, the shift in economic policies that all the nations have adopted have affected the degree and form of welfare cutbacks very differently.

TABLE 5.2 Degree of selectivity in welfare provisions 1984 (percentages)

	Denmark	Finland	Norway	Sweden
Share of retired on public second layer pensions[1]	47	69	35	65
Child allowance recipients as per cent of all families with children[2]	53	100	100	100
Share of total sickness payments through public social insurance[3]	45–55	100	65–75	100
Waiting days in sickness insurance	1	7	0	1

[1] Defined as recipients of public second layer pensions for old age in 1984.
[2] Recipients of full child allowance. Denmark is the only country which uses income test on child allowances.
[3] Calculated as the number of sick days covered by public health insurance payments. In Denmark the first 13 weeks of sick leave excluding the first day are paid through the employer. In Norway two weeks are covered by employers. Finland has seven waiting days in its public sickness insurance, but in most industries these days are compensated at the expense of the employer.

DO POLITICS MATTER?

At the beginning of the 1980s Denmark, Norway and Sweden had all replaced Social Democratic minority governments with non-socialist coalitions (Paloheimo, 1984). To a large extent these new coalitions came into power on programmes critical of the welfare state and the role of the state in general. In all four countries the Conservative and Liberal parties increased their share of the electorate while the populist agrarian Centre parties diminished (Mackie and Rose, 1982) – see Table 5.1. It is also evident that the Conservative parties changed their profile from a paternal positive welfare state position into a neo-liberal conservative one. Even within the Liberal parties a shift towards more negative welfare views can be noted.

Differences in the political situation cannot in a simple manner explain why Denmark and Norway carried through more severe welfare cuts than Sweden and Finland. In Sweden, two consecutive periods of 'bourgeois' governments from 1976 to 1982 only had a marginal effect on welfare policies. There were some attempts at cutbacks in the health insurance and pension systems that did not pass through the Parliament.

While these indicators of political strength do not show any systematic relationship to welfare reduction, there is of course a possibility that the Danish and Norwegian Conservatives and Liberals were more aggressively against public welfare than their Finnish or Swedish colleagues.

That may explain the Norwegian case, but it remains to be explained why Norwegian Conservatives should be more reluctant to maintain welfare than for example Swedish Conservatives. It should be added that the Social Democrats in each of the nations also proposed cost-reducing measures in social welfare and to some degree accomplished cuts during their time in government in Denmark, Norway and Sweden.

The political situation in Finland is more complicated and cannot be used to explain changes over time as the country has been governed for many years by large coalitions including almost all the parties. It seems plausible that this kind of government construction fosters political stability in general and makes social policies in particular less vulnerable to change. As the same group of parties agreed to the major welfare reforms of the 1970s, they are less inclined to suggest far-reaching reductions a few years later.

To sum up, it must be said that politics matter in that non-socialist governments have been more active to reduce the costs for public welfare. However, differences between the nations in terms of size and content of welfare cuts are not easy to explain by party composition in governments or by the length of time in power of non-socialist governments. In all four nations the political right was both willing and formally able to accomplish welfare reductions, but the degree of success varied.

WELFARE CONSTRUCTION AS AN EXPLANATION OF WELFARE STABILITY

To simplify the argument, Denmark and to a lesser extent Norway are regarded here as cases of active welfare reduction and Finland and Sweden as more stable. Economics and politics can only partly explain these differences. In this section factors endogenous to the welfare system itself are scrutinised for their ability to explain what happened to social security during the recession in Scandinavia.

Three factors seem important; first, the degree of selectivity in public welfare programmes (see Table 5.2); second, the distribution of the financial burden between individuals, industry and state; and third, the labour market orientation or work ethic of social security programmes.

Denmark has traditionally had stronger selective mechanisms in its public welfare system than Finland, Norway and Sweden. Denmark kept income tests longer in its pension system and has a much larger non-public insurance sector. Unlike the other Nordic nations, Denmark has always had income tests in its child allowances. Private as well as employment-based insurance systems are more common in Denmark. Norway has a weaker second-layer public pension system compared to Finland and Sweden, but is in general closer to Sweden in terms of universalism than it is to Denmark.

The reason why selectivity decreases stability in the public welfare system is that it fosters the growth of private insurance and employers' organised systems. Once such structures are created, they constitute an

TABLE 5.3 Distribution of finance of public social welfare expenses (percentages)

	1975				1984			
	State	Local state[1]	Employers	Individuals	State	Local state	Employers	Individuals
Denmark	64	24	10	2	53	32	11	4
Finland	24	15	52	10	34	15	44	7
Norway	14	16	47	23	29	17	35	19
Sweden	36	29	24	11	23	28	48	1

[1] Local authorities as well as regional bodies collect personal taxes separately. Local authorities are primarily responsible for child care, care of the aged and personal social services. Regional bodies are the prime organisers of health services. Both are subsidised over the national budget.

argument against the growth of universal welfare programmes in the areas of health and pensions. If large sections of the population are covered by individual insurance, these groups are often prepared to accept reductions in public welfare and are unwilling to support the extension of public social security. The room for political manoeuvre is larger the more divided the welfare structure is.

Financing social security is a much ignored issue in the sociology of welfare despite the fact that there are interesting differences between nations and despite its impact on the construction of welfare. Denmark is the only Scandinavian nation that relies almost entirely on general taxes to finance its welfare programmes. The other three nations have different mixes of shared financial structures involving taxes, individual and employers' contributions (see Table 5.3). Norway has a relatively high degree of individual fees. In Sweden and Finland employers pay somewhat more than half of total social security costs through separate employers' fees.

There are two reasons why shared financial burdens seem to foster stability. The most obvious reason is that the vulnerability of finances is smaller with three different sources of income. These are not necessarily affected simultaneously during a recession. A specific reason is how the cost debate was formed in the early 1980s. In all the Scandinavian countries the economic problem was seen in terms of the public economy rather than in terms of the cost burden of the industrial sector. The fact is that profit levels continued to be high during the recession while public deficits grew. Thus, the cost argument to implement cutbacks was weakened in Finland and Sweden as the major income was not taxes but employers' contributions. Social security in Denmark was completely dependent on

TABLE 5.4 Distribution of costs for labour market policies in the Nordic countries 1979 and 1984 (percentages)

	Denmark 1979	Denmark 1984	Finland 1979	Finland 1984	Norway 1979	Norway 1984	Sweden 1979	Sweden 1984
Unemployment benefits	84	64	33	34	43	50	10	30
Labour market policies	16	36	67	66	57	50	90	70
Expenditure per person 16–64 years of age (Sw Kr)	2750	8460	850	1790	380	2250	2160	3870

general revenue and consequently extremely vulnerable in this respect.

A third aspect of public social security that seems to affect stability is the degree to which the system is linked to labour market performance or seen as a support system for groups excluded from productive life.

Despite the change over time and differences in total costs the coupling effect is quite obvious. Active labour market policies constitute a much higher share of total spending on labour market policies in Finland and Sweden than Denmark and Norway (Table 5.4). Denmark and Norway spend about two-thirds of their labour market activities on passive measures such as cash payments for the unemployed, whereas Finland and Sweden spend about one-third on such benefits. In Finland and Sweden large efforts are made to improve the education of the unemployed, other manpower policies, support to regional redistribution of the labour force and support to industries.

Not only may these policies affect the numbers of unemployed and in that way limit the cost of social security, they also create a strong work ethic in the system as a whole. This work ethic is also visible in the way other social security provisions are strictly linked to the labour market performance of the individual, in particular in Finland and Sweden. The Danish system is more generous in its compensation levels, duration of benefits and access for the non-working population as compared to Finland, Norway and Sweden. The fact that the welfare system is based on the labour market performance of the individual to such a high degree may be criticised as this created large differences between parts of the population, but it is effective in maintaining stability and at least partly facilitates an overall homogeneity in social security conditions.

FACTORS CONTRIBUTING TO SOCIAL SECURITY STABILITY

Social security of the kind that was created in Scandinavia has a number of distinctive features that are tested in an economic recession. In this context the capacity to survive a tougher economic and political climate is certainly important. The ability of public social security to create social integration or social conflict is another aspect. This includes the ability of a particular social security system to create redistribution and equality.

Public social security, which is directed towards all citizens through high labour market participation and universal social security provisions, is very robust against serious retrenchments. Extensive and expensive public social security seems paradoxically more stable than a selective one. However, this is conditional on two other major patterns. The cost burden should ideally be shared between state, employers and individuals to weaken the budget argument when the public economy is unbalanced. Furthermore, to be effective and legitimate, social security of this kind should foster labour market participation through active labour market policies. Thus, it is not the fact that public welfare is extensive that makes it relatively unaffected by the recession. As the differences between the Scandinavian nations show, universality, shared financial structures and strong work orientation are favourable to stability.

Stability is an important characteristic of public social security, but the construction of social welfare must also be judged from the point of view of class solidarity and redistribution. Few admirers of the Scandinavian models are aware of the fact that these public social security systems are very much based on what Titmuss called 'the industrial welfare model'. This means that social security conditions for the individual are closely linked to their labour market value. This social security work ethic is particularly strong in Finland and Sweden. Previous or present income, length of employment and expected duration of employment are important factors in determining whether the individual will become a member of the more rewarding parts of the system and receive more substantial benefits from it (Marklund and Svallfors, 1987).

The advantage of this construction is that few employed people, blue or white collar, have strong incentives to join private insurance systems for protection. The negative side is that groups outside the labour market, and they do exist even in Scandinavia, are given only second-rate conditions. Some are not eligible for benefits at all and most only for low flat-rate benefits. Another effect of this construction is its limited capability to create redistribution of income. As benefits in the central parts of the social security system are strictly linked to income, there will not be much redistribution. Only at the very bottom and the very top, where the income relation to benefits is set aside, is there a formal redistribution.

This issue is closely linked to the class basis and political functions of Scandinavian social policy. Denmark, Finland, Norway and Sweden are in general in the same family of large public welfare systems. But they have managed to create inter-class solidarity rather differently. Whereas Denmark in particular has a system that fosters conflict, the other three largely seem to support the idea of a large class unit between all employed. Despite the fact that Danish welfare provisions are in most cases the most generous of all the Scandinavian nations, it has less support and representatives of classes have rather different opinions about it. One reason is the lower level of universality so that large sections of high income earners, even among skilled workers, are excluded through income tests. Another reason is probably a stronger feeling of free riding as larger shares of the total costs are directed to clients rather than to workers. To some degree similar patterns occur in Norway. Finland and Sweden have both created unitary social security systems that are extremely popular among blue collar workers as well as among public and private white collar groups. There are differences in popularity among the different segments but there is a strong and supportive majority that gives very little opening for political attempts to make welfare cuts.

6
SALAMI TACTICS AND THE AUSTRALIAN WELFARE STATE

PETER TRAVERS

Mr Rakosi describes one stage of it as 'salami tactics', by which slices of the Small-holders Party were cut away and its strength worn down

The Times, 19 May 1952

CREEPING UNIVERSALISM

In 1908, seven years after the federation of the six colonies that formed Australia, the Invalid and Old-Age Pensions Act was passed by the Federal Parliament. This Act set the pattern for the structure of what would later evolve into the Australian welfare state. The old-age pension was to be a means-tested, flat-rate pension, paid from general revenue. There would be no special contributions from individuals, employers, or government. There was general bi-partisan support for the Bill, and it was hailed by the Parliamentarians with some enthusiasm. One Labor member concluded his speech with the words 'we offer an example to European countries. As an Australian, I glory in the fact that every European nation has its eye on Australia and New Zealand' (Commonwealth Parliamentary Debate (CPD), 2 June 1908, p. 1, 1953). This rhetoric was partly correct. Australia was indeed being watched, but with apprehension. Its non-contributory stance met with the disapproval of the Conference on Social Insurance at The Hague in 1910 (Kewley, 1973, p. 101). The continuing interest in 'Australian exceptionalism' in the field of social security has rarely been based on admiration. Australia has precisely that marginal structure that is so often associated with welfare backlash (Korpi, 1980).

However, a claim has been made by Goodin and Le Grand that suggests that selectivity is more difficult to sustain than is commonly thought. They have used Australia as an extreme testing ground for their thesis of the 'middle class capture' of the welfare state. Their argument is that programmes which were initially tightly targeted on the poor are, over time, increasingly invaded by the non-poor. They found strong evidence between 1940 and 1981 of 'creeping universalism' operating even in Australia

(Goodin and Le Grand, 1987).

Goodin and Le Grand are themselves guarded as to whether they think 'creeping universalism' is a good thing or a bad thing (*ibid.*, p. 218). If one's goal is egalitarian, then it is probably a bad thing, but not necessarily if one sees poverty relief as the chief aim. Goodin has more recently elaborated his view that the welfare state should have the aim of *at least* benefiting the poor, rather than the New Right's vision of its being *only* for the poor. Since he sees the beneficial involvement of the non-poor as largely inevitable, he resigns himself to it, and welcomes the welfare state in spite of it (Goodin, 1988, p. 19). In this chapter I do not propose to pursue that debate. I will focus, rather, on the prior question of the fact of creeping universalism and the mechanism by which it is said to occur.

The Goodin and Le Grand argument is in two parts. First, the growing involvement of the non-poor in three programmes is established. Second, explanatory mechanisms are discussed.

The three programmes examined are the old-age pension, the invalid pension, and the Class B widows' pension (principally for older women without dependent children). These three are chosen partly because of the availability of data, and partly because they are assumed to be programmes from which the non-poor might hope to benefit. Their argument does not extend to programmes in which the non-poor see no likely interest (Goodin and Le Grand 1987, p. 115).

This limitation is a major weakness of the thesis. For one thing, its circularity makes it difficult to falsify. Counter-examples could always be dismissed as involving programmes in which the non-poor have no interest. This weakness is also apparent when we come to the next strand in the argument, the very risky assumption that extended coverage means extended coverage of the non-poor. An examination of three programmes in isolation masks the very large movement *between* programmes, such as from unemployment benefit to the invalid pension. There is no reason to believe that the formerly unemployed were not poor.

On this very shaky basis, Goodin and Le Grand have no difficulty demonstrating the first part of their argument, especially with regard to old-age and invalid pensions. The old-age pension was received by just over 40 per cent of the aged population (women aged 60 and over; men aged 65 and over) in 1940, rising to 76 per cent in 1981. If one accepts that estimates of the invalid population are meaningful, coverage rose from below 50 per cent in 1940 to 88 per cent in 1981. Coverage by the Class B widows' pension showed a marginal increase.

The second part of their argument in which they attribute the growth in coverage principally to behavioural change on the part of the non-poor is even more contentious.

Goodin and Le Grand examine four mechanisms whereby pension coverage might be extended: boundary issues, where similar groups are added to those already favoured by the pension; bureaucratic empire building; behavioural change, whereby the non-poor arrange their affairs to qualify as poor; political change, whereby the non-poor lobby to be included. The test of the probable mechanism is simplified by the fact that the first, second and fourth mechanisms would all imply a relaxation of the means test. If there has been none, behavioural change wins by default.

The maximum income permitted under the relevant means tests has, in fact, varied very little over the period in question when it is taken as a proportion of per capita GDP (Goodin and Le Gran, 1987, p. 121). Thus, it is claimed, there is evidence that the means test has not been relaxed. I find this unconvincing. If we accept a constant proportion of per capita GDP as an adequate indicator, it does indeed show that one aspect of the means tests has not varied. However, it does not capture very significant variations in the means tests on both the age and invalid pensions introduced in 1961 (tests on property and income were merged); 1969 (the 'tapered' means test, i.e. only half of every dollar above the permissible income was considered as means); 1973 (abolition of the means test for those aged over 75) and 1975 (abolition of the means test for those aged 70-74). These last two changes alone were followed by coverage soaring from 62 per cent in 1973 to 74 per cent in 1976 (Department of Social Security (DSS), *Ten Year Statistical Summary*). It is quite unconvincing to argue that this is the result of behavioural change rather than relaxation of the means test.

To sum up, although Goodin and Le Grand can claim some plausibility for a theory of expanded coverage between 1940 and 1981, their claim that the principal explanatory mechanism is behavioural change is singularly unconvincing. I will now argue that policy changes played a decisive role. This will be a prelude to discussing the events of the 1980s when policy changes reversed the trend noted by Goodin and Le Grand.

THE HISTORICAL LEGACY

The selective structure of Australian social security and the absence of a contributory system give the impression of a needs-based system tied to poverty relief. This impression is compounded by the focus on poverty that has been especially evident in the major welfare lobby groups such as the Australian Council of Social Service and the Brotherhood of St Laurence. The poverty lines devised in connection with the Commission of Inquiry into Poverty (the Henderson Inquiry) of 1972-5 have achieved quasi-official status and widespread popular acceptance. Their use was implicit in a much-publicised (and much ridiculed) 1987 Labor electoral promise that 'by 1990 no child need live in poverty'. Yet this is a far cry from attitudes at the turn of the century when the present structure was devised.

The Invalid and Old-Age Pensions Act of 1908, which was to play a decisive role in setting the tone for subsequent social security legislation, was itself based largely on the New South Wales Old-Age Pensions Act of 1900. This Bill had wide bi-partisan support, though there was dissent by some Labor members who opposed means testing (Kewley, 1973, p. 46).

The issue that raised most passion was that the pension should be seen as a right rather than as a charity. In tones reminiscent of Proudhon, Labor members in particular argued that the aged poor are poor because of injustice (New South Wales Parliamentary Debates (NSWPD) 14 Nov 1900, 4973, 4991, 4998, 5440).

The chief argument in favour of universalism was that a means test would penalise thrift and would cause stigma (*ibid.*, 4984). However, the argument that the pension was a right and not a charity, a proposition on which there was general agreement, was turned against the proponents of universality. Universalism was too heavy a price to pay for the avoidance of stigma, since the issue was a pension and not pauperism. 'It is not a gratuity, it is not pauperism, it is something which a man has earned and which he is entitled to' (*ibid.*, 4969).

On the financing side, a contributory system similar to Germany's was rejected on the grounds that it would penalise the sick, the feeble and women. Moreover, a large proportion of the Australian work-force was engaged in casual, seasonal labour, and would not be in a position to make regular contributions (*ibid.*, 4968).

When the federal old-age pension legislation was debated in 1908, the issue of means testing did not loom large. Labor members who in principle favoured universalism supported the Bill as a step in the right direction (*CPD*, 4 June 1908, p. 12021).

Financing of the federal old-age pension by means of a contributory scheme was not seen as a serious possibility at this stage, largely because the newly federated Commonwealth had very limited possibilities of raising new taxes. In addition, Labor pressed its customary claim that the right to the pension was based on prior contributions to the wealth of the nation, rather than on contributions to an insurance scheme (*CPD*, 4 June 1908, p. 12021).

To sum up, at this crucial stage of the development of the Australian welfare state, Labor was arguing against selectivity and against a contributory scheme, but generally agreed that a universal scheme was not a realistic possibility in the short term. At this stage it was the Conservatives who were more likely to oppose the principal of universalism.

The 1908 legislation was decisive in that the centrepiece of all subsequent legislation, the old-age pension, was actually set in place on a non-contributory, selective basis. Those two basic principles have now remained intact for 80 years, despite numerous attempts from both sides of politics, to abolish selectivity, either with or without a contributory system.

One source of ambiguity within the labour movement in this early period was the overlapping issues of universality and the method of funding universal benefits. Labor was generally opposed to contributory schemes, and there was little support at the 1912 conference of the Party, when Labor was in office at the Federal level, for a proposal to introduce a comprehensive, contributory social insurance scheme. Yet the same party delegates were strongly in favour of the payment of universal benefits from general revenue on the analogy of free education (Kewley, 1973, p. 102).

For the next thirty years, moves to introduce contributory pensions came overwhelmingly from the conservative side of politics. None of these contributory schemes ever came to fruition, even though a National Insurance Act was actually passed and proclaimed in July 1938. It was to cover old-age pensions, disablement, medical and sickness benefits, though not unemployment. It was bitterly opposed by a diverse array that included a variety of interests and ideologies, among them the Labor Party, unions, the medical profession, Communists and anti-socialists (Watts, 1987, p. 16). In the face of this opposition, and also because of the growing demands on defence expenditure, the Government lost heart and abandoned the project.

MODIFICATIONS TO SELECTIVITY

The modern welfare state in Australia is generally seen to date from the Unemployment and Sickness Benefits Act of 1944, the crowning achievement of the Curtin Labor Government. The benefits provided under the Act followed the now established pattern of being selective. However, instead of being funded from general revenue, a National Welfare Fund was set aside, and an additional tax in the form of a social services contribution was levied from 1945 to 1950. This had the predictable effect of causing intense resentment on the part of those excluded from all or most of the social service benefits. The numerous modifications to the selectivity of pensions and benefits since that date simply resulted in new groups seeing themselves as unfairly treated (Kewley, 1973, p. 405). It is not surprising that both sides of politics have sought electoral support from these disaffected non-pensioners by periodically promising to abolish the means test, at least on the old-age pension. This reached a high point in 1972 when both parties promised to take immediate steps to dismantle the means test.

So why was the decision made in 1972? It was an election year, there was a favourable economic climate, and an idiosyncratic Minister responsible for social security had forced the issue.

Gruen has drawn attention to the effect of elections on government spending, especially elections a government fears losing. In its last budget before losing office in 1972, the McMahon Liberal Government increased outlays by a massive 6.3 per cent in real terms – an action Gruen (1985) describes as an attempt at 'wholesale bribery of the electorate'. Spending on the aged was a prominent feature of this increase.

It should also be noted that 1972 marked the end of the post-war boom. In 1972, the ratio of spending on unemployment benefits to spending on the old-age pension was 1:26; by 1978, the year coverage began to contract, the ratio was 1:4. Real expenditure on unemployment benefits multiplied a phenomenal 15-fold in that period (DSS *Ten Year Statistical Summary*). A universal old-age pension seemed affordable in 1972 to a degree that has not been matched in subsequent years.

The propensity of governments to increase spending prior to elections and the favourable economic climate do not explain why specifically the old-age pension was chosen for such generous treatment. For that we must look to the Minister responsible for social security in 1971-2, W. C. Wentworth, an outspoken anti-Communist crusader who proved to be equally outspoken in his personal campaign to abolish the means test. To the acute embarrassment of his own party, he refused to let the issue rest (Kewley, 1973, p. 407). Wentworth prevailed, and in August 1972 the Government promised to abolish the means test within three years. After 23 years in the political wilderness, the Labor party was equally determined to woo middle-class voters, and immediately matched the government promise with a commitment to do likewise if elected.

Labor was duly elected in December 1972, and began the dismantling process in 1973. Pension coverage of the aged population peaked at 76 per cent (adjusted to 80.3 if recipients of veterans' pensions are included) in 1980/81 (Saunders, 1987a). This happens to be the year in which Goodin and Le Grand conclude their study.

Contributory Schemes

Though moves towards universality had thus achieved some success by the mid-1970s, parallel attempts to introduce contributory schemes have proven singularly unsuccessful. I have already alluded to the failed attempts by Conservative Governments in the 1920s and 1930s. The Chifley Labor Government made a half-hearted examination of national superannuation in 1947, though Chifley himself was not enthusiastic and preferred to concentrate resources on the poor (Kewley, 1973, p. 292). The Menzies Liberal Government also examined contributory systems, but shelved them by 1954 on the ground of cost (Kewley, 1973, p. 254). The Whitlam Labor Government appointed a committee of inquiry into national superannuation in 1973 (Hancock Committee) which advocated a national scheme in its final report in 1976 (Hancock, 1976). Its proposal to abolish the means test was not supported by the Australian Council of Social Service, the Brotherhood of St Laurence, or by the Chairman of the Committee of Inquiry into Poverty (*ibid.*, p. 15). The Liberal Government in power in 1976 rejected its recommendations outright, once again, mainly on the grounds of cost.

To conclude this section, it can be seen that both sides of politics have periodically favoured a universal old-age pension. Initially, it was Labor that strongly supported universalism, though there is also a long Labor tradition of resistance to middle-class pensions. There was a long process of attrition as policy decisions sliced away at the means test. Finally, by the mid-1970s, the debate on means testing seemed to be over, as steps were well under way to dismantle all means testing on the old-age pension. There was certainly 'creeping universalism', though not of a kind that can be attributed to behavioural changes among the non-poor.

What also emerges from this historical discussion is that there has been no consensus as to the purpose of the welfare state. Throughout the entire period, the focus has oscillated between the relief of poverty and community recognition of citizens' contributions to that community.

Finally, the role of policy has been paramount, reaching a climax in 1972 with the first steps towards the dismantling of the means test on the old-age pension. I will now move on to the 1980s and ask whether the trend towards universalism has continued and in what way policy decisions have influenced that trend.

AUSTRALIA IN THE 1980s

The Economic Context: Boom and Crisis

The Australian economy has had mixed fortunes during the 1980s. Real growth has been high compared to other OECD countries, as have growth in employment and in real household disposable income. On the other hand, a labour market crisis occurred in the early part of the decade and a balance of payments crisis in recent years.

The present Labor Government was elected in March 1983 at the height of the labour market crisis. Labor's macro-economic policy then, as now, was based on an Accord with the Australian Council of Trade Unions (ACTU) whereby wage demands were restrained with a view to promoting growth in employment (for the text of the Accord see National Economic Summit Conference, 1983). The 1983 Labor election promise of '500,000 new jobs during our first term of office' was easily fulfilled.

A second crisis occurred in 1986/7 with a rapid decline in the terms of trade, that is in the ratio of the foreign currency price of exports to imports. Foreign debt increased threefold between 1983 and 1987, while the deficit on the current account increased dramatically (Treasury 1988, Tables 21, 23 and 28).

Government response to the second crisis was to restrain spending. Social security was cut along with all expenditure, but not at the same rate. In real terms, social security outlays in 1988 were only marginally less than in the peak year, 1985 (DSS *Ten Year Statistical Summary*).

The Political Context

The Hawke Labor Government elected in March 1983 was determined to show itself not only as a more competent economic manager than the previous Whitlam Labor Government (1972-5), but also in comparison to the Fraser Liberal Government (1975-83). A key part of this strategy was the Accord between the political and industrial wings of the labour movement referred to above. Its stated aim was to fight inflation and unemployment simultaneously. Though it has elements of European corporatist strategies, it has not succeeded in becoming a truly tripartite agreement between government, employers and unions.

The Accord is relevant to social security expenditure in several ways. The 'social wage' was to be taken into consideration in all negotiations on prices and incomes; the fight against unemployment had first priority and a national superannuation scheme was to be given immediate 'consideration'. Despite constant predictions of its imminent demise, the Accord has in fact endured for six years. It is being constantly re-negotiated, especially when it was no longer possible for the original promise of indexation of wages to be sustained. As we shall see, these negotiations have included specific trade-offs between wage-rises and superannuation and family payments.

Creeping Universalism or Salami Tactics?

We left Goodin and Le Grand on the eve of the election of the Hawke Labor Government with their convincing account that the old-age pension at least seemed to be moving towards universal provision, and their unconvincing account that this was due primarily to behavioural change among the non-poor.

The most notable developments under the Hawke Government have been the re-imposition of the means tests on the old-age pension that were being phased out in the 1970s, the imposition for the first time of an income test in family allowances, the one major universal programme in the Australian social security system, and the phasing out entirely of the Class B widows' pension. The old-age pension may also be affected in the longer term by moves in the field of occupational superannuation. In contrast to these restrictive measures, there have also been very substantial moves to abolish child poverty.

The first moves to back-track on the abolition of the means test on the old-age pension came as early as 1978 under the Fraser Government when, on the grounds of economic necessity, the means test-free pension for those aged 70 and over was frozen at its current nominal level. Two months after the election of the Hawke Government, the Treasurer announced the re-introduction of an income test on pensions for those aged 70 and over. His explanation was one that was to be repeated frequently in subsequent years: 'That problem (of providing decent support for the aged) has been almost totally bedevilled by the way in which the available resources have been sprayed about indiscriminately' (*CPD*, 19 May 1983, p. 806). An even more significant step towards reversing the decisions of the 1970s was the introduction of an assets test from 1985. This last move was prompted by factors that accord entirely with the Goodin and Le Grand theory. Very significant numbers of the non-poor aged were making use of capital appreciation schemes to render themselves eligible under the income test. What sits less easily with the Goodin and Le Grand theory is that the newly-elected Government acted decisively, in the face of intense political

Salami tactics and the Australian welfare state

opposition from those affected, to end this practice. Coverage by the old-age pension has declined from 76 per cent in 1981 to 61 per cent in 1988.

Can the entire decline in coverage be attributed to the harsher means test alone? That would be too strong a claim. Some of the decline is a temporary feature of a 'bulge' during this period in the numbers of ex-service personnel becoming eligible for the separate veterans' pension (DSS, Australia, 1988). There might also be an increase in affluent people in the aged population. However, it is highly unlikely that either of these factors could account for the bulk of the dramatic decline in age pension coverage.

The second move was the imposition for the first time of an income test on the family allowance payment that had previously been a genuinely universal payment for all children under 16. On the ground that resources should be targeted to those in greatest need, an income test (at a very high level) was applied from November 1987. The cut-off point is indexed to inflation, and in its first year of operation, the previously universal coverage declined by only 8 per cent (*ibid.*, p. 76). There was very little adverse political comment when the income test was introduced. Despite the wide constituency having an interest in this universal payment, few argued for the principle of universalism. It seemed, rather, to be the case that a universal payment in an otherwise selective system appeared as an anomaly. There was simply no lobby to sustain the case for universalism.

One of Goodin and Le Grand's three examples of creeping universalism was the Class B widows' pension paid principally to older women without dependent children. This is being phased out entirely on the grounds that women and men should be treated equally by the social security system. Women in this category will in future have to join the labour force, or rely on the same unemployment or other benefits as men.

In the original version of the Accord between the Labor Party and the ACTU in 1983, there was a carefully worded promise to give 'immediate priority (to the) consideration of the possible role for a national superannuation scheme'. What actually emerged was something very different. In 1985, the ACTU endorsed a campaign for universal superannuation cover of the Australian work-force (Foster, 1988, p. 205). In the 1986 re-negotiation of the Accord ('The Accord Mark II') at the time of the balance of payments crisis, it became impossible to sustain the original promise of wage-indexation. As a trade-off, the union movement accepted a package that included a 'wage-tax trade-off', and payments for increased productivity taking the form of the equivalent of a three per cent wage rise in the form of employer-funded superannuation. Occupational superannuation rather than a national scheme was thus given a major boost. There was a dramatic rise in the percentage of employed people who have some superannuation cover. However, many of these recent entrants to superannuation will receive meagre benefits, and far more expect to have the age pension rather than superannuation as their principal source of income in retirement (Australian Bureau of Statistics (ABS), 1988, Table 3).

What are the long-term consequences for the old-age pension of this notable move towards occupational superannuation? At the very least it can be said that the displacement of the old-age pension by superannuation as the principal source of retirement income is now on the political agenda. The prestigious Economic Planning Advisory Council (EPAC) foreshadowed this in a recent discussion of the adverse effects on savings of the means test on the old-age pension. With rather chilling logic, it pointed out that a solution would be to tighten the means test. Fewer people would then receive the pension, and thus fewer would have their behaviour affected. The pension could then be focused on poverty alleviation, while income maintenance would be the function of private savings and superannuation (EPAC, 1988, p. 54). Similarly, the Social Security Review, after stating categorically that the opportunity for introducing a national superannuation scheme had passed, recommended a dual system of means tested (but substantially increased) age pensions, and occupational superannuation (Foster, 1988, p. 183). This proposal is very much in keeping with the Hawke Government's consistent policy of focusing the social security system on poverty alleviation.

Social Security and Poverty Alleviation

The examples given so far of social policy developments in the 1980s might well give the impression merely of cost-cutting. However, that would overlook the very notable increases in expenditure that have been made in the name of eliminating poverty.

The standard pension rate has been raised, and is close to achieving yet another Accord goal: that it should be 25 per cent of average weekly earnings. The pension rate has been indexed to inflation since 1977, though the lag between rises in the cost of living and adjustment of the pension could be considerable. This lag was reduced by 12 weeks as from 1990.

Though the pensions paid to adults have been protected against inflation since 1977, this has not been the case with the child support component of pensions and benefits. This was redressed in a substantial package introduced in April 1989 in fulfilment of a government promise to 'eliminate child poverty by 1990'. Family allowances have been increased markedly, though in real terms they are still lower than when introduced in 1976. However, a very notable breakthrough is that these payments are now for the first time indexed.

A further component in the child-poverty package was a large increase in the size of the family allowance supplement payments that are made to low income workers. This resulted from the wage bargaining process with the union movement where the widening of benefits for low-income workers has been a crucial element in the acceptance of limited wage rises (Treasurer's April Economic Statement, 12 April 1989). We have already seen how occupational superannuation was used in 1986 in a similar fashion. But the use of a social security programme in this context is a new departure.

What all these moves add up to is a major strengthening of the focus of social security on poverty alleviation. Within this framework, notable success can be claimed. It is a far cry from the 'middle class capture' theory. What we have seen, rather, is the consolidation of a selective social security system.

The Purposes of Social Security

A recent critic of Goodin and Le Grand has described their theory as perverse on the grounds that it evaluates the welfare state on the sole criterion of how efficiently the poor are assisted by the non-poor, whereas one should expect the welfare state to represent a compromise between competing aims (Marmor, 1989).

I have described such competing aims in Australian political debate and practice. There has never been a resolution to the rival claims based on poverty-relief as opposed to, say, community provision in the face of contingencies of life that can befall all, rich and poor alike.

A striking feature of political debate in the 1980s is the extent to which the anti-poverty focus now dominates. Though their rhetoric differs, both sides of politics now judge programmes on their efficiency in targetting the poor.

The only political voice questioning this mainstream consensus is coming from the newly formed Grey Power movement, a grouping based principally among people affected by the means test on the old-age pension. Their overall political programme is such that they have been described by the leader of the Australian Democrats as 'geriatric fascists' (*The Weekend Australian*, 11-12 Feb 1989, p. 25). It is too early to tell if this movement will amount to anything, and whether it may succeed in wringing some concessions from the major parties. Its existence does make clear, however, that the consensus is not complete.

Despite the dissenting voice of Grey Power, I would argue that the mainstream consensus on the aims of the welfare state is now so strong that it is increasingly difficult to sustain Marmor's criticism of the Goodin and Le Grand theory in Australia. Experience of the political ease with which an income test was imposed on family allowances in 1987 illustrates the extent to which Goodin and Le Grand's central premise is now broadly accepted in Australian political debate. In other worlds, the basic assumption is that the welfare state should be judged by how efficiently the non-poor assist the poor. That is a new development.

THE FUTURE

This chapter has shown that the expanding coverage by the Australian social security system has been reversed in the 1980s. Can one go further, though, and predict whether coverage will continue to shrink, or will it be held constant at present levels, or will once again expand as in the recent past? To answer that, it must first be made clear whether the mechanism for expansion and contraction is primarily behavioural or political.

Political Explanations and Behavioural Explanations

In the course of this chapter, I have questioned the validity of Goodin and Le Grand's behavioural explanation for the undoubted expansion of coverage that took place up to 1981. It is not a question of denying that people 'arrange their affairs' to qualify for eligibility for means-tested pensions. They undoubtedly do. The question is the extent to which policy intervention can over-ride this expansionary tendency. The Australian experience in recent years is surely that policy intervention can be very effective. That can be illustrated with reference to the invalid pension, one of the areas where Goodin and Le Grand found expanded coverage. The recent estimates of outlays on the invalid pension and sickness benefit by the Department of Finance show that expansion has continued up to 1988/9, but is projected to decline up to 1991/2. Coverage depends on a variety of policy factors. Rapid growth in coverage coincides with high unemployment, as the sick and disabled find it harder to get jobs. Growth in coverage between 1972 and 1987 was five times higher for men than for women, reflecting in part the availability of alternative income-maintenance programmes for women, and women's earlier retirement age. Coverage depends crucially on policy decisions as to how disability is defined. The 1980s have seen first an increase and then a decrease in the consideration given to socio-economic, as distinct from medical, grounds. Sometimes the Department of Social Security goes too far. A 1987 change to guidelines saw so many rejected that the rules were subsequently relaxed somewhat (Finance, 1988, p. 167).

Overall, the Department of Finance estimates that policy decisions over the three years to 1988 to target 'greatest need' in the area of social security income programmes have resulted in expenditure being 4 per cent lower than it would otherwise have been (*ibid.*, p. 186). It does not follow, however, that this rate of attrition will continue. That will depend on the economic and political context.

The Economic Context

It would be difficult to establish the case that coverage will continue to shrink on grounds of economic necessity alone. What can be established is the very large increase in expenditure on certain programmes that will be needed if coverage does not shrink. Commenting on the Department of Finance Forward Estimates, Saunders has taken the period 1975/6 to 2021, and asks what would be involved in the case of the old-age pension if coverage is held constant at present levels, while the rate of increase in real benefits continues to grow at 1 per cent a year. Expenditure would have to grow in real terms at 3 per cent a year, compared to an annual average growth of 1.3 per cent a year since 1975/6 (Saunders, 1989). Even with no growth in real benefit rates, expenditure would have to grow by 2 per cent a year. That may seem an impossibly large rate of increase, but it is offset somewhat by declines in other areas of social spending.

Australia's population structure is relatively favourable in terms of dependency ratios compared to most OECD countries. Moreover, Australia's participation rates are lower than in most OECD countries, so there is room for expansion, especially in the case of women (EPAC, 1988, p. 28). The EPAC study of all social spending, both at national and at state levels, predicts, on most of its assumptions, modest increases in the ratio of social spending to GDP. However, it concludes that the prospects up to the year 2021 are 'not unduly alarming' (*ibid.*, p. 28). Among the various options EPAC canvasses before reaching that relatively optimistic conclusion are cutting the level of benefits, and further restricting coverage.

Cutting the level of benefits (e.g. by restricting increases to the rate of inflation rather than to rises in productivity) would mean pensioners falling further behind community living standards. In view of current practice, and especially in view of the present anti-poverty consensus, that seems an unlikely policy choice for either side of politics. It is far easier to argue that pension rates should be maintained, but should be targeted to the 'genuinely poor'.

The Political Context: The Anti-Poverty Consensus

It does not necessarily follow from a focus on poverty-relief that coverage will shrink. The argument can certainly be made that adequate help to the poor will only come by expanding coverage. Saunders, for instance, has argued that Australia's low ranking in international studies of the redistributive effect of income maintenance programmes is directly related to its high selectivity (Saunders, 1987b). However, at the political level, this argument lacks appeal in the face of the more populist demand of the Federal Treasurer that resources should not be 'sprayed about indiscriminately'.

The real significance of the shift in attitude I have noted is that a whole set of arguments for universal provision as a good in its own right, that even recently was common in Australia, is now carrying little weight. The once common argument for the old-age pension as a right for all is now associated with fringe political groups. This means that the potential for coalitions between varied groups having a common interest in expanding coverage has now greatly diminished.

The focus on poverty provides a ready-made legitimation for policy decisions to restrict present social security coverage. The favoured mechanism for restricting coverage may not, however, be means testing. It has been pointed out that it is far easier to make savings when one starts from the generous base of most OECD countries than from Australia's already restrictive system. Even recent experience in Australia has involved starting from a relatively high coverage base (universal in the case of family allowance and close to universal for pensioners aged 70 and over) (Finance, 1988, p. 186; OECD, 1988c). There is clearly room to tighten means testing on family allowance, where coverage is still above 90 per cent. But the Department of Finance points out that for old-age pensions in particular, a continual tightening of the means test will involve an interaction with the income tax system that produces extremely high marginal tax rates (Finance, 1988, p. 186). If the aim is to encourage private saving, and less reliance on the old-age pension, it may not make sense to tighten the means test beyond a certain point.

For these reasons, though the salami process that further restricts coverage is likely to continue, there will be more emphasis on mechanisms other than means testing, such as changes in the retirement age and in definitions of invalidity and unemployment, and on the use of incentives to switch to semi-public schemes such as occupational superannuation.

DISCUSSION

Esping-Andersen (1989) has questioned the usefulness of categorising welfare states in a linear fashion in terms of their expenditure. He suggests we look, rather, at clusters of regime-types, three of which can be clearly identified: the liberal, the corporatist, and the social democratic. Australia is seen as 'exceedingly close to the bourgeois-liberal ideal-type', with Austria, France, Germany and Italy representing the corporatist, and the Scandinavian countries the social democratic model.

If we examine the chief characteristics of the liberal model, Esping-Andersen's categorisation of Australia appears correct. Under the liberal regime-type, means tests dominate, provision is mainly for low-income groups, entitlements are strict, benefits are modest and there are heavy subsidies to private welfare schemes. This results in minimal de-commodification (i.e. there are very restricted possibilities of opting out of work), in equality of poverty among recipients, and in class political dualism between public and private welfare. It is in relation to these last two outcomes – equality of poverty and public/private dualism – that important reservations must be made.

Though the ideal-type liberal model might be expected to result in equality of poverty and stigma among recipients, this is not yet the case in Australia. Thus, even though an assets test now applies to the old-age pension, the principal family home is exempted. With no less than 84 per cent of married old-age pensioners owning their homes, their material circumstances differ markedly from those of, say, supporting parent beneficiaries and unemployment benefit recipients (ABS, 1986). This difference is less apparent if one looks only at the cash level of pensions.

Old-age pension recipients also deviate from the liberal model in the level of esteem they enjoy, something which no political party can afford to ignore. This is in part related to the historical legacy according to which they still retain the image of honoured creators of the nation's wealth. The moves towards universalism noted by Goodin and Le Grand undoubtedly contributed to this lack of stigma. In this sense, the old-age pensioners stand in marked contrast to groups such as single parents and the unemployed to whom the liberal model applies in its full rigour.

The developments since 1983 under a Labor Government have produced only minor deviations from the basic liberal model. It is significant that the moves towards greater adequacy of benefit levels have been carried out above all in the name of eliminating *child* poverty. The Labor Government's use of Swedish-style terminology, such as 'active labour-market policy', has yet to be applied in practice. The terminology itself is sufficiently ambiguous to be compatible both with de-commodification and with harsher use of work tests.

The Australian welfare state still defies simple categorisation. I have argued that the 1980s have seen something like a political consensus that has resulted in its poor-law features emerging ever more sharply. This may well result eventually in the 'equality of poverty' that the ideal-type liberal model would predict. However, the anomalous situation of old-age pensioners remains for the present, and as long as it remains, there is the potential for challenges to the liberal model.

7
IRREGULAR EMPLOYMENT PATTERNS AND THE LOOSE NET OF SOCIAL SECURITY: SOME FINDINGS ON THE WEST GERMAN DEVELOPMENT

KARL HINRICHS

INTRODUCTION

In West Germany as in most other OECD countries, *labour market flexibility* has developed into a catchword and a prominent political issue in the controversy about how to reduce the number of unemployed (which is still hovering around two million) and how to speed up the job generation process.[1] It is stated that the West German labour market is too rigid, especially if compared with the United States' 'employment miracle' which is considered to be due to the efficacy of 'unchained' market forces. Thus, to overcome the 'classical' unemployment problem, more flexibility and deregulation is required. According to the protagonists of enhanced flexibility the prevailing wage structure has to be adapted to meet the productivity and scarcity of different categories of workers and to increase labour mobility. The wage bill of the employers has to be freed from 'non-wage costs' (e.g. by lower social security contributions) and jobs should be more 'fluid', i.e. employers' costs of dismissals have to be reduced. Moreover, in order to increase the utilisation of machinery, obstacles to more shift work, work at weekends and other 'abnormal' working time patterns have to be removed, and the distribution of employees' working hours should be smoothly adapted to the fluctuations in production to help to lower unit labour costs (Himmelreich, 1988; Vaubel,1989).

However, there are good reasons to question the assumption that more dynamism is prevented by an increasingly over-regulated and inflexible labour market (Buttler,1986, pp. 25-44; Franz,1989) or that the West German labour market is, in general, the most 'inflexible' among OECD countries (Klau and Mittelstädt, 1986). Nevertheless, the Conservative-Liberal government has responded to neo-liberal doctrines and employers' demands for more flexibility when enacting several deregulations, the most important of which so far was the *Beschäftigungsförderungsgesetz* from 1985.[2] Further de-/re-regulations (e.g. a new law on working hours) have reached the stage of parliamentary discussion or can be expected to appear on the legislative agenda. Moreover, the employers gained in collective bargaining themselves (especially on more flexible working hours – see Hinrichs,1990), and they extended their capacity to shape the labour process by utilising unregulated segments of employment more frequently (e.g. certain forms of part-time work or sub-contracting). Partly assisted by the alterations *within* the system of regulating the employment relationship, the proportion of irregular employment patterns has increased over the last decade.

However, if there are irregular employment patterns there have to be regular employment patterns from which the former deviate in one or more respects. The changing composition of employment patterns in favour of the irregular ones has enjoyed lively discussion under the heading 'erosion of the standard employment relationship' (*Normalarbeitsverhältnis*) after the publication of Ulrich Mückenberger's seminal article in 1985 (for examples see Bosch, 1986; Besters, 1988; Bäcker,1988). Since then the phrase *Normalarbeitsverhältnis* has become a key word when the future of industrial relations and the 'work society' is concerned. Hence, in the following section I will discuss the development, the main elements and the functions of the 'Standard Employment Relationship' (SER) as a societal arrangement of production and reproduction. Of special interest is the connection between the SER and the social security system. I will then examine certain recent developments in the West German labour market. The spread of various irregular employment patterns, however, is not solely due to endeavours of employers. As will be demonstrated, the SER has become too narrow a 'corset' to accommodate the needs of a very differently composed labour force. Next I will turn to the consequences of the 'erosion' of the SER. The formation of 'new poverty' and precarious income situations are the result of the growing polarisation between a well-protected core of the labour force and marginalised groups on the verge of the labour market. Finally, two alternatives to deal with the partial erosion of the SER are tentatively explored.

THE DEVELOPMENT AND THE FUNCTIONS OF THE 'STANDARD EMPLOYMENT RELATIONSHIP' (SER)

Polanyi stated that no society could stand the effects of an unbounded ('self-regulating') labour market where the fictitious commodity 'labour power' is bought and sold without its own destruction – not 'even for the shortest stretch of time'. Society would have to protect itself from 'demolition' by social legislation, factory laws, social insurances and further standards and regulations and, thus, retain the main functions of the labour market (Polanyi, 1957, pp. 73, 76 and 163–177). This is not the place to elaborate on the driving forces behind the development of labour and social policy, the conflicts and controversies, but, it was the interplay of the state's intervention into the working of the labour market, the achievements of collective bargaining and the rules of social custom that brought about the SER and its successive refinements. While the 'self-regulating' labour market was a result of the movement 'from Status to Contract' (Maine, 1959, p. 141), the development of the SER in the course of industrialisation meant a reversal when the labour contract was gradually enriched with individual and collective status rights regulating dependent labour and its exchange with capital. Almost everywhere attempts to safeguard the long-term 'marketability' of labour power and to prevent the disastrous downward spiral of wages when labourers compete in selling their labour power started with limitations of working hours, regulations concerning the work of women and children and measures to improve occupational safety. However, when certain stages to establish the SER had been reached or whether legislation or trade unions were the most influential during this process, varied between the nations.

Labour policy dealing with the central interests of labour – working conditions, wages and stability of employment – is thus the first of three hierarchically ordered institutional elements of the security structure grouped around the SER. Second, resting upon dependent employment under 'normal' conditions, although separately organised, social insurance policy provides income substitution for well-defined circumstances (i.e. typical risks of wage labour) where employees are temporarily unable to earn a market income (sickness, unemployment) or are no longer expected to do so (invalidity, retirement). The institution of poor-relief (supplementary benefits) constitutes the third element within the SER arrangement. Earning a market income has priority over benefits from the social insurance systems and the normative point of reference of supplementary benefits is the reproduction through employment as well. In its character as a subsidiary (means-tested) income and in the determination of the (maximum) level of supplementary benefits the dominance of the SER shows up. While the level of social insurance benefits is tied to (former) earned income (or to contributions respectively), supplementary benefits are granted according to individual needs. However, the principle of 'less eligibility' demonstrates the esteem and priority of employment (Leibfried and Tennstedt, 1985b; Mückenberger, 1985, pp. 415-8).

Together, labour and social policy constitute the SER as a 'prevailing fiction' (Mückenberger, 1985, pp. 422 and 432-3). This societal arrangement of dependent employment is assumed to be regularly found in reality and, at the same time, in a normative sense it signifies something that 'should be' although the SER has never covered 100 per cent of the dependent labour force. There has always been day-labour, seasonal work and other kinds of marginal employment beside contracts empirically coming up to the SER. Because of this difference the SER has always been only a 'fiction'. Nevertheless, as a point of reference this societal 'model' of dependent employment has guided (further) labour and social policies, it has structured images of oneself and others, expectations, the perception of deviations (e.g. from a 'normal biography') etc. And last but not least, the SER functioned to internalise workers' willingness to engage in continuous, disciplined and dependent employment as a life-long necessity when it superseded alternative human activities and conceptions of life as inferior (Mückenberger,1989a pp. 212–3).

The overall power imbalance between the supply and demand of the labour market was not abolished by the emergence and successive refinements of the SER. This would have meant the termination of the relationship of exchange between capital and labour since the possibility to extract effective 'labour' from 'labour power' (which is inseparably connected with the living owner even after its sale) rests upon unequally distributed strategic market options placing the employees at a disadvantage of which one of the most important is that the wage dependent worker cannot 'wait' to sell his labour power (Offe and Hinrichs, 1985). However, this power imbalance has been reduced and, thus, the SER protected the workers from the worst effects of the 'self-regulating' labour market. It limited arbitrariness and the absolute dominance of the owners of capital and, thus, improved the efficiency of the labour market processes. Therefore, the interventions into the 'free' labour market also served the long-term interests of capital when they enabled the market to unfold its productive potentials.

So far, I have not touched on the 'content' of the SER. What are its key elements? The items listed below take pattern from those named by Mückenberger (1985, pp. 422–9), Däubler (1988) and Zachert (1988) and might still not be complete (as well as uncontested). First of all, the concept of the SER implies continuity and stability of employment; it is supposed that dependent work is performed from the end of education until retirement at a certain age. The contract of employment is, in principle, unlimited which does not exclude the (permanent) risk of dismissal or to terminate the contract by one's own will. Involuntary interruptions of employment signify only temporary, short-term spells of unemployment. With the length of service and, sometimes, with age the stability of employment increases (e.g. improved dismissal provisions or other 'seniority' rights). Therefore, 'continuity' and 'stability' refer to the notion that the SER includes a 'career'; improving the position within the wage hierarchy, occupational advancement etc. be it with one and the same employer or in the course of changing to other employers.

Moreover, the SER means full coverage by all legal protection and participation rights (some of which improve with the size of the employing firm), encompassing rights to the results of collective bargaining and full entitlement to occupational benefits (e.g. pensions) and procedures (e.g. participation in qualification schemes). If there are individual deviations and negotiations, they are exclusively concerned with improvements 'above' certain standards. Especially, 'normal' employment is full-time employment according to the prevailing standards and this also signifies employment with only *one* employer (in a firm and not at home). The standardised working hours arrangement which is part of the

SER includes the fixation of a certain number of 'normal' working hours as well as a regulated and even distribution of these hours. This functions as a protection of employees' non-working time (leisure) when differentiated from predictable and regular working hours and it draws a clear distinction between 'normal hours' and overtime. Foremost by custom it is secured that a 'job' is a 'full-time job' and that employers do not tailor jobs according to some economic calculus which would not provide a 'living wage'. Since it is presumed that, according to qualification and seniority/age, wages are fixed, this implies that even employees with the lowest wage-rate and working full-time earn an income sufficient to maintain the needs of a nuclear family (husband, wife and one child).

As mentioned above, benefits from the social insurance systems are tied to the duration of employment and the level of former earnings. If the former employment corresponded to 'normal' condition regularly, these benefits secure the subsistence, although on a lower level. However, the SER discriminates against those employees who are unable to meet the conditions of 'normal' employment or who prefer to deviate from this pattern. The disadvantages concern all or only a few aspects of the employment relationship and subsequently the access to and the level of social insurance benefits.

Predominantly, women are affected because the SER is clearly 'gender biased' (for some examples, see Hinrichs, 1989, pp. 13–4). As a societal arrangement of production and reproduction it rests upon the conception of the 'male breadwinner family', and the establishment of the SER constituted or stabilised the 'female homemaker family' as the opposite side of the coin (Davis, 1984). As is well known, the assignment of household and family work to the wife still hampers her continuous and stable (full-time) employment.

But employees who do not want to meet the conditions of the SER are also discriminated against. With the unparalleled rise of real incomes after World War II, the expansion of the welfare state, extended schooling etc., class identities and class-related traditions have been fading in their importance for shaping one's life. This has led to an individualisation of experiences, situations and conceptions of life, enhanced self-competence (and necessity) to organise one's own life and a pluralisation of life styles. The fading of the 'modal' (male) employee as the centre of the SER means that for an increasing part of the labour force potential this arrangement has become too narrow a 'corset' to accommodate diverse biographical situations, more fluid life plans, and conceptions of non-linear occupational careers. First of all, these 'deviating' preferences are related to working hours. There is much evidence that working full-time over one's whole occupational life is becoming less attractive as compared with other non-linear patterns (Hinrichs, 1990). Certainly, very often the desire for part-time work (or interruption of employment altogether) stems from obligations in the non-occupational sphere, especially for married women, but, these preferences also emerge from 'new' conceptions of (family) life, i.e. they extend to men as well.

However, employers are much more active in striving to blast the overall prevalence of the SER. In the past, they benefitted from the SER arrangement that directed competition in a productive way, provided social stability and a calculable framework for economic growth because it transformed the 'bazaar' type labour market into a regular 'market' with standardised prices for a typified supply that rendered possible economically rational comparisons and decisions and relieved the exchange between capital and labour from an unregulated and permanent conflict (Lederer and Marschak, 1927, p 116). In view of markets becoming more turbulent and decreasingly dominated by mass-production for capacious demand, cycles of investment and product innovation getting shorter and international competition growing fiercer, 'Labor as a Quasi-Fixed Factor of Production' (Oi, 1962) is no longer adequate to adapt to changes, fluctuations and risks in the industrial sector as well as in the growing service sector with its specific conditions of production (e.g. non-storable) and profile of demand (e.g. less predictable). The strategic re-orientation is enhanced if foreign competitors can operate in a comparatively more 'flexible' environment (Barkin, 1987). However, deregulation and 'strengthening market forces' as measures to increase firms' capacity to adapt to new challenges mostly do not come up to those terms. Preponderantly, changes *within* the system of regulation are at stake – variations of the type (substantial/procedural), the level (e.g. from legislative to collective bargaining), the objects or subjects of regulation (Buttler, 1986, pp. 12, 24 and 49). But those alterations do not meet the interests of employers and employees in a like manner and, therefore, unions regard demands for 'more flexibility' as an attack on the protective functions of the SER. They fear that a flexible 'fringe' could replace ever larger parts of the internal labour force without loss in efficiency. Although 'rational' employers can by no means be interested in overrunning the institutions for non-price coordination of the exchange of labour altogether (and thereby all stable employment relationships – Buttler, 1986, pp. 41–2 and 45–9) their strategic reorientation and utilisation of given options for more 'flexibility' have already resulted in an increased number of irregular employment patterns.

THE CHANGING LABOUR MARKET: IRREGULAR EMPLOYMENT AND DESTABILISED CAREERS

The patterns of irregular employment I want to deal with in the following pages are not altogether new, but have grown in importance and are looked upon differently under the auspices of continuing mass unemployment and enhanced interest of employers for more 'flexibility'. They are part-time work, fixed-term contracts, temporary work (Leiharbeit) and certain forms of self-employment ('false self-employed', 'teleworking').

Furthermore, shifts within the stock of the registered unemployed and the problems for unemployed to return to stable employment are examined. Unfortunately, the available statistics on all these forms of irregular employment do not provide satisfactory information to render possible a valid estimation of the overall development.

Part-time work does not fulfil the criteria of the SER with regard to working hours. Coherent with 'subnormal' working hours, 'marginal' part-time jobs especially (below 20 hours per week) offer no or only limited social protection and entitlements to the results of collective bargaining and customary fringe benefits or career prospects. Part-time jobs increased most during the years of a very tight labour market (late 60s/early 70s) when firms were compelled to offer those jobs in order to attract women not able or prepared to enter the labour market on a full-time basis due to gender specific distribution of family work. According to the *Mikrozensus*, 12.8 per cent of all persons in dependent employment were part-timers in 1988 (i.e. worked less than 36 hours per week). Part-time employment still remained almost purely a 'women's affair'; the proportion of women was 92 per cent, and 83 per cent of them were married. That is, about half of the employed married women were working part-time. However, only 7.4 per cent of all female part-timers in dependent employment did so involuntarily because they were not able to find a full-time job (Heidenreich, 1989, p. 337).

This does not imply that – apart from those 7.4 per cent involuntary part-timers – full-time and part-time employed women are satisfied with their current number of 'normal' working hours; about one third of full-time employed women would like to change to ('regular') part-time (for a time or constantly). Mainly, they prefer weekly hours within the range of 20 to 34 hours. This is also true for those women already working part-time. Women with 'marginal' or 'unprotected' part-time contracts especially want to work longer hours (Bielenski and Strümpel, 1988; Brinkmann, 1989a).

But whereas only employees with strong market power are able to overcome employers' reluctance to come up to the preferences of women (and an increasing number of mainly well-educated men) for 'protected' part-time work, employers themselves offer more part-time jobs below certain thresholds of the liability to social insurance contributions or to be covered by legal and collective regulations. For them, this type of 'irregular' employment involves comparatively lower total hourly wage costs and provides more 'flexibility'. Unquestionably, because of these advantages employers have split up normal full-time jobs (e.g. in the service industries, especially in retail trade). Therefore, the number of full-time employed has almost stagnated over the last fifteen years and the increase in total employment is mainly due to more ('unprotected') part-timers. Very often, married women (with younger children) when re-entering the labour market have to accept those overwhelmingly low-grade part-time jobs as the only option open to them. However, these 'marginal' part-time jobs are not, in general, precarious in the sense that they are less stable, and 'unprotected' part-timers are not confined to those jobs. Generally they constitute a passage, a bridge to enter regular part-time work or full-time employment according to the SER and, hence, matching certain biographical situations (Büchtemann and Quack, 1989, pp. 111–3, 119–20 and 125–9, Schupp, 1989).

Therefore the criticism that 'regular' and especially 'marginal' part-time work does not provide an income sufficient to run an independent household is somewhat misleading. Approximately 80 per cent of the female part-timers live in 'traditional' families where the spouse earns a full-time income. Mostly, in this family constellation a second full-time income is not presently necessary, although very often the wife's part-time income constitutes an indispensable part of the household income (Büchtemann and Quack, 1989, pp. 123–5) and, moreover, in future the wife will be dependent on the husband's pension because of low entitlements of her own due to longer spells of non-employment, 'unprotected' part-time work or lower contributions while having a 'regular' part-time job.

If permanent employment is considered to be an essential of the SER, it is evident that a fixed-term contract of employment is 'irregular'. The *Beschäftigungsförderungsgesetz* extended the opportunity to conclude those contracts for up to 18 months. The Government argued that firms should be given the opportunity to meet not yet calculable surplus-demand for labour by hiring employees on fixed-term contracts instead of increasing overtime. The unions argued that this 'present' to the employers would not result in more job opportunities but would lead to more insecurity and a weakening of the position *vis-à-vis* the employer on the part of the employees and a perforation of protection against dismissal.

While the net employment effects of the facility to hire employees on fixed-term contracts seem to be rather small, the proportion of employees on fixed-term contracts increased. In the private sector they made up 4 per cent in 1984, 6.3 per cent in 1986, and 5.6 per cent in 1988. Since most of those contracts are concluded within six months or less, many more employees are actually affected within one given year; in the private sector about one third of all new recruitment is made on a fixed-term basis. But only a small fraction of private firms make (extensive) use of fixed-term contracts, and most of those contracts would have been possible even without the extended latitude created by the *Beschäftigungsförderungsgesetz* (Büchtemann, 1989, pp. 549–51). All available data demonstrate that more women are hired on fixed-term contracts than men, part-timers more than full-time employees, younger employees more than prime-aged employees and unskilled and low-skilled workers more than qualified employees. Although the risk of becoming unemployed is considerably higher than for employees hired on a permanent basis right from the beginning, for about half of those initially on fixed-term contract it is a 'bridge' to slip into permanent employment (Büchtemann and Quack, 1989, pp. 117–8 and 131–7).

However, the results of studies undertaken to evaluate the *Beschäftigungsförderungsgesetz* differ over the extent to which employees on fixed-term contracts suffer from insecurity and stress to meet the management's expectations with regard to efficiency, loyalty, punctuality etc.; whether customary rules and the validity of informal norms beyond the change of formal rights had become eroded; or whether employers' extended grip on employees with little market power had deepened the split between the internal labour force and those employees on the verge. Burgbacher *et al*. (1989) as well as Linne and Voswinkel (1989) find the unions' apprehensions mainly confirmed while Büchtemann's (1989) conclusions are less negative (see also Rudolph, 1987; Büchtemann and Höland, 1989).

Temporary (or agency) work is not 'irregular' employment *per se*. However, since those services from temporary employment agencies are called on to meet peak demands and short-term labour shortages, in general, temporary workers' employment is unstable. Although there was a steady increase in the number of temporary workers employed on a certain reference day (June 30) since 1983 (25, 702) a figure of 87, 743 in 1988 (Krüger, 1987, p. 427; *Amtliche Nachrichten der Bundesanstalt für Arbeit*, Nr. 2/1989, p. 165) does not pose a serious threat to the SER. However, according to calculations carried out by the *Deutscher Gewerkschaftsbund*, due to the high turnover about 200,000 temporary workers had been employed with the agencies during 1987. Longitudinal data reveals that many of the temporary workers (especially unskilled) are fluctuating between those jobs and unemployment and do not succeed in terminating their discontinuous employment career (Brose *et al.*, 1989).

Temporary work is closely regulated by law; notwithstanding, the agencies very often violate their employees' definite rights and entitlements (Kock, 1989, pp. 25 and 28–30) and, what is more, in this business an unknown number of agencies without a permit are bustling about. Since they cautiously try to conceal their illegal activities (or avoid the infringement of laws by 'contracts for service'), there are no reliable estimates about the number of illegal temporary workers. Many of them are foreigners without an employment permit and, thus, especially liable for any kind of exploitation (Krüger, 1987).

The legal part of temporary work has changed its functions during the last years (which explains its expansion). It is no longer mainly an instrument to overcome firms' unforeseeable and unstable labour demand, rather more and more temporary work is used as a strategy to reduce costs and to externalise risks. The prolongation of the maximum period to 'hire' a single temporary worker up to six months worked as a further impulse. Together with employment on fixed-term contracts and 'marginal' part-time work it is used to reduce the 'core' work force down to a minimum and to build a flexible, cost-saving fringe around it (Krüger, 1987, pp. 429–32; Kock, 1989, pp. 480–1).

Due to structural changes the absolute number and the relative share of self-employed continuously declined. Since the mid-seventies this downward trend has come to a halt and even reversed. Outside the agricultural sector, the number of self-employed has increased from 1.752 million in 1976 up to 1.997 million in 1987 (Büchtemann and Quack, 1989, p. 113). As such, to leave the 'shelter' of the SER voluntarily and to start one's own business is neither precarious nor 'irregular' employment. However, not every 'self-employed' person out of this expanded category corresponds to the traditional notion. This is true for the false self-employed workers. They show the negative characteristics of both the employee and the self-employed status. In the course of reorganisation processes aimed at improving flexibility and minimising costs, risks and commitments, foremost firms in the insurance, transport and construction sector 'offer' the chance to become self-employed to some of their employees. Very often they 'support' the start of the business of their former employees when they lease or sell the means of production to them (Bögenhold, 1987, pp. 86–92; Mayer and Paasch, 1987). Although formally self-employed, *de facto* these workers remain dependent. Normally, the former employer remains the sole or chief customer of their products or services which places him in a powerful position to determine the terms of delivery (this is especially true in the retail trade where several companies have shifted to some kind of 'franchise system'). To provide for social security (health insurance, contributions to the pension system) and to earn as much (or more) as before, the false self-employed worker has to turn to 'self-exploitation', i.e. not to call on former statutory or collective entitlements and benefits (vacation, maximum hours, sickness pay etc.) which the former employer has been released from.

Threatening or actual unemployment has driven many of these false self-employed workers into this type of employment. To an increasing extent this is the background for other founders of their own small-scale business as well. But this does not guarantee stability and a secure income; increasing stock figures of self-employed conceal that the 'life expectancy' of firms is decreasing. There are about 300, 000 persons per year starting their own business and nearly as many who give it up. Most of them had been running a one-man-business (Bögenhold, 1987, pp. 22–3 and 27–30).

A marginal phenomenon is still that kind of employment which has been vividly discussed as 'new outwork' or 'teleworking'. Outwork deviates from the SER since it is not performed in a firm and, thus, lacks a direct subordinate relation between management and employee. While 'traditional' outwork (which is continuously declining) is concentrated in the manufacturing sector, 'telework' is decentralised service work; word and data processing, software programming etc. Almost unanimously it is concluded that firm-based work need not be expected to dissolve and telework will not expand very much (Dostal, 1985; Hegner, 1987). Therefore, it should not represent a further threat to the SER.

Much more important, especially with regard to social security and the incidence of precarious income situations, are changes in the working of the labour market which threaten the continuity and stability of employment as the major characteristics of the SER. As with some of the aforementioned types of irregular employment patterns, these changes are closely related to persistent high unemployment. Since 1982 unemployment in West Germany no longer means 'short intervals of standing by, with the certainty that very soon one will be wanted either in one's old job again or in a new job that is within one's powers' (Beveridge, 1944, p. 125). A higher level of employment on the one hand and almost constant unemployment figures on the other hand imply that the stock of registered unemployed has been 'sifted' several times and the 'sediment' of hard-core unemployed who do not meet the heightened expectations of the demand side is growing. Among the registered unemployed in September 1981 there were 12.9 per cent with a current spell of unemployment of one year and over; in September 1988 this percentage rose up to 32.6, and the share of unemployed being registered for two years and over quadrupled from 3.9 per cent in 1981 to 16.5 per cent in 1988.

Older job-seekers, those without vocational training and/or low formal education and the physically handicapped are especially affected by long-term unemployment (Brinkmann, 1989b). The results of a panel-study (Schupp, 1988) underline the relevance of long-term and recurrent unemployment amounting to an ever greater share of the overall unemployment problem. Only 47 out of one hundred unemployed in 1984 were employed in 1987 (21 of them having a fixed-term contract; one quarter worked in an occupation for which they were not trained); 15 had been constantly unemployed, another 16 were unemployed again after they had taken up employment (once or repeatedly), and 22 were no longer members of the labour force in 1987. Among the latter, women were overrepresented, i.e. after becoming 'discouraged' they returned to their traditional role as householders to a great extent.

Another recent study (Karr and John, 1989) focussing on recurrent and cumulative unemployment (the total duration of various spells of individual unemployment) confirms these findings. Both recurrent and cumulative unemployment have steadily increased during the period of observation (1977–1986), i.e. although there is a high inflow into and outflow from the unemployment register, the burden of unemployment is concentrated on a relatively small fraction of the labour force. This is due to a higher frequency of employment/unemployment; the duration of the single intervals of unemployment is getting longer while the periods of employment are getting shorter. This refers to the fact that, very often and more often than in the past, the incidence of unemployment 'infects' the

Irregular employment patterns

unemployed with the risk of recurrent intervals of unemployment and, thus, with the threat of a destabilised and downward directed occupational career. Being denied the chances to escape this 'revolving door' not only implies financial hardships during the intervals of unemployment but, most probably, also the risk of a precarious income situation after (enforced early) retirement (see later).

Beside growing disparities between a core of employees in stable jobs and those members of the labour force whose stability and continuity of employment is seriously threatened, we observe growing disparities between regions (especially along a 'north–south axis') which the study of Karr and John (1989) points out as well. In those regions with a continuously high unemployment rate (and a smaller increase in the level of employment) the intervals of single unemployment spells are longer and, thus, cumulative unemployment is higher. These disparities present a serious burden to the municipalities. While having less revenue than municipalities in prospering areas, they have higher expenditures on social assistance to cover the needs of the unemployed (and their families) who do not or no longer qualify for sufficient unemployment benefits (Lompe and Pollmann, 1986; Heinelt, 1989).

From the preceding results of this section we can conclude that although the available data on the prevalence of irregular employment patterns and destabilised occupational careers do not allow an exact quantitative statement, there is nothing like a rapidly progressing 'erosion' of the standardised employment relationship. Men, preferably performing qualified work in large-scale firms (with a higher degree of formal and customary 'seniority rules') in the industrial sector, who acted as the focal point of reference in the process of establishing the SER, have not been affected to any great extent by the recent developments. Even the structural shift towards the service sector, which is assumed to provide somewhat different conditions with regard to the stability of employment, wage levels and wage differentials, has not been accompanied by major changes. Despite the increase of irregular employment patterns – of which not all are precarious, have been accepted involuntarily and represent permanent traps – and ongoing processes of 'marginalisation' under the auspices of high unemployment, the SER is empirical reality for the majority of the male labour force.

Because of the gender specific distribution of irregular employment patterns women have, paradoxically, benefitted from the recent development, though almost exclusively in a quantitative sense. If employers had not turned to irregular employment patterns, not nearly so many jobs would have been supplied, and these (fewer) jobs meeting the criteria of the SER would not have been completely available to women under the still given conditions of women performing the bulk of family work. Certainly, the employers' strategy to make the exchange of labour more flexible has not favoured women in a qualitative sense, since these jobs regularly involve an under-utililisation of skills, disadvantages with regard to career prospects, social security entitlements and working (time) conditions. And especially part-time work favoured the continuance of asymmetrical responsibilities for unpaid work at home (Triest and van Doorne-Huiskes, 1988). However, to improve the 'quality', e.g. by extending liability to social security contributions and further protection to all part-time jobs, would entail the risk of a diminishing number of those jobs supplied when stripped of the conditions favourable to employers.

Apparently, the 'deregulation rat race' between EC countries leading to an extension of irregular employment patterns has not yet progressed very far in the Federal Republic. Why is this so? It is not possible to give a complete answer here, but a fast and linear dissolution of the SER in the Federal Republic is checked by the high degree of 'juridification' (Verrechtlichung) of the German system of industrial relations. It includes an extensive substantial legal intervention into the exchange of labour (which is not easy to overturn *in toto* and, thus, guarantees some continuity) as well as procedural regulations strengthening the role of the bodies of labour's interest representation (works councils and unions). Having built up encompassing organisational structures, the unions retained their strength and their membership during the crisis of the labour market, and the climate between the 'social partners' is still guided by cooperation rather than conflict. As technical innovation and industrial modernisation were never hampered by the unions, so demands for greater flexibility are not rejected altogether. The collective agreements on working time reduction in 1984 and thereafter which included regulated working time flexibility as an element of the compromise may be one example. On the industrial level certain limits and procedures were defined which have to be observed when management and works councils agree upon the application of the opportunities provided (Hinrichs, 1990).

Nevertheless, the emergence of irregular employment patterns in an environment of persistent mass unemployment has influenced the level of social security and led to many more households suffering from 'new poverty'.

OUTSIDE THE STANDARD EMPLOYMENT RELATIONSHIP: PROCESSES OF IMPOVERISHMENT

In almost every occupation a full-time job guarantees a net income sufficient to lift a couple with one child above the official poverty line. In 1984 the number of 'working poor' was not a serious problem in West Germany (Welzmüller, 1986). It should not have changed very much since then and this is due to the fact that almost every employee is covered by collective agreements (and, therefore, no 'minimum wage' fixed by the state or some kind of 'wage council' exists). However, unemployment benefits (Arbeitslosengeld) and the even lower unemployment assistance

(Arbeitslosenhilfe), which are both related to former earnings, might not be sufficient to prevent poverty if the unemployed person qualifies at all for those transfers. Whether unemployed persons might actually be eligible for supplementary benefits (Sozialhilfe) depends on the type of household he or she lives in. Therefore, the distribution of the unemployed with regard to the type of household is important.

In 1988 unemployment was highest among single persons (especially divorced men and women). An unemployment rate above the average was also true for married women (11.4 per cent). It was more than twice as high as the rate for married men (5.0 per cent) (Heidenreich, 1989, p. 333). To a certain extent this should be due to still valid selection patterns of management and works councils when dismissals are at stake ('youngsters and women first, the family men last'). This distribution of unemployment according to family status has not changed over the last fifteen years although the number of unemployed has increased tremendously since 1980 (WISTA, 1981, p 658; Mayer, 1988, p. 854). Therefore, a greater number of households are endangered by poverty. However, this risk is comparatively low if it is not the head of the household who becomes unemployed, but rather the wife or grown-up children who are affected (Klein, 1987; Mayer, 1988, p. 860).

Exceptional financial hardships and, very often, precarious income situations arise if the only member of the household (in the case of a one-person-household) or the head of the household (households of couples or of single parents with dependent children) becomes unemployed. These cases add up to about 55 per cent of the 2.35 million unemployed in 1987 (Mayer, 1988, p. 859). An extreme deterioration occurred among the households of couples with unemployed husbands; to an increasing extent the wife is also unemployed and to a decreasing extent the wife contributes to the family income. In 1980 there were only 17, 000 families with *both* spouses unemployed; in 1987 this figure rose up to 65, 000. While in 1980 as well as in 1987 in nearly half of the families with an employed husband the wife was employed as well, the share of gainfully employed women married to an unemployed husband fell from 40 to 30 per cent (WISTA, 1981, pp. 661–2; Mayer, 1988, p. 859). Therefore, to a great extent they should be entitled to receive supplementary benefits or already do so (Mayer, 1988, pp. 858 and 860–1; Klein, 1987).

Hence, the share of recipients to whom supplementary benefits are granted because of 'unemployment' as the main reason for income insufficiency has increased from about 10 per cent in 1980 up to 32.7 per cent in 1987 (corresponding to 436, 400 households). 265, 300 of these households were not (or are no longer) entitled to receive unemployment benefits (Deininger, 1989, pp. 540–1 and 543).

The latter figure as well as the increase in the absolute number and the relative proportion of the unemployed receiving supplementary benefits are due to two developments. First, the duration of unemployment has increased. How long (and if at all) the unemployed are entitled to unemployment benefits depends on the duration of preceding employment. When they no longer qualify for this type of benefit the lower unemployment assistance is paid (after enduring a means test). Second, and probably more important, since 1975 there have been several restrictions with regard to the entitlement to both unemployment benefits and assistance, as well as (selective) reductions of the *level* of benefits (Reichsbund, 1986), i.e. an increasing proportion of the unemployed are not eligible for benefits after losing their job and if they qualify they receive relatively less than in former years. In 1975 only 19 per cent of the *newly* unemployed persons received no benefits at all; in 1986 the figure had risen up to 25 per cent. Related to the stock of registered unemployed meanwhile, the proportion of those without benefits amounts to about 40 per cent (Kühl, 1989, p. 11). This means, as another study points out (Cramer, 1987), that a decreasing share of the aggregated periods of unemployment is covered by payments from the Federal Labour Office. Moreover, although the formal replacement rate of net wages is 63 per cent for Arbeitslosengeld and 56 per cent for Arbeitslosenhilfe (unemployed with at least one child receive 68 or 58 per cent respectively) *de facto* the recipient of Arbeitslosengeld receives only 54 per cent of his or her former net income. The figure for the recipient of Arbeitslosenhilfe is 45 per cent (IAB, 1988, pp. 2–3). Therefore, it is not surprising that while real disposable income of *all* private households increased by 25 per cent between 1970 and 1986 (real wage increased by 20 per cent), households headed by someone unemployed who actually receives Arbeitslosengeld or Arbeitslosenhilfe suffered a loss of about 12 per cent in real terms of which the greater part came off between 1982 and 1986 (IAB, 1988, p. 5).

Unemployment often results in a serious reduction of current income compared with previous earnings and, thus, very often establishes a claim to (additional) supplementary benefits. Moreover, with regard to retirement, longer intervals of unemployment definitely affect the statutory pension one can expect since the pension is calculated to a lower rate during phases of unemployment. Occupational pension schemes reward stable and continuous employment as well. Very often certain labour force categories are not included in those schemes *per se* (mainly, the 'irregularly' employed) and employees with a short length of job tenure do not fulfil the preservation requirements of their claims to an occupational pension after retirement.

The recent changes in the qualifying conditions for unemployment benefits (and their level) have favoured employees with stable jobs coming up to the SER or, at least, have not affected them negatively. By contrast the growing part of the labour force which does not fulfil the criteria of continuity and stability is increasingly excluded from the general systems of social security and shifted to the 'bottom' of the hierarchically ordered arrangement of reproduction. They are instead more and more dependent on social transfers which are related to individual cases, i.e. to means tested benefits (Mückenberger, 1986, pp. 40–1). This development signifies a strengthening of the 'normative fiction' of the SER. It is one aspect of the growing 'polarisation' between the 'core' of employees whose jobs are coming up to the SER and the no longer negligible 'fringe' of the labour force experiencing recurrent/long-term unemployment or working irregularly as described above. While the former is sitting more comfortably, the 'fringe' is worse off and, moreover, it 'cushions' the favourable position of the 'core' labour force while bearing the greater part of the risks which emanate from fluctuations in the demand for labour.

'DROPPING' OR 'PRESERVING': THE FUTURE OF THE STANDARD EMPLOYMENT RELATIONSHIP

Mückenberger (1985, pp. 466–7 and 470–2) argues that (1) full employment cannot be attained again in the future, (2) the reproduction of society based on the SER as the 'normal' case is no longer conceivable (3) because of the 'unavoidable decline' of the SER as an empirical regularity and as a normative focus ('prevailing fiction'), attempts to preserve and to restore the SER are without prospects and conservative and (4) it is thus much more promising to turn to a new societal arrangement that supersedes the SER. The offensive strategy would be to strive for some kind of 'guaranteed minimum income' (GMI). Mückenberger is probably right that full employment of the kind lasting until the early seventies is out of reach for the rest of this century. However, the preceding chapters have demonstrated that there is not an accelerating 'erosion' of the SER. Moreover, it is questionable whether concepts of a GMI are actually appropriate to succeed the traditional (or reformed) arrangements of individual and collective reproduction.

It is not possible to discuss here the many arguments that have been raised against the GMI concepts. The counter-arguments relate to the question of how to bring about some kind of GMI in a parliamentary democracy governed by the 'majority rule' ('vested interests' and 'status quo orientation' resulting from uncertainties about favouring/injuring effects are only two catch-phrases). Furthermore, they refer to the effects (work incentives, outcome of such a momentous diversion of revenues and transfers) and to the level of benefits, the burden to be borne by the employed. And especially unionist writers like Bäcker (1988; pp. 611–7) advocate the opinion that a GMI would not improve the situation of those members of the labour force who are already placed at a disadvantage. Involuntary non-employment cannot be expected to be abolished altogether and the distribution of chances to get access to desirable jobs would not change.

As was pointed out above, the SER no longer meets the changed biographical conceptions, the diversity of life situations, the heterogeneity of preferences, etc. (to this extent one can easily agree with Mückenberger, 1989a, pp. 217–8). Saying the SER is becoming increasingly 'outmoded' furthermore implies that, in view of the rising labour force participation of married women, a 'job' does not necessarily have to provide a 'family wage' in each case and at any time. Finally, if one provided every citizen with a more or less comfortable amount of money (independent of his/her preparedness to take up paid employment), one would have to renounce the chance to influence the application of time not spent in paid employment for socially useful purposes. These are the starting-points for an alternative to GMI concepts: at present (and according to the SER arrangement) there are only two ways to gain command over financial income; either gainful employment or certain well-defined inabilities to perform paid work which establish a claim to receive benefits which replace earnings. All other persons receive status-derived means of maintenance (by marriage or dependency as it is true for children). It is the idea of a supply-side policy to expand the situations which found an entitlement to money income, i.e. to develop policies by which attractive life situations as an alternative to full-time employment are financed. This policy is aimed at creating 'occasions' to make the transitions between full-time employment and (temporary) part-time or non-employment more 'fluid' (Lutz, 1988).

The 'occasions' are those where activities considered as socially useful are performed during periods not spent in paid work and thus constitute a *legitimate* reason to receive publicly financed support. To recognise child-raising as such a task and to offer non-contributory credits for pension entitlement as well as to enact a paternal leave as an option for mothers and fathers are first steps (although the flat-rate benefits paid during this leave are far from generous). It is conceivable to extend those regulations to unpaid work done to take care of elderly or handicapped persons (either at home or in the context of voluntary associations). These examples do not cover all the potential occasions for providing subsistence while not, or not full-time, employed. Furthermore, one can think of 'guaranteed individual options' to reduce the number of hours worked or to interrupt employment for a certain period for any personal reason and at one's own 'expense' (i.e. foregone earnings). Laying claim to these options would also reduce the amount of labour supply and, hence, improve the employment situation. These innovations would 'exploit' the increasing willingness to deviate from a linear full-time career in a positive way. Although it preserves the SER as a kind of 'yardstick', this policy is suitable to modify this arrangement in a direction that means collective and individual progress by extended options and a de-centred role of paid employment.

NOTES

1. For a discussion of the recent developments in several OECD countries cf. the contributions in *Labour and Society* 12 (1987), No. 1 (January) and in Rodgers and Rodgers, 1989; for comparative studies (including Great Britain and West Germany) cf. Casey *et al.*, 1989; Grahl and Teague, 1989.
2. Among others, this law gave employers more latitude to employ persons on fixed-term contracts and to make use of temporary workers, and it reduced the cost of dismissals (for a discussion see Mückenberger, 1985, pp. 457–63). It must not be mixed up with the Arbeitsförderungsgesetz (Labour Promotion Act) from 1969 which regulates the tasks of the Federal Labour Office.

8
PULL-DOWN EFFECTS, UNEMPLOYMENT AND INTERESTS IN THE WELFARE STATE
HEINER GANSSMANN

INTRODUCTION

What follows is a sequel to a previous attempt to describe and analyse interests in the welfare state (Ganssmann and Weggler, 1989). Perhaps I should stress right at the outset that I do not believe that analysing welfare states in terms of interests will *per se* result in a satisfying theory of the welfare state. On the one hand, there are difficulties inherent in the concept of interests.[1] On the other hand, referring to interests and corresponding actions does not make much sense without some understanding of the conditions and constraints for actions resulting from systemic properties.[2] Thus, the following discussion of interests and the adoption of the perspective of actors has the limited purpose of assessing the welfare state's potential for change, especially in terms of the chances of a reversal of the well-established trend towards increased social marginalisation.

'Social marginalisation' refers to processes by which a considerable part of the population is pushed into a 'worst-off' position (in terms of income, status, etc.) and kept there. The main mechanism is long-term unemployment, which involves a downward career. The longer it lasts, the lower are the chances of returning to stable, full-time employment and the lower is the level of protection provided by the welfare state, which in turn deepens the separation of the long-term unemployed from the rest of society. Apart from what social marginalisation means for those subjected to it, it implies a fragmentation of society which has traditionally been perceived as endangering its stability. By contrast, we are more inclined nowadays to attribute a stabilising function to fragmentation, but this issue lies beyond the scope of this chapter, whose underlying theme is the future nature of the welfare state. Can the welfare state contribute to reversing the trend towards increased marginalisation or is it unable to oppose the trend?

Our previous results do not induce much optimism. Only a considerable increase in 'solidarity' between the marginalised groups and the mass of the wage-earning population could lead to a reversal of the current trend. However, apart from the appeal to altruistic or traditional norms, what reasons would there be for the (relatively) privileged to act in solidarity with the marginalised? Can the appeal to the interests of rational actors result in such solidarity?

A positive answer may be found by looking for 'pull-down effects' in the welfare state. The term refers to those effects of social interdependencies which tie the position of the worst-off to the position of the better-off such that the deterioration of the position of the worst-off has a negative impact on the position of the better-off, even if they are rather remote actors or groups. 'Pull-down effects' could be constitutive for solidarity: given a link between two groups (or actors) resulting in a potential pull-down effect, it is in the (selfish) interest of the privileged to prevent the deterioration of the position of the worst-off, if their expected loss due to the pull-down effect is greater than the costs of supporting the worst-off. Although pull-down effects may exist in a number of social policy areas, the following- exploration is concerned with demonstrating the plausibility of the idea of pull-down effects by looking at the connection between income distribution and unemployment.

ILLUSTRATION: MARX'S 'INDUSTRIAL RESERVE ARMY'

Marx's concept of the 'industrial reserve army' provides an example of the type of argument needed to support the idea of pull-down effects. Marx argued that the 'production' of the industrial reserve army due to labour-saving innovations has several advantages for capitalist enterprises. The unemployed in the industrial reserve army exercise competitive pressure on the employed so that work discipline is enhanced, absenteeism is discouraged and wage increases are prevented, while at the same time capital accumulation gains relative independence from labour supply restrictions. The overall constellation is assumed to be such that whatever is good for capital is bad for workers, and vice versa.

In this constellation it is in the interest of those who have a job to support moves towards full employment. For workers, full employment will lower both the risk and the costs of losing their jobs and increase their power to resist management pressures. Thus, full employment will improve the bargaining position of the active labour-force, where the bargaining objectives include not just wages but also working conditions. By contrast, the existence and the growth of the industrial reserve army results in pull-down effects on working conditions and wages even for those workers who have relatively safe jobs. So they have reasons for solidarity with the unemployed, insofar as supporting them reduces downward pressures (assuming that there are no feasible methods of getting rid of the unemployed without restoring full employment).[3]

But this is not the whole picture: achieving full employment is not likely to be costless, either for labour or for capital. If 'solidarity' in the sense of supporting moves towards full employment has costs for the active labour force, the matter turns into one of weighing the relative costs of solidarity against non-solidarity. If, as the traditional neo-classical argument has it, the restoration of full employment presupposes (real) wage reductions[4], the issue turns simply into one of comparing (expected) wage losses with those costs of pull-down effects which are born by the active labour force.

The example of Marx's industrial reserve army points to some of the difficulties involved in arguing for solidarity founded on self-interest. But it also illustrates quite well the concept of pull-down effects. If they are indeed part of the present social constellation in West Germany, arguments in favour of supporting those who are currently marginalised could point to the potential benefits of such solidarity not just for the supported, but also for the supporters. The advantage of such arguments over the appeal to altruism is, perhaps, that stable support for the worst-off is more likely if it can be founded on the self-interest rather than the benevolence of the better-off.

UNEMPLOYMENT AND THE PULL-DOWN EFFECT IN INCOME DISTRIBUTION

In this chapter, I shall examine a potential candidate for the pull-down effect which is quite accessible empirically: the effect of persistently high unemployment on the income distribution between wages and profits. The evidence for West Germany points to a negative correlation between the share of (net) wages and salaries[5] in national income and the rate of unemployment; the higher the rate of unemployment, the lower the share of (net) wages (see Figure 8.1).

There are various ways of interpreting this correlation. One is simply that higher unemployment means less wage-earners and less work performed[6], so that labour's share in national income decreases because the volume of work performed decreases. This is wrong, because the role of the unemployed as former (and potential future) producers is neglected.[7] If the share of wages in national income decreases as unemployment increases, this is not simply the result of the changed volume of work. So what are the relevant factors? There may be others, but let me begin with two.

The first has to do with the welfare state and the question of who pays for the support of the unemployed. Unemployment insurance contributions (presently 4 per cent of gross wages in West Germany) are part of the wage bill. The rate has doubled compared to the mid-seventies. Since the employed support the unemployed by financing unemployment benefits via their insurance contributions, it is not surprising that the share of net wages in national income is depressed by high unemployment. The higher unemployment is, the more is (*ceteris paribus*) deducted from the wage bill to support the unemployed. This argument, while basically correct[8], does not explain the nature and extent of the distributional shift in West Germany. It implies that an increasing gap between gross and net

Pull-down effects in the welfare state

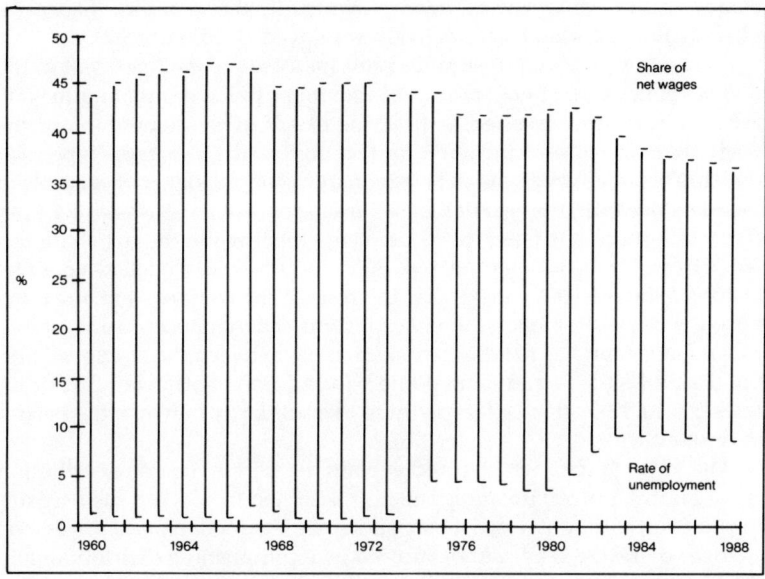

Figure 8.1 Net wages (as a percentage of national income) and the rate of unemployment. (*Sources*: Statistisches Bundesamt, 1987; Dorow *et al.*, 1989)

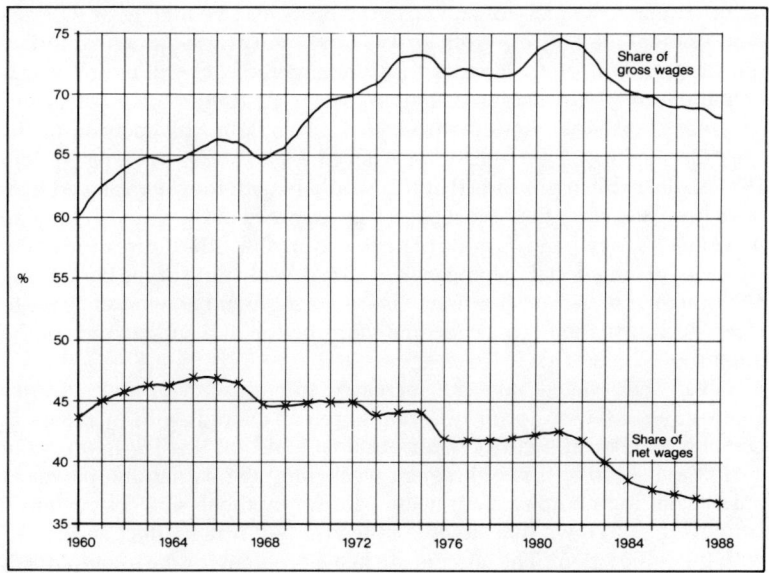

Figure 8.2 Gross and net wages as shares of national income

wages results from growing unemployment if, and as far as, the unemployed are supported by the actively employed (see Figure 8.2).[9]

That unemployment insurance rates increased from 2 per cent in the mid seventies to 4.6 per cent in 1984 illustrates this argument quite well. What remains unexplained is, first, the extent of the depression of the wage share in national income[10], and secondly, that a 'scissor'-type relationship between gross and net wage shares[11] was no longer observable in the 80s; since 1981, the year of the maximum share of gross wages (74.4 per cent), this share has fallen to 68 per cent (1988) while the net share has fallen from 42.6 to 36.6 per cent (see Figure 8.2). So the two fell in a parallel fashion. Nonetheless, considering interests in the welfare state, the issue raised is relevant, namely, whether income maintenance during unemployment is (and has to be) a zero-sum-game between the employed and the unemployed. A zero-sum game would imply a strict conflict of interests, with little chance for anything like solidarity between the parties in the conflict.

The second factor which could explain the shift in income distribution is bargaining power: unemployment is assumed to weaken the bargaining position of unions. Even if they anticipate productivity and price-level changes correctly, they cannot succeed in accomplishing distributionally neutral wage-increases. The main reason is that the traditional bargaining weapon of unions, threatening a strike, is not as threatening under conditions of mass unemployment. But why, if striking workers are not easily replaceable by strike-breakers nowadays (largely because of legal regulations)? The risk of job-loss for strike activists may be higher, or workers (and unions) may refrain from strikes (and limit wage-demands) if they see the survival of their enterprise endangered. Or strikes for wage-demands may be considered illegitimate in a situation of mass unemployment by the workers themselves. (In this light, the decision of the West German metal workers union to strike for a 35 hour working week in 1984 on the explicit grounds that this would benefit the unemployed may have been less risky than most observers assumed at the time.) Taking all these factors together, it is quite plausible to attribute the depression of the wage share in national income mainly to the weakening of the bargaining position of unions. In a situation of mass unemployment, workers have to face a decline in their (gross) income share, on top of having to pay for the unemployed.

Given that wages have not increased in step with productivity increases and inflation (or, if net wages are considered, with increases in taxation and social security contributions) and that this lag is probably attributable both to unemployment weakening the bargaining power of unions and to unemployment being paid for by those who are currently employed, it follows that there is indeed a pull-down effect associated with unemployment. The latter is not just a problem for the unemployed, it is also detrimental to the interests of those not directly threatened by it (even if they do not realise this). Thus, both the employed and the unemployed have an interest in full employment.

The same point can be made simply by relying on the familiar law of supply and demand; if the supply of labour-power is greater than the demand, wages as the price of labour-power come under downward pressure. Since full employment is the best environment for resisting this pressure, all those who have to sell their labour-power have a *prima facie* interest not only in full employment but even in an excess demand for labour-power.[12]

THE EMPLOYED AND THE UNEMPLOYED

However simplistic the logic of supply and demand may be, it brings in a new aspect; the extent to which the downward pressure on wages becomes effective is a matter of competition among the sellers of labour power, so their own actions influence the strength of the pull-down effect. According to the simple[13] neoclassical tradition, perfect competition among sellers would lower the price of labour-power until supply equalled demand and wages corresponded to the marginal productivity of labour. This reveals a difference in interests between the employed, who will want full employment but not at the cost of reducing (real) wages, and the unemployed, who will probably want jobs even if they have to accept lower wages. How important is this difference of interests?

In the simple neoclassical story, unemployment is described as an excess supply of labour power at the going 'price', the given wage level. Sellers and buyers have, apart from a common interest in a functioning labour market, opposing interests. Sellers want to sell dear, buyers want to buy cheap. Unemployment puts sellers at a disadvantage. Wages have to go down to clear the market. Competition normally takes care of this. Sellers will bid the price down. Full employment will be restored.

This simple story can be made more complicated in several ways. Labour-power is not a homogeneous commodity, so there will be different sub-markets and wage levels. Competition may be limited, either through market segmentation or because coalitions among sellers and buyers are formed or because existing contracts and legal restrictions serve as barriers to entry. The transaction between buyers and sellers of labour-power is not completed on the market, but only when work is performed and wages are spent, so there is the problem that the wage-contract does not sufficiently regulate work performance or consumption possibilities. All these (and more) complications have been extensively discussed in the literature on wages and unemployment, mostly in the effort to explain why the restoration of full employment via the normal market mechanism does not happen in the real world.

Going back to the difference in interests between the currently successful sellers of labour-power and the unemployed, it is evidently in the interest of the employed to limit 'price'-competition among sellers to protect themselves against wage losses. Basically, there are two ways to accomplish this; by pushing competitors out of the labour-market or blocking their access to it (for example, by sending 'guest'-workers back home or forcing women back into housework) or by greater unionisation. Unions press for collective wage contracts which exclude or limit the possibilities for the unemployed to bid down wages as a way of getting a job. Management interests may converge with union interests because management has incomplete information about individual workers; firms may prefer collective wage contracts with relatively high wages to individual, flexible, market-responsive wage formation, because the latter involves high search and control costs.[14]

For the unemployed (or those wanting to climb the job pyramid), all these barriers resulting from limited competition on the labour market still leave open the possibility of competing in terms of qualifications and (promised) job performance. Can the unemployed be competitive in these terms? Or do those who currently have jobs protect themselves by contracts or customs (rules like 'first in, last out', for example)? If not, do they have to compete preventatively by improving their own qualifications and job performance?

With the available, highly aggregated data it is difficult if not impossible to answer these questions. However, it is quite clear that the level of qualifications of the employed has increased considerably during the period of mass unemployment. Whether this is due to the sorting out of the non-qualified into long-term unemployment or to competition-enforced 'adaptive upgrading' of those entering and holding jobs[15] is difficult to determine. While the higher level of qualification (which may in part have come about quite independently of labour-market conditions) can to some extent be interpreted as the effect of stiffer competition for jobs, there is also evidence that protective devices are at work. For example, the fact that in 1986 unemployment for men was lowest for the age group between 45 and 50 for all levels of qualification (Tessaring, 1988, p. 189) suggests some mechanism of social closure which protects this group more effectively against competition than other groups. So it is quite likely that all three factors are at work simultaneously: the longer unemployment lasts, the more it functions as a filter, forcing the least competitive out of the work-force; average levels of qualifications increase, partly because a section of the better qualified is pushed down in the job hierarchy, partly because those who enter jobs have to be better qualified (even if their qualifications are not actually needed); and to some extent at least, those who hold jobs (and have held them for a while) are able to protect themselves against new entrants, thus reducing their own risk of unemployment.

Nonetheless, the changes in income distribution indicate in a summary fashion that all these (and possibly other) ways of limiting and channelling competition are not sufficient to counter the wage depressing effects of unemployment. In relative terms, labour has become cheaper; although it is performed by better qualified personnel, it can be bought with a smaller share of national income. So it is plausible that there is a pull-down effect at work. To leave a considerable part of the working population unemployed has a depressing effect on the income share of those who succeed in selling their labour-power.

For the simple neoclassical way of telling the story of unemployment, this result raises a puzzle. Any pull-down effect on wages due to unemployment should eliminate itself; since labour has clearly become relatively cheaper, employment should have increased significantly. However, it has not.[16] Either one can explain this in the neoclassical spirit by arguing that labour has not become cheap enough yet, or one can abandon the neoclassical frame of reference. An alternative way of looking at unemployment also throws some light on the interests involved in unemployment insurance.

Suppose the number of jobs was adjusted (by whatever means) to be always smaller than the number of those wanting them. Getting a job would be a game of the musical chairs type. In each labour market transaction period, some would be left without a job and no amount of competitive bidding, whatever the means of competition, would alter this result. So rather than spoiling the market for each other by bidding down prices, sellers of labour-power could be better-off if they agreed to limit competition by offering a side-contract to those who cannot sell in the current transaction period, a side-contract that the winners in the game should compensate the losers. Unemployment insurance can be considered as such a side-contract; the employed pay the unemployed for refraining from all-out competition for jobs. For the employed, paying 'insurance' contributions is worthwhile as long as they do not exceed the losses they would have to expect if full-fledged competition started.[17] For the unemployed, unemployment relief, by establishing a lower limit for wage demands, is a sort of protection against damaging their own long-term interests, at least as long as unemployment relief guarantees survival.

But, of course, instead of playing a rather expensive variant of musical chairs, all who offer labour-power for sale would prefer to change the rules of the game; why not adapt the number of jobs to the number of those seeking jobs? Compared with that possibility, unemployment insurance is a second-best solution, especially because it does not prevent the pull-down effect on wages. Full employment would be preferred. But, outside the simple neoclassical framework, accomplishing full employment is not a matter which sellers of labour-power can settle by themselves.

Before entering into a discussion of the relevant interests of other agents, it is worth referring back to the beginning of the argument. There, the idea that pull-down effects could provide reasons for solidarity on 'rational' grounds, because they define an area of common interest among those negatively affected was put forward. So far, all the arguments concerning the interests of sellers of labour power point to such a common interest in full employment. But there is not much evidence that this common interest really matters. While there seem to be enough reasons for increased and renewed solidarity among the employed and the unemployed, for a combined effort to push for full-employment, scarcely anything (and certainly nothing decisive) along these lines is happening. So we end up in a situation familiar from a host of analyses in terms of 'objective' interests; agents just do not do what the theoretical observer expects them to do. It would seem to follow either that agents are irrational, misinformed, or subjected to false ideologies, or that something is wrong with the analysis of their interests. However, there may be another explanation for the discrepancy between observed and theoretically expected actions. The analysis simply may not have been pushed far enough to cover different layers and types of interests.

Since much of what follows is more or less speculative I shall take it for granted, for the sake of the argument, that all wage-earners have a common interest in full employment. What would follow from such a common interest? Is it not something quite abstract, quite remote from the everyday lives of the people concerned? Are there not countervailing interests connected with the issue of unemployment versus full employment (for example, interests in price stability) which raise the question of priorities? Are there not other agents and groups of agents whose interests and actions are crucial when it comes to dealing with the consequences of unemployment?

INDIVIDUAL INTERESTS AND MACROSOCIAL GOALS

I shall take up these questions one by one. First, it makes sense to conclude that all wage-earners (and perhaps not only them) have a common interest in full employment if they are all affected negatively by unemployment – unless one wants to restrict (which does not seem sensible) the usage of the term 'interest' to those concerns which agents can directly influence by their own actions. This is not the case with concern for full employment, or democracy or a well-organised social security system or any macro-social or macro-economic event or state. In other words, an interest in full employment is an interest in a state of the economy which cannot be brought about immediately by the actions of those affected by unemployment. For the interests of those immediately concerned to have an impact, they must be bundled and organised. In this sense, an interest in full employment is indeed an interest in something abstract and remote from what people can do and do do as individuals. For example, individual workers can react to unemployment, or the threat of it, with all sorts of individually realisable strategies; by improving their qualifications, their job performance or their reputation. Whether they are successful or not depends only to a limited extent on their own actions. If a steel plant is closed, the individual performance of a steel worker is no longer relevant. However, these individually realisable strategies are competitive; if only 10 per cent of the workers are fired, it may pay to be among the better performing 90 per cent. So in this sense, individually realisable strategies are rational.

However, they do not cancel out pull-down effects. The individually rational, competitive strategy helps an individual to be better off than their competitors. But, in general, it does not help if the losses of some members of a group worsen the position of the whole group, as happens in the case of the effects of unemployment on wages. Losses are unevenly distributed, to be sure, and it is certainly preferable to be among those who lose least, i.e. by not becoming unemployed. But losses are still losses. If the smaller losses are recognisably due to the bigger ones, there is a manifest common interest in eliminating losses in general. With unemployment, this requires the restoration of full employment. To pursue this interest, however, presupposes organisation (on several levels), because it requires actions on a level beyond the reach of individuals as such.

It may well be the case that the resources needed to build an organisation, in terms of effort, time, money, etc., outweigh the losses incurred. Then it is obviously not worthwhile to organise. It may also be that the risks of failure despite organisation are too great. And there may be other obstacles which prevent people from pursuing common interests by way of organisation (like the notorious 'free rider' syndrome). But I do not want to explain the birth of organisations by starting from a sort of social zero point. Organisations to pursue collective interests exist, from grass roots groups to nation states and beyond. Leaving aside issues such as the tendency of organisations to develop some kind of autonomy against the interests of members, it follows from the analysis of members' interests that the workers' organisations will wish to pursue the goal of full employment. However, they do not control the economic and political means to achieve full employment.

Stable full employment, as a macro-social goal state, can either come about spontaneously (but if that were regularly the case, there would not be much of a problem) as a result of decentralised economic decision-making. Or it can be brought about by political decisions influencing economic processes in the necessary direction. Neither of these levels of decision-making are normally controllable by workers' organisations. The first level is under capitalist control, while access to the second one is regulated by the political system, normally in the form of electoral competition between political parties. So the interest in full employment, as expressed in union activities, encounters other interests; those of capital and its functionaries and those operative in the political system.

OTHER INTERESTS

From Marx (1867) to Kalecki (1943) to Vogt (1986) it has been argued (within quite different theoretical frameworks) that unemployment is in the capitalist interest, for quite straightforward reasons; competition for jobs by the unemployed and the increased risk of losing a job result in pressure to lower wages and in increased work discipline and performance. The threat of losing a job is more of a deterrent the higher the resulting expected costs are for workers and it is more effective than management control of work performance. For the 'normal' worker, the expected costs of unemployment will vary with the rate of unemployment. The amount of unemployment needed to fulfil this function for capitalist interests is not necessarily very high, just enough to make the threat of job loss credible and to reduce the prospects of immediately finding a new job. Since unemployment insurance lowers the difference between income with and without a job, it limits the effectiveness of unemployment as a disciplinary and wage depressing device[18], so that earnings replacement by means of unemployment insurance is against capitalist interests (although there are other effects of unemployment insurance which are beneficial for capitalist interests, for example maintaining labour-power reserves by preventing immiseration).

According to this account of capitalist interests, the interests of all those who have to sell their labour are symmetrically opposed to those of capitalists. Beyond the common interest of sellers of labour-power in their opposition to buyers, however, they may not – as we have seen – have much in common. Those who have a job want to keep it, those who do not have one want one. However, this conflict of interests can be dampened by organisational means to limit competition among sellers of labour power, and by unions demanding full employment.

What happens when interests between business and labour organisations clash can be reconstructed by looking at the costs of full employment for both sides. In the not so good old days, Keynes promised full employment not only without wage loss, but with income gains for all (except perhaps rentiers). Thus he promised the (socially) cost-free resolution of the conflict of interests about unemployment However, deficit-financed demand management by the state as the means of fulfilling the Keynesian promise has proved rather ineffective, at least unless it is accompanied by labour market policies responding to changing economic structures and overcoming shortages of skilled labour and immobility. As we know by now, these policies are not without cost. While full employment can be realised even in post-Keynesian times, and there is no 'natural' pairing of capitalism and unemployment, as the examples of Sweden, Switzerland and Japan show, full employment can only be restored if some social class or group can be persuaded to bear the cost of effective employment policies. If that is not possible, the stalemate results in unemployment despite the possibility of abolishing it.

Pull-down effects in the welfare state

So who can be made to bear those costs? For any group or coalition, it would be economically rational to accept them if the alternative, unemployment, was even more expensive. These costs are difficult, if not impossible to calculate, but nonetheless the strategic options seem quite clear; the successful sellers of labour-power compare current wages minus (their share of) unemployment costs with (expected) full employment wages minus adaptation costs. The unemployed compare unemployment benefits to expected wages. The capitalist buyers of labour-power compare their current profits to expected full-employment profits. The rest of the population (economically either directly dependent on economic agents or living from welfare state organised transfers) compare current income to that expected with full employment.

A further complication (to make things a little more realistic) can now be introduced. If unemployment works as a disciplinary device, full employment implies less work discipline and poorer work performance; workers work more like they want to work, not like capitalists want them to. Labour productivity would decline to some extent. Workers would benefit from this, but they and everyone else would have to live with a somewhat lower output. However, there would be more heads and hands at work, so that the loss in productivity could be more than offset by the increase in volume. Full employment national income would probably be higher 5–10 per cent than unemployment national income despite lower productivity. Since in our type of society, (almost) everybody prefers more to less, full employment is preferred, unless either transition costs are higher than expected benefits or the decline in shares for some offsets the increase in the size of the pie.

Estimating the income shares in moving from unemployment to full employment does not present much of a problem for two groups; the unemployed increase their share once they move into jobs while the capitalist share declines (that follows from the shift from a buyer's to a seller's labour market, and its consequences for bargaining power). So capital-owners are unlikely to bear the costs of full employment policies voluntarily.

Things are more difficult with the two other groups; those who are currently employed and those who depend on income transfers. Sellers of labour-power (as a group) will probably increase their gross share due to their better bargaining position in a situation of full employment, once this is established. They could win the support of those who are dependent on transfer incomes if the gains from full employment are divided between wage earners and welfare state clients (as they normally are, given the current rules linking pensions to wages). Of course, this logic of side payments does not only apply to one side in the conflict of interests. In addition, there are the costs of the transition, i.e. of installing full employment policies, to be taken into account. These costs may not be 'given', but may be subject to manipulation, either by political forces or by coordinated capitalist action.

The possibility of side payments points to two issues that need further exploration:

1. Capital and labour, or business and labour organisations, having conflicting interests, can attempt to influence each other and third parties by redistributing the gains of decisions in their favour. This was referred to above when unemployment insurance was considered as the outcome of a side-contract between sellers of labour-power.
2. Social security arrangements, as institutionalised forms of redistribution, may be analysed as the outcome of attempts to win coalition partners in the conflict between labour and capital, or as attempts to influence the strength of opposing interests.

The last point may be illustrated again by referring to unemployment insurance and the determination of benefit levels. For the currently successful sellers of labour-power, the strategic variable in the conflict about unemployment is a comparison of the cost of achieving full employment with the cost of unemployment. It follows that the lower cost of unemployment makes full employment relatively less attractive (and vice versa). Lower (direct) costs of unemployment, assuming they fall on the employed in the form of unemployment insurance contributions, can be achieved in two ways; by reducing the volume of unemployment at given costs per head or by reducing costs per head at the given volume. The first way is irrelevant in the present context, but the second one offers a strategic option for capitalists. The interest of those currently in full employment can be served by lowering unemployment benefits (per head) and thus reducing the costs of unemployment to them. Again, this is merely to illustrate the complications which come up once we consider interests not just as given, but subject to influences by conflicting groups which correspond to each other.

To close this chapter (but not the further investigation of interests in the welfare state), consider the additional complication resulting from the fact that lowering unemployment benefits is not a strategic option that can be directly realised by capitalists, but a matter of political decision making. This leads to the more general problem of how political processes are influenced by economic interests and how, in turn, the latter are modified by political decisions.

POLITICS AND UNEMPLOYMENT

Sellers of labour power, as economic agents, do not control the political means requisite to move an economy from one characterised by unemployment to one of full employment. In the same way, capitalists do not control unemployment insurance (which may stand as an example for the whole social security system) and cannot themselves adjust benefit levels according to their interests. Both labour and capital have to address the political system, either as interest groups or, at least, as voters. The question is whether and to what extent agents in the political system will opt for taking the political decisions in support of either capital or labour interests.

Although it is not possible to enter into a fully-fledged discussion of this question, one point must be stressed; the political process cannot be understood as merely a passive reflection of economic interests. Rather, political agents have their own interests, most prominently the interest in power. Given a democratic system, politicians have to win elections to gain or maintain access to power. So they will do what is in the interest of economic agents only if this is compatible with their own interests to win elections. Among other things this means that the particularity of the interest served by a particular decision must be concealed.

Obviously, the best decisions are those that can be grounded in the common good or the public interest or, at least, the interest of the majority. Thus, it seems natural that all political parties will have an interest in full employment. Capitalist interests are those of a minority. The majority of economic agents, the sellers of labour-power, also function as the majority of voters. Thus, for a politician to maximise votes, it is a must to pledge to fight unemployment. Some may go as far as to represent unemployment as a necessary, but temporary evil, the cure that is necessary to restore full employment. But even then, the emphasis is on 'temporary'. We can expect that all participants in the political game will refer to full employment as a norm. Therefore, their common interest in full employment does not establish much of a distinction among political parties.

On top of this, voting as the mode of articulation of interests vis-à-vis the political system is quite unsuitable as a means of pursuing single 'issues'. Parties offer different policy 'packages' and the decision to vote becomes one of deciding among such packages according to the priorities shown in party manifestos or past political actions. With regard to unemployment and its recent history in West Germany, the problem for voters is that neither of the major parties has credibly made full employment its top priority. The era of Keynesian optimism ended in the stagflation of the mid-seventies. The Social Democrats were taught a practical lesson on the veto powers of capital, and now shy away from offering any strategy towards full employment that would be acceptable for the majority of those who are currently employed. The Christian Democrats have been more concerned with manipulating unemployment statistics than with active intervention in the labour market.

Thus, the situation that sellers of labour-power face as voters is one where all parties pledge to fight unemployment but none offer any policy which convinces the majority of voters that full employment can be restored. Recent West German election results show that this situation might induce another pull-down effect of unemployment. The surprising gains of right-wing parties could be the result not only of the above average propensity of the unemployed to vote for 'radical' parties, but also of a widespread dissatisfaction with the way in which the dominant parties have handled the problem of mass unemployment and its consequences. But analysing this sort of pull-down effect would demand another chapter.

APPENDIX: A NOTE ON INTERESTS

Much could be said about the concept of interests. Here it will be used in the following sense: Saying 'x is in the interest of A' means that agent A prefers the situation to which event x belongs to the situation without x. Thus, interests express preferences. The nature of the 'objects' ordered according to preferences does not matter, be they things of material wealth or a hierarchy of norms. When interests are attributed to an agent by an observer, the latter must implicitly refer both to the agent's preference ordering and to his capacity for goal-oriented behaviour. The observer can go wrong, but this risk does not prevent the attribution of interests, either in everyday interaction, or in scientific discourse. Since all agents can observe other agents, they will attribute interests to others and will, at the same time, articulate their own. They will communicate about each other in terms of interests, at least in some social contexts. In some other contexts, this may be inappropriate, for example, when we ask: 'What were A_i's interests in falling in love with A_j?' The articulation and attribution of interests presume an instrumental attitude which is not the only possible attitude we can have towards other persons or towards inanimate objects. One issue this raises is how we arrive at instrumental, goal-oriented attitudes and to what extent and for what reasons other attitudes are transformed into instrumental ones. Intuitively, it seems plausible that the range of instrumental, interest-oriented strategic action is socially limited and this may be an advantage for arguments referring to interests. Universally applicable concepts tend to become empty.

The exercise of attributing 'objective' interests may involve 'a rationalistic prejudice' (Weber, 1972, p. 3) in the sense of assuming real agents to be rational. Such a prejudice rules when we take it for granted that agents' 'subjective' interests should be identical with those attributed by us as observers. Despite the danger of such confusions, reconstructing rational interests is a useful step of analysis, because such a reconstruction allows us to distinguish clearly between what people do and what we as observers would expect them to do 'in their own, best interest'. As the next step, this difference itself may be turned into the explanandum etc.

While this justification for using a concept of rational interests is formally correct, it is also a bit naïve. One can read economic theory, especially the neoclassical tradition, as a theory of rational interests. The development of the theory shows that the difference between what rational and real agents do never quite makes it to become the explanandum. On the the contrary, the inclination has been to explore the implications of the (rather restrictive) rationality assumption in an in-

Pull-down effects in the welfare state

creasingly formalised framework, exchanging rigour for realism.

Thus, any use of a concept of rational interests in social analysis can lead one straight into the neoclassical framework, insofar as one aims for logically watertight arguments. But there seems to be a trade-off. The security of conclusions is only obtainable at the cost of diminishing empirical relevance. If that is too high a price, what could be alternative uses of the concept of interests? The extreme alternative would be to refrain from '(re-)constructing' interests altogether. Instead of asking what would be rational for an agent in a given situation (described by an observer) we can simply ask the agent what his or her interests are.

We can discover subjectively defined interests using opinion research, etc. This alternative, which leaves little room for (explicit) theorising, is even less attractive than the neoclassical one. What remains between the two is some kind of muddling through, with opportunity costs in both directions.

NOTES

1. For some remarks on these difficulties see the appendix.
2. The merits of a functional analysis of welfare states are discussed (and perhaps demonstrated) in Ganssmann, 1988.
3. P. van Parijs convinced me that my built-in moralism prevented me from seeing this alternative. For example, the unemployed can be sent to war to get themselves killed.
4. Real wage reductions may not be feasible, as Keynesians would point out.
5. In the rest of this chapter, I will, for the sake of brevity, refer to wages when I mean wages *and* salaries and to workers when I mean workers *and* white collar employees, female and male.
6. From 1980 to 1987, the total annual volume of work declined by 5.6 per cent, from 45,942 to 43,373 million hours. The fact that during the same time, the number of economically active workers declined only by 1.7 per cent indicates that less work is performed per head per year (Tessaring, 1988, p. 178).
7. Fewer workers receive a smaller total wage, but they also produce less. If wages increase in line with productivity and inflation, the share of wages and profits will remain the same.
8. If the total number of the employed decreases, the total wage bill decreases, while the share of gross wages in national income may remain unchanged. Since more unemployed receive benefits deducted from wages as unemployment insurance contributions, the rate has to increase if the level of benefits is maintained. The result is a widening gap between gross and net wages (and a corresponding gap between their shares in national income).
9. In the West German system this is not the case. Only about 42 per cent of the unemployed received contribution-financed unemployment relief (Arbeitslosengeld) in 1988 whereas 23.6 per cent received means-tested support (Arbeitslosenhilfe) financed out of the federal budget. As an aside, note the recent shift in these shares; in 1986, 35.9 per cent received Arbeitslosengeld and 27 per cent received Arbeitslosenhilfe. The shift is mostly due to

legislative change in favour of the older unemployed, who can now receive Arbeitslosengeld for a longer period. For the federal Government, this has the welcome side-effect of relieving the federal budget (and the general taxpayer), making wage-earners carry a larger share of the burden of unemployment.

10. A parallel argument holds for other parts of the social security system and helps to explain the extent of the distributional shift; if the ratio of the retired (receiving pensions) to the actively employed (paying social security contributions) increases, the gap between gross and net wages increases.

11. Of course, this is not to say that an observable 'scissor' relationship between the development of gross and net wages is solely or even predominantly due to increasing unemployment insurance contributions; their size is small relative to taxes and other social security contributions.

12. The interests of others in unemployment versus full employment will be discussed below.

13. Since the neoclassical theoretical apparatus is increasingly used to formulate ideas which do not quite fit into the traditionally harmonious picture of self-regulating, welfare-maximising markets, I use the term 'simple' to denote the tradition.

14. These themes are discussed in the 'efficiency wage' literature. For a survey see Gerlach and Hübler, 1985.

15. The share of those without vocational training in the economically active population declined by almost 10 per cent from 1976 (33.4 per cent) to 1985 (23.9 per cent). At the same time the rate of unemployment of unskilled labour (not counting those currently in training) increased from 7.5 per cent (1975) to 18.4 per cent (1987) (Tessaring, 1988 p. 189f).

16. Conservative commentators recently stressed that the number of jobs in the West German economy has increased significantly and that continuing high unemployment was mostly due to increased labour-force participation, especially by women. However, both in terms of absolute numbers and of the participation rate, the West German economy has (as of 1988) not reattained the pre-mid-seventies employment figures.

17. Unemployment insurance also has the function of a genuine insurance against the risk of temporary job loss. But if getting a new job were only a matter of bidding wages down – given that one could survive at the resulting wage level – why would somebody capable of working need insurance?

18. 'In part as a result of the social policies of the Keynesian accommodation, the neutral rate of unemployment – the unemployment rate at which the share of labor wages as a claim on net output neither rises nor falls – has drifted upward. Ever more unemployment is needed to maintain a given level of power of capital over labor.' (Bowles and Gintis, 1986, p. 61).

9
GENDER, CLASS AND THE WELFARE STATE: THE CASE OF INCOME SECURITY IN AUSTRALIA*

SHEILA SHAVER

When feminism has raised questions about the state, questions have invariably also been raised about class and the relation between gender and class. This trilogy of terms invokes a triangle of conceptual relationships. For most of its history discussion of the welfare state has privileged the relationship between state and class. It is only in the last decade that feminists have forced recognition that the welfare state is also deeply implicated in a politics of gender.

The first feminist analyses of the welfare state called attention to areas of history and policy not mentioned in decades of class analysis. Thus Elizabeth Wilson (1977) pointed to the woman-to-woman character of the archetypal welfare transaction. Hilary Land (1976) showed how the Beveridge legacy reinforced a sexual division of labour taking women's dependency for granted. Linda Gordon (1976) documented state resistance to women's demands for autonomous control of their bodies and fertility. These and related themes have since been expanded in feminist accounts of a variety of welfare states (for example, Baldock and Cass, 1983; Nelson, 1984; Ungerson, 1985).

Feminist theory and politics have nevertheless remained undeservedly marginal to mainstream debate about the welfare state and its contemporary restructuring. No doubt this is partly attributable to plain intellectual sexism; not all writers want to face the fundamental questions raised by feminist social science (Harding and Hintikka, 1983). But perhaps feminist theory must also take some responsibility, both for inadequacies in the analyses offered to date and for abandoning public politics for the more exotic enticements of subjectivity, sexuality and semiotics (Segal, 1987). These important beginnings, now more than ten years old, have developed little beyond their first formulations, and while vital policy debates ensue, theoretical discussion of gender and the welfare state has lately all but ceased.

To a large extent this is because the paradigm which seemed most

---

* This chapter was originally published in *Feminist Review* 32 (June 1989), and is included in the present collection with the editors' kind permission.

promising, combining Marxist analysis of class and the capitalist state with feminist analysis of gender and social reproduction, has failed to meet feminist criticism of its theory and politics. The Marxist/feminist paradigm attempted to fill gaps in Marxism by adding theoretical terms for family, the sexual division of labour and formation of the gendered human subject. It presented the social structures of the private sphere as ordering gender and family relations around the reproduction of capitalist labour power. The welfare state was portrayed as 'public patriarchy' supporting, compensating for, or replacing the private variety (Brown, 1981). While capitalists appropriated the economic benefits of patriarchy, men enjoyed its private fruits.

This framework allowed little or no autonomy to gender in the conceptual triangle of gender, class and state, reducing gender relations to a subsystem in the cycle of capital, and male power to an abstract system of property. The account was 'gender blind' (Hartmann, 1981a). Marxism's categories were too little questioned, and feminism's too superficially applied. There have been relatively few attempts to theorise gender and state independently of class (MacKinnon, 1983): for the welfare state at least, the politics of class are too salient to be ignored. But neither can gender simply be grafted onto an independently constructed analysis of class and state. The trilogy of concepts must be reworked together. This chapter attempts to begin such a reworking.

In an earlier paper, 'Sex and Money in the Welfare State' (Shaver, 1983), I applied the Marxist/feminist paradigm to the centrepiece of the Australian welfare state and its tax/transfer system of income security. The analysis which resulted was quite powerful in some respects. It showed how pensions, benefits and allowances assume and reinforce a sexual division of labour in which males are defined as workers and breadwinners and females as dependent spouses primarily responsible for the domestic care of others. Moreover the structure of the tax/transfer system replicates the sexual division of labour at societal level, redistributing money from male worker-taxpayers to female dependants defined as mothers, wives and ex-wives. Nevertheless the analysis was both functionalist and reductionist. The key relation was between state and class, with the state acting to ensure the cycle of production and accumulation. The relation between state and gender followed from this understanding, with the state underpinning the family in the reproduction of labour power. The analysis subsumed gender politics in a self-maintaining system of functionally necessary interventions in production and reproduction. This was not a fatal flaw in a one-time examination of income security and taxation, which do after all form a system; there is a sense in which the welfare state does serve these ends and interests. But the theoretical closures built into the analysis left me incapable of explaining why such an arrangement has arisen in Australia, how it has changed over its history, and why it differs from income security in most other advanced capitalist states. These are, of course, the most interesting questions and the most significant for political action.

The timeless circularity of this analysis had something to do with the particular Marxism it drew on, incorporating the stubborn functionalism of the Althusserian reading then current among feminist interpreters of the welfare state (Wilson,1977; McIntosh, 1978). But it was not due only to this. The problem was also at least partly a result of its method, treating the income security system as an instance of the patriarchal capitalist state. The structures and functions of the whole were read back onto the part, assuming that what had been shown about the welfare state on a macro level was replicated in an individual subsystem. This method had two effects. It compounded the problem of functionalism, obscuring the historical specificity of diverse and changing welfare arrangements and precluding, among other things, comparison of welfare provisions as more or less oppressive. It also combined function and intention. Function properly belongs to the abstract level of system needs, whereas intention refers to human actors as empirical individuals or social groups. While abstract system imperatives may define the limits of possible action they cannot account for the actualities of power and process in welfare politics.

These closures can be overcome by situating the analysis at the level of the particular institution, abandoning *a priori* assumptions about the unity of the state and the integration of its parts. By disaggregating the study of the welfare state, each of its apparatuses can be afforded a specific history, framework of internal relations and series of connections with other social structures (Hansot and Tyack, 1988). In the case of income security this allows its connections with the wider structures of class and gender to be seen as problematic subjects for analysis in their own right. Its processes of political construction can be examined in relation to the stakes and power of conflicting social groups. The capacity of the income security system to mediate class and gender relations can be compared over time and with other state structures such as health, education and labour law. Its most significant relations with other social institutions, principally labour market and family, have a distinctive history and politics.

Functional relations can not be treated as straightforwardly determinant. Class and gender are primary sources of the social tension and conflict which welfare provisions mediate, and are correspondingly central to the institutional structures which comprise the welfare state. These tensions and conflicts have functional origins in the organisation of the capitalist social economy around wage labour. In principle, lack of access to an alternative form of subsistence compels individuals to sell their labour power, in actuality not all labour power is effectively saleable, with potentially disruptive consequences for social order. Welfare provisions serve to manage this disjunction (Piven and Cloward, 1971; Gough, 1979, p. 47). Also, labour markets determine the value of labour power of individuals as individuals without regard for the consumption needs of the domestic unit; in actuality the reproduction of labour power is organised within family units of variable sizes and composition. Welfare transfers also mediate this contradiction (McIntosh, 1978, p. 271; Gough, 1979, pp. 48–9).

These underlying tensions may indeed create the basis for welfare intervention, but they do not, in themselves ensure that functional requisites are actually fulfilled (Gough, 1979, p. 50; McIntosh, 1978). Neither do they explain the form, scale or content of welfare provision. These are socially determined through the political institutions of liberal democracy, which have generated widely differing welfare systems at different times and in different societies. We need an analysis treating the income security system as historically constructed in the day-to-day legislative and bureaucratic politics of the welfare state. Functional relationships set limits to these politics but do not determine their specifics within those limits.

Nelson has observed that claiming benefits from the state is as much a political as an administrative relationship, and that beneficiary status is connected with voters' evaluations of government performance. She concludes that 'modern political life includes distributive as well as classically democratic components' (Nelson, 1984, pp. 217 and 224). Both components, beneficiary status and voter participation, have bases in gender as well as in class and income. T. H. Marshall's (1963) 'social rights' refer to the structural side of the same relationship between citizen and state. Marshall's theory was that the evolution of civil and political rights in the eighteenth and nineteenth centuries gave rise in the twentieth to social 'citizenship' the right to 'live the life of a civilised being according to the standards prevailing in the society' (*ibid.*, p. 74), primarily through public education and the social services. While civil and political rights were clearly compatible with the simultaneous evolution of English industrial capitalism, social rights were potentially in conflict with its basic framework of economic inequality. Because the representative basis of parliamentary democracy had become essentially individual, the equality of social citizenship was self-limiting and the (imperfect) equality of social rights in citizenship was complementary to economic inequality. Feminist critiques of the welfare state have shown that these rights also embody structures of gender inequality.

The income security system is a framework, historically and politically constructed, which defines legitimate claims to social rights. Social rights, once in existence, have become objects of budgetary and ballot box politics. Hence their terms, conditions and values are always subject to contention among competing policy agendas and citizen constituencies. Welfare politics operate through contending claims about relative needs, economic efficiency, and distributive justice. Their ambit almost always cuts across the ideological divide between the public domain of the market and the private domain of home and family. Thus class and gender are together engaged in situational concert.

This approach invites us to see income security provisions as simultaneously 'classed' and 'gendered'. Following Smith (1983) and Phillips (1987), it understands capitalism and patriarchy as mutually constitutive forms of domination, dimensions of each other; gender and gender relations are integral to the social organisation of class, and class is similarly constitutive of gender. This is true of the 'public' institutions of the welfare state, of the 'private' structures of the social economy in which it intervenes, and of the relations constructed between them.

Provisions are 'classed' in the way they articulate income security with labour markets and social relationships derived from employment. The establishment of a social right to subsistence income effectively decommodifies labour power, providing sustenance without labour market obligation (Esping-Andersen, 1987). The terms and conditions under which labour power is decommodified are political constructions of class relations. Gender and family are basic elements in these terms and conditions, both immediately in a labour market structured by a deeply-rooted sexual division of labour and secondarily in enduring mechanisms of class inheritance such as wealth, education and social connection, racial and ethnic subordination. Welfare provisions are 'gendered' in the way they articulate income security with family structure and dependency relations. Social rights to subsistence or supplementary income reflect and reconstruct relations between men and women in terms of marriage, fertility, parenthood, kinship. These rights establish a framework of breadwinner and dependency statuses for men and women institutionalised through the welfare state (Shaver, 1983). The actual social meaning of dependency is strongly affected by class. This is expressed in class structuring of its provisions through means tests on income and property, differential class entitlement through 'welfare' and 'taxation' expenditures, and most concretely in the prospect of actually being subjected to the controlling forces of the welfare state.

The political institutions of Australian liberal democracy originated in class conflict, and class interests remain the salient framework of electoral politics. The Australian welfare state has, in line with other changes, meant a reconstruction of class relations (Shaver, 1987, p. 431). The politics of decommodification define the role of the state in regulating labour force obligation and apportioning the social burden of its cost. While class has been a visible point of conflict in welfare politics, gender has been a point of covert agreement across the political spectrum. Its very invisibility reflects the tension in liberal thought between woman as dependant and woman as citizen (Brennan and Pateman, 1979; Nelson, 1984). The politics of family income support operate through liberal democratic institutions under male control and have until recently made no distinction between the interests of the family unit and the interests of women.

Gender and class do not give a full analysis of the structure of domination exercised through the welfare state. Race and ethnicity are at least as important. The Australian welfare state began with colonisation of the Aboriginal people, and the twentieth century construction of its framework of social rights with their exclusion. Its history of immigration and social policy tells another story of social and cultural domination in the terms of membership in its 'imagined community' (Anderson, 1983). Other welfare states also embody forms of racial and ethnic domination. However, it is not appropriate to try to incorporate these dimensions of analysis in the present argument. Its focus on income security leaves out other racially specific welfare apparatuses 'protecting' and assimilating Aboriginal and immigrant groups. Beckett (1987) has described the Australian state's relation to indigenous peoples as 'welfare colonialism'. This powerful analysis is beyond the scope of this chapter, which must therefore stand incomplete.

The Australian income security system has developed within the principles of social assistance established at the Federation of the national state early this century. As a result it differs from income security systems in the United Kingdom and the United States in some important respects. It is first of all a more unitary system, providing virtually all coverage within a single framework of revenue and entitlement. This distinguishes it from the more common arrangement in which a secondary, residual system of social assistance underpins primary coverage grounded in principles of social insurance. Both British and American income security have this more usual character. Administered wholly by the Commonwealth government, responsibility is not divided among levels of government as in the American federal system. As a social assistance system Australian income security is wholly financed from the consolidated revenues of the federal government, of which income taxes make up a comparatively large share. There are no levies on employers or employees of the kind applied to social insurance in the United Kingdom or the United States, and no corresponding attachment of eligibility for or levels of benefits to a contributory history. The system of benefits which results has been characterised as 'state charity' (Dickey, 1980), and its purpose is more singly defined in terms of the relief of poverty than the complex amalgam of social and individual equity which structures British and American income security. Although it has not always been the case, eligibility for virtually all pensions and benefits now depends on a means test as determined by the income of the nuclear family unit and for many benefits also by capital, excluding owner occupied housing. Benefits are flat-rate, with no earnings or contributions-related component, and include allowances for dependent spouse and children.

The discussion to follow identifies key structures of Australian income security and examines the way they articulate class and gender relations. These key structures are the categories used to define the life contingencies for which benefits are provided and the universal and selective (means-tested) determinations of eligibility within categories. Virtually all pensions, benefits and allowances have both class and gender dimensions built into these categorical and universal/selective specifications which link eligibility for income security with the surrounding structures of labour market, economy and family. These specifications are reworked continuously and incrementally in legislative revision and bureaucratic application. The interconnections of class and gender in income security are thus also subject to continuous historical reconstruction. At a broader level, the income security system sets up circuits of redistribution between interest groups formed on the basis of income, family form and life cycle. These engage income security with the wider politics of Australian capitalist patriarchy.

CATEGORICAL ELIGIBILITY AND THE DECOMMODIFICATION OF LABOUR POWER

The fundamental point of departure in Australian income security is the idea that certain specified categories of person should be eligible for subsistence income from the state. Each of its component pensions or benefits is defined in terms of personal and circumstantial criteria, such as old age, widowhood or unemployment, upon which eligibility depends. The history of the Australian welfare state is often represented as a series of developments, largely extensions, in the range and interpretation of these categories (Kewley, 1973). Categorical definitions are basic to British social insurance (Ogus, 1982, pp. 202–32) and to the contributory and most means-tested tiers of American provision (Rainwater, Rein and Schwartz, 1986, pp. 165–72 and 188–92).

This categorical framework defines the nexus between income security and labour market; the categories express at once social conditions of access to welfare[1] provision and political limits to the institution of wage labour (Piven and Cloward, 1971, pp. 123–46). Because categorical terms apply to both personal attributes and social circumstances, decommodification of labour power clearly engages social structures of gender as well as class. This is the case whether terms of eligibility for benefit are the same or different for men and women. Politically debated, legislated and bureaucratically interpreted, each category has a political history in both dimensions.

Most categorical terms of Australian income security revolve around the obligation of able-bodied, prime-age workers to participate in paid employment. The aged were the first group of workers to be accorded the social right to income from the state. They had been the largest group cared for through nineteenth century charity, and the end of the century saw an emerging alliance between liberal reform movements and the new Australian Labor Party (ALP) over the demand for an age pension. The category was initially defined in 1908 Commonwealth legislation as aged 65 or more for both men and women, with women becoming eligible at age 60 in 1910. Aboriginal and 'Asiatic' persons were excluded. Among further restrictions were good moral character, disqualifying men or women having deserted spouse or children (Kewley, 1973, pp. 74–5). The invalid pension grew out of the same political and legislative processes and was closely modelled on it.

The establishment of maternity allowance in 1912 represented a new departure in income security; a cash subsidy was to be provided not on the grounds of wage labour but of motherhood. The measure emerged less from any articulated political demand than from the conjunction of electoral politics with ideological panic about 'race suicide' (Kewley, 1973, pp. 99–109). The same racial exclusions applied. The allowance was a onetime grant upon the birth of a child, payable to the mother. Both married and unmarried women were eligible without test of character or of means.

During the inter-war period, when Britain and the US were establishing systems based on insurance principles, Australian development was paralysed by class conflict over welfare finance. The only new benefits were for ex-servicemen. World War II put income security back on the political agenda, this time as a pragmatic political device of wartime unity. Once again a surprise political tactic seized on motherhood. As in Britain (Land, 1976, pp. 113–6), the introduction of child endowment was a device to restrain male wages (Kewley, 1973, pp. 190–1). This was a regular weekly payment acknowledging the extra cost of children. Though free of means testing it applied only to parents having more than one child, because the family wage was supposed to support one or two already. Like maternity allowance the benefit has since been paid to the mother, who is entitled regardless of marital status. This was the first benefit extended to Aboriginal women.

The war-time Labor government revamped Australian income security, retaining the social assistance basis and adding important new categories of benefit. Two developments are of particular importance. New South Wales had instituted a widow's pension in the 1920s. A Commonwealth pension, repeatedly aborted in the battles over contributory finance, now became a war-time symbol of social justice to come. In caring for their children these women were performing a 'national service' (Shaver, 1987, pp. 420–1). The 1942 Commonwealth pension was available to married women, *de jure* or *de facto*, whose husbands had died or deserted, who had not remarried, and who were either responsible for the care of one or more dependent children or had reached the age of 50, subject to a means test. Widowed or deserted men in similar circumstances were not eligible. This was the first time prime-age labour power was decommodified, and the first time subsistence income was provided on grounds of family responsibility.

Unemployment benefit took similar impetus from the years of delay and the war-time moment. It became a key symbol also of Labor's commitment to full employment and the welfare state. Men and women were equally eligible (Shaver, 1987, pp. 422–5). A parallel sickness benefit and an essentially discretionary catch-all special benefit were also established.

Few changes were made to the categories of income security during the period of post-war expansion. Most important was supporting parent's allowance, established for single and deserting women solely responsible for dependent children in 1973 and extended to men in 1977. The Whitlam Labor Government was responding to pressure from women's and welfare lobbies about the anomalous treatment of single and other supporting mothers dependent on the more penurious provision of state governments (who in turn saw their support as properly the responsibility of the federal government).[2] In effect the new provision for supporting mothers gave all female parents the same access to pension income regardless of marital history. The subsequent extension of supporting parent's benefit to men followed a vocal campaign by single fathers and established equivalent social rights for single parents of both sexes. The Whitlam Government also introduced the handicapped child's allowance in 1974. The benefit is a supplement to child endowment, and is also paid to the mother. It provides a cash supplement to a mother or other guardian caring for a handicapped child in the home. In 1982 family income supplement was introduced, extending pension allowances for dependent children to poor non-pensioner parents. It too is paid to the mother.

Since the advent of fiscal crisis, governments have begun to narrow categorical boundaries and to abolish categories of welfare provision altogether. In 1978 the Fraser Conservative Government abolished the maternity allowance. The Hawke Labor Government has shortened the period of child dependency entitling widows and supporting parents to pension and has begun the gradual abolition of widow's pension for older widows. Widowhood, divorce or desertion without responsibility for dependent children are no longer to be grounds for the decommodification of labour power.

There is a broad developmental logic in the categories structuring Australian income security. The range of categories established for income security payments has been slowly extended to provide for a widening range of individuals and circumstances, covering broadly the same span as in Britain and America. Within this framework a dual structure has emerged, with one group of benefits providing subsistence income maintenance (full decommodification of labour power) and another providing income supplementation (partial decommodification).

By the beginning of the post-war period income maintenance provision had come to include two different kinds of provision. One concerns conditions directly tied to labour market and class structure, such as age, invalidity and unemployment. For these benefits categorical terms are broadly similar to those applied in both British and American income security in age, gender and circumstantial criteria. The other concerns the somewhat different condition of widowhood and single parenthood, where gender and family have been independently prominent grounds for the decommodification of labour power. Here Australian provision has differed, providing subsistence for widows without dependent children at markedly younger ages than either Britain or America and for single parents without the obligation to seek paid employment often applied to their American counterparts. In both cases the historical trend has been for income maintenance categories to become defined in formally equal terms between men and women. Most important here are the extension of income support to male single parents and the phasing out of pensions for older widows. With these changes the Australian pension system makes relatively few gender distinctions, the most significant remaining difference being earlier access to the age pension for women. This also continues to be the case in Britain (Land, 1976, pp. 53–56).

Family income supplementation categories have changed much less, and their ideological specifications have continued to represent the mother as recipient and guardian. This representation has become the basis of a secondary income security model for measures directed to 'family' welfare with close resemblance to British income security, where similar allowances for maternity and child benefits and a family income supplement exist. American income security has no counterpart to this model; there are no family allowances, and income supplementation for the working poor is provided mainly through the non-categorical food stamps programme.

'NEED' AND ALLOCATIVE POLITICS: MEANS-TESTING AND THE FAMILY UNIT

A second key feature of Australian income security is its near total reliance on the basic allocative principle of relative economic need. While categorical eligibility is common to most income security systems, need rarely plays the central allocative role it does in Australia (Saunders, 1987c, pp. 411–8). Both British and American income security base primary allocation on contributory entitlement, and only secondary forms of supplementary provision use needs criteria. Thus British social insurance provides benefits made up of flat-rate and earnings-related components for age, widowhood, disability, sickness and unemployment based on contributory history, but where the social insurance payment is inadequate or contributory entitlement is absent these often have to be increased or replaced by means-tested supplementary benefits. American social security, administered by the federal Government, is similarly underpinned by Aid to Families with Dependent Children, food stamps and other means-tested benefits provided through state and local government.

In Australia the needs principle has always been two dimensional, measuring both volume of resources and composition of the unit dependent on them. The primary vehicle for needs-based allocation between family units has been means testing in relation to income and/or property, constructed to compare relative economic need on a family unit basis. Pensions and benefits carry structures of rates and allowances, scaling payments according to the size and composition of the family unit.

Through its linkages with labour market and life cycle, needs allocation joins income security with underlying structures of gender and class. The means test specifies the point of interchange between privately gained resources and publicly provided income within the particular category of eligibility. It marks the junction between economic and state power for a given social group. Its family unit basis codes assumptions about marriage, kinship and life cycle into this nexus. Most significant for gender relations is the assumption that husband and wife have equal shares in all economic resources.

The establishment of Commonwealth old age and invalid pensions set up the dual economic and family framework for selective allocation from which all later formulations have derived. Namely, while pension entitlement would be a 'right' this would be qualified by a test of need as measured by both income and property. Equal pensions would be paid to single and married persons but the eligibility of married claimants would be tested on the combined means of both. The suggestion that relatives other than spouses should be obliged to contribute to the support of pensioners was rejected (Kewley,1973, pp. 74–5, 91).

The maternity allowance was universal and ostensibly free of class feeling, but the debate which ensued from it was not. Payment to the mother was justified in terms of the fiscal profligacy of the working class husband. More broadly, the electoral popularity of the measure kicked off the 30-year debate on the 'contributory question' and class interests in the finance of social security. The non-Labor parties quickly became committed to contributory social insurance. Various schemes reiterated both class and gender principles. The contributory basis was appropriate for a society in which class division was a settled reality, the working class would pay for its income security protection while the link of benefit to contribution would teach foresight and thrift. The contributory basis also embodied expectations about the sexual division of labour, carrying the framework of the family wage into the income security system. Women were to contribute at lower rates, reflecting parities in the wage system drawn up in wage arbitration.

In the event the war gave Labor the opportunity to have its way with social security. While the ALP had opposed only the first of these two principles, its own wartime interpretation of 'contributory' finance actually broke more clearly with the second. Labor had always favoured finance from a progressive income tax. During the war it established a tax/transfer framework which earmarked a share of income tax as a 'social services contribution'. Because the income tax base now extended deeply into the working class, the practical result of the new framework was not unlike contributory finance (Watts, 1980). The ideological connection between individual contribution and benefit was, however, absent. Nor was the sexual division of labour so unambiguously encoded in social provision. Access to benefits did not depend on individual contribution, either one's own or through a spouse, but derived directly from personal membership in the national community (Shaver, 1987, pp. 42–7). In the ALP version of income security weaker parallels with the family wage were embodied in allowances enabling pensioner 'breadwinners' to provide for a dependent spouse and children (*ibid.*, 1987, pp. 421). Family wage concepts were embodied, too, in the principle of means-testing; the new social rights of Labor's welfare state were measured against the income and property of the family unit without regard to individual shares, access or control. Family was now sharply defined as married couple or single parent and dependent children.

Labor's (unacknowledged) resolution of the contributory question allowed the selectivity of the income security system to be progressively weakened over the years of the long boom and Conservative Government. The contradiction between universal taxpayer and selective pensioner statuses gave rise to a politics of envy among those denied eligibility for benefits by the means-test (Shaver, 1984, pp. 302–3). The means test for the age pension was successively weakened. The prosperity of the period had precisely the opposite effect on means testing for unemployment and sickness benefits. Unemployment was low and few depended on these benefits for long, so the test was not an issue. While means-test limits for the age and invalid pensions increased by ten times between 1947 and 1972, limits for unemployment benefit increased only three-fold. The same period also saw steady expansion in the range and distribution of family benefits. Child endowment for the first child in the family became an important political symbol for universalism in child provision. Less popularly, the changes included the introduction of differential rates for single and married old age pensioners recognising the higher costs of living alone.

Australia's long period of post-war growth ended in the early 1970s, hitting the Whitlam Government in mid-term. A confused decade of reaction ensued. Labor embarked on and then abandoned the abolition of the means-test for the old age pension. The Fraser Government had greater enthusiasm for cutbacks, but not before it had weakened the means-test for large asset holders. It also extended tax concessions for children in increased child endowment payments, renamed family allowances, giving poor parents the tax benefit previously available only at higher income levels.

Most recently the Hawke Government has reasserted the needs principle in widespread rationalisation of income security. It has tightened means-tests for the old age pension and closed assets loopholes. It has also applied a means-test to the family allowance. Having long represented horizontal equity between taxpayers with and without children, family allowance is now a means-tested welfare provision. Other child benefits are to be reintegrated in a new, tighter framework of means-testing. The government has also begun to reconstruct single parent provision around enforced child maintenance by noncustodial parents.

The development of needs-based allocation in Australian income security has seen three types of provision emerge. Entitlement to long-term income maintenance has been extended up the income scale. Means-tests for the old age pension, which provide the paradigm for long-term categories of income maintenance, though now tightening, remain liberal enough for 78 per cent of eligible age groups to receive at least part pension. At the same time most pensioners qualify at full rate, and those without private resources are marginally poor. As the old age pension approached universality, it came to resemble the British pension, paying flat-rate benefits at an ostensibly adequate minimum level. Ironically, while the Australian pension reverted to selectivism its British counterpart was being reconstructed as earnings-related. Both the Australian old age pension and British supplementary benefit, which many British pensioners in fact require, are ideologically defined as means-tested 'rights' (Shaver,1984; Rainwater *et al.*, 1986, pp. 185–6). Although their earnings-related basis is heavily boosted at low income levels, American social security payments to the elderly are perceived as property rights flowing from past contributions.

The same means-test framework has applied to the Australian widow's pension and supporting parent's allowance. In the hostile employment climate, 'single parenthood on the pension' has become a common outcome of divorce among virtually all income groups, and increasingly among male as well as female custodial parents (Social Security Review, 1987, pp. 40–43). A very high proportion of the women in this position is poor (Cass, 1985), and means-test 'poverty traps' deter them from supplementing the pension with part-time employment. At the same time the unitary framework of Australian income security has meant that single parents, especially women, have greater equality of treatment and individual autonomy of entitlement. American and British single parents are divided into widows whose entitlements stem from the contributions of their husbands, and other single parents with less regular marital histories whose relation to the state is more direct but whose eligibility for support falls to secondary means-tested programmes.

While long-term income maintenance has been extended to middle income groups, Australian short-term provisions for unemployment and sickness have remained much more tightly restricted. Again the unitary basis of Australian income security gives these provisions a distinctive character. The insurance bases of British and American unemployment compensation obviate means-testing but also limit the period for which insurance-based compensation is available. In contrast Australian provision makes little distinction between short and long-term beneficiaries, but family unit means-testing makes the rights of claimants subject to the employment status of marital partners, largely precluding access to benefit for married women.

Historically universal, Australian payments supplementing family income are currently being reconstructed as means-tested benefits. As in Britain (Rainwater *et al.*, 1986, p. 144), family allowances have been allowed to decline in real value while poverty-targetted child supplements are integrated and increased. Piggy-backed on family allowance, these benefits share its expectations about the special responsibility of motherhood.

THE INCOME SECURITY SYSTEM AND THE POLITICS OF REDISTRIBUTION

The categorical and allocative terms of Australian income security establish frameworks of relative economic need, labour force attributes and familial dependencies for the decommodification of labour power. The income security system is defined in its financial circuits of revenue and expenditure, where this framework situates income security within a larger political economy of redistribution. The double redistribution by income and by family structure and life cycle links income security with structures of class and gender. Class interests in income security are embodied in the terms of trade of tax and benefit among income groups ('vertical redistribution'), and more generally in the legal and ideological construction of entitlement. Gender and life cycle interests are embodied in the framework of income pooling and family dependencies inscribed in the family unit basis of income security provision, and are expressed in a calculus of exchange between family and life cycle groups ('horizontal redistribution').

Circuits of redistribution define limits to the decommodification of labour power through welfare payments. These circuits express both structural contours of the welfare state and social boundaries between public and private power. They describe, for example, the scale of the welfare state, its accommodation of class conflict and its biopolitical agenda.

In principle there are functional limits to state intervention beyond which key structures of the existing social order would be jeopardised. It has been argued, for example, that functional limits of this kind explain changing access to dole payments over the trade cycle (Piven and Cloward, 1971), the forms taken by welfare concessions to the working class (Gough, 1979, pp. 64–9) and the existence of the cohabitation rule (Shaver, 1983, p. 155). But in practice functional limits are too broad to explain the determination of specific institutional arrangements. This is true of the relation between the political and the economic. Gough (1979, pp. 102–27) has observed, for instance, that the scale of welfare expenditure which the capitalist economy can accommodate depends on how it is financed. It is also true of the relation between family and economy.

McIntosh (1978) argues that in important respects the family household system is not adequately functional for capitalism, requiring the welfare state to replace as much as to underpin it.

The socially effective limits to state intervention are not functional but more immediately historical and political. These limits are contested between and among interest groups constituted through the circuits of redistribution in income security. Australia's formulation of means-tested social rights makes these redistributions particularly salient in political debate about comparative equity within claimant groups. Tax payments are submerged in general revenue and confer little public sense of entitlement, while benefits are rationed publicly with visible social boundaries between those eligible for and excluded from benefit. These tensions have been variously expressed, in a drift toward universalism during the long boom and an attack on 'middle class welfare' since the advent of fiscal crisis. A similar dynamic has also operated with respect to family and dependency provisions of the double redistribution.

The Labor legislation of the 1940s established income security on a tax/transfer basis in which a share of (nominally progressive) tax revenues was redirected to income security recipients. This transformation changed the political and economic calculus of class and gender in Australian income security. The contributory question had been argued in terms of class interests and class solidarities. The non-Labor parties were adamant that any scheme must be, and be seen to be, paid for by the working class. Labor's determined preference for finance through direct taxation was a demand for a 'ransom of capital'. The terms of debate were in important respects illusory (Shaver, 1987, p. 419), but deeply felt nonetheless. Questions about gender, family and dependency arose from within the contributory debate and drew little attention in their own right; it was taken for granted that the eligibility of married women, and likewise widows, would depend primarily on the contributions of their husbands.

Labor's welfare state was built on Keynesian demand management for full male employment. Income security was a complement to full employment policies, mildly redistributive at the lowest income levels (Kewley, 1973, pp. 234–54; Watts, 1980). Marshall (1963) observed that equality in social rights serves to support and legitimate inequality in economic rewards. Social rights are thus as much an extension as a modification of class society. The new tax/transfer system established institutional mechanisms for a double redistribution between income and life cycle groups, and these became the basis of a new post-war politics. Both class and gender relations were affected. What had been argued in terms of equity between classes was now institutionalised as parities among income groups. What had been recognised as legitimate conditions of dependency were now integrated in a structure of transfers based on age, family and life cycle. The claimant status of men and women was more nearly equivalent than proposed in earlier contributory schemes, but the access of both continued to be determined on a married couple basis. The system as a whole redistributed income from taxpayers defined as individuals to recipients treated as members of family units (Shaver, 1983).

The initial contours of the income security system were altered incrementally over the long period of post-war prosperity, and although the structural basis of the system was little changed there were significant shifts of emphasis within it. Welfare monies were spread increasingly widely and thinly. By the late 1960s the tax structure as a whole effected little vertical redistribution (Bentley, Collins and Drane, 1974; Podder and Kakwani, 1975). With the redistributive capacity of the tax/transfer system depending almost exclusively on the concentration of expenditure among low-income recipients through the means test, the calculus of class benefit shifted toward middle-income groups. The calculus of gender, family and life cycle changed much less.

The collapse of economic growth and full employment brought a crisis of legitimacy for Keynesian economic policy and the welfare state. In Australia this coincided with the break-up of 23 years of parliamentary rule by conservative parties and the practical possibility of a Labor government. It coincided also with the emergence of new forms of political organisation including a politically organised women's movement. Having committed itself to social justice through expanded circuits of redistribution, the Whitlam Government initially moved to expand the depth and coverage of income security. This responded both to demands for larger, universal pensions and women's demands for family and single parent provision. By mid-term, however, it was moving to constrain the growth of the welfare state.

Expenditure commitments have been trimmed repeatedly since. Both parties have retreated from 1970s commitment to universalism, speaking instead of priority for the poor. Yet while governments have sought to reduce expenditure the effects of recession have combined with other factors, most importantly rising numbers of single parent families, to push up demand for welfare spending. The share of social security in total federal government outlays continued to rise until 1983/4 and the advent of the Hawke Labor Government. While the current reconstruction has strengthened the welfare floor, mainly through increases in benefits to children, it has elsewhere weakened the circuits of redistribution. The level and distribution of welfare benefits have been contracted while tax reform measures are reducing rates of income tax, especially for higher income groups. More recently it has begun to reduce horizontal redistribution and the flow of funds to children and single parents. Social security spending has been wound back to its 1977/8 share of total outlays.

Australian income security has been built around a double redistribution among income groups and among family structure and life-cycle groups, with the second dimension by far the most significant. Like Australia, the United Kingdom and the United States spend a comparatively small proportion of gross domestic product on social security (Saunders, 1987c, p. 411). International comparison of the redistributive effects of welfare spending raises more complexities than can be dealt with here, but it is reasonable to suggest that the overall patterns of redistribution are broadly similar in all three countries, with horizontal redistribution much more significant than vertical. Rainwater *et al.*, (1986, pp. 147–51), for example, show this pattern for both British and American transfers to families in mid life cycle.

Australia's unitary tax/transfer system constructs welfare politics as relatively straightforward expressions of age, income, race and ethnicity, gender and family composition. The more complex amalgams of social insurance and means tested systems of both British and American income security create further bases of political division. Australian income taxation, for example, is applied to the income of individuals with relatively little distinction between the tax treatment of husbands and wives; there is a substantial rebate to a taxpayer maintaining a dependent spouse, but income splitting is not generally available. Individuals confront the benefit side of the system as members of a family unit. British and American income security is financed from combinations of levies on employment income and income taxes. Until recently British social insurance allowed married women to decline to contribute (the 'married woman's option'), and even now their benefits from equal contributions are less (Land and Parker, 1978, pp. 339–40). American social security requires equal contributions from employed wives but their benefits are not similarly individualised (Kamerman and Kahn, 1978, p. 445). Both systems credit dependent women with nominal contributions during periods of full-time child care. In both countries income taxes apply to the married couple, and although options exist for taxing partners separately the structure implicitly favours joint taxation of couples of breadwinner and dependent spouse (Land and Parker, 1978, pp. 342–3; Kamerman and Kahn, 1978, pp. 450–1). Means-tested benefits in both countries assess resources and determine benefits in terms of the family unit. These more multiplex circuits of revenue and expenditure in turn set up more complex interplays between income security and the gender and class structures of labour market and family.

CONCLUSION

Class and gender are closely integrated in Australian income security; in defining its provisions they also define each other. In income security as elsewhere gender and class describe structures of domination. Indeed one reason welfare is interesting is that it represents both alleviation of oppression and a mode of social control in its own right.

As gender and class define each other, both also define and are defined by the welfare state. This is why the state cannot be understood as simply patriarchal (MacKinnon, 1983) or straightforwardly capitalist (Gough, 1979) as its functions and concrete political forms embody the mutual interactions of patriarchal capitalism so must our conceptual understandings. We can begin to see some of these processes of mutual interaction in the case of Australian income security, where a key institution of the welfare state is simultaneously classed and gendered. The class and gender relations expressed through its categorical and allocative frameworks have grown out of and reshaped connections with labour market, family and wider social economy.

The trilogy of relations between gender, class and state also inheres in its substructures of income maintenance and family income supplementation. Income maintenance provisions have common forms of connection with the class basis of a gendered labour market. Terms for the decommodification of labour power set limits to the exigencies of the labour market, but release from employers' demands subjects the claimant to the more direct powers of the state. These more direct powers have their own subtext of class and gender control in what Fraser (1987) calls the 'juridical-administrative-therapeutic state apparatus'. She has pointed to its American manifestation in largely separate systems of 'masculine' provisions defining claimants as workers, ideological possessive individuals and bearers of social rights of citizenship, and 'feminine' provisions portraying claimants as dependent clients whose benefits derive from family need not individual rights.

Australian income maintenance has a parallel but more weakly differentiated gender subtext, with 'masculine' benefits directly tied to labour market and economy, such as age, invalidity and unemployment, and 'feminine' provisions for widowhood and single parenthood where gender and family are independently prominent bases of entitlement. Both forms are more clearly imbued with an ethos of individual right, largely ideological, yet simultaneously more uniformly mediated by family through the assumptions of the means test. Moreover there has been an increasing historical tendency for income maintenance categories to become defined in formally equal terms between male and female claimants. This is most marked in the treatment of single parents.

By contrast, family income supplementation provisions have been written in a language of gender with class as subtext. Historically, measures such as maternity benefit and family allowance appropriated motherhood as vehicle of class and wage politics. With the fiscal crisis, text and subtext have been reversed and extension of these benefits has been accompanied by their redefinition from measures for horizontal equity between taxpayers with and without children, in which all income groups appropriately shared, to measures for vertical redistribution and poverty relief. Indeed we were promised that relatively small increases would abolish child poverty by 1990 (Howe, 1987)!

Gender, class and the welfare state

None of this means that Australian income security is necessarily less capitalist, less patriachal or even less oppressive than the income security systems of other advanced capitalist nations. Indeed it is all these things, but in quite specific ways particular to Australia and particular to its given historical circumstances. It is these national and historical variations which an adequate theory of gender, class and the welfare state must be able to illuminate.

NOTES

1. In American usage 'welfare' refers only to means-tested social assistance and contrasts with 'social security' benefits based on social insurance principles; in that country the term often carries derogatory connotations. The term has a more general meaning in Australia where this distinction does not apply and negative connotations, while not entirely absent, are more muted. In the present analysis 'welfare' refers to income security benefits generally, including those provided through both social insurance and social assistance principles.
2. At the same time it formalised the 'cohabitation' rule denying benefits to single parents residing with a heterosexual partner, on the grounds that to do otherwise would treat them more favourably than a legally married couple (Jordan, 1981, 1–38). Similar rules operate in both British Supplementary Benefit (Fairbairns, 1985; Donnison, 1985) and American Aid to Families with Dependent Children (Piven and Cloward, 1971, p. 127).

10
THE PARTICULARISM OF WEST GERMAN WELFARE CAPITALISM: THE CASE OF WOMEN'S SOCIAL SECURITY*

STEPHAN LEIFBRIED AND ILONA OSTNER

Welfare state analysis relies too easily on a sort of universal model of welfare with the peculiarities of national welfare state cultures often eradicated. Welfare states are tradition-bound and embedded in cultural patterns and are not easily made out in quantitative approaches. As an outcome of political development and struggle, these traditions provide a hegemonic, institutionalised framework for political discourse. While certain arguments, interests and actors are allowed, others are restricted. Focusing on women's social security we will try to outline how the German welfare state is tradition-bound and particular and we will do this in a comparative framework.

FEMINISATION OF POVERTY AND MARGINALITY IN THE WEST – SIMILARITIES AND DIFFERENCES

In all western societies women are more likely to suffer from poverty or at least from being marginalised from mainstream society. Many women are marginalised *and* poor. Modern western societies share common features; they tend to impoverish women and to render women and women's work invisible . Moreover, women are often denied full citizenship rights and equality with men. But there are differences in the extent of continuous and systematic feminisation of poverty and marginality (Gerhard, Schwarzer and Slupik, 1988; Riedmüller and Kickbusch, 1982; Jones and Jónasdottir, 1988; Ostner, 1990).

'Marginality' can be described as a lack of income and economic well being, and as being partly excluded from good qualifications and job opportunities. Furthermore, marginalised people often suffer from bad living conditions such as crowded or poor housing, as well as a lack of spatial and ecological resources such as air, light, silence, 'nature', 'beauty', public transport and similar public goods. Marginalised women suffer, in addition, from restricted access to public amenities and discourses, such as

---

* We are grateful to Mary Langan for her critique, for pressing for conceptual clarity and for her help in de-teutonising our English draft. All mistakes are now transparently ours.

walking through parks, enjoying leisure time in pubs and contributing to the production of ideas and symbols, that is, to the 'common' culture. It is mainly men who, as journalists, preachers, etc., build the public sphere and the moral economy, developing symbols in which women are treated as objects and not as individual and independent actors.

Mainstream theorising identifies poverty simply as a lack of income or of material resources in general. This is only partly true for women. Money allows choice and provides options, but social participation involves more than just money. A woman might have sufficient income but nevertheless experience marginality and poverty; well-to-do households do not necessarily prevent married women's poverty. Feminists have started to argue against the notion of the family as a 'joint utility' and a realm of fairness and solidarity (Okin, 1989). It is not a natural given that 'family' income is equally distributed between all adults or all family members (Pahl, 1980, 1983). Even if this is true, an equal share in income does not abolish wives' social dependency on husbands. If a woman is old or if she is a single mother, then marginality is likely to coincide with income poverty. If a woman is single (living without a man) and no longer young, then she even more likely to experience both marginality and poverty in the FRG.[1] To put the point another way, a stable and lasting marriage is generally still a very important long-term insurance against poverty for the majority of women.

Poverty in old age is mainly a female issue. The lower average pensions of women are often explained by the fact that women do not have – or, according to neo-classical 'preference/choice' theories, do not opt for – a continuous work career. But this does not fully explain the considerable difference between male and female pensions. Restricted opportunities – and not unrestricted choice – in the labour market combined with significantly lower wages – due also to a continuous loss of qualification after each reentry into the labour market – explain poverty, as we will show later.

Women's poverty in old age is common to all western societies. Sometimes it is robustly incorporated into welfare traditionalism, into a particular welfare state logic which is resistant to any change that could seriously challenge the system of social stratification. Trying to confront this inflexible structure is like 'tilting at windmills'. Such is the case in West Germany.

Irrespective of national and cultural differences, western welfare states and their social policies have regulated the lives of citizens, explicitly and implicitly, in such a way that women – and not men – are exposed more systematically to the risks of poverty and marginalisation in their life course. This leads to a series of paradoxes for women (Pateman, 1988a; Ostner, 1986, 1990):

- Women are protected as men's dependants but it is women whom others depend upon – and they receive only precarious forms of gratification in return.
- Furthermore, those who care daily will be those who, in their future, can

seldom rely on being cared for themselves. This is an issue quite independent of women's precarious income status: caring thus marginalises the carer and cared-for in a mutual relationship of 'dependency'.
- Finally and ironically, in many cases women's individual wage work – though normally (for men) the means of gaining independence in a market society – does not grant them independence from their husbands nor from welfare state tutelage. On average they just do not earn enough.

The welfare state has emerged from and functions in a market economy. It does not replace the market but limits the inequalities of distribution or of participation resulting from it. According to Goodin (1988) the welfare state protects 'the vulnerable' in a market economy. It is the family that does the main work of protecting the vulnerable; mainly women as mothers, children, the handicapped and the elderly (Zaretsky, 1982). Social policies are therefore designed to preserve and reproduce the family as an institution providing well-being and welfare. Women are regarded as 'generalised mothers', who are less available for employment. They, and not men, get caught in a 'prisoners' dilemma'. More often than men, women have to accept the prevailing working conditions to avoid a further deterioration of their standard of living or work. As Okin (1989) argues, Goodin does not recognise that the family might and empirically does involve a 'no choice' situation and a 'prisoner's dilemma' for women and children. Western societies have successfully identified protection and justice with family life and ignored the injustice and inequality which may result from being dependent.

Of course there are differences between western societies or welfare states. Modern societies differ in their constitutive 'welfare mix'.[2] These are an outcome of welfare traditions and political struggles, which are specific to each country. In a 'welfare mix' three distinctive ways of providing goods and services are blended. Provision may occur through the market, the state, or through private households and families, and, in the latter, mainly through female labour. The prevailing and dominant form of allocation is the market. Modern western societies can be distinguished according to the stress they place on market, state or family provision, or on their combination. The kind of mix also helps to explain the extent to which women are available to participate in the labour market. It explains whether women are helped and encouraged, or hindered and discouraged, to participate full-time, part-time, regularly or irregularly. These issues are shaped in policy arenas such as social security, labour market, education and tax regulation.

Western societies differ according to the extent to which they are socially differentiated and 'individualised'[3] and to the extent to which the social role and status of women is differentiated. Societies differ in the way women are treated as individuals with rights of their own, for example with a right to earn a living under equal conditions. Are women perceived and treated primarily as appendages of others? Does 'being a woman' immediately denote being a mother, daughter or wife? Is there a separate symbolic and logical notion which allows for female individualisation first – without reference to a 'significant other' as it exists for males? These questions are central to analysing the ongoing process of modernisation, but they will be answered differently for each western country. Modernisation first 'freed' men from traditional links. It has led to a relative diversity of men's lives in a separate, mainly male, sphere. Women have a less or no differentiated social status in the female sphere (Ostner, 1986). This is true at least in the West German case. For more than a century different types of welfare states have hindered or promoted women's individualised status leading to a greater diversity of women's lives but also to more dissimilarity and inequality between women.

Women's labour market participation has always been a salient indicator of the degree to which women's status has been individualised. Figure 10.1 reveals strong national differences in European societies, due to the extent to which women are treated as individuals or as family and household members. Greece is a traditional society with a low but stable female labour market participation. We assume that women play an important role in a subsistence economy. Denmark has the opposite characteristics. The diagram shows a decline in employment for women between the ages of 24 and 34. It does not distinguish between full-time and part-time employment. Empirical data suggest that women re-enter the labour market mainly on a part-time basis.

Though all modern societies tend to impoverish women and render them marginal, specific welfare mixes promise, produce or sometimes even guarantee them social participation together with a relatively equal share of income and social security.

This chapter tries to explain some of the peculiarities of the West German welfare state, its traditions[4] and impact on women's social security (see also Ostner, 1990). We do this by placing Germany in a West European context and also by contrasting it mainly with the USA.[5]

WEST GERMANY'S WELFARE STATE COMPARED – MODELS AND DATA

To understand West Germany's welfare state we can make a useful start with some distinctions made by Catherine Jones (1985) in her analysis of western welfare states. Jones looks separately at two dimensions; quantitative aspects of welfare state policies and social spending (in kind, services, cash) and qualitative aspects, for example the different *foci* in social policy (individuals first versus society first). Social spending may then be assessed relative to prevailing social policy orientations in different countries. Jones offers two distinctive *foci* in policy orientation. The first prevails in West Germany and the USA, where the focus is on market, achievement and 'contributory principles' in social security, thus on a 'society first' (pp. 332–334) approach and not on individual needs univer-

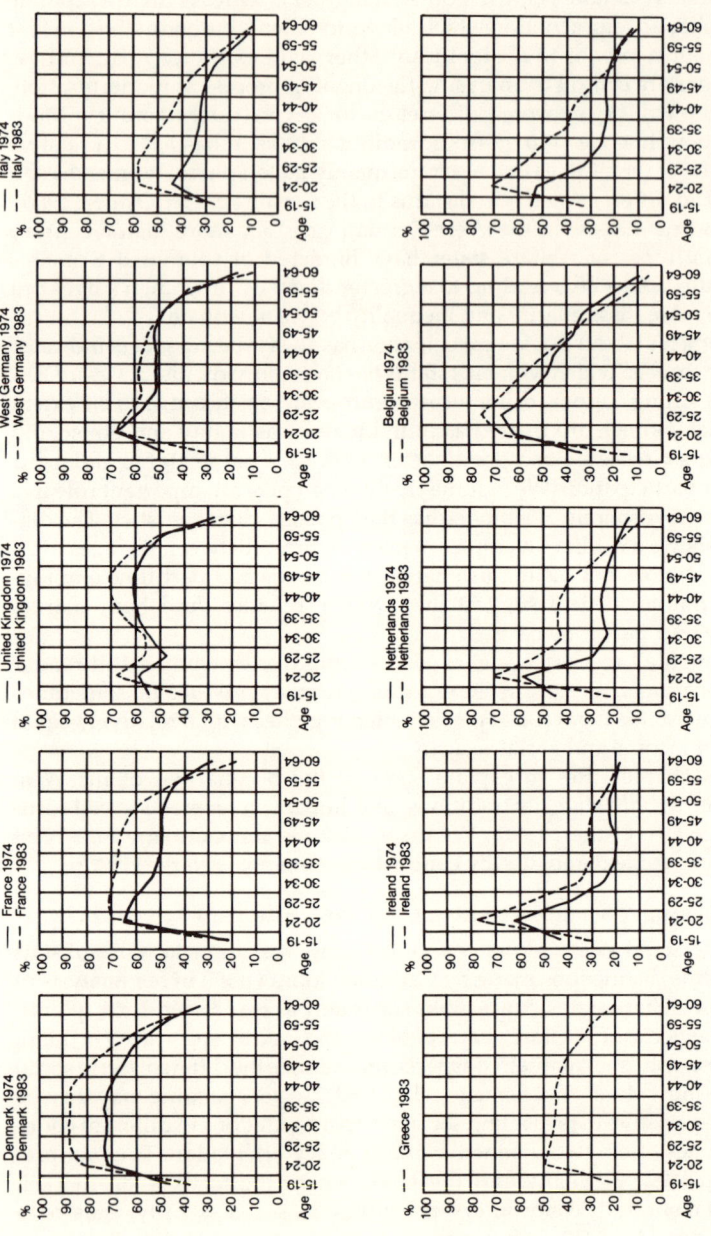

Figure 10.1 Labour market participation of women in a life course perspective and by age. (Source: Bach and Brinkmann, 1986, p. 361.)

sally conceived. The emphasis is placed not on a welfare or social ethic, but rather on a system's integration approach and a market ethic. The second focus is to be found in the UK and Sweden, with an 'individuals first' approach to social policy, 'with egalitarian/compensatory and citizenwide forms of social provision' (p. 334). Thus, Jones distinguishes between welfare *capitalist* and *welfare* capitalist countries.

West German data suggests that the FRG belongs to the 'society first' league with an achievement/contribution type of welfare state infrastructure. About 95 percent of all Germans are insured or protected against sickness and accidents and 85 per cent are insured in pension schemes. Unemployment insurance is also widespread, though less inclusive. Characteristic elements of the West German welfare state in the West European context are set out below (for these OECD statistics, see especially Alber, 1988a, pp. 14 onwards if no other sources are given).

The West German welfare state is oriented strongly towards social security transfers, towards delivering monetary transfers. In 1980 62.2 per cent of all West German social welfare expenditures went in this direction against the West European average of 56.5 per cent. In this respect Germany belongs to the 'major league' with Austria and Belgium. This monetary slant, with transfers being channelled through the contribution nexus, makes West Germany – similarly to the USA – a welfare *capitalist* country stressing the linkage with the work record. The results of primary distribution in the labour market are corrected only at the margin, and the hierarchy obtained in the labour market is basically reproduced in social security. The redistributive potential of the German welfare state between classes is quite small. Most redistribution takes place within the wage earning class – and there from individual workers to families. Social ethic programmes are in constant danger of becoming residual, second tier, stigmatising marginalised groups (the German 'Sozialhilfe', social assistance).

Universal schooling in the FRG ends after fourth grade at the age of 10. Despite reforms, the tertiary (university) education system is much smaller than it is in the USA and more highly class selective. In 1980 16.6 per cent of expenditure went into education, in contrast to a European average of 21.6 per cent. Germany thus leads the 'minor league' of spenders, grouped only with Austria.

Germany has a longstanding tradition of 'dual education', a rather sophisticated system of apprenticeships provided mainly by firms and enterprises supported by selective state schooling. This educational mix helps to explain some of the strength of the German economy. It has been able to guarantee relatively stable careers for those who successfully obtain occupational status after passing through the different levels of the certification system.

This rather pre-modern, artisan-craftish 'estatist'[6] tradition of qualification for the majority of the labour force can be traced back to medieval times with its 'corporative' features, the estates and the guilds and their system of education. It was reconstructed in the late nineteenth century as an outcome of bargaining between artisans, workers trained as craftsmen in the industrial system, their unions and the Prussian State. This history gives some background to the male character of the West German labour market and to its impermeability for women.[7] It also partly shows how the German welfare state was able to reduce its spending on education and training the labour force. The German qualifications, certification, and licensing system are still characterised by a traditional, quasi-estatist, craft-oriented approach.

The West German qualifications system contributes to what in West German sociological debates is called the 'incomplete modernisation' of West German society, a process which has been co-produced and reinforced by welfare policies for more than a century. This 'partial modernisation' of the labour market allows the German welfare state 'to lay back' calmly, capitalising on these well entrenched traditions.

This system tends to nourish the fiction of abundant and incessant job opportunities for those lucky enough to be able to move within its boundaries. This renders the beneficiaries inflexible in case of unemployment, and thus tends to induce long-term unemployment rather than short-term adjustment. The system also tends to inhibit entry from outside, which often means entry by women. The West German labour force may thus be described as split, with only narrow connecting passageways. There is a privileged, male-dominated, normal ('primary') sector and another ('secondary') sector made up of casual workers with precarious job opportunities. This split between 'insiders' and 'outsiders' becomes even more decisive as West Germany has been facing a serious crisis of the labour market since the mid-seventies. This crisis may look modest in a macro perspective when Germany is compared with other countries. It is, however, quite serious in the German micro perspective because even a mild crisis intensifies if it is up against the built-in traditional inflexibility of the certification system.

Welfare state spending in West Germany focuses on securing the wage earner in *his* – not her – place, not on investing in social mobility (Heidenheimer, 1981). To put this another way, since educational expenditure only contributes to equality of opportunity, 'insuring inequality' via social security is not attenuated substantially by compensatory investments in education.[8] Social policies guarantee 'status maintenance'.

Health expenditure in West Germany (21.2 per cent) conform approximately to the west European average (21.9 per cent), the system being basically public. Recent work by Alber (1988b) suggests that in Germany cost containment 'crises' are more manageable. A public regime of health care facilitates expansion as well as contraction and assures reversibility.

According to Jones, the FRG and the USA are welfare *capitalist* societies. It therefore makes sense to discuss the two countries together. However

The case of women's social security

there are some crucial differences. For the USA Table 10.1 shows a high increase in service jobs (+27.1 per cent) and a comparatively stable industrial sector. While industrial employment has declined (-14.6 per cent) in the FRG, there is a rather modest increase in service employment (+8.9 per cent) compared to the USA. The UK looks as if it were moving towards a post-industrial economy with a high decline in generally male industrial jobs and an increase in service jobs (+9.9 per cent). This increase does not compensate for the losses, and it presumably consists of mainly part-time jobs for women.

In the early eighties every fifth person in the USA was employed in the general field of social services, whereas only 12 per cent were so employed in West Germany. As recently as 1970 West Germany employed only 7.9 per cent of its labour force in the the social services, whereas the USA employed 8 per cent in education alone. In all sectors, i.e. adding health and other social services, the USA employed 14.8 per cent (Riede *et al.*, 1988, p. 300, Table 1[9]). Though both countries can be considered as belonging to the welfare *capitalist* league, which stresses the market-employment-contribution-nexus, they differ most strongly in the extent to which social services are delivered by state, market or private households. There is, surprisingly, no significant difference in the share of social services delivered by the state (about 50 per cent in both countries). However, services delivered through the market take up the other half in the USA but comprise only 20 per cent in West Germany, where the remainder is delivered by 'intermediaries', mostly by welfare associations.

A further, dramatic expansion of the West German social service sector – at the state, intermediary or market level – is not to be expected; services have gained in relative weight over time but the state's role in the social services, at least in their delivery, is decreasing. The 'service state' in Germany has a low profile which needs to be explained by factors external to the welfare state. As we said earlier, there is still an intact, though 'rudimentary household economy', producing services beyond market and state mostly through women's work at home. The state does not systematically provide full time schooling or kindergartens, day care or other public help for dependent groups. West Germany is built on an 'ancillary culture of care' which emphasises that women should provide the caring services. This is buttressed by attitudes and beliefs about who is to care for whom and how, and about the proper responsibility for care. These attitudes are still basically traditional, that is, they are focused on the 'household economy' and not on the state or the marketplace. All these factors are mutually reinforcing.

In addition, as Table 10.2 shows, the tax (and contribution) burden in West Germany (38.7 per cent) is close to a Western European average (38.5 per cent) and thus not high enough – as for example in Sweden (53.1 per cent) – to provide, universal social services. Furthermore, West Germany's wages do not have a wide enough spread to ensure that basic services,

TABLE 10.1 Employment in Agriculture, Industry and Services in OECD Countries

	Agriculture		Industry		Services	
	Share in Civil Employment (1)	Changes 1973–1982 (2)	Share in Civil Employment (3)	Changes 1973–1982 (4)	Share in Civil Employment (5)	Changes 1973–1982 (6)
Australia	6.0	-3.3	29.8	-7.1	63.8	+23.6
Austria	10.0	-17.9	39.9	+3.1	50.0	+15.2
Belgium	3.0	-24.3	33.4	-21.1	63.6	13.9
Canada	5.2	-2.6	26.5	+5.1	68.2	+32.0
Denmark	7.3		29.3		63.3	
Finland	13.2	-15.4	33.8	+4.2	53.0	+23.5
France	8.3	-26.5	34.6	-12.3	57.2	+17.8
FR of Germany	5.5	-28.2	42.7	-14.6	51.8	+8.9
Ireland	17.1	-24.6	30.7	+8.6	52.2	+29.2
Italy	12.4	-27.1	37.0	+1.7	50.6	+28.4
Japan	9.7	-22.3	34.9	+0.4	55.4	20.4
Netherlands	5.0	-6.5	30.2	-8.2	64.8	+15.7
New Zealand	11.2	+10.9	32.6	+0.2	56.2	+17.9
Norway	8.0	-17.5	29.4	+2.1	62.5	+34.4
Portugal	25.3	-23.9	37.3	+13.2	37.5	+28.1
Spain	18.3		33.9		47.8	
Sweden	5.6	-14.5	30.3	-10.5	64.1	+24.5
Switzerland	7.1	-13.4	38.4	-17.5	54.5	+7.3
UK	2.7	-12.3	34.7	-21.9	62.6	+9.9
USA	3.6	-0.1	28.4	+0.1	68.0	+27.1
Average	9.2	-15.0	33.4	-4.1	57.4	+21.0
Variation Coefficient	0.605		0.122		0.137	

Australia: estimates for August 1973 **Austria**: including armed forces; changes 1974 to 1982, as figures for years previous to 1974 are not strictly comparable, due to a modification of a design of the sample **Belgium**: year of reference is 1981; mid-year estimates **Denmark**: years of reference are 1976 and 1981. Due to a change in the reference period, figures from 1976 onwards are not strictly comparable with those of previous years **Finland**: age group 15 to 74 **Ireland**: estimates for April of each year **Japan**: 'Services' includes persons with not adequately defined activities; in 1982 approximately 140,000 persons **Netherlands**: years of reference are 1975 and 1981, estimates at 1st of January. No data available previous to 1975 **New Zealand**: data refer to April 1973 and February 1981 **Norway**: including armed forces **Portugal**: data refer to the 2nd half of 1974 and 1982, not comparable with years previous to 1974 **Spain**: estimates at 4th quarter, in 1980 the minimum age limit for a person to be included in the labour force was raised from 14 to 16 years, therefore 1982 data are not comparable with those previous to 1980 **Sweden**: including certain categories of the permanent military personnel **United Kingdom**: mid-year estimates, data for 1973 are provisional.

Source: Scharpf, 1986, p. 5

TABLE 10.2 Taxes and Social Security Contributions as Shares in GNP, Wage Differentials in Manufacturing Industries, Employment in Private and Public Services in OECD Countries, 1978

	Taxes and Social Security Contributions as Shares in GNP	Wage Differentials[1] in Manufacturing	Private Services (ISIC 6+ 9–OECD[2]) Shares in Population	Public Services (OECD)[2] 15 to 64
Australia		1.2	13.7	16.8
Austria	40.8	2.1	13.5	11.7
Belgium	42.3	2.2	17.0	9.8
Canada	33.3	2.2	20.9	12.6
Denmark	41.9	1.5	16.7	8.9
France	39.5	1.5	16.7	8.9
F.R. of Germany	38.7	1.8	13.9	9.1
Japan	21.5	2.4	24.4	4.5
Netherlands	48.7	1.8	17.1	7.6
Norway	46.6	1.5	17.7	15.1
Sweden	53.1	1.4	14.8	22.6
United Kingdom	34.3	1.4	16.8	14.9
USA	30.0	2.5	23.2	10.8
Average	38.5	1.8	17.7	12.1

Notes: [1] Ratio of wages paid in highest-wage and lowest-wage branches in manufacturing industries (ISIC major division 3, at 3-digit level; ILO data). [2] Private services: ISIC major division 6 (wholesale and retail trade, and restaurants and hotels) and 9 (community, social, and personal services) minus public sector employment of column 4; Public Services: OECD calculations, share of the public sector in total employment, recalculated as share in population 15 to 64 years (OECD, Employment in the Public Sectors, p. 12, Table I).
Source: Scharpf, 1986, p. 11.

which would need to be provided cheaply through the market, could be afforded by the 'normal' consumer and would thus present a mass market (the differential is only 1.8 and thus equal to the European average). Instead such services are quite expensive and can only be afforded by the few (Scharpf, 1986). These services can be afforded by most in the USA, where wages are spread more radically (differential 2.5), taxes are lower (30.0 per cent) and where private services are ranking near the top (23.2 per cent) while public services rank medium (10.8 per cent versus an average of 12.1 per cent).

The many crucial differences between the USA and West Germany suggest that it may be helpful to employ distinctions other than the very useful ones provided by Jones. Moreover there may be other ways of understanding, for example, the British tendencies towards an American 'residual' welfare state or of extrapolating the possible outcomes of recent Swedish restructuring of welfare provision.

We can distinguish four different social policy, and especially poverty, regimes (Leibfried, 1990) or 'worlds of welfare' (Esping-Andersen, 1990). Esping-Andersen talks about three western models in his discussion of the welfare states as they emerged in fully developed capitalist market economies. There are, however, also the rudimentarily developed welfare states in what might be called the 'Latin rim' countries in Europe. The move towards Western capitalism in Eastern Europe may lead to new, additional types, though it looks as if a unified Germany will only generalise the West German welfare state model with all its implications for women, women's work and social security.

Let us examine the four basic models.[10] First, there is the 'modern' welfare state which best fits Scandinavia. Since the Second World War Scandinavian societies have emphasised the right to work for everyone. This is demonstrated in Table 10.3 which shows a very high percentage of 'employed' people, especially women.

The focus of the modern (Scandinavian) welfare state is on *services*, not on monetary transfers. Universalism dominates, though not primarily as a mode of income redistribution which is uncoupled from the work sphere, but rather as a mode of organising a full employment 'modern' work society. The focus on services fosters employment for practically everyone, including women. The welfare state is in the first place an employer, mainly for women, providing jobs in the field of care and subsidising the entry of both women and men into (different segments of) the labour market.[11]

Taken together, these features (the right to work supported by considerable services, jobs provided massively by the state as service provider and high female labour force integration) provide the elements of what one might call at first sight a 'modern' welfare state. Titmuss (1987) would have spoken of an 'institutional-redistributive welfare state' and would have paid no regard to women's situation. We use the term 'modern' here to indicate the degree of women's individualisation. Titmuss' term is more suitable for a society where man's status is by far the most 'individualised' and women, especially wives and mothers, are treated rather as men's appendices.

The costs incurred by the modern type of welfare state are high: high tax burdens, and expensive services, whether they are provided through state or market (see Table 10.2 under Sweden). There are very few ways for women to 'opt out' of the labour market – since equal pay policy has been successful in undoing the 'family wage'. Such a state generally needs a very high degree of compliance and consent. Women's labour force integration is achieved through a high level of segregation of industries ('female

TABLE 10.3 Women's Labour Force Participation[1]

	Women's Labour Market Participation Rate (in % of all Women Aged 15–64)					Women's Employment Share (in % of All Employment)		General Labour Market Participation Rate[2]	
	1966	1970	1975	1980	1986	1966	1986	1966	1986
Sweden	55.3	59.4	67.6	74.1	78.3	37.2	46.5	73.4	81.3
Denmark	55.1	58.0	63.5		76.5	37.7	45.3	75.0	82.5
Finland	61.9	61.4	65.6	70.1	73.5	43.7	48.2	74.5	77.7
Norway			53.3	62.3	71.0		43.8		79.3
USA	45.4	48.9	53.2	59.7	64.9	35.6	44.4	66.6	74.8
Canada	39.7	43.2	50.0	57.2	63.5	31.3	42.8	63.9	74.3
UK	49.9	50.7	55.1	58.3	61.0	35.2	42.6	73.0	74.5
Japan	56.2	55.4	51.7	54.9	57.4	39.8	39.8	71.1	72.4
France	46.4	48.3	51.2	54.4	55.3	35.1	41.8	67.3	65.8
Australia	42.7	46.5	50.1	52.7	54.1	30.2	38.5	69.1	69.9
Switzerland	51.5	52.3	51.9	54.1	53.9	33.4	37.1	78.1	71.8
Austria		48.7	47.6	48.7	51.7	38.4[3]	39.7	67.7	66.3
Belgium	38.6	40.2	44.0	48.2	51.3	31.7	38.8	63.1	63.4
FRG	48.5	48.1	49.6	50.0	50.3	36.9	39.1	70.2	65.1
Italy	33.4	33.5	34.6	39.6	42.3	28.2	33.1	60.7	60.5
Netherlands				31.0	35.4	41.1		34.5	58.3

Notes: [1]The percentages relate to all employed including the registered unemployed. The countries in the table are listed in the order of the female labour market participation rate of 1986. The countries selected are the highly industrialised OECD member states. New Zealand has not been included because its data is too scant. All this data should be viewed with some hesitation: the data given by the OECD, the EC or the ILO on one and the same topic diverge – and none of these are necessarily identical with national statistical data sources. Nevertheless the data is exact enough to gauge for general trends and country contrasts. [2] In % of population aged 15 to 64. [3]1968
Source: Becker, 1989, p. 23.

branches') and jobs within industries. Thus, 'modern' does *not* denote 'gender equality' in the strict sense but refers to a process which individualises women without necessarily narrowing the gender hierarchy in the labour market, or the gender gap. Quite the reverse might be true. A modern welfare state and society promotes the diversification of the lives of women and men in separate, gendered spheres across the board, including the labour market.

The second type, the Bismarck type, best describes Germany and Austria, and France to a limited extent. On the one hand it emphasises capitalist economic development and productivity, on the other the family is seen as a 'one-voice one-heart venture'. Both of these approaches are realised mainly by 'paying off' social problems, i.e. by compensating those who are defined as less productive than the fit-white-male-skilled-'normal' employee or those who are not productive at all. This type of welfare state does not focus so much on rendering people capable of at least partly supporting themselves. This model stresses (monetary) transfer programmes *not* services, all its rehabilitative ideology notwithstanding. The welfare state is a compensator of first resort, not an employer of first resort. In contrast to the 'modern' type, the notion of 'social citizenship' or that of 'universalism' or inclusion is strongly biased towards compensation ('pay off'). There are two contrasting 'classed' types of universal claims; those for the needy and those for the (formerly) employed.

The Bismarck countries are 'Janus headed'; individualised men are facing less individualised women. In the first case the focus is on labour market integration, related productivity and social security programmes compensating for any undeserved loss of productivity ('man power') and related risks. In the second case the family is thought to be the provider of the first resort for welfare and of compensating programmes for families and women in families at risk or in need. Consequently, these countries have a low service industry profile and only an average tax level (Table 10.2). The truly disadvantaged in this model are the average single employed women; the average married *un*employed woman is often much better off during the whole life course than any other average female category. In general those individuals who are not continuously available to the labour market and not integrated in a family or similar support system are in a bad position.

West Germany's national welfare state in a comparative context can be classified as focusing on transfers – like the USA federal welfare state – but not on services – as do the UK and Sweden. But it can also be classified – unlike the USA and like Sweden – as belonging more to the 'high spenders'. One might hold Germany to be the example of an all-out effort to design social policy for the 'market' as well as status maintenance – an effort that was only viable historically when universal (male) access to a wage earning position was guaranteed.

The third, 'Anglo-American' type refers mainly to the USA residual welfare state. In this model policies force people to enter the labour market under any conditions. The state is not perceived as an employer at all but rather as the compensator of last resort. Nowadays, the UK seems to approximate more to the *residual* model. The Anglo-Saxon approach is equally distant from the German 'compensatory regime' and the Scandinavian 'work society regime' (Leibfried, 1990). To reach the level of a kind of 'normal' welfare state and to break away from harsh residualism, the USA would have to go beyond Food Stamps and introduce at least a universal system of cash social assistance instead of a categorical welfare system. Its categories are built in such a way that welfare disappears the closer one gets to the labour market and only consolidates in proximity to the 'deserving poor' (Taylor-Gooby, 1988).

In the 'residual' model women are treated as individuals – the same as men. But the same treatment is quite the opposite of equal treatment. It neglects crucial differences, for example, in a market economy to be a parent is to be less free and, thus, less productive. The truly disadvantaged in this model are those who do not fit the notion of being the same; mothers, wives, handicapped and sick people, those who are in need of support or compensation. Social programmes in this model are strictly targeted and 'means-tested'.

The 'Latin rim' countries constitute at best welfare states in *statu nascendi*. In fact, they stress residualism, forcing people to enter the labour market under a kind of *laissez-faire* condition while still relying on older traditions of self-help provided by traditional support systems and the church. They do not show a general tendency to disaggregate women's status. Individualisation is limited to educated middle and upper-class women. Figure 10.1 and Table 10.1 suggest that many women in, for example, Greece or Italy earn their living as rural or manufacturing homeworkers, invisible in any labour statistics, relying on their families in old age.

WOMEN'S STATUS, WOMEN'S WORK – THE LAST DECADES

The weak profile of the West German 'service society' or 'service state' and the belief – held by both women and men – that services should be delivered at least part-time by families, mainly by women[12], requires a more detailed analysis of how the German labour market functions.

In recent years West German social scientists have discussed the crisis of 'normal wage work' (Mückenberger, 1989b). 'Normal' refers to qualified, secure, full-time and continuous white male labour market activity. This type of work has become increasingly scarce today even for men. Thus a social security system which is built on the 'wage labour – contribution nexus' is jeopardised. The notion of a normal wage worker's career continues to inform the outlook of politicians, administrators as well as male wage earners and their unions.

When the fiction of the normal wage worker's career was socially constructed it rested on the following premises (Flesch, 1901); in a modern acquisitive society, which is centred around the market, people are sufficiently provided with goods and services through property or wage earning or as members of households. Social assistance, any welfare state intervention, was to be subsidiary, only a residual provision. In the German model of a modern society women have been thought of only as backing up men. Men, who have such care available in *their* own households, thus become unremittingly and flexibly available to enter the labour market. This is true for more or less all Western societies. In the German case, this gendered social division was supported by family policies which have helped to establish and uphold the idea of the 'immobile' woman

TABLE 10.4 Popular Concepts about the Ideal Gendered Division of Labour and the Preferences of Men in Respect to the Spouse Role in 7 EC-Countries (1987 in %)

	Ideal Division of Labour			Men's Preferences	
	Equality	Partial Equality	Traditional	Working Woman	Homemaker
Denmark	53	26	12	58	23
United Kingdom	48	31	18	50	40
France	45	28	24	53	41
Belgium	34	30	25	50	35
FRG	26	34	32	31	59
Italy	42	31	25	51	43
Netherlands	43	28	23	42	40
Average of the 12 EC Countries	41	29	25	47	43

Note: The response 'no answer' has not been computed in the table.
Source: Becker, 1989, p. 31.

waiting and caring at home.

'Returning home' ('no one is there to welcome the returning people') was one post-War slogan. It influenced the idea of the immobile woman at home and the successive family policies of the 50s and 60s. From a comparative point of view, the peculiarities of opening and closing hours of kindergartens, schools and shops are striking features of West Germany. School, which ends on one day after two hours, the next after six, but always at lunch time, presupposes the immobile woman waiting at home with a cooked lunch. The sanctioned expectation 'to return home to somebody' has become second nature to many women or, at least, one side of a continuous double-bind for women. Here, in part, we have an explanation for the comparatively low level of state and market provided services in West Germany. Here too, perhaps, is the explanation for the delayed invasion of microwaves in West German kitchens, or the relatively small consumption of take-away or fast food in family homes.

Table 10.4 reports on views held in the populations of 7 EC-countries on the principles according to which the division of labour in the family should be organised. Male preferences in West Germany are rather conservative in the European spectrum. In the GDR, with East German women supposedly being more emancipated than their West German counterparts[13], a poll focusing on parents' opinions of where a child should properly be cared for brought familiar results, when seen from the West German perspective; most men and women answered that a child up to the

TABLE 10.5 Women's Labour Force Participation Rate by Age Cohort 1966–1985

	Age 15–24			Age 25–54			Age 55–64		
	1966	1975	1985	1966	1975	1985	1966	1975	1985
Sweden	60.2	66.2	66.4	57.4	74.3	88.9	42.2	49.6	59.9
Finland	53.4	48.9	54.9	68.7	78.0	86.7	50.4	44.4	52.9
USA	46.1	57.1	63.7	45.9	55.0	69.5	40.9	40.7	41.7
UK	61.0	56.4	63.1	49.9	61.3	67.0	37.1	40.3	34.1
Japan[1]	52.1	45.6	43.2	56.3	52.3	60.3	45.9	43.7	45.3
France	51.5	45.6	40.3	45.8	57.3	68.9	40.5	35.9	31.0
FRG	67.7	58.6	53.3	45.9	51.6	56.4	30.5	24.8	23.9
Netherlands		49.1	48.8		28.7	46.8		14.3	14.5
Italy[2]	36.6	31.6	40.7	28.0	31.3	43.8	13.4	8.5	10.5

Notes: [1] The labour force participation rate of women older than 65 in 1985 was still 15%. [2] The age groups here are 15–24, 25–59, 60–64.
Source: Becker, 1989, p. 27.

age of three should be cared for full time at home by the mother. East German women have experienced employment and motherhood as a triple burden. Before unification child minders were consistently badly paid and frequently quit their jobs. Thus, there was a scarcity of childminders in day care institutions, and too many children were cared for by too few frustrated childminders. Women had to queue for goods and they, rarely the men, did the housework. Finally, women worked full-time. Women's triple burden and men's tendency to refuse to help are an outcome of an equality strategy which has remained abstract. In the GDR a 'sameness strategy' was implemented in a highly fragmented society. Such a strategy ignores the fact that women and men are equal but different. German unification will give GDR women the right not to be primarily part of the labour force but to be mothers and wives. They may enjoy a new 'optionality', at least for a while.

That women are less individualised in West Germany may be explained by the feudal, estatist tradition which has always created barriers to women entering the labour market, for example in the qualification and occupation system. What are the implications of this for women's employment and the related social security system? The integration of women into the German Labour market can be defined as 'integration by segregation' (see Table 10.5). Women now make up only 38 per cent of the labour force. Female employment has oscillated between 36 and 38 per cent in the last hundred years. Only 52 per cent of all women available for employment are actually employed in West Germany (Bakker, 1988, p. 19 and Table 10.1.[14] The unemployment rate for women is 11 per cent; for both women and men it is 9 per cent. The rate is low because the discouragement of

TABLE 10.6 Women in Part-Time Work 1973–1985

	% of Women in the Labour Force			% of All Part-Time Workers		
	1973	1979	1985	1973	1979	1985
Sweden	38.8	46.2	46.2	88.0	85.2	84.6
Denmark	45.1	46.3	44.7	86.8	86.9	84.7
Finland	10.5	10.6	12.5	72.8	74.7	72.1
Norway			54.8			
USA	23.8	34.1	23.3	68.4	69.8	70.3
United Kingdom	39.1	39.0	42.4	90.9	92.9	89.6
Japan	14.7	18.4	21.1	60.9	64.5	70.7
France	14.7	17.0	20.1	77.9	82.0	84.6
Belgium	10.2	16.5	19.8	82.3	83.3	84.0
FRG	24.4	27.6	30.0	89.0	91.6	91.9
Italy	14.0	10.6	9.6	58.4	61.4	64.8
Netherlands	26.2	31.7	50.3	80.2	82.5	7.4

Source: Becker, 1989, p. 28.

women from participating in the labour force is built into the system.

Women make up 93 per cent of the insured part-time employed. This does not include uninsured, precarious jobs. In 1960 4 per cent of all (insured) jobs were part-time (see Table 10. 6). In 1975 the rate was 12 per cent. By 1987 the rate of part-time jobs had increased to 14 per cent. The growth of insured part-time work thus seems to have significantly slowed down. Meanwhile Kurz-Scherf has found a boom in the part-time uninsured sector (1989). The growth of insured part-time work thus seems to have stagnated, whereas the growth of uninsured part-time employment seems to have boomed (Kurz-Scherf, 1989).

Women compete with women in the labour market, and not with men. Both women and men have lost full-time jobs in their respective labour market segments, but women have gained some part-time jobs. The typical employed woman nowadays is middle aged, married and a mother and works increasingly in a discontinuous way. Her peers a century ago were likely to be young and unmarried.

Although more women enter the labour market and earn their income, this does not necessarily mean that they can earn their own living or contribute to the pension system so that poverty in old age will be prevented. Female wage work is generally on a lower level than a normal male worker's career. A woman still has to rely, at least in a supplementary fashion, on a man's income or, in the last instance, on assistance by the state. The state becomes a kind of 'universal husband equivalent' ('ideeller Gesamtehemann').

As far as women's potential occupational prospects are concerned, it is

TABLE 10.7 Employment Growth in Traditional and Post-Industrial Industries (annual average % growth)

	Germany 1961–84	Sweden 1964–84	USA 1960–1984
Industrial			
Agriculture	-2.6	-2.7	-1.5
Manufacturing[a]	-0.6	-0.7	1.0
Neutral			
Distribution[b]	0.0	0.1	2.0
Government[c]	3.8	3.0	0.9
Personal Services	0.0	-0.1	2.3
Post-Industrial			
Producer Services[d]	4.2	5.0	7.9
Health, Education and Welfare	4.8	8.6	6.2
'Fun' Services[e]	1.1	1.6	7.2
Total Post-Industrial Employment	3.5	6.7	6.7
Total Employment	-0.1	0.8	2.4

Notes: [a] Includes all extractive and transformative industries [b] Includes retail and wholesale, transport, and communications [c] Includes public administration and non-welfare related Government activities (military, police, sanitation, etc.) [d] Includes business services, finance, insurance, and real estate [e] Includes recreation and leisure, eating, drinking, and lodging
Source: Esping-Andersen, 1990, p. 199.

worthwhile noting some trends in the German labour market (see Table 10.7, and Esping-Andersen, 1988 and 1990). The FRG differs significantly from the USA and Sweden regarding structural changes in 'post-industrial' societies.

In general West Germany has experienced a decline in the number of jobs. It continues to have a high number of traditional industrial (male) jobs. The service sector, which is the main provider of jobs for women in other countries, is relatively underdeveloped. The labour market is highly segregated by gender and, compared to the USA and Sweden, women have not done well in gaining entry to a generally declining labour market. As we showed in Figure 10.1, the trends only indicate a marginal increase in service jobs, whether they are provided by the market or the state. There has been a small increase in jobs in the public sector over the last twenty years, but any further increase is threatened by policies aiming at 'refamilisation' and at 'decommodification' of service work. Esping-Andersen (1988) succinctly summarises some of the trends in the West German labour market and the implications for women:

German post-industrialism is one with jobless growth. Instead of creating new dimensions of stratification between job-classes or employment sectors, a variant of the 'insider-outsider' phenomenon seems the most likely to evolve... As a part of an implicit accord between business, trade unions and government, Germany's response to deindustrialization was to shed manpower via retirement and unemployment programs, and by encouraging guest workers to return. This, of course, resulted in a much slimmer workforce and enhanced productivity. With the additional lack of incentives for female labour supply, the result is a diminishing, yet highly productive, workforce supporting a growing but unproductive outsider population... To support housewives, male earners must rely on high net take home pay; to support the welfare state clientele, the employed will have to pay heavy taxes. And this is where the greatest potential for a conflict axis appears. (*ibid*. p. 33)

The potential for West German women today is limited in a number of crucial respects. They are not fully individualised as potential wage labourers who can secure their livelihood independently. Policies *vis à vis* family, education, social security and taxes discourage high female participation in the labour market. Women thus have to manage as 'freelancers' with little public support or incentive.

Poverty in old age provides a good example of the 'particularism of the West German social security system.[15] In the Federal Republic 'poverty in old age' is synonymous with 'poverty of women'. In 1986 86.3 per cent of former female industrial workers ('Arbeiterinnen') and 60 per cent of the female white collar employees ('Angestellte') received pensions lower than DM 900 a month, a level equal to or just below the official poverty line ('Sozialhilfeniveau').

One might argue that most German women are protected by marriage and do not have to rely exclusively on their individually achieved pension. But even as widows women do not enjoy abundant social security, often stereotyped as 'Überversorgung'; 'overprotection'. Former women workers only reach a cumulative average pension of DM 1,190 a month, less than the average male worker's pension. The cumulative pension of retired women who have been white collar employees at least approaches the average male employee's individual pension of DM 1,840 a month (Wichert, 1988, p. 183).

That poverty in old age (mainly for women) is a central problem is even more striking when contrasted with the size of the West German pension scheme. The West German pension scheme is the transfer programme which dominates all other transfers (41.2 per cent versus the European average of 35.3 per cent). Other special German features in transfers are that veterans' and related benefits amount to 4.1 per cent versus 1.3 per cent in the West European average. Welfare expenditure amounts to 3.6 per cent versus 9.5 per cent in the West European average. The latter point is most interesting when one looks at the United Kingdom (15.7 per cent), Sweden (16.8 per cent) and Denmark (24.2 per cent). Though the German percentage is likely to have grown in the eighties the league patterns will not have changed. Since pension payments are the 'achievement' and contribution oriented programmes of the West German welfare state, their predominance is a good expression for the the German version of a welfare capitalist hegemony in welfare state structure. Social policy in West Germany does not only transfer results of the market in a social security trajectory, but, together with the qualifications system, it also maintains, amplifies and constitutionalises status. Social institutions are split into three large sectors (public servants, white collar, blue collar), each with separate and somewhat different systems of pension and health security. Beyond that, disability (and pension) insurance, and to a lesser extent unemployment insurance, protect each sector and their varied internal subdivisions from what is perceived as social mobility downwards ('Arbeits- und Berufsunfähigkeit'). Thus market logic and status logic are already fused in the labour market. Social policy continues this pattern – and 'constitutionalises' it through institutionalisation and entrenchment of status entitlements – partly excluding women as non-normal wage earners.

In financing social security the contribution principle is firmly anchored in West Germany (34 per cent versus 19.1 per cent in the West European average), thus linking the discriminatory structure of the labour market and its hierarchy of wages and privileges more firmly to hierarchy building in the 'social wage sector' in Germany than in the rest of Europe. The state has a low share of 28.9 per cent of the social budget in the GNP in Germany versus 40.2 per cent in the West European average. However, the state share is most likely to grow, especially in the dominant area of pensions in the near future.

Women are incorporated into the pension system basically at three levels – through the general 'contribution nexus' either independently or as dependants, and through some (comparatively low) premiums attached to the work of 'child raising', if such work is done instead of participating in the labour market. There is a special remedial programme which deals with discrimination of women in the labour market. Certain pensions are paid according to a minimum wage standard which is subsequently used to raise pensions (Gerhard-Teuschner, 1989).

WELFARE STATE RETRENCHMENT AND WOMEN'S LIFE – AN OUTLOOK

If one examines welfare state spending, its share in West Germany's Gross Domestic Product etc., the welfare state as it has developed from the 50s to the early 70s today seems basically intact, though somewhat scaled down.

Major cuts occurred after 1975 (Bieback, 1985[16]; Kohl, 1986[17]). But their effect need not be alarming, especially if compared with welfare state performance in Western Europe (Alber 1988a; pp. 13ff). The share of social expenditure in the 'Bruttoinlandsprodukt' (GDP) grew steadily until 1975

– starting with 19 per cent in 1950 and ending at around 34 per cent in 1975. Since then this share, and the share of state spending in general, has been 'frozen' through retrenchment policy (Alber, 1988a, pp. 53ff, p. 253). The rising trend of social expenditure shares was already broken in the mid-seventies, with expenditure still growing. In the 1980s, especially after the change of government in 1982, the trend in rising real expenditure was also broken. Real expenditure was cut first in pensions after 1977, then in sickness insurance after 1981. Retrenchment in unemployment (post-1975) and welfare (1981–1985) is not as easily transformed into a spending freeze, since total social needs are also growing, leading to real expenditure growth. Overall, social expenditure has only marginally increased in the early 1980s falling for the first time from 610 billion DM in 1982 to 608.5 billion DM in 1983 (Alber, 1988a, pp. 254ff). For Alber this amounts only to consolidation. But what may appear as stalemate or consolidation may also be part of a process of the 'gradual redefinition of welfare and the welfare state, which, in our view, has been potentially much more detrimental and long lasting than actual curtailments and concrete cuts' (Markovits and Halfmann, 1988, p. 96–97). These shifts are not as easy to make out as cuts in spending because they have not yet restructured policy systematically. But they create a climate leading to 'tunnel vision' which demarcates the terrain for future action.

A slow and silent corrosion of universalism has occurred in the West German welfare state in the sense of a welfare state's 'universal' provision for the needs of all, not in the sense of a universal structure of gender-neutral entitlement. This process is more difficult to perceive in West Germany than in the UK because universality has never been the primary formal maxim of social policy institutionalisation here. It is formally of only residual importance in 'welfare' policy, i.e. poverty policy. Nevertheless universalism holds true at the level of welfare state and welfare society relief systems, that is as long as everybody has access to a decent job and thus to the social security state.

Universality is corroded by a sort of decremental 'policy creep'[18] in the design of social welfare programmes. If we focus on some arenas of welfare state power 'the' welfare state disappears. There is not just a diversity of welfare states (Moran, 1988, p. 413) but there is also a diversity within the welfare state. Different policy regimes or arenas may flower or stay more or less in position, whereas others are strained beyond capacity. A welfare crisis therefore would not necessarily be one of 'the welfare state' but could be contained in one arena only and might even be displaced further into other parts of 'welfare society'. So high unemployment of a permanent nature – hovering around 10 per cent – is covered less and less by unemployment insurance, which may even amass a huge surplus.

Unemployment involves what we have called the 'insider'–'outsider' split. According to this split three types of people are treated differentially:
1. Those who will presumably never experience unemployment.

2. Those who will be unemployed once, or occasionally more than once, but will find jobs again easily.
3. Those who will be exposed to continuous unemployment spells with little or no chance of getting back into the labour market's 'main stream' and are forced to rely increasingly on family networks. This group includes many women and faces the brunt of the welfare cutbacks.

In West Germany a 'labouristic' orientation has been central to the welfare state. This has held well, giving way only where labour market attachment itself is already at risk, i.e. within unemployment insurance. Furthermore the programme for the traditional deserving poor; the blind, disabled etc., have more or less held their place. What has been hit most is the wide area between 'stable employment' and 'undeserved poverty', that is, the working poor or those employable poor unable to find a job.

In West Germany we can observe a process in which the distance between a mostly male norm, including 'normal' social security, and the 'last safety net' of social assistance and unemployment insurance is increased. The inclusiveness of the social policy system is thus decreased generally. Status maintenance still aims at those already better off and stays intact. A contingent but downward-bound safety net exists for those who are outside stable employment. This process especially affects women. It may reach new dimensions in a unified Germany (Bäcker and Steffen, 1990). Unification only builds on the 'West German model' and attempts a positive integration of a society and an economy whose state of development is more similar to the Mezzogiorno of Italy than to West Germany. This again may emphasise polarisation in the welfare state structure and it might radicalise the development to such a point that a two-tiered, two-class welfare state will be more fully revealed.

NOTES

1. If a woman is from an ethnic minority, for example from the Greek or Turkish community in the FRG, she might enjoy the support of her family. But her access to the opportunities of a modern Western society is even more restricted than for native German women. This is true to an even greater extent for disabled or chronically sick women.
2. The history of these different welfare cultures is only rarely studied. Two studies (Ritter, 1989; Geyer, 1983) approach the subject with England and Germany being the major topic.
3. See Zapf *et al.*, 1987 on the discussion about 'individualisation' and social policy in the FRG.
4. On the formation of the West German welfare state in general see Tennstedt, 1983. On the parallel formation of poverty and local social policy see Sachsse and Tennstedt, 1988.
5. We have learned much about the situation in the USA from McLanahan and Sørensen, 1987 and their later work.
6. 'Estatist' refers to today's quasi-feudal division of society into 'estates'. 'Corporatist' only transports some of this meaning, but

does not denote the feudal heritage of the German tradition we would like to stress here.
7. The entry to the system is controlled by the two major actors in the labour market; by male dominated unions and by – no less male – entrepreneurs.
8. Thus maybe those welfare states which did not take the educational route have to accommodate *more* inequality within social security.
9. In 1981 the US employed 19.3 per cent of all employees in social services (45.1 per cent in education; 42 per cent in health; 12.9 per cent in other social services), whereas in West Germany only 12.6 per cent were so employed of which 35.4 per cent were in education, 44.4 percent in health and 20.3 per cent in other social services. Whereas education is the major service in the US, health and other social services dominate the German welfare state's service delivery. Also, state domination of service delivery does not differ much in Germany (53.7 per cent in 1982) from the US (49.2 per cent in 1981), mainly due to the 'nationalisation' of the major education sector in the US (Reide *et al*, 1988, p. 300).
10. It should be kept in mind that the four models were originally developed by looking at 'the' welfare state from a 'poverty angle' only.
11. Rainwater, Rein, and Schwartz (1986) have explored the comparative dimension of the transfer/service mix and its connection to gender status (with Sweden and Germany being among the countries studied).
12. This belief may be traced back to the bourgeois women's movement of the nineteenth century. Its culture of 'social or organised motherhood' ('geistige Mütterlichkeit') was conceived as lying outside the sphere of market and state intervention.
13. In the GDR, for four decades, women had been systematically incorporated into full employment status (93 per cent participation rate) with child care becoming a complete public and company responsibility (Schwarze, Gornig and Steinhöfel, 1990).
14. In the USA 64 per cent of all employable women are employed. These differences could be much larger if, in women's life course, one were to differentiate according to full-time and part-time employment status.
15. It is mainly Kohl (1987) who is analysing poverty in old age comparatively (centring on the UK, Germany, Switzerland and Sweden), though not its specific gendered structure.
16. Bieback takes more of an institutional legal perspective on the cuts.
17. On the British situation we have consulted the outsider's view of Pierson, 1988.
18. See Klein and O'Higgins, 1988, pp. 220, 223 for a different version of this process.

11
MEANS-TESTING IN EUROPE: A GROWING CONCERN
WIM VAN OORSCHOT AND JOHN SCHELL

INTRODUCTION

For several reasons 'means-testing' is an interesting subject for sociological analysis and research. To make this clear we first present a brief outline of our conception of the sociology of social security.[1]

Our starting point in defining the sociology of social security is the basic sociological problem of the (im)balance between societal order on the one hand and the autonomy of individual action on the other. This basic problem, which has engaged Western thinkers for more than 300 years and is central to the work of many contemporary sociologists[2], implies that there is a fundamental tension between the interests, expectations and actions of a collectivity and those of the individuals that constitute it. Social institutions, i.e. typical structures of relations between individuals based on a set of values, rules and common practices, are the instruments through which society and individuals are linked to each other. They have the important function of balancing, i.e. coordinating and integrating, the expectations and actions of both 'parties', and attempting to promote their interests at the same time. For us, sociology in its broadest sense is the discipline that describes and explains the development of social institutions and their functioning with regard to the balancing of collective and individual interests, expectations and actions.

From this point of view, the sociology of social security is the branch of sociology which takes the institution of social security as its subject. This institution has to balance societal and individual needs for security which result from the dynamics of economic, socio-cultural and demographic change. Adopting this frame of reference, attention can be paid to the historical process of the modernisation of the institution of social security, i.e. to the processes of structural differentiation and cultural generalisation. Here processes like professionalisation, growing state intervention, the subsequent inclusion of different social groups into the social security system, and the shift from charity to benefits as of right can be studied. Attention can also be paid to contemporary problems in the field of social security. Under the heading of 'system-security and actor-security', general problems like the tension between the needs for collective solidarity and individual freedom, between the credibility of the overall system and the way in which individuals make use of social security benefits, and between the efficiency of implementing social security and the achievement of justice in individual cases can be discussed. Attention can also be paid to the functioning of specific elements in the overall institution of social security. One such element is means-testing.

Means-testing in social security is of considerable interest to sociologists. One of the reasons for this is that means-tested benefits are by their nature targeted at the poor, i.e. at the social category that is most vulnerable to social exclusion. This is of great significance because problems of social integration are of fundamental importance for sociology. Another important reason is that, in the case of means-testing, the problems which are related to the balancing functions of social security are most clearly manifested.

In the first section of this chapter we will elaborate on these problems, showing that, although the practice of means-testing in social security is attractive in modern society, its effects tend to be counterproductive to what we regard as the broader aims of the welfare state, i.e. doing away with poverty, injustice and dependency, and integrating all groups and classes into society. Thus, the first section focuses on the functions and dysfunctions of means-testing. In the second section, we proceed with an empirical analysis of recent developments in six selected European countries which have in the last 15 years led to a continuous growth in the number of persons dependent on means-tested benefits. In the concluding section, we discuss, in broad terms, some implications of this trend.

FUNCTIONS AND DYSFUNCTIONS OF THE MEANS-TEST

We speak of means-tested benefits when entitlement to the benefit, and/or the amount of benefit to which claimants are entitled, depends on the financial resources of claimants and/or their household. Thus, means-testing, as an administrative method, has the function of allocating benefits to claimants on the basis of their financial resources. Alternative methods of administration include allocating benefits on the basis of age (as in pension schemes), physical status (as in disablement benefit schemes), previous earnings and/or individual work history (as in unemployment benefit schemes), marital status (as in widows pension schemes) and the number of dependent children (as in child benefit schemes). However, it is clear that means-testing also has other social and economic functions. First, means-testing can be used as a way of limiting social expenditure. It is cheaper for society to pay benefits only to those members of a group who have financial resources below a certain level than to all members of a group, irrespective of their resources. Second, means-tests have the effect of flattening the distribution of income since they contribute to social equality. Third, means-tests are specifically used to target income or resources to those individuals or households in society who are regarded as 'the truly needy'. The test of means implies that the income or resources to be distributed only reach those people whose own means fall below the income standard set in the benefit scheme. This standard is in most cases equal to a level of income which the government regards as a subsistence minimum. Thus, means-testing is an instrument of distributing income or resources to the poor in society.

Although Deacon and Bradshaw (1983) argue that these functions can legitimate the means-test for both 'right' and 'left' on the political spectrum (flattening of the income distribution being especially appealing to the left, the targeting of the truly needy to the right, while the relative cheapness of the selective means-test, as opposed to universalistic measures, attracts politicians on both sides) we believe that means-testing in social security is more closely related to the ideology of the right, with its emphasis on minimal collective arrangements supplemented by private insurance, than to that of the left, with its emphasis on broad and solidary collective arrangements. In this respect we should note that the growth in the clientele of means-tested benefits, as described later in this chapter, is related to the rise of the New Right in the 1980s in Great Britain and, to a lesser extent, in the Netherlands. What Deacon and Bradshaw make clear, however, is that means-testing, as an instrument for redistributing income and resources to the poor can have a broad political legitimation. Furthermore, means-testing is believed to encourage the spirit of self-responsibility, something that is highly valued in Western industrialised and market-oriented societies (see Foster, 1983; Leibfried, 1976; Taylor-Gooby, 1976). This also implies that means-testing has a broad societal legitimation. Why then is it likely to be a controversial instrument?

The answer to this question is that means-testing in general has the effect of stigmatising beneficiaries, and of contributing to non-take-up and the 'poverty trap'. Now, for everyone who is of the opinion that the broad aim of social policy should be to do away with poverty and social injustice and to integrate all groups and classes into society on the basis of equality, these three general effects of means-testing constitute severe dysfunctions. Stigmatisation is counterproductive to social integration, non-take-up leads to injustice and contributes to individuals and households being in poverty, while the poverty trap tends to keep individuals and households in poverty and dependent on society.

In the rest of this section we will describe why the effects mentioned above are inherent to means-testing. First, we discuss the poverty trap. Second, we elaborate on the socially divisive character of means-testing. Finally, we pay special attention to the problem of non-take-up.

The poverty trap

Because eligibility to a means-tested benefit and/or the amount of benefit received depends on income, a rise in income has the effect that the benefit is reduced or withdrawn. When this occurs only a part of the gross increase in income remains as an increase in net disposable income. This is partly due to means-testing and partly to two other factors that consume part of any gross increase in income: income tax and social insurance contributions. This difference between gross and net increases in income can act as a disincentive for people to become better off, either by finding a job or by changing their job or skill-level. People for whom the difference between gross and net increases in income acts as a disincentive are said to be 'trapped by poverty' (we used a broad conception of the 'poverty trap').[3]

The poverty trap can in practice affect a wide range of incomes which is why Bradshaw speaks of a 'poverty plateau' (Deacon and Bradshaw, 1983). This is indicated by the fact that, in 1982–3, a British family earning £120 per week could be no better off than another family earning £70 per week (Deacon and Bradshaw, 1983). A similar situation existed in the Netherlands. When the minimum wage level is indexed to 100, then the gross modal wage had an index of 152 in 1984–5. After deduction of taxes and insurance contributions, the modal wage index decreased to 130. Then, because of the fact that modal wage earners receive a lower amount of means-tested housing subsidies and education allowances than households with a minimum income, the index decreased further to 109.[4]

In the Netherlands there is little empirical evidence about the disincentive effects of the poverty trap, and what evidence there is is conflicting. According to Deacon and Bradshaw (1983) and to Beenstock (1987), this applies for the United Kingdom as well.[5] Although there are arguments suggesting that these effects are not as important as is sometimes believed (e.g. because some people do not have real opportunities to become better off, money is not all that counts, or because the matter is too complex for people to make rational decisions about whether extra efforts are worthwhile or not), data about the size of the poverty trap and the number of people affected by it make it quite inconceivable that these effects will be entirely absent. Deacon and Bradshaw (1983, pp. 150–175) present some data for the United Kingdom.[6] In 1982–3, incomes at or below the needs allowance for means-tested housing benefit had a theoretical marginal tax rate of 71.75 per cent (i.e. of an increase in gross income of one currency unit (£1) 28.25 per cent would remain as net disposable income). In this rate (calculated without regard to the loss of Family Income Supplement and its passport benefits), income tax had a marginal tax rate of 30 per cent, national insurance contributions 8.75 per cent and means-tested housing benefits 33.50 per cent. Incomes just above the needs allowance had a comparable marginal tax rate of 66.75 per cent. In November 1982, 139,000 families were receiving the means-tested Family Income Supplement (FIS), of which about 80 per cent were also paying taxes and therefore subject to marginal tax rates in excess of 100 per cent. In this, FIS had a marginal tax rate of 50 per cent. In 1980, 530,000 pensioners were receiving means-tested housing benefits. Most of these would therefore have been subject to a minimum marginal tax rate of at least 66.75 per cent. For 1980

TABLE 11.1 Marginal rates as a percentage of an increase of 1 currency unit in gross income for different income levels in 1984–5 in the Netherlands (households with one income)

	I	II	III
Minimum wage	100	100	100
Modal wage	60	80	90–125
1.5 x modal wage	55	55	64–90
2 x modal wage	55	55	55–80
3 x modal wage	63	63	63
4 x modal wage	72	72	72

I: The effect of taxes, insurance contributions and means-tested lump-sum social assistance benefit
II: The effect of I plus means-tested housing benefits
III: The effect of I and II plus means-tested education allowances

Source: Ministry of Social Affairs and Employment, 1986, Table 4.8, p. 35

it was estimated that 700,000 tax units had marginal tax rates of over 50 per cent. In the Netherlands the theoretical marginal tax rates are also very high, as is shown in Table 11.1.

Table 11.1 shows that households with one income between the minimum and the modal wage, face very high marginal tax rates. In some cases they can exceed 100 per cent – an increase in gross income can actually lead to a decrease in net disposable income. Means-tested benefits play a significant role in the poverty trap experienced by the lowest income groups. It should be noted that, in 1985, 40 per cent of the employed labour force in the Netherlands earned between the minimum and the modal wage[7] and that, in 1984, 80 per cent of all claimants of income maintenance schemes (composed of pensioners, the unemployed, the disabled, widows and social assistance claimants), received a benefit at or near the minimum wage level.[8] This does not, however, mean that all of these individuals and households face the same marginal rate. This is because they are not all entitled to all of the means-tested benefits, and do not all receive the same amounts of benefits (the amount of housing benefit depends not only on income but also on the amount of rent paid, and not all households have children for whom they could receive an education allowance).

These figures make it clear that in the Netherlands, as well as in the United Kingdom, large numbers of individuals and households are faced with high marginal tax rates if they try to become better off than they are. Means-tested benefits play a significant role in this poverty trap, especially for groups with incomes below modal or average levels.

Means-testing and social division

When trying to describe the ultimate character of social policy, Titmuss

(1970, p. 212) quoted with assent the way Boulding (1967, p. 7) defined social policy as 'centred in those institutions that create integration and discourage alienation.' This view of social policy implies that its central aim is to integrate all groups and classes into society. That is, to provide for all citizens the prerequisites for participating in society as full members. This may not only require a redistribution of economic welfare from the 'rich' to the 'poor', but also that a positive identity, or self-esteem, of the individual citizen is promoted and protected (Kaufmann, 1970). Means-testing, as an instrument of social policy, tends to do a poor job with respect both to the economic and the socio-cultural prerequisites for integration.

With regard to the economic aspect of the integration problem, the contribution that means-tested benefits make to the poverty trap is to restrict individuals or households from making full use of their productive capacity, i.e. their capacity to generate economic welfare, not only for themselves, but also for society as a whole. As will be explained later, non-take-up is inherent to means-tested benefits and can contribute to the extent of poverty.

With regard to the socio-cultural aspect of the integration problem, there is a broad consensus among scholars of social policy that means-testing is highly intertwined with the problem of stigmatisation (see Titmuss,1968; Pinker, 1971; Waxman, 1983; Davies and Reddin, 1978; Deacon and Bradshaw, 1983). The term stigma refers to 'an attribute that is deeply discrediting' (Goffman, 1974, p. 3). Stigmatisation of individuals means in essence that a negative social identity is attached to them or, as Goffman (1974, p. 5.) puts it: 'we believe the person with a stigma is not quite human'. Stigmatisation thus implies social exclusion, i.e. 'discrimination, through which we effectively, if often unthinkingly, reduce his (the stigmatised person's) life chances'. Because, as symbolic interaction made clear, much of what we think we are comes from what we believe that others think we are, this implies that stigmatised persons will find it very hard to construct or uphold a sense of self-esteem. No doubt this will have a negative effect on stigmatised persons own efforts to become integrated in society. From Goffman's notes on stigma it becomes clear why, due to its relation to the stigmatisation of beneficiaries, means-testing detracts from the integrative aim of social policy. The question remains why means-testing and stigmatisation of beneficiaries are related.

At the most general level it can be argued that in so far as being in poverty is a discrediting attribute, i.e. a stigma, dependence on benefits or services that are specifically targeted at the poor will be related to stigmatisation. In addition, means-testing itself contains several discrediting elements. First, claiming a means-tested benefit makes it evident that a person is not able to secure sufficient economic welfare on his or her own. This runs counter to the ethic of self-sufficiency which, as we stated earlier, is highly valued in Western, industrialised and market-oriented societies. Or, as Parker (1975, p. 150) puts it: 'The significance of such an arrangement (means-testing) is that rights depend on declaring and establishing some degree of financial poverty, a situation widely viewed in capitalist societies with suspicion, disapproval and hostility'. Claiming a means-tested benefit is thus likely to be seen as deviance from prevailing norms, which in turn can be grounds for stigmatisation and the loss of self esteem. Second, in the administration of means-tested benefits, discretion and the control of potential fraud play a much more important and (to all actors involved) visible role than in the administration of non-means-tested benefits. Being seen as potentially fraudulent is in itself discrediting. The existence of discretion implies that the decision on whether or not to grant a claim is at least in part dependent on the administrator's evaluation of the applicant and the circumstances which led to the claim. This subjective element gives the administrator moral and cognitive power over the applicant, which is likely to invoke a feeling of inferiority on the claimant's part. Control of potential fraud, discretion and the detailed investigation of many aspects of the claimant's personal affairs and relationships are all elements in administration that are likely to reduce the extent to which a benefit is perceived as being given 'as of right'. Where a benefit is not seen as a right but as a form of charity, it will invoke feelings of shame and inferiority. As Simmel already noted in 1908: 'die Gedrückheit, die Beschämung, die Deklassierung durch das Almosen hebt sich für ihn [der Arme] in dem Maße auf, in dem es ihm nicht aus Barmherzigkeit, Pflichtgefühl oder Zweckmäßigkeit gewährt wird, sondern er es fordern darf.' (Simmel, 1908, p. 456) ('the humiliation, shame and loss of status ["declassement"] brought about by the acceptance of charity are alleviated for him [the poor man] to the extent that it [the benefit] is not granted out of compassion or a sense of duty or even expediency but rather because he has a valid claim to it.')

In this respect it is important to note that citizenship would appear to be only an abstract principle on which the use of means-tested benefits can be morally justified (Parker, 1975). However, the abstractness of this principle is bound to make it a weak base for the perception of means-tested benefits as being as of right. In fact, the finding of Coughlin (1980) that in eight Western industrialised nations expenditure on public assistance (which in all these countries is the main means-tested benefit) received much less support from the public, compared with expenditures on old age, sickness, disablement, family support and unemployment benefits, indicates that the principle of citizenship has a weak societal legitimisation. Moral justification for receiving a benefit is much easier to provide in the case of non-means-tested benefits, where benefits are 'earned' or 'deserved' because of contributions paid or where, according to Offe (1988, p. 219), 'it is much easier to conceive of a broad and inclusive alliance of potential beneficiaries ... (since 'all of us' expect to be old and sick in the future)'. In both cases the moral base can be found in the more concrete principle of reciprocity. Reciprocity is not only one of the strongest mechanisms for social integration and cohesion (Münch, 1984) but, according to Pinker (1971), is also a prerequisite for the maintenance of self-respect in any system or relation of exchange. Because of the fact that many receivers of means-tested benefits have no means to 'reciprocate', except through citizenship, they are bound to lose self-respect and become stigmatised.

Non-take-up

'Non-take-up' refers to the phenomenon of people who are eligible for a social security benefit but are not receiving it, or only receiving it in part. It is clear that the occurrence of non-take-up implies the failure of a scheme to achieve its goals since the benefit does not reach all the individuals or households it is supposed to reach. But as Deacon and Bradshaw (1983, p.122) note: 'Take-up is not just a technical issue concerned with the effective delivery of welfare'.[9] Non-take-up also implies social injustice, because of the difference in the extent that citizens receive what they are entitled to. Within social security, an institution that is to a large extent based on ideas of justice, this aspect of non-take-up represents a remarkable dysfunction. Non-take-up can also be the reason for people being in poverty. In fact, in the United Kingdom and in West Germany non-take-up came to be seen as a social problem as a result of the outcomes of empirical research into poverty. Townsend (1957) and Cole and Utting (1962) reported on the relationship between non-take-up and poverty, based on their studies into the circumstances of old people in Britain. Knechtel (1960) first reported the relationship between non-take-up and poverty in West Germany and was followed by Blume (1970). In the Netherlands, this relationship has only recently received attention from poverty researchers (Oude Engberink, 1984; Berghman and Muffels, 1988).

Our own conclusion, based on an international review of take-up research (van Oorschot and Kolkhuis Tancke, 1989), is that take-up has not been the subject of empirical research in the majority of European countries. This is the case in Belgium, Denmark, Finland, France, Italy, Luxembourg, Sweden and Switzerland. Some empirical research has been carried out in the Netherlands and in West Germany. The United Kingdom occupies a unique position among European countries with regard to research on take-up. Since the 1960s, many studies have been carried out, nationally as well as locally, and almost all of the existing means-tested benefits have been subjected to research.[10]

British experience indicates that non-take-up is confined to and is inherent in means-tested benefits. Why is this? To answer the question we will have to look at the *reasons* for non-take-up. In the international review of take-up research referred to above (van Oorschot and Kolkhuis Tancke, 1989), an inventory of different factors affecting the take-up of benefits was constructed. These factors were classified on three levels: on the level of the benefit scheme itself, on the level of administration and on the client level.[11] The probability of non-take-up was found to be greater in *schemes* which:
- have a high 'density' of rules and guidelines

- contain complex rules
- contain vague entitlement criteria
- contain a means-test
- are aimed at groups in society which are the subject of negative valuation
- supplement other sources of income
- leave the initiative to initiate the claiming process fully to the claimants themselves.

Factors which, on the level of *administration*, enhance the probability of non-take-up are:
- procedures for handling claims that are experienced by claimants as humiliating or degrading
- the combination of 'service' and 'fraud control' functions
- poor quality communication with clients, resulting in the provision of insufficient information and advice
- poor quality decision making, e.g. taking decisions on the basis of insufficient information or on the basis of client-stereotyping
- poor quality administrative procedures
- using complex application forms
- poor cooperation with other relevant agencies
- incorrect interpretation of the rules by administrators.

On the *client* level, relevant factors are:
- ignorance of the existence of the scheme
- insufficient knowledge and incorrect interpretations of entitlement criteria
- insufficient knowledge of the appropriate claiming process and of administrative procedures
- fear of stigmatisation and humiliation
- negative attitudes towards being dependent on society
- an attitude that the 'whole business is not worth the effort'
- experiencing difficulties in completing forms and in gathering the required information.

The relationship between means-testing and non-take-up becomes clear when it is realised that in means-tested benefit schemes, factors from these different levels tend to occur in combination. Means-tested benefits often contain complex rules concerning what is counted as 'means', what part of available means are to be taken into account, and whose means are to be considered. Most means-tests are not based on individual means, but on household means. What makes up a 'household' is often vaguely defined and can leave considerable scope for discretion, as well as adding to the complexity of the scheme. At the level of administration, complexity and vagueness are likely to increase the occurrence of mistakes, incorrect interpretation of rules, insufficient gathering of information on which decisions are based, stereotyping of clients, the use of complex forms, etc. On the client level, complexity is likely to induce false perceptions of eligibility or of the amount of entitlement, to obscure the claiming process and administrative procedures, and to pose problems in gathering the required information. Another important characteristic of means-tested benefits which is relevant for non-take-up is that they are in general aimed at 'the poor', i.e. at a social category that is still likely to be stigmatised (Waxman, 1983). Claiming a means-tested benefit is therefore likely to induce a fear of stigmatisation and a feeling of degradation, which can form a serious barrier to claiming (see Hartmann, 1981a; van Bijsterveldt, 1975). The feeling of degradation is likely to be intensified by the combination of the administrative functions of providing a 'service' and controlling potential fraud, a combination which is characteristic of the administration of means-tested benefits and services (Howe, 1985; Knegt, 1986).

A GROWING CLIENTELE FOR MEANS-TESTED BENEFITS

Having shown that the use of means-testing tends to be dysfunctional with regard to the broader aims of social policy, the question of the extent of the role that is played by means-tested benefits in social security becomes relevant. The greater this role, the greater the societal impact of these dysfunctions and the more seriously one can question whether the institution of social security fulfils its balancing function in modern society adequately.

In this section we will address the role played by means-tested benefits in social security, taking as an indicator the number of citizens who are dependent on means-tested schemes. The period considered is from the early 1970s to the mid 1980s, the period in which Western welfare states witnessed their first major crisis. The countries analysed are Belgium, France, Ireland, the Federal Republic of Germany, the Netherlands and the United Kingdom. These countries were the subject of an international juridical comparison of the means-test (Schell and Pieters, 1989).

The starting point for this analysis is that two general factors account for the number of citizens eligible for a social security benefit: processes in society which have an influence on whether people meet the conditions for eligibility of existing benefits, and political decisions which set and alter these conditions. An economic process like increasing unemployment enhances *ceteris paribus* the number of people eligible for unemployment benefits; a political decision such as an extension of the minimum duration of previous employment as a condition of entitlement for unemployment benefit is likely to lower *ceteris paribus* the number of people who are entitled to that benefit.

Our analyses led us to the conclusion that in all the countries considered, with the exception of Belgium, there has been a continuous growth in the clientele of means-tested benefits. In part, this growth is a result of the growth in unemployment and the number of one-parent families which took place in the 1970s and 1980s in all the selected countries. In part, it is a consequence of policy measures which were taken in the 1980s to control

TABLE 11.2 Unemployment: number (x 1000) / percentage of total labour force

	1970	1975	1980	1985
Belgium	71	175	322	506
	1.9	4.4	7.7	12.0
France	530	901	1467	2442
	2.5	4.0	6.3	10.2
Germany (Fed. Rep.)	149	1075	889	2304
	0.6	4.0	3.3	8.3
Ireland	65	84	91	226
	5.8	7.3	7.3	17.4
Netherlands	47	260	326	634
	1.0	5.2	6.0	10.9
United Kingdom	555	838	1513	3179
	2.2	3.2	5.6	11.5

Source: OECD 1988, Table 5.1, p. 30

and cut back social security expenditures in response to the economic crisis of this period, and to adjust national social security systems to the EC directives on the equal treatment of men and women. Measures were taken which widened the range of existing means-tests, which introduced means-testing in formerly non-means-tested schemes, and which lowered the levels of social insurance benefits. In this section we present data relating to these developments in the selected countries. First we present data on unemployment and one-parent families, and, second, data on the policy measures.

Societal processes

Unemployment
We first consider the development of unemployment and its implications for social assistance. Table 11.2 sets out the unemployment figures of the selected countries for the period between 1970 and 1985, as a percentage of the total labour force. During the worldwide economic recession of the mid 1970s to the early 1980s, unemployment rates increased dramatically in all the countries under consideration The relative increase in unemployment during this period was lowest in Ireland but only because the percentage of unemployed in Ireland was already high in 1970.

Unemployment insurance benefits, which are non-means-tested and based on contributions paid during periods of employment, existed in all the countries considered. Relevant here, however, is the fact that at least

TABLE 11.3 Youth unemployment (unemployed < 25 years of age): numbers (x 1000) / percentage of total unemployed

	1970(a)	1975(a)	1980(a)	1985(b)
Belgium	20.3	108.0	176.1	195.0
	25.4	44.0	41.4	43.9
France	84.9	484.4	735.9	944.0
	31.5	47.7	46.4	38.4
Germany (Fed. Rep.)	18.2	287.4	224.6	562.0
	18.7	28.6	27.3	24.4
Ireland			27.9	72.0
			25.2	31.0
The Netherlands	14.7	87.2	131.3	286.0
	31.5	41.3	47.2	37.6
Great Britain		362.4	855.0	1236.0
		36.6	41.4	37.8

Source: Eurostat, Employment and Unemployment, 1983 and 1988
(a): October figures
(b): annual averages

two groups of unemployed persons[12] are, in general, not entitled, or are only temporarily entitled to unemployment insurance benefits. These two groups are the young unemployed of 24 years old or less (school leavers and young people without any or with very little work experience) and the long-term unemployed.

In none of countries that we are concerned with here are there any unemployment insurance benefits for the young unemployed (Koditz, 1981). In some countries, like France, Ireland, the Netherlands and the United Kingdom, young unemployed persons are, because of their unemployment status, eligible for means-tested assistance, eligibility and/or the amount of benefit depending on conditions like their age, whether they are living with their parents or on their own, and the duration of the period of unemployment. In other countries, like West Germany, financial assistance for young unemployed persons on the grounds of their unemployment is totally lacking. Only if they cannot rely on their parents are they entitled to means-tested social assistance. Belgium was again an exception because young unemployed persons can claim a tax-based, non-means-tested benefit, where the amount of benefit depends on age and educational level. However in recent years benefit levels have been cut. Table 11.3 shows that in the period between 1970 and 1985, youth unemployment formed a large proportion of total unemployment, ranging from 18.7 per

TABLE 11.4 Long-term unemployment (12 months and over) as percentage of total unemployed (October-figures)

	1975	1980	1985
Belgium	35.9	46.2	58.1
France	11.1	22.3	30.4
Germany (Fed. Rep.)	9.6	17.0	31.0
Ireland		31.6	43.8
Netherlands	22.6(a)	21.1	53.9
United Kingdom	16.6(a)	19.4	41.3

Source: Eurostat, Employment and Unemployment, 1983 and 1988
(a): 1976-figure

cent in 1970 in West Germany to 31.5 per cent in France and the Netherlands, and in 1985 from 24.4 per cent in West Germany to 43.9 per cent in Belgium.[13] Now, if unemployment increases and a large proportion of the unemployed are young people who can only rely on social assistance, then an increase in unemployment must *ceteris paribus* contribute to an increase in the size of the clientele of means-tested social assistance schemes.

A similar situation applies to the long-term unemployed. Table 11.4 shows that in all the countries considered, the proportion of long-term unemployed among the unemployed was relatively high in 1975/6, especially in Belgium and the Netherlands. In all countries this proportion increased steadily in the following decade leading to higher percentages, ranging from 30.4 per cent in France to 58.1 per cent in Belgium, in 1985. Because of the fact that in all the selected countries with the exception of Belgium, entitlement to unemployment insurance benefit runs out after a certain period, this growth in long-term unemployment also contributed to the growth in the number of persons dependent on assistance. In the early 1980s, the period of entitlement varied from 12 months in the United Kingdom, West Germany and France (longer for those over 50 years of age) to 15 months in Ireland (6 months for those under 18 years of age) and 30 months in the Netherlands (Walsh, 1982). Having exhausted their entitlement to unemployment insurance, the long-term unemployed in all these countries become eligible for means-tested social assistance. Belgium was again the exception because there is no fixed limit on the length of time an unemployed person is entitled to receive state unemployment benefit.

Millar (1988) provides some comparative data which show that the developments discussed so far have indeed led to a growing proportion of the unemployed receiving social assistance benefits instead of, or in addition to, unemployment insurance benefits. In 1971, 27 per cent of

TABLE 11.5 One-parent families: number (x 1000) / index

	1970	1971	1975	1980	1981	1982	1983	1984
Belgium	167				213			
	100				127			
France			776			887		
			100			114		
Germany			736	868		927		
(Fed. Rep.)			100	118		126		
Ireland			22			30		
			100			136		
Netherlands		170			214		246	
		100			126		145	
United Kingdom		570		870				940
		100		153				165

Source: O'Higgins, 1987, Table 1, p. 6.

unemployed persons in the United Kingdom received only means-tested supplementary benefit; in 1986 this figure had grown to 59 per cent. Between 1974 and 1984 the proportion of unemployed persons receiving insurance benefits in West Germany fell from 60 per cent to 38 per cent, and the proportion receiving assistance benefits rose from 7 per cent to 26 per cent (Lawson, 1986 quoted in Millar, 1988). Between 1970 and 1985, the proportion of unemployed persons receiving assistance in the Netherlands rose from 13 per cent to 61 per cent (Roebroek and Berben, 1988). Millar speaks of 'the "drift" away from contributory and towards means-tested benefits' with regard to the type of benefits received by unemployed persons in the United Kingdom. With this in mind, and with Belgium as an exception, this drift can be seen as a European trend.

One-parent families
Next to the growth in unemployment another development that has occurred in all the selected countries in the 1970s and 1980s is the growth in the number of one-parent families. Table 11.5 illustrates this trend.

In general, according to O'Higgins (1987), a small proportion of one parent families, ranging from 10–20 per cent in countries like Belgium, France, the Netherlands and the United Kingdom, have a male head. The large majority of one-parent families are headed by a female. In general a large proportion of these females are unemployed. The proportions were 67.4 per cent in Belgium in 1981, 23.8 per cent in France in 1982, 40.5 per cent in West Germany in 1982, 61 per cent in the United Kingdom in 1982/4

Means-testing in Europe

TABLE 11.6 Social assistance beneficiaries: number (x 1000) / index

	1970	1975	1979	1980	1982
Belgium			20		31
			100		159
Germany(Fed Rep.)	1508	2159		2266	
	100	143		150	
Ireland	188	230		229	
	100	122		122	
Netherlands	299	429			495
	100	143			166
United Kingdom	2740	2790			4270
	100	102			156

Source: Flora, Vol. 4, 1987 (Tables on 'welfare clienteles' in country-sections)

(O'Higgins, 1987, Table 10, pp. 27–8), and 86 per cent in the Netherlands in 1983 (Boos, 1987, Table 18, p. 50). Within the group of female heads of one-parent families, the proportion of widows was relatively small – it was 24 per cent in the United Kingdom in the early 1970s and has decreased somewhat since then. In the Netherlands and France, the proportion decreased over this period from about 50 per cent to about 40 per cent in the Netherlands and 30 per cent in France. O'Higgins concludes that, in countries like Belgium, France, Ireland, West Germany, the Netherlands and the United Kingdom, there was a general decrease in the proportion of widows as female heads of one-parent families between the 1970s and the early 1980s. It follows that the proportion of unmarried, deserted and divorced wives as female heads of one-parent families must have increased. Thus, the general picture that emerges from this rather scattered information is that, in the countries concerned, large proportions of one-parent families have as a head of household an unemployed and unmarried, deserted or divorced woman. With the exception of the deserted wife's benefit in Ireland, non-means-tested insurance benefits do not exist for this group in any of the countries considered. In so far as these families do not have other sources of income, they will be dependent on a social assistance benefit. This is why we believe that the growth in one-parent families must have contributed to a growth in the number of persons dependent on social assistance.

One conclusion from this is that in all but one of the selected countries, all of which are members of the European Community, the growth of unemployment and the increasing incidence of long term and youth unemployment, together with the growth in the number of one-parent

TABLE 11.7 Social beneficiaries in the United Kingdom: percentages

	1970*	1975*	1980*	1984–85**
Elderly	69.0	60.4	54.2	39.8
Unemployed	8.7	19.4	24.2	42.0
Sick	11.8	8.7	6.6	6.0
One-parent families	6.9	9.9	10.1	10.4
Other	2.9	1.7	1.7	1.8
Total	100	100	100	100

Sources: * Flora, 1986/7, Vol. 4, Table 11, p. 401
** calculations on Table 15.13 (p. 270) in Government's Expenditure Plans 1988–9 to 1990, Cm 288-II, 1988

families resulted in an increasing number of unemployed and one-parent families becoming dependent on social assistance in the 1970s and 1980s. Belgium was the only exception to this general trend. Because of the unlimited duration of unemployment insurance benefits and the availability of non-means-tested benefits for the young unemployed, the effect of the growth in unemployment on the number of social assistance beneficiaries in this country was quite small.

The analysis outlined above is supported by relevant data relating to the number of people receiving social assistance in the countries considered, and by data about the composition of recipients of social assistance in the Netherlands and the United Kingdom. As Table 11.6 shows, there was a marked increase in the total number of recipients of social assistance in each of the countries considered in the period between the 1970s and 1980.[14] Tables 11.7 and 11.8 show that in the 1970s and 1980s in the United Kingdom and the Netherlands the proportion of unemployed among those dependent on social assistance increased sharply, and that the proportion of one-parent families also increased, albeit to a lesser extent.

Political decisions[15]

In the foregoing discussion, we have seen that certain societal processes caused a shift within the social security system from social insurance to social assistance. It should be noted that the reason why these societal processes actually had this effect was that the existing social insurance schemes were not constructed with these processes in mind. Of course, national legislators could always have made the necessary adjustments, for example by prolonging the period of entitlement to unemployment benefit. The fact that, in most cases, nothing of the kind was done itself constitutes a political decision. Indeed, instead of improving the existing social insurance schemes in order to adapt them to the changing conditions in society, the opposite direction was sometimes followed. Two types of

TABLE 11.8 Social assistance beneficiaries in the Netherlands: percentages

	1971	1974	1980	1986
General assistance	96	91	73	34
Of which:				
Two-parent families	30	28	9	11
One-parent families with female head	38	40	61	64
Single male	5	7	8	5
Single female	27	25	26	34
Assistance for unemployed	4	9	27	66
Total	100	100	100	100

Source: calculations on Tables 1, 2 and 3 in Jansen, 1988, pp. 39–41.

political decisions can be distinguished here: cutting back insurance benefits and tightening entitlement conditions.

Cutbacks in social insurance benefits have taken place in several countries. Such cutbacks can be realised either by lowering the earnings-replacement ratio of the benefits or by reducing the role of earnings-related supplements to flat-rate benefits.

Examples of the decrease of the earnings-replacement ratio can be found both in West Germany and the Netherlands. In the latter, unemployment, sickness and invalidity insurance for workers until a few years ago provided for earnings-related benefits at an earnings-replacement ratio of 80 per cent. In 1985–6 the ratio was reduced to 70 per cent, a measure that made a most significant contribution to the policy of cost-saving on public expenditure. In West Germany, the 1984 Budget Supplement Law (*Haushaltsbegleitgesetz*) reduced the earnings-replacement rate for unemployment insurance from 68 per cent to 63 per cent for beneficiaries without children. Comparable cutbacks had previously been introduced for special categories of unemployment insurance beneficiaries, like those receiving an educational training allowance or a benefit during rehabilitation.

Examples of reductions in the role of earnings-related additions to flat-rate benefits can be found in the British and Irish systems. In the United Kingdom, earnings-related supplements for both sickness and unemployment benefit were abolished in 1982, while entitlements under the State Earnings-related Pensions Scheme (SERPS) were reduced in 1986. In Ireland, earnings-related supplements to unemployment, sickness and maternity benefits were reduced in 1983 and the supplement to unemployment benefit for part-time workers was abolished. At the same time the maximum amount of benefit, that is flat-rate benefit together with the earnings-related supplement, was set at 75 per cent of previous earnings instead of 100 per cent as before. The maximum amount of maternity benefit was reduced from 80 per cent to 70 per cent of previous earnings. In all these cases, the effect of the cutbacks was the same: recipients of social insurance benefits were forced to become dependent on means-tested additions.

The tightening of entitlement conditions also took place in several of the countries considered. In West Germany, for example, tighter conditions for entitlement to unemployment benefit were introduced in 1981 and these were further tightened in 1983. In comparison with the original rules, the contribution periods which claimants had to satisfy were tripled. A comparable change occurred in both the Netherlands and the United Kingdom, where, in 1981 and 1988 respectively, the contribution conditions for entitlement to unemployment benefit were made significantly more onerous. Finally, in Ireland, a change in the law in 1987 increased the contribution conditions for all short-term benefits.

One consequence of these changes in contribution conditions is that fewer people will be entitled to social insurance benefits. Where the number of contributions paid or credited also influences the period of entitlement, a further consequence is that this will on average be shorter. Because of this, more people will be dependent on means-tested benefits and will be dependent on them for longer.

In search of the motivation for these reductions in the scope of social insurance, one will only find an expressed need for cost-saving on public expenditure, and thus on social security. One will look in vain for a more fundamental appreciation of the consequences of the shift from insurance to assistance.

A political decision that clearly constitutes an increase of the role of means-testing is the introduction of means-tests into an existing social security scheme or a new scheme. Decisions of this kind can be found in several of the countries considered.

The Dutch system contains two examples. The first one concerns the minimum income guarantee in the unemployment, sickness and invalidity insurance schemes. Previously these insurance schemes themselves provided for a non-means-tested minimum benefit level, although the guarantee was restricted to people in full-time work. Between 1983 and 1985, as part of its cost-saving measures, the Dutch Government restricted the minimum income guarantee to people with dependent family members. In that context means-tested family additions were introduced. In 1987, the relevant provisions were transferred to a separate scheme, the Supplements Act (*Toeslagenwet*). In so doing, the Dutch Government intended to make a clearer distinction between earnings replacement on the one hand and a minimum income guarantee on the other. Second, a means-test was introduced into the Old Age Insurance Act (*Algemene Ouderdomswet*). The immediate cause was the requirement to treat men and women equally for social security purposes, an obligation imposed by the European Commission's Third Equality Directive (79/7/EEC). Previously, married men with a partner younger than 65 were entitled to a pension (for a married couple) corresponding to 100 per cent of the minimum wage at the age of 65. Married women of 65 with a partner younger than that were not entitled to a pension at all, unless the woman was the breadwinner in the family. In order to satisfy the equal treatment requirement, it was decided that, at the age of 65, men and women would both be entitled to a basic non-means-tested pension of 70 per cent of minimum wage (the pension for persons living alone). For pensioners with a partner younger than 65, the law provides for a means-tested addition of 30 per cent of minimum wage on top of the non-means-tested 70 per cent.

The equal treatment of men and women was also the reason for introducing means-tests into the West German accident, invalidity and old age insurance schemes. It affects entitlement to a survivor's pension. Previously, men were not entitled to this pension, but according to the Federal Administrative Law (*Bundesverfassungsgericht*) (BVefGE39, 169), this was held to be contrary to the constitutional principle of equality. The German Government wanted the equalisation to be cost neutral but this was possible only by making the pension rights for both men and women means-tested.[16] A second example of the introduction of new means-tests into West German social security provisions can be found in the child benefit scheme (*Kindergeld*). As part of the reduction of public expenditure, Kindergeld for the second child was made partly means-tested. A third example is the means-test attached to the entitlement to *Erziehungsgeld*, a benefit for a parent who raises a child younger than one year old and who, for that reason, is not able to work in full-time employment. The benefit is state-financed and was only recently introduced.

The equal treatment of men and women was also the reason for introducing a new means-test in Ireland. Here the entitlement to adult dependent additions on top of the basic insurance benefits was made means-tested with the coming into force of the Social Welfare (No.2) Act 1985. Before the change a woman was regarded as dependent on her husband if she lived with him. A man on the other hand was only regarded as dependent on his wife if, due to physical or mental handicap, he was not able to support himself and was actually wholly or partly supported by his wife. In the new formula this unequal treatment is removed.[17] Together with the introduction of the new concept of the adult dependent, some new rules were introduced into the unemployment assistance scheme in order to cover the costs of equal treatment. Of particular importance is the aggregation rule in the application of the means-test in the unemployment assistance scheme, according to which the means of both spouses are aggregated, whereas before only the means of the beneficiary was taken into account.[18] The introduction of the Irish Family Income Supplement Scheme is a somewhat less recent example of a new social security scheme that provides for means-tested entitlements to benefits.

What applies to the Irish Family Income Supplement Scheme applies equally to its British counterpart (now called the Family Credit Scheme) which was introduced at the beginning of the seventies. In the recent changes in British social security, a further increase of selectivity was one of the policy aims. In that respect two non-means-tested benefits were abolished, the maternity grant and the death grant: people who have not taken the necessary precautions in relation to birth or death are now dependent on the Social Fund. The introduction of the Social Fund itself constitutes the clearest example of increased selectivity, since entitlement to payments for special costs is subject to considerably more administrative discretion.

Considering the cases in which new means-tests were introduced, it is striking that the requirement of equal treatment of men and women constitutes an autonomous reason for the increase in means-testing. Without exception, equal treatment was realised by reducing the entitlements of the previously most favoured groups by submitting these entitlements to a means-test.[19] The means-test, as it were, was needed to finance the costs of equal treatment. Here again a more fundamental or ideological reflection on the use of the means-test is missing. The only discussion it gave rise to was in West Germany and concerned the acceptability of means-testing in social insurance schemes. This is a very important discussion because it can be argued that, with the introduction of means-tests into social insurance schemes, the distinction between social assistance and social insurance becomes considerably less clear.[20]

We have illustrated the political decisions with examples from the British, Irish, German and Dutch social security systems. Does this mean that in Belgium and France political decisions of the kind mentioned did not occur?

For Belgium, it can be said that in its social security system the relation between social insurance and social assistance has always been clear. Social assistance has never played more than a residual role: both expenditure on social assistance and the number of beneficiaries are, compared to the corresponding figures for social insurance, very low.[21] In spite of the fact that dependence on the social security system as a whole has increased enormously in recent years, a shift from social insurance to social assistance has not occurred. Two structural elements in the Belgian social insurance schemes are of decisive importance. In the first place, these schemes provide for minimum benefits that normally exceed the level of social assistance.[22] A second, already mentioned characteristic, concerns unemployment insurance, in particular the unlimited duration of entitlement to benefit. However, even where social insurance has kept its central position within the system, it did not remain unaffected. Here, special attention should be paid to the introduction of a new benefit category within the unemployment insurance scheme. Where before a distinction was made between breadwinners and other beneficiaries, the latter are now divided into people living alone and people living with others. The aim is to identify people having a partner with an income. From the third year of entitlement on, unemployment insurance benefit for people living together is lower than for people living alone.[23] Although, in strict terms, this does not entail the introduction of a means-test, the new benefit category is very much related to it, since, although an actual test of means does not take place, account is taken of the presence of other means in the household.[24]

The French case is rather difficult to evaluate. Here a shift from social insurance to social assistance as a consequence of political decisions is very hard to trace, because the role of social assistance remains extremely unclear. French social assistance is split up into many local and regional schemes and adequate national information is very difficult to obtain. Until 1989, a national social assistance scheme was actually missing.

CONCLUDING REMARKS

In this chapter, means-testing is identified as an interesting subject for sociological analysis. Its functions and dysfunctions with regard to the broader aims of social policy are discussed. The societal impact of the dysfunctional consequences of means-testing is seen to depend on the number of people receiving means-tested benefits. Both the evidence relating to societal processes (growing numbers of long-term and young unemployed persons, and of one-parent families) and that relating to political decisions (cutbacks in social insurance benefits, tightening entitlement conditions and the introduction of new means-tests), show that, from the 1970s onwards, the role of means-testing has increased sharply in all the European countries considered, with the single exception of Belgium. On this basis one can say that there has been a European trend from universal social insurance to selective means-tested assistance. Although the possible economic, political and socio-cultural implications of this trend are not yet clear, some general comments may be put forward.

First, from a sociological point of view, one could say that the trend identified above, combined with the dysfunctional consequences of means-testing, i.e. its influence on poverty trap problems, non-take-up and social exclusion, implies that the institution of social security is fulfilling its balancing or integrating function less adequately. Means-tested social assistance may be an adequate 'safety-net' instrument in social security when its application is necessary in exceptional cases and for short periods between an individual's loss of one 'secure' socio-economic position and the achieving of another. However, relying on means-testing as the major means of guaranteeing a minimum income for a large group of citizens who are dependent on it for long periods of time testifies to a preoccupation with short-term, mainly economic, interests and a related neglect of long-term needs for social integration and participation.

Second, although one can argue that the period from 1970 onwards, in which modern welfare states witnessed their first major economic crises, has not led to 'a crisis of the welfare state' itself (Alber, 1988c), the trend identified above would imply a loss in the quality of the welfare state for the many citizens whose socio-economic chances are, or will become in the future, primarily dependent on social security benefits. For, compared with social insurance benefits, means-tested social assistance benefits in general imply lower amounts of benefit, stronger and more intrusive controls over personal circumstances and activities, more complex obstacles to the realisation of rights, fewer opportunities and incentives to become better off and a greater chance of beneficiaries being seen (and treated) as second-rate citizens.

Third, from a socio-political point of view, the trend identified above implies a new dimension in the relation between the welfare state and those of its citizens who are or are likely to become dependent on social security. In the case of non-means-tested social insurance schemes, especially in continental social security systems, this relation is mediated by institutional bodies, constituted by trade unions, employers organisations and independent organisations of professionals, which have a say in the distribution of rights and duties between the State and (potential) beneficiaries.

With the growth of means-tested social security schemes this relation is institutionally uncoupled due to the fact that in such schemes policy-making, financing and administration are in general completely in the hands of the state. Together with the fact that a strong collective movement of social assistance claimants does not exist in any of the European countries considered, the trend identified above implies that these states are now confronted with a large group of 'institutionally naked' citizens, i.e. citizens with no institutional back-up in their relationship with the state who are at the same time in a position of strong socio-economic dependency. This means that these claimants are wholly dependent for their life-chances on the state's notion of 'social citizenship'. The big question is whether this notion will develop into a basis from which a better quality of life can be achieved than is at present the case for the large number of citizens who are dependent on means-tested benefits.

As yet we have our doubts about this. Developing this notion of social citizenship in relation to social security would require a fundamental and ideological discussion of the aims and premises of the overall social security system in general and those of the different types of social security schemes in particular. However, as may have become clear from our discussion of political decisions, in dealing with the question of means-testing, European governments have been much more concerned with cost-saving than with fundamental and ideological arguments.

NOTES
1. Sigg's conclusion from the results of several conferences in the 1960s, that 'a sociology of social security worthy of the name has not developed' (Sigg, 1986, p. 285) is another reason for focussing attention on the definition of this sub-discipline.
2. This question goes back to the writings of Thomas Hobbes in the seventeenth century, Adam Smith and Jean Jacques Rousseau in the eighteenth century, Emile Durkheim, August Comte, Max Weber, George Simmel and Vilfredo Pareto in the late nineteenth and early twentieth centuries, and is central in the work of George Herbert Mead, Talcott Parsons, Jürgen Habermas and Anthony Giddens in the twentieth century.
3. It has become customary to differentiate between the 'poverty trap' and the 'unemployment trap' i.e. between the disincentive effects of the working of the tax-benefit system for those in work and for those out of work (Parker, 1982; Deacon and Bradshaw, 1983). In this section of the chapter, where the core problem is whether means-tested benefits can have disincentive effects, whether they are in or out of work, this distinction is of no relevance. Dilnot et al., (1984) confine the use of the poverty trap to situations in which households can make themselves even worse off by increasing their income. This restricted conception leads them to the finding that in 1982/3, relatively few British households were 'trapped in poverty'.
4. Ministry of Social Affairs and Employment (1986, Table 4.10, p. 37); the calculations were made for a two-parent family with one male earner and two children.
5. According to Millar (1988), disincentives to work will certainly be real for women who are married to, or otherwise form a household with, an unemployed man who is in receipt of a means-tested benefit. When household resources, instead of individual resources, are the subject of means-testing, which is the case with most means-tested benefits in Europe, such women will have very low financial incentives to take a job.
6. For more detailed British data see Parker (1982) and Dilnot et al. (1984).
7. Ministry of Social Affairs and Employment (1986, Table 4.4, p. 29).
8. Ministry of Social Affairs and Employment (1985, Table 3.10, p. 28).
9. Although some problems in the delivery of welfare, i.e. in the implementation of welfare programmes, may just be of a technical nature, many implementation problems are related to an underlying 'passivity of the administration' toward the delivery of services to citizens by the state (Ringeling, 1981). According to Ringeling this passivity is a remnant of the liberal theory of the state in which the citizen is regarded as an actor, equal to the state, consciously choosing between alternatives on the basis of full information. Empirical evidence concerning the reasons for non-take-up indicates that this citizen-model does not reflect reality very well.
10. For reviews of the British research, see Corden (1983); Falkingham (1985); van Oorschot and Kolkhuis Tancke (1989); and Craig (1991). For figures on the rates of take-up of social security benefits in the different countries mentioned, see van Oorschot (1990).

11. Although the various factors influencing take-up can be distinguished analytically and can be classified into different levels, it is clear from the research literature that in practice the reasons for non-take-up form a very complex whole. Models in which these factors are integrated do exist (for example, see Kerr, 1983), but in the context of this chapter we do not think it necessary to elaborate on them. For such an elaboration, followed by a critique and further elaboration based on recent Dutch research, see van Oorschot (1990).
12. It can be expected that other groups of unemployed persons will be dependent on social assistance. For example, in most countries not all of the members of the labour force are covered by unemployment insurance schemes. In 1975, 60 per cent of the French labour force was covered, 77 per cent in West Germany and 80 per cent in the United Kingdom (Walsh, 1982). Persons who are not covered and become unemployed will be dependent on other sources of income. In some cases this will be the income of family members, in other cases it will be social assistance benefits. Another group that may need a means-tested supplement to earnings-related insurance benefits is the group of former part-time workers. In the Netherlands, where unemployment and disablement insurance benefits are limited to 70 per cent of previous earnings, many unemployed or disabled part-time workers receive a level of insurance benefit which is less than the minimum social assistance benefit. In most cases such persons can therefore claim a means-tested supplement, which brings their income up to the minimum social assistance level.
13. We must add that, for countries like West Germany, where there is no financial assistance for young unemployed persons on the grounds of their unemployment, the figures cited probably underestimate the number and rate of youth unemployment (Koditz, 1981). For, if it is assumed that unemployment is defined in terms of those unemployed persons who are actually registered and that the receipt of financial assistance is an incentive for 'signing on', it is probable that in West Germany many young unemployed persons do not actually register as unemployed.
14. Although the trend is clear in all the countries considered, we must note that the figures presented in Table 11.6 are estimates based on the countrywide tables in Flora (1987, Vol. 4). Because of this, these figures are not strictly comparable between countries.
15. This paragraph draws on the results of an international juridical comparison of the means-test in several European countries. This study is reported in Schell and Pieters (1989).
16. The change in legislation gave rise to an extensive and fundamental discussion in the German literature about whether means-testing should be regarded as allowable under an insurance scheme. See, for example, the special issue of the magazine *Deutsche Rentenversicherung* of May 1985.
17. The spouse of a beneficiary who is wholly or partly maintained by the latter is now regarded as an adult dependent. However, a spouse who is in full-time employment or is entitled to, or actually in receipt of, a social security benefit is excluded. In the Social Welfare (Adult Dependant) Regulations, S.I. No. 369 of 1986, this legal definition is in fact restricted somewhat. According to these regulations a spouse who is working but whose weekly income

Means-testing in Europe

does not exceed a certain amount (£50) as well as a spouse who is entitled to disablement benefit, death benefit or orphan's pension is regarded as an adult dependant. The legitimacy of the regulations is questionable.

18. In Ireland, the view is taken that, in line with the decision of the High Court of 19th January 1988 in *Hyland* v. *Minister for Social Welfare*, the aggregation-rule is contrary to the constitutional obligation of the State to protect the family (see Whyte, 1989).

19. It is true that these means-tests are not as severe as the 'traditional' means-tests in social assistance schemes, since only earned income is taken into account, and then only in so far as it exceeds a rather high threshold. However, in light of the ruling of the European Court of Justice in the *Teuling* case (30/85), one could argue that the requirements of the equal treatment directive require a more severe means-test in order to prevent the scheme from discriminating indirectly.

20. Less clear is the way that previous developments have already led to a *rapprochement* of the two types of schemes. We refer to the fact that social insurance schemes are now very often partly financed out of general taxation and that the level of benefits for large categories of people is the same under social insurance and social assistance schemes.

21. See the statistics in this chapter and in Cantillon *et al.* (1987, pp. 280–1).

22. The minimum income guarantee is certainly not perfect: in the old age and survivors pension schemes the further condition that one has to give up a full-time job causes many problems.

23. Of all beneficiaries, no less than 80 per cent are considered to be living together (Cantillon *et al.*, 1987, p. 230).

24. The introduction of this new benefit category is seen as an example of the increase in the family related character of social security benefits (Cantillon *et al.*, 1987, pp. 193-4). It exemplifies a development that would lead to a weakening of the insurance character of social security (Cantillon *et al.*, 1987, p. 221).

12
THE PARADOX OF MANAGING DISCRETIONARY WORKERS IN SOCIAL WELFARE POLICY*

MICHAEL LIPSKY

The new welfare reform legislation in the United States, the Family Support Act of 1988, has significant implications for welfare administration. The implementation of the Act, which emphasises restoring recipients to the work rolls, calls for States to provide education, training and jobs to what eventually should be a majority of recipients, to provide day-care and continue health benefits, and to increase recipients' cooperation with child support enforcement. Successful implementation of the Act will require capable, imaginative and resourceful workers. In addition to mastering the usual complex and seemingly everchanging regulations and procedures, workers will also have to be knowledgeable about employment and training, become analysts of clients' interests, strengths and weaknesses, and serve as effective counsellors to individuals attempting difficult life changes.

It is ironic to observers of the American welfare scene that the new law will require more of the very people who were regarded as the problem in welfare administration a short time ago, when welfare workers and their imagined excessive sympathy for clients were considered major contributors to excessive welfare spending. In this chapter the terms 'welfare' and 'social welfare' are used broadly to refer to income support programmes for dependent populations. The signature programme in the United States is Aid to Families with Dependent Children (AFDC), which receives the bulk of attention and is the focus of the Family Support Act reforms. The Food Stamp Program and disability provisions of the Social Security Act also fall under this designation. The term 'social security' widely used outside the United States for such programme, in American usage is usually restricted to refer to the old age income support programme that goes by that name.

---

* I am grateful to Larry Best, Evelyn Brodkin, and Jolie Bain Pillsbury for their help in developing this chapter. The account of the Massachusetts ET Choices programme is based primarily on my conversations with principals and observations of the programme from its inception to 1988, while I was a consultant to the Massachusetts Department of Public Welfare.

If the new legislation is to be implemented effectively there must be a reorientation away from recent exclusive emphasis on procedural accuracy and bureaucratic discipline and toward a professional orientation where capacity for prudent judgement and skillful interactions with clients are given greater weight. But this may not be so easy to accomplish. Public welfare workers are often thought of as typical of those street-level bureaucrats whose discretion and autonomy are protected by the nature of their jobs, and who are therefore likely to be able to resist policy directives enunciated by higher authorities (Lipsky, 1980).

The question arises, then, as both a practical and theoretical matter: can management techniques be developed to ensure that welfare workers produce substantially different outcomes? In particular, can management techniques ensure that they achieve policy objectives requiring more effective interactions with clients as well as objectives that call for tighter fiscal and administrative controls? These questions seem particularly salient for analysts who accept that 'street-level bureaucrats' exercise wide discretion and are uncertain about whether management techniques can be developed to ensure that they achieve effective policy outcomes.

DISCRETION AS A COMPONENT OF SOCIAL WELFARE POLICY ADMINISTRATION

In an impressive range of welfare state policies, the residual discretion enjoyed by workers who interact with and make decisions about clients results in workers effectively 'making policy'. They effectively 'make policy' not in the sense that they articulate core objectives or develop mechanisms to achieve those objectives. Rather, they make policy in the sense that the aggregation of their separate discretionary and unsanctioned behaviour adds up to patterned agency behaviour overall. The underlying explanation of this proposition aids our understanding of why this should be so. Social welfare workers, as well as teachers, police officers and other public employees who interact with citizens, behave in ways that are unsanctioned, sometimes even contradicting official policy, because the structure of their jobs makes it impossible fully to achieve the expectations of the work. Resources (primarily of time, money, human resources or skills) are inadequate to the tasks they are expected to perform. Goals and objectives may be conflicting or ambiguous. Job performance is extremely difficult to assess in the areas that matter most. Moreover, work with clients is often particularly stressful because of high volume and the complexity of the task, and the need to interact with a client population that can be highly reactive to their intervention.

When confronted with these conditions, welfare workers will try to salvage their jobs by developing routines that promote fulfilment of at least a part of what is expected of them, as well as their own sense of well-being. They will try to perform in as acceptable a fashion as they can, but will also deviate from official expectations in the process. These individual solutions to work pressures, I have argued, 'add up' effectively to form public policy (Lipsky, 1980).

Thus the policy that a welfare agency delivers is not fully comprehended by its budgetary allocations, authorising statutes, regulations and official procedures. One must also take into account the solutions workers invent to cope with abusive clients, high workloads and the pressures that result from having to command hundreds of rules and procedures and fit them responsibly to individual clients.

It is no accident that welfare workers act with discretion in a vast number of policy areas. On the contrary, it is essential to social welfare policy and administration that they do so. This is the case, most obviously, because the nature of the jobs they perform require that human judgement is, to use a medical metaphor, exercised in diagnosis, prescription and treatment of clients. To elaborate, in social welfare policies workers, and not regulations, guidelines or computers, must assess the complex nature of the presenting client and his or her situation, the relationship between the presenting client and the range of programme options and possibilities once eligibility has been determined, and (in the generic case of street-level bureaucracy) determine and implement a course of action.

It is critical to understanding the nature of many social welfare policies that a substantial part of their legitimacy is associated with their apparent responsiveness. Welfare societies seem to want social welfare programmes to take into account factors that may not be reduced to programmed formats, whether the issue is making diagnoses of lower back pain and emotional stress, or counselling welfare recipients into appropriate employment referrals. They want a world which differentiates between different kinds of needs and different life circumstances. Indeed, social welfare programme depend, as Lance Leibman and Richard Stewart write about the Social Security Disability programme in the United States, 'on a widespread public belief that benefits are individual entitlements that must be honoured through appropriate procedures' (Leibman and Stewart, 1983; Mashaw, 1983).

In many States, the complementary beliefs that social welfare expenditures are excessively burdensome and that cheaters permeate and are tolerated on the rolls have led them to try to constrain costs by simplifying rules and then holding welfare workers to greater account. But these developments can only be taken so far before the substantive character of welfare systems becomes fundamentally challenged. And they are wholly inconsistent with more recent reform initiatives to help people leave the rolls through education and training.

Although street-level bureaucracies may be characterised by an irreducible discretionary role there is a danger that this insight will be taken to an extreme. The discovery that lower-level workers effectively make policy does not absolve the executive of responsibility for policy outcomes. The lesson that street-level bureaucrats exercise irreducible discretion

The paradox of managing discretionary workers 215

must not be that executives are powerless, but that executives must fit management tools to the task at hand.

Of course, in areas that have nothing to do with street-level workers, higher-level executives have always made policy. These policy makers play critical roles of resource allocation and deployment. Payment levels, eligibility standards and determinations of acceptable proof of eligibility, for example, are clearly matters of executive, and legislative action; that have little to do with street-level workers. Other things being equal, a ten per cent increase in basic grant levels should have no effect on welfare workers' conduct.

Higher-level executives also play critical roles in determining the extent to which discretion will play a major part in service delivery. The key purpose of programmed formats to guide client intake, for example, is to reduce worker discretion. At the other extreme, public agencies may promote professionalism as the legitimate way to make allocative decisions, thereby eliminating or displacing many of the conflicts that street-level bureaucrats typically encounter (Lipsky, 1980). However, these developments are not all that I mean when I say that higher-level executives must develop management tools to conform to the realities of street-level policy delivery. I mean as well that top policy makers can and do influence the outcomes of street-level discretion by shaping the work environment in which workers perform without intruding excessively into their discretionary decision space. Administrators may be charged with sharing responsibility for the aggregate outcomes of street-level bureaucracies, even if they cannot dictate individual outcomes.

Recognition of the role of higher-level executives in shaping policy is critical to understanding the politics of street-level bureaucracy. Analysts of public sector management have come to realise that the values distributed in social welfare systems are not only determined by higher-level executives through top-down decisions. But neither are they determined entirely by street-level bureaucrats exercising discretionary judgment. To operate on any other premise would be to make the mistake of conceiving higher-level executives simply as mechanical actors in a world determined largely by street-level workers who themselves are in some sense victims of the system that employs them. Failure to understand the role of top policy makers shaping the discretionary context also leads to making the analysis of street-level bureaucracy appear to be insensitive to larger political realities, although it is readily observable that public services such as welfare systems, schools and police departments, although often deeply resistant, do change over time in response to political pressures

But how do higher-level executives affect policy when they cannot intrude into the discretionary decision itself? Imagine the modern manager who believes that his or her agency is putting out decisions that are insufficiently responsive to preferred policy directions, yet is ultimately constrained by law, labour agreements, political opposition and worker solidarity from dictating decisions or otherwise compromising the role of the street-level worker in determinations about individual clients. A manager subject to these constraints and motivated to change his or her agency's performance, having exhausted opportunities to directly affect outcomes, will attempt to increase the *probability* that outcomes on the whole will be more favourable to the preferred policy direction.

In the following pages I discuss three cases which illustrate the ways public officials have confronted the paradox of managing street-level workers; influencing their behaviour without directly challenging their discretion. The cases include two in which administrators sought to restrict discretionary behaviour, and one in which they attempted to encourage it.

REDUCING OVERALL PROGRAMME GENEROSITY WHILE RETAINING WORKER DISCRETION

Let us imagine a continuum on which we can arrange income transfer entitlement programmes according to the extent of agency worker discretion. At one end of the continuum would be programmes for which entitlement criteria are relatively straightforward. Examples might be veteran benefits, old age assistance, or child allowances. There may be some problems of proof at the margin (demonstrating veteran status or age may be difficult for some people; the status of children whose parents have separated may cause some difficulties), but overall the reliance on discretionary judgment in such programmes is low. In such programmes policy changes overwhelmingly can be effected at the legislative and regulation-writing stages of the policy process.

A different matter entirely is presented at the other end of the spectrum, when outreach, evaluation of evidence, obtaining client cooperation, and judgments about properly characterising the evidence are more typical. Two cases of programmes involving considerable discretion are the Aid to Families with Dependent Children (AFDC) programme, the basic family assistance programme in the United States, and the Social Security Disability Insurance (SSDI) programme, which provides income support in the United States for the physically and mentally disabled who cannot participate in the workforce. In the first, questions of existing income, assets, and willingness and readiness to participate in the work force leaves AFDC an entitlement programme that places substantial discretionary burdens on intake and case maintenance workers. Similarly, the ambiguity and subjectivity of many disabling conditions make disability insurance an entitlement programme dependent upon discretionary judgment of workers (Stone, 1984).

Social welfare policy makers who seek to lower the fiscal burden of social welfare programmes may move straightforwardly to cut benefits and narrow eligibility criteria, and may prevail depending upon the political climate. However, those who would reduce the size and scope of the welfare state encounter limits in cutting back on social welfare

The paradox of managing discretionary workers

expenditures through legislative actions. Citizens are ambivalent: they tend to approve of individual social welfare policies even while expressing preferences overall for reduced tax burdens (Kuttner, 1980). Moreover, except for some fringe cases (for example, perhaps, affluent recipients of untaxed American social security payments, who could well pay taxes on social security income) (Ford Foundation, 1989), it is hard to portray payment levels as excessively generous.

Citizens tend to express opposition to AFDC, but not because this support programme for mothers and children is perceived as too generous to legitimate recipients. The programme is vulnerable rather because it is thought to tolerate or encourage shirking of work, and because of the belief promoted by anti-welfare advocates that programme administration is too weak to exclude undeserving claimants. In the latter case and somewhat in the former, it is not that the programme is poorly conceived, it is that too many ineligibles have taken advantage of it. This critique allows the critic simultaneously to accept the legitimacy of the programme in principle while assailing its administration.

The critique has other political advantages. It scapegoats clients and workers while giving the appearance of supporting the deserving poor and other unambiguously needy people. And it allows an attack on the extent of welfare state benefits to take place in the hidden recesses of administrative reform rather than in the full glare of legislative and rule-making activities where programme advocates can more effectively rally support against the attack (Lipsky, 1984).

How do top policy-makers, who believe that the programme is acceptably targeted but too poorly administered to catch welfare cheats and advantage-takers, reduce programme generosity? There are many possibilities, including recruiting workers less sympathetic to clients, speeding up and fragmenting the work so that employees are unable fully to attend to individual clients, and strengthening public agencies' audit capacity. From the point of view of this chapter however, more interesting are ways that policy makers try to change the probabilities of individual outcomes by shaping the environment in which street-level workers operate.

Error reduction in AFDC

A chance to observe such efforts arose in the case of implementation of the federal 'quality control' initiative in the AFDC programme (Brodkin, 1986). The mechanism employed by the federal government to reduce State welfare rolls in the 1970s and early 1980s through quality control was engagingly simple. In essence, it operated by penalising States for excessive errors, but defined errors exclusively as inaccuracies that resulted in what was defined as wrongful spending. The error rate was determined by counting only errors committed when workers were considered insufficiently vigilant, that is, when they admitted ineligibles to the rolls, failed to obtain required verifications, or awarded recipients too much money.

What might be called 'errors of stringency', that is, wrongly denying eligible applicants, or underpaying recipients, were not counted in the error rate (Mendeloff, 1977).

Predictably, Massachusetts and other States undertook a series of corrective actions in order to avoid severe fiscal sanctions and the political liability of being regarded as incompetent, which the persistence of a high 'error rate' implied. State campaigns against error consisted of strategies that were exclusively directed toward inducing workers to be tougher, and to lean in the direction of refusing claims if there was any uncertainty. In Massachusetts the Welfare Department pursued activities that increased the frequency of case redeterminations, demands for documentation and adherence to procedural standards. It initiated administrative 'blitzes' to root out paper errors. Ambiguities in documentation, flexibility in accepting alternative verifications and trust in client claims were all reduced. Under the old system, workers would hold cases open while documentation of continued eligibility was being collected. Under the new campaign, workers would close cases even though they knew the clients were eligible and they would be returned to the rolls as soon as documentation was forthcoming. The new reforms, although ostensibly neutral in their impact, were in reality structurally biased in ways that favoured tighter controls and reduced programme flexibility.

Massachusetts succeeded in substantially reducing its error rate, from 25 per cent to 8 per cent in two years. However, an array of indirect evidence, including the high rate of reversals of caseworker decisions by hearing officers and the large number of cases reinstated retroactively from the date they were dropped, suggest that during the most severe error rate campaigns, eligible recipients were wrongly removed from the rolls. Many more paid a heavy price in increased difficulties in demonstrating eligibility. It might be argued that State officials were only pawns once the federal 'game' had been set, but this is not entirely true. State officials, driven by what they saw as simply a neutral administrative demand without redistributive consequences, disliked throwing the agency into turmoil but were relatively indifferent about and largely ignorant of negative consequences for recipients. It is important to bear in mind that Welfare Department executives made choices about how they would proceed, and might have made different choices if they had been more concerned about the consequences for welfare clients.

Controlling appeals in disability insurance

Excessive liberality in the Social Security Disability Insurance (SSDI) programme was the subject of similar concerns of Federal officials in the late 1970s and early 1980s. They were troubled by the steeply upward trend in SSDI expenditures over time. Recipients served by the programme had gone from one million in 1961 to three million by 1972, peaking at 4.8 million by 1978 (Social Security Bulletin, 1983). In response, the Reagan

Administration created a crisis by accelerating the schedule for investigating the continuing disability of beneficiaries. The initiative permitted examiners to disregard the previous criterion of whether medical improvement had taken place, and to proceed only on the basis of whether ongoing functioning for the purposes of employment was possible. In the first year of the initiative, over 130,000 beneficiaries were dropped from the SSDI rolls, including a disproportionate number of mentally impaired individuals who might be expected to require special consideration in case reviews because their impairment directly affected their ability to participate effectively in the reviews.

The Administration also tried to reduce the disability rolls by focusing on the independence of Administrative Law Judges (ALJs). The ALJs, who hear appeals from original examiners' decisions *de novo*, were targeted because they tended to find in favour of appellants in over half of the cases that came before them (Mashaw, 1983; Mezey, 1988). Although there is some controversy over the motivation of Federal officials in trying to bring the entirely discretionary system of ALJ hearings under control, it is clear that administrators attempted to bring the ALJs into line and thereby reduce expenditures. They used the following strategies:

1. 'Clarifying' the disability standard to make it apparently more objective, with the overt intention of making application of the standard more routine. The Social Security Administration (SSA) developed a protocol (known as the 'grid') that made assignment of disability status apparently more automatic. However, the new protocol did not diminish discretion by ALJs so much as it shifted discretionary judgments into new forms. Some aspects of SSDI decision-making became more routine, but now hearing examiners and ALJS had to decide under what circumstances the newly elaborated standards actually applied.
2. Tracking and publicising individual judges' reversal rates to highlight the high degree of reversals as well as to suggest the legitimacy of a 'normal' set of caseload outcomes. The SSA then sought to 'counsel' those judges who were most deviant from the norm. While the typical ALJ reversed denials in over half the cases, some judges had 90 per cent reversal rates.
3. Imposing quality control standards on ALJ decisions since presumably more objective referents would now be introduced. Judges most out of line with the newly established norm would receive the most attention. (There was some evidence that those ALJs with the highest reversal rate were also those who were most 'error prone'. This was vigorously resisted by ALJs, who maintained that their independence, guaranteed under the Administrative Procedures Act, would be compromised if such bureaucratic control procedures were pursued.
4. Establishing goals for timely settlement of claims. This compromised the independence of the ALJs by forcing them to produce decisions under greater pressure. The 'speed-up' constrained ALJs' ability to

gather and bring a wide range of evidence to bear on cases. Coupled with restrictions on funds to purchase expert testimony, the predictable result for disability recipients, according to Jerry Mashaw, would be 'cases lacking certain required and perhaps producible evidence [would] be classified as denials so that they may be decided. A demand for objectivity [and timely decision-making], without changes in the resources devoted to processing, tends to produce stringency' (Mashaw, 1983)

5. Administrative Law Judges were not the only targets of the crackdown. The Reagan Administration sought to have SSA desk reviewers recover monies from clients who were alleged to have been overpaid without interviewing the clients and without informing them of their right to request a waiver of overpayment recovery. Emphasis on recovering funds was ascendant. According to John Harris, President of the national organisation of SSA employees charged with this responsibility, 'the worker is told to think of herself as a bill collector...' (Best, 1989).

The SSA also restricted testimony from personal physicians who might be expected to advocate for their patients' interests, and manipulated initial reviews in other ways. Throughout the 1980s, despite congressional hearings and legislation designed to clarify public expectations of the SSD programme, the Administration sought bureaucratic, technical ways to bring under control what it regarded as excessively liberal provisions of the law.

LINKS BETWEEN REDUCING GENEROSITY AND CONTROLLING BUREAUCRATIC CLIMATE

It would be fairly easy to proliferate examples of efforts to achieve cost savings by constraining street-level bureaucrats while maintaining the sanctity of the discretionary encounter. Virtually every entitlement programme in the United States has been subject to quality control initiatives. In the health care field the story could be repeated as well. Diagnostic Related Groups, Health Maintenance Organisations, mandatory second opinions and other innovations are all efforts to change the structure of incentives under which physicians and hospitals operate, without directly challenging the right of the physician to make the ultimate judgment on patient care.

How does one explain that structuring the bureaucratic climate appears to be largely a matter of concern for policymakers worried about excessive programme generosity? It is not surprising that in a period of perceived fiscal crisis and conservative social policy, efforts directed toward influencing the structure of bureaucratic decision-making should be directed toward spending curbs. There may be a general tendency in social welfare programmes dependent upon discretionary judgments to expand, because among other things discretionary actors tend to find in favour of the ambiguous case while legislators tend to support the inclusion of excluded

The paradox of managing discretionary workers

groups at the margin of eligibility (Stone, 1984). If this is the case it may be understandable that controlling the bureaucratic climate in favour of welfare stringency is typical, because mechanisms to support greater programme generosity are already in place. However, at least in theory structuring the bureaucratic climate is not an approach available exclusively to social welfare administrators striving to limit outlays. In theory it is an approach equally available in programme that seek to expand worker discretion and initiative.

INFLUENCING WORKER DISCRETION TO INCREASE OVERALL PROGRAMME RESPONSIVENESS

An opportunity to examine the workings of a welfare bureaucracy that strived to *increase* workers' responsiveness to clients comes with an initiative taken, once again, by the Massachusetts Department of Public Welfare (DPW), beginning in 1983. The case bears directly upon the likely requirements of a welfare workforce operating under the new American employment and training initiatives.

The State welfare administration, as described above, had been confronted in the early 1980s with the prospect of paying substantial penalties for failing to bring down the error rate in accordance with federal requirements. The high error rate, however, was only one of the reasons that the Department sought to deprofessionalise welfare work. Its executives also believed that trained social workers tended to be excessively sympathetic toward clients, and that high degrees of discretion allowed them to favour clients inappropriately. To reduce errors which operated in favour of clients, prior to 1983 the Department had taken a number of steps in addition to the previously described error reduction initiatives:

1. Workers were taken off caseloads and instead given work according to a computer-generated schedule of the next required action of the service unit. In contrast to a caseload system, under the new system a worker would only infrequently interact with clients he/she had seen before.
2. The Department ceased to seek workers with social work backgrounds and career interests, but defined entry level jobs instead more as requiring the skills of accountants. Individuals with different orientations as well as lower levels of educational achievement were consequently recruited. Rewriting the administrative guidelines for AFDC was thought to be necessary not only to reduce the sorts of matters that might result in recorded 'errors', but also to assist a work force that was thought to be getting less and less able.
3. At about this time, but unrelated to quality control issues, the State was completing a reorganisation of administrative functions that would relocate the social service activities of the Welfare Department, notably child protection, foster care and adoption services, in a new Department of Social Services. Most welfare department employees who wanted to

work in these areas, including assistance payments workers, were allowed to choose the new agency as their place of work. This had the significant if unintended result of still further depriving the DPW of its social work-oriented contingent.

These changes and others may have been undertaken for the reasonable goal of reducing the State's error rate, or for unrelated reasons. But the signals to the workers conveyed an additional message: the Department was concerned with timely and accurate payment, nothing more.

When, in 1983, Governor Michael Dukakis took office for his second term after a four-year hiatus, he was particularly concerned about his standing with liberals and welfare advocates. With this in mind he was highly supportive of the efforts of Charles Atkins, his new Commissioner of Public Welfare, and his staff, to redesign the work and welfare initiative. The goal of the redesigned programme was to help people who wanted to leave the roll get off welfare. But instead of forcing recipients off welfare through punitive work requirements or requiring them to engage in meaningless work-search activities, the new programme would recruit people to it because it offered them desirable opportunities and helped them prepare for future employment (Department of Public Welfare, 1986). It also had to meet federal requirements or at least be consistent with federal requirement waivers. This initiative was to become the ET Choices (ET for Employment and Training) programme or, more colloquially among State insiders, simply ET.

ET was to attract considerable attention as interest in work and welfare reform at the federal level grew and finally peaked in 1988. It was a programme that appeared to indicate that recipient preferences could be respected; indeed, that they might be crucial to programme success. As such the programme represented an important counterpoint to other work and welfare experiments that were founded upon the notion that recipients must be forced to participate (Gueron, 1986). ET became famous when Governor Dukakis began to campaign for President on the basis of his success in creating this and several other state programme.

As finally designed, ET offered welfare recipients three main service components: assessment and career planning (an intake activity normally followed by another option); training and placement services (including job search, skills training and supported work, a programme in which recipients' wages are subsidised when they are hired as probationers) and further education in preparation for work. The availability of each component varied, depending upon the mix of State and federal financial support that had been allocated to that component. In addition, the programme offered child care assistance, transportation subsidies, and ongoing Medicaid benefits, recognising that without these components most recipients would find it too costly or risky to participate voluntarily.

It was one thing to eliminate some important obstacles to recipient participation. It was another, in the absence of a requirement to participate, to induce recipients to volunteer for the programme. This is where the attitude and behaviour of welfare workers toward recipients became critical. If recipients were to be persuaded to participate (particularly at the beginning when the programme had no reputation to speak of and 'word-of-mouth' was not operable), they had to be recruited.

It is no easy matter to induce a welfare recipient with few employment-related skills and a low self-image to believe that the State's programme to help him or her gain self-sufficiency is plausible and worth the personal and financial risks. Simply mailing a flyer about the programme along with the bi-weekly cheque was unlikely to provide sufficient incentive to induce participation. For ET to succeed, workers had to establish rapport with recipients, engage them in discussion about matters unrelated to the recipient's primary concern of getting on welfare or getting through a redetermination interview, persuade them to investigate the programme (usually through an interview with an ET specialist), and support and reassure the recipient through the fits and starts of trying to get off welfare.

The Welfare Department had to turn a harassed and demoralised staff that had recently been under great pressure to end welfare fraud and abuse into a work force that accepted helping recipients was one of its primary roles. It had to do so relatively quickly if the new State-wide programme was to prosper.

The Department largely succeeded in turning the staff around by providing the same sort of signals that in other circumstances, as previously described, have been used to increase programme stringency. A list of management innovations introduced to obtain workers' cooperation with and implementation of a more complex conception of the job (Behn, 1987) is set out below. Some of the developments were not exclusively related to ET.

1. To hold workers and supervisors accountable, the agency each year established a negotiated list of ten goals. Each administrative unit then identified a unit target consistent with each goal. Each administrator, including all welfare area directors (the directors of the agency's field offices, where clients actually apply, are interviewed, etc.,) were held responsible for their area's goal achievement. ET placement was one of the top goals. Now that ET placements were being measured, office directors could hold supervisors, and through supervisors, individual workers, accountable for ET placement achievements. (This approach was used throughout the agency, for every important agency goal, including error rate reduction.) Now that supervisors were being held accountable for achieving goals, upper level management could expect subordinates to innovate, as local conditions dictated, in order to achieve their targets.
2. For various reasons, including holding workers accountable for clients, the Department restored the caseload system so that every worker now had responsibility for individual cases. This created the minimal con-

ditions for caring about clients. It also made workers more resourceful, because they were now in a position to learn what individual clients thought were the critical barriers to their participation in ET. (The caseload system became even more important when the Department began to counsel recipients into a new Medicaid prepaid health initiative, and into greater cooperation with child support enforcement authorities.)
3. Client-to-staff ratios were established considerably below the maximum negotiated in the union contract, somewhat freeing workers from crushing caseload burdens and creating some goodwill among workers toward the Department.
4. The Department established and publicised a general message that indicated it intended to do business differently. Commissioner Atkins' first public action was to fire the holdover General Counsel for saying that providing recipients with emergency shelter was not the Department's job. His initial general theme focused on the importance of 'compassion' in official actions. Later, the agency promoted the (unusual) notion that the Department's task was not to maintain recipients' income at the below-poverty Massachusetts AFDC support levels, but was to get people 'out of poverty' – through ET, increased child support payments, and other initiatives.
5. The Department and the Governor made unusual efforts to communicate widely the high priority that was to be given to ET tasks. The Department pursued a public relations campaign, unprecedented for a welfare department, agency executives believed, to market the programme to recipients, workers, and potential employers. Meanwhile, favourable publicity about initial successes, including favourable and heralded actions of the Governor, contributed to the growing notion among Departmental personnel that the programme was important.
6. Several actions of the Department were directed generally toward improving the status of Departmental employees, in a sense offering collective employment benefits in implicit exchange for acceptance of increased responsibilities. Area directors were given significant salary increases in exchange for the expectation that they would for the first time manage the output of their area units. Efforts were made to endow welfare work with greater respect. Line workers went from being Financial Assistance Workers (FAWs), reflective of the discredited recent emphasis of the agency, to Financial Assistance Social Workers (FASWs), reflecting the new expectations. Regional gatherings of line workers were initiated to rally them to the agency's mission and demonstrate recognition of the Department's dependence on worker performance. The Department initiated a series of internal service awards and for the first time began actively to recognise the contributions of individual workers in symbolic ways.
7. Respect for workers and clients was also demonstrated by a campaign

The paradox of managing discretionary workers

to relocate or refurbish most of the welfare offices around the state that, like prisons and mental hospitals, had been neglected over the years. Symbolic of its importance as a State agency in the second Dukakis administration, the Department was able to move its executive offices and some of its central office staff out of Boston's sleazy 'combat zone' to a prestigious site a block away overlooking the Boston Common.

The general philosophy of the agency, reflected in a myriad of executive statements and actions, was that its performance ultimately depended upon the performance of line workers, that they could and would achieve reasonable departmental expectations if the expectations were clearly articulated, success was measurable, and they were given the resources to succeed. It is important to bear in mind that the agency continued to pursue complex goals. Achieving ET placements had to be accomplished while keeping the error rate down and providing for the homeless. Some of these objectives did not have a direct impact on individual welfare workers but maintaining a low error rate certainly did. The agency also continued to be responsive to its political and policy environments. It changed the ET goal from placements as such, to placements with earnings of at least five (and later six) dollars per hour when an internal evaluation of the programme revealed that ET graduates returned to welfare because they were not becoming financially independent.

CLIMATE CONTROL: DOING SOMETHING ABOUT THE BUREAUCRATIC WEATHER

The cases described here are not strictly comparable. Efforts to expand the initiative taken by welfare department workers do not seem to be entirely similar to efforts to constrain decision-making about individual cases. The ET model calls for establishing goals and then allowing supervisors leeway in order to achieve those goals; the cost containment campaigns took opposite tacks.

Yet the cases do bear comparison. In all three policy areas executives conceived policy objectives in which they needed to change the patterns of administrative behaviour without directly requiring workers to act differently in any particular case. Moreover, cost containment through administration *could* have been pursued with a more open model of setting goals and holding supervisors to those targets. Indeed, this was the approach the Massachusetts Department of Public Welfare eventually took toward error rate reduction during the same period that it was pursuing the ET initiative.

If the comparability of the cases is accepted we may use them to suggest generalisations about executive actions that appear to be consistent with public objectives of guiding street-level actions without fatally compromising worker autonomy.
1. No single action is more powerful than establishing an operational standard against which to measure worker performance. Establishing

the standard radically clarifies what are otherwise jobs with greater role ambiguities and conflicts. Although workers can undermine policy objectives through 'creaming' and other performance enhancement techniques to secure high ratings, establishing a measure, and then guarding it with quality control checks, is a powerful tool for influencing street-level performance.

2. The threat of sanctions or the prospects of reward must be substantial and credible if workers are expected to behave in ways indicated by the new standards. Sanctions such as disciplinary reviews (in the stringency cases) and achievement of personal and work unit rewards seem to be surprisingly potent from the perspective of analysts who might have thought more severe accountability sanctions were required.

3. To rely on workers' discretion to a greater degree is to promote professionalism, and *vice versa*. It follows that manipulating the trappings of professionalism and demonstrations of respect for workers contribute to successful implementation of new policy initiatives in welfare policy. Deprofessionalisation, both materially and symbolically reducing the respect for the office and for the decisions of street-level workers, may contribute to bending discretionary actions toward the preferences of the bureaucratic centre. But the costs are high in terms of reduced policy responsiveness.

4. A critical aspect of workers' performance in jobs involving discretion is the extent to which positive opportunities and resources for clients are truly available. Previous studies have indicated that street-level workers apprehend the actual choices available to clients and make determinations accordingly. For example, special education evaluations tend to produce diagnoses that conform to the kinds of specialists available to work with handicapped children (Weatherley, 1979). Judges sentence criminals according to the availability of sentencing alternatives (Lipsky, 1980). In the case of ET clients, support by workers for their clients was encouraged by the availability of new client opportunities. We may hypothesise that agencies will have difficulty in encouraging worker initiative if new opportunities for clients are more apparent than real.

5. Several aspects of these efforts to reshape workers' discretionary behaviour appear to be related to the potency and consistency of the message put out by the agency to reflect its philosophy. At the same time that the agencies tried to shape worker discretion they undertook traditional bureaucratic initiatives to increase or decrease recipient benefits. Workers perceived that the pressures they were experiencing were part of more broadly-based campaigns. Again this observation is consistent with the notion that reducing ambiguities in public agencies is a useful tool in shaping discretionary bureaucratic behaviour.

In sum, two general themes seem to be struck in this effort to shape discretionary behaviour. One is the clarity of agency expectations, the measurability of outcomes, and the deployment and rewards and sanctions for conforming and non-conforming performance for individual workers. The second is the clarity and credibility of the agency's broader message concerning its balance between helpfulness and stringency toward clients as a whole.

CONCLUSION

The three cases discussed in this chapter provide convincing evidence that administrative discretion remains central to the delivery of social welfare policy. Yet this is not the way in which welfare policy is normally treated in the Press or is perceived by the public. Most public discussion focuses on payment levels, eligibility issues, and such like. These are the public matters which shape social welfare policy and are given the most conspicuous treatment. It is sometimes forgotten that welfare programmes are finally placed in the field only when they are implemented through administrations whose structures, as they bear on those who have to implement them, have not been determined at the legislative level. On the contrary, the politics of structuring welfare administration takes place out of the public spotlight, in executive quarters and around the negotiating tables of the agency's staff. Meanwhile, those who have to carry out the policy are located in remote field offices far away from the places where the content of their work is the subject of scrutiny. Agency directors making policy for field staff would be well advised as planning proceeds to bring the perspective of the field to the table (Elmore, 1979).

Policy-makers and economists might wish it were otherwise, but it seems clear that in the implementation of social welfare programmes there remains an irreducible extent to which worker discretion cannot be eradicated. Application of systems of eligibility, verification and payment schedules is complex because the systems are deliberately responsive to a variety of presenting situations.

Although social welfare systems have an irreducible discretionary core, welfare administrators, nonetheless, regularly attempt to influence their workers' behaviour. They do so by trying to influence their agencies' bureaucratic climates to change the aggregate direction of outcomes while leaving the core of individual decisions beyond the reach of bureaucratic scrutiny. The objective of such efforts is to change the probability that individual worker judgments will be made in ways that are favourable to preferred departmental directions. The executive hopes not to eliminate all generous (or stringent) behaviour, but instead to shift the balance in the preferred direction. In this sense structuring the bureaucratic climate, as discussed here, represents a compromise with the structure of street-level work realities.

These attempts indeed can be moderately successful. Yet they will be constrained by workers' resistance to having their jobs redefined, particularly if the redefinition is not accompanied by changes in procedures or new resources for workers, or new opportunities for clients. They will also be constrained by the structure of the programmes. No matter how much discretion workers exercise, there will still be relatively unambiguous cases of eligibility or ineligibility. In employment outreach, there will still be unemployable recipients, no matter how resourceful the programmes are.

Social welfare systems, in the United States and elsewhere, have been moving toward greater simplicity with an attendant reduction in the need for worker discretion. However, the conservative emphasis on work requirements combined with liberal support for allocation of funds for education and training, has led to a reorientation of American Welfare Programmes. Thus we may be in for a period of increased dependence on service delivery personnel in welfare and these workers will have to be even more able in the future. The days of single solutions to persistent poverty in the United States, such as a negative income tax, are over. In the place of such monolithic solutions have arisen proposals that combine a variety of programme into patchworks that promise to relieve poverty only when pieced together (Ellwood, 1988; The Ford Foundation, 1989). Such proposals, particularly if they involve a work component, and whether or not they are mandatory or quasi-voluntary, will require more discretion among workers who will have to move clients among and between the patchwork pieces. These developments place the management of discretion among social welfare workers at the centre of welfare system reform.

13
THE SOCIAL SHAPING OF INFORMATION TECHNOLOGY: COMPUTERISATION AND THE ADMINISTRATION OF SOCIAL SECURITY*

MICHAEL ADLER AND ROY SAINSBURY

INTRODUCTION – THE SOCIAL SHAPING OF TECHNOLOGY

Social scientists have tended to concentrate on the 'effects' of technology, on the 'impact' of technological change on society. This is a perfectly valid concern, but it leaves a prior, and perhaps more important question unanswered. What has shaped the technology that is having these effects? What has caused and is causing the technological changes whose impact we are experiencing? (MacKenzie and Wajcman, 1985, p. 2)

The Operational Strategy, the Department of Social Security's (DSS) massive programme for the computerisation of the entire social security system, is the largest civil application of new technology in Europe (Otton, 1984).[1] In this paper we analyse the Operational Strategy as an important example of technological change, by considering the ways in which forces inside and outside the DSS have influenced its development.[2] We also examine the opportunities for organisational innovation which it has created and assess those options which appear to have been opened up and those which seem to have been foreclosed. Using the analytical framework developed by Mashaw (1983) we argue that the Operational Strategy has promoted a particular (bureaucratic) view of what good administration comprises. Finally we present, as an example of an attempt at social shaping, the results of a consultative exercise that we carried out for the DSS (Adler and Sainsbury, 1990) which investigated the potential of computerisation for improving the quality of service to the public. The

---

* The research on which this chapter is based was funded by the Department of Social Security. The views expressed in the chapter represent those of the authors and do not necessarily reflect those of the Department. We are grateful to the Department for its financial support and to Wendy Faulkner, Nigel Gilbert, Bjørn Hvinden, Donald MacKenzie, Martin Partington, Adrian Sinfield and several unnamed Departmental officials for their helpful comments on the paper. An earlier version of this paper was discussed at the Social Security Workshop held at the London School of Economics on 23 February 1990.

results suggest that although participants in the exercise strongly supported improvements in bureaucratic efficiency, they did not favour a more bureaucratised service and would have preferred a different balance with other (professional and juridical) values.

ADMINISTRATIVE JUSTICE AND SOCIAL SECURITY

Criticisms of the administration of social security have been many and varied. From within the DSS there are concerns about administrative costs and the efficiency of procedures which are articulated in the annual Public Expenditure White Papers (see, for example, Cm 1014, 1990, paras. 66–70). Claimants are more concerned with delays in receiving benefits, errors in calculations, and their personal treatment in dealing with the DSS. Their opinions have been sampled systematically (Berthoud, 1984; National Audit Office, 1988) and described more impressionistically (Beltram, 1984; Cooper, 1985). Other criticisms, particularly from those who come into contact with the social security system on behalf of claimants, bemoan the lack of effective rights accorded claimants (Bull, 1984; Allbeson and Smith, 1984; Craig, 1989). Further criticism emerges from the Chief Adjudication Officer, whose job it is to monitor the adjudication standards of the DSS and the Department of Employment, that officials frequently fail to adhere to the principles of sound legal decision-making (Sainsbury, 1989). According to Mashaw (1983), these varied criticisms reflect three normative conceptions or models of administrative justice, i.e. three ideal types of what good administration should comprise.[3] The three models, whilst not mutually exclusive, are highly competitive; 'the internal logic of any one of them tends to drive the characteristics of the others from the field as it works itself out in concrete situations' (Mashaw, 1983, p. 23).

In the first model, which he calls 'bureaucratic rationality', Mashaw argues that the administrative goal should be a system for deciding true and false claims at least possible cost, i.e. decision-making should be accurate and cost-effective. The emphasis is factual and technocratic; individual decision-makers must apply a set of rules to the facts to determine the eligibility of a claim, and managers must develop the cheapest appropriate mechanisms for this to be achieved.

Mashaw calls his second model 'professional treatment'. Since 'the goal of the professional is to serve the client' (Mashaw, 1983, p. 26), administration should be explicitly client-oriented:

> it would seek to provide those services ... that the client needed to improve his well-being and perhaps regain his self-sufficiency (Mashaw, 1983, p. 27).

Using techniques of personal examination and counselling, concern for the individual's overall circumstances would override strict adherence to any rules for deciding eligibility, an approach Mashaw calls 'holistic'.

Thirdly, Mashaw defines a 'moral judgement' model, the essence of which is the resolution of 'disputes about rights, about the allocation of benefits and burdens' (Mashaw, 1983, p. 29). Its most familiar manifestations are in civil and criminal trials. However, decision-making does not merely require finding facts and applying law, it also requires judgements about worth and preference, i.e. about values. Hence, decision-making from this perspective is 'value-defining' (Mashaw, 1983, p. 29). When interests and values conflict, the question to be decided is not only what the 'truth' of a situation is but whose interests and values are to be preferred. So, the central issue in adjudicating cases is

> the deservingness of some or all of the parties in the context of certain events, transactions or relationships that give rise to a claim (Mashaw, 1983, p. 30).

If we examine the aims of the Operational Strategy, and the way in which the DSS has addressed each one, it will become clear that computerisation aims to strengthen bureaucratic as distinct from professional and juridical conceptions of administrative justice.

TECHNOLOGICAL SOLUTIONS TO ORGANISATIONAL PROBLEMS

In 1982 the Department of Health and Social Security (as it then was) published its plans to computerise the whole social security system in *Social Security Operational Strategy: a Framework for the Future* (DHSS, 1982).[4] Quoting an earlier Departmental working paper (DHSS, 1980b), it pointed out 'that social security operations were under considerable strain, which was likely to continue, but that advances in computer and telecommunications technology were creating new opportunities for advance during the 1980s'. The Operational Strategy had three fundamental objectives (DHSS, 1982, p. 1):

1. To improve operational efficiency, reduce administrative costs and increase the flexibility of the operational system to respond to changing requirements.
2. To improve the quality of service to the public, e.g. by treating customers in a less compartmentalised benefit-by-benefit manner and more as 'whole persons' with a range of possible social security business, and by improving the provision of information to the public.
3. To modernise and improve the work of social security staff.

In *A Framework for the Future* the Department also outlined some of the main parameters of the programme. These comprised:

1. Movement towards a unitary claimant database which, in order to avoid excessive size, would be divided into geographical segments linked through a Departmental Central Index (DCI).
2. The adoption of a functional approach to the processing of claims to benefit which would bring together the various common functions, e.g. collating evidence, determining entitlement and implementing decisions, which apply to all benefits.
3. The development of a three-tier system comprising the DCI, area computer centres, where claimant records would be located, and a

network of local offices containing interactive terminals which would constitute the main means of access to the system.
4. A phased programme of implementation in which a number of discrete projects would be implemented in an incremental manner. Fourteen projects were identified at this stage and a number of additional projects were subsequently added in the light of changes to the social security system.

The Operational Strategy can be summarised, according to O'Higgins (1984) as 'a response ... to the problems of cost, size, duplication and complexity' which characterised the administration of social security.

Of the three fundamental objectives mentioned above, the first reflects the interests of the organisation, the second reflects the interests of the customer, while the third reflects the interests of the smaller remaining number of staff. From the outset the DSS has paid greatest attention to the first, the technical task of setting up the necessary hardware and software (Dyerson and Roper, 1989). It has also attempted to construct job specifications which go some way to achieving the third objective (DHSS, 1988b). In this way there is an assumption that if the system is right and the staff are happy, then an improvement in quality of service to the claimant will automatically follow.

'TOP-DOWN' AND 'BOTTOM-UP' APPROACHES TO POLICY-MAKING

One of the reasons why bureaucratic concerns have dominated the development of the Operational Strategy is that the DSS has adopted a 'top-down' approach to policy-making by giving priority to administrative rationalisation, rather than a 'bottom-up' approach in which the system would have been designed to meet the needs and reflect the circumstances of social security claimants.[5] Although the 'top-down' approach to policy-making is clearly the one currently favoured by the government, and was the approach adopted by the DHSS in its recent review of social security provisions (Adler, 1988), it was not always clear that it would be the dominant approach in this case. In the early 1980s the DHSS took over and improved a computer-based welfare benefits information system which had been designed by Nigel Gilbert of the University of Surrey for use by members of the public. The system was evaluated by Epstein (1984) for the DHSS but, in spite of a favourable reaction from the public,[6] the DHSS withdrew its support and took out of service the prototype machines which had been installed in DHSS offices, local Citizens Advice Bureaux, a social services office and a supermarket (Dawson, Buckland and Gilbert, 1990).

Nevertheless, as part of the Alvey programme, a five-year collaborative programme between government, industry, and the universities (Alvey, 1982), the DHSS commissioned, in 1984, the development of a Demonstrator Project. The project comprised the development of four distinct, but complementary 'demonstrators', i.e. adaptations of information technology which would demonstrate what could be achieved, rather than the development of systems which were ready for implementation. Two demonstrators, one designed to assist local social security offices to improve the quality of their decision-making, and one to assist policymakers in drafting social security regulations, were developed by teams drawn from the computer firms ICL and Logica, and from the University of Lancaster and Imperial College, London. The other two demonstrators were 'expert systems' and specifically claimant-oriented.[7]

Developed by the University of Surrey, they comprised an interactive programme to assist claimants with completing forms, and an advice package, intended for those who advise and assist claimants. They provided an opportunity to examine carefully what 'users' might want from a welfare benefits information system, whether they would welcome using computers to obtain information, and who would be likely to use such systems if they were to be provided. In designing these expert systems, it is clear that the Alvey researchers adopted a bottom-up approach by, for example, drawing on a small survey of social security claimants which investigated perceptions of new technology and attitudes towards a computer-based welfare benefits system (Dawson, Buckland and Gilbert, 1990).

However, the DSS appears never to have worked closely with the Alvey researchers and the projects were not carried forward beyond the 'demonstration' stage. A distinctly 'bottom-up' approach seems, therefore, to have had little impact on the DSS.

REDISCOVERING THE OPERATIONAL STRATEGY AND QUALITY OF SERVICE

The lack of commitment to using the strengths of computerisation for the benefit of claimants apparent from the Alvey project is reflected in the DSS's initial failure to address the second objective of the Operational Strategy. This is not to imply that the Department had ignored the service to its claimants entirely. For example, resources had been allocated over several years to improve the physical condition of local offices. In addition the DSS continues to develop its own 'Quality Assessment Package' (QAP), a combination of performance measures (such as waiting times in offices, and the quality of interviews by counter staff) and a customer opinion survey. The QAP is primarily intended for the use of management in setting performance targets and the results are not widely disseminated.[8] The Department has also published an internal report by officials which addressed the problem of low staff morale and poor standards of service in local offices (DSS, 1988c, the 'Moodie Report').

However, these initiatives have largely been pursued independently of the Operational Strategy. Furthermore, in spite of numerous rhetorical references to the 'whole person concept', the Strategy document contained little evidence that much thought had been given to what this might mean.[9]

The impetus for the rediscovery of computerisation's potential contribution to quality of service came from the National Audit Office's (NAO) scrutiny of the implementation of the Operational Strategy (NAO, 1989). Its report criticised delays in the completion of individual projects and the Department's response to them. In particular it found a 117 per cent increase in costs (which rose from £784m in 1982 to £1,700m in 1988) and a 54 per cent decrease in savings (which fell from £1,006m in 1982 to £463m in 1988).[10] The NAO considered that the escalating costs of the Operational Strategy were so serious as to call into question the financial viability of the entire strategy unless improvements in the quality of service, which it recommended in an earlier report (NAO,1988), were taken into account.[11]

PUTTING THE 'WHOLE PERSON' CONCEPT INTO PRACTICE

When the Department became aware of the content of the NAO Report it recognised that little thought had been given, since *A Framework for the Future* in 1982, to what the 'whole person' concept might mean in practice. In response we were commissioned by the DSS to investigate its possible interpretations and implications. In full our terms of reference were as follows:
1. To give some substance to the notion of 'quality of service' by specifying those aspects of service to the public which are most salient.
2. To identify the range of possible interpretations which can be given to the 'whole person' concept.
3. To develop a small number of viable organisational models which could be run on an experimental basis in different local offices.
4. To suggest a set of evaluation criteria in terms of which these models and the Operational Strategy as a whole could be assessed.[12]

It was clear that these terms of reference involved a set of highly normative questions about which we ourselves held strong views and could quite easily have written at great length. However, we were sure that the DSS did not have any particular interest in the views of two university researchers. Rather, we set out systematically to collect and collate the views of a cross-section of informed opinion and by so doing to identify a consensus, where there was one, and a set of coherent alternatives, where more than one view commanded support. It is also clear that these research objectives entailed a substantial modification of the DSS's implicit technological determinism, (i.e. of the assumption, referred to above, that if the system was right and the staff were happy an improvement in quality of service would necessarily follow) in that they implied that an elaboration of the notion of 'quality of service' could lead to experimentation and organisational innovation.

THE CONSULTATIVE EXERCISE

The procedure we chose to adopt is known as the *Delphi Method* (Delbecq *et al.*, 1974; Linstone and Turoff, 1975). Briefly, the Delphi Method consists of a series of questionnaires which require panels of experts to evaluate a number of policy options in a structured way. Their responses to an initial questionnaire are collated and fed back to the panels who are asked to consider them carefully before responding to a second questionnaire. The process enables respondents to reconsider their own responses in the light of arguments which they themselves may not previously have thought of and can be repeated as many times as is considered necessary. The technique is a very effective means of canvassing informed opinion, identifying areas of agreement and disagreement, isolating ideas which need further clarification and developing and refining policy options. It is also a flexible technique which can be adapted to suit the particular research question. In our study respondents were approached twice. Because the Delphi technique is a process of 'distillation' the results of the exercise presented below are from the second questionnaire.

Each questionnaire was divided into sections containing a number of policy options. Respondents were invited to comment in their own words on any or all of the policy options, to identify advantages and disadvantages, to modify the options, to argue in favour or against any of them, and to raise new policy options for consideration. Where appropriate, respondents were invited to assess the *desirability* and *feasibility* of each of the policy options according to two five-point scales as follows:

Desirability
very desirable	+2
desirable	+1
neither desirable nor undesirable	0
undesirable	−1
very undesirable	−2

Feasibility
definitely feasible	+2
possibly feasible	+1
neither feasible nor infeasible	0
possibly infeasible	−1
definitely infeasible	−2

It was important to assess the desirability of policy options in the light of their feasibility. Therefore respondents were also asked to rank the overall importance of the policy options in each section.

Our selection of participants reflected our wish not to seek only the views of those involved in the formulation or implementation of the Operational Strategy, but to canvass a much wider range of opinion. Sampling was problematic since there was no natural population which could act as a sampling frame. The participants were therefore selected to represent the main interest groups and all shades of opinion. We identified four main sub-groups of experts from which to draw our sample:
1. *DSS staff*: including policy-makers and systems analysts from the

Operational Strategy team, local office staff and representatives from DSS trade unions.
2. *Welfare rights/pressure groups:* this group comprised individuals who in some way represent claimants, including pressure groups, welfare rights workers, Citizens Advice Bureaux, Consumer Councils, and local authority Social Work/Social Service departments.
3. *Academics and researchers:* including those with an interest in the administration of social security and in the application of information technology to case-level decision-making.
4. *Other organisations:* this group included individuals with experience of large organisations, such as banks and building societies, and individuals with knowledge and experience of social security administration in the USA, Belgium, Australia and Norway.

Out of the 70 people who agreed to take part we received 56 replies to the first questionnaire, and 43 to the second questionnaire, comprising 11 DSS personnel, 11 welfare rights officers and representatives of pressure groups, 11 academics and researchers, and 10 persons with backgrounds in other organisations or overseas social security administrations.

It will be noted that we did not attempt to canvass the views of claimants directly. This is because the Delphi technique assumes a level of expertise that few claimants can be expected to have. This is not to deny that it would have been helpful to canvass their views by other means. Unfortunately, it was not possible to organise a claimant survey within the time and resources that were available to us. Nevertheless, many of our respondents, particularly those from welfare rights organisations and pressure groups, explicitly adopted a claimant perspective.[13]

The policy options which we asked our panels to address in the two questionnaires[14] were based on the view that the whole person concept could embrace a range of meanings depending on what are regarded as desirable and legitimate activities for the DSS in its administration of the social security system. It seemed to us that the Department could either restrict itself to a *re-active* approach (by merely processing the claims presented to it) or, in addition, adopt some form of *pro-active* role (for example, by providing information, advice and guidance to individual claimants, developing multi-purpose claim procedures, providing help with budgeting or offering to refer claimants to appropriate welfare services). In addition, we argued that 'quality of service' had two dimensions which could be distinguished from each other. On the one hand, it could be taken to refer to the range of provisions provided for the claimant as a social security customer; on the other, it could refer to the treatment of the claimant by the staff of the DSS, i.e. to the idea of *being of service* rather than *providing a service*. This distinction was used as the basis for two of the sections in the Delphi questionnaires.

The social shaping of information technology 237

RESULTS FROM THE CONSULTATIVE EXERCISE

The first section was called 'Span of Departmental Activities' and referred to sixteen specific activities which the DSS either undertakes at present or could undertake in the future. Since we were interested in how broad a role our respondents thought the Department should adopt and where they thought the boundaries between social security and other services and activities should be drawn, we included questions on the provision of money advice, help with budgeting, negotiation with creditors and referral to other agencies; questions on the provision of information, the development of multi-purpose claim procedures, the encouragement of participation in decision-making; as well as questions on the prompt and accurate assessment of claims.

Most of the policy options were regarded as desirable and feasible. Speed and accuracy of claims processing received the highest desirability ratings and were ranked first and second in terms of overall importance. Very high priority was attached to the provision of comprehensive information on benefits and how to claim them, and for explaining how decisions are reached, which were ranked third and fourth. High priority was also attached to the development of multi-purpose claim procedures, to safeguarding the confidentiality of claimant data held on computer, and, interestingly, to greater involvement by the DSS in national and local take-up campaigns. By comparison, much lower priority was given to extending the Department's role through the provision of money advice, budgeting facilities or welfare advice, or even through referrals to agencies providing these services.

The second section, entitled 'Treatment of the Claimant', was concerned with quality of service in the sense of being *of* service. It covered issues such as courtesy, privacy, accessibility, convenience and impartiality. Although all seven policy options were regarded as desirable and feasible, highest priority was given to ensuring that staff treat claimants with courtesy and understanding, and to dealing promptly with claimants who call at the local office. Ensuring that staff treat claimants impartially, that claimants can, if they wish, be dealt with in private, and improving the cleanliness and comfort of waiting areas, formed a middle group. Improving access to local offices for elderly and disabled claimants and extending their opening hours were ranked much lower in overall importance.

It is clear that the operationalisation of the 'whole person' concept will be shaped by financial and technical considerations as well as by whatever is thought to be the legitimate or desirable span of Departmental activities. However, once a choice has been made, there will be implications for the interface between the public and the staff of the Department and for the internal organisation of the office. The introduction of new technology will influence this interface and the internal organisation of the local office in such a way as to promote a particular version of the 'whole person' concept. Two sections of the Delphi questionnaires addressed organisational questions.

The section called 'Organisational Issues' included sixteen questions on the integration of separate assessment procedures for unemployment benefit and housing benefit, the location of offices and their internal organisation, the provision of automated banking facilities, and the need for professional training of staff.

Again most of the policy options were thought of as desirable and feasible. Opening more local offices to serve smaller communities, organising the staff into integrated working groups[15] which could deal with the whole range of benefits and assigning claimants to a team of officers were ranked respectively first, third and fourth equal. Very high priority was attached to the provision of independent courses of training for social security staff which was ranked second. High priority was attached to the provision of an expanded home visiting service, ranked fourth equal, and an improved telephone service ranked seventh. There was considerable support for DSS assessing claims for unemployment benefit, but very little for it assessing claims for housing benefit or for the Department of Employment assessing claims for income support for the unemployed. Very low priority was attached to the development of automated banking facilities for social security claimants.

The section entitled 'Organisational Strategies' asked respondents to assess four organisational models (see Appendix 1) which the DSS put forward for discussion in a Departmental report on *New Technology, Job Design and Organisation* (DHSS, 1988b). These four models all refer to the internal organisation of local social security offices and differ in the extent to which they maintain specialised roles. The immediate adoption of Organisational Model D as the basis for the DSS organising its operations was ranked first, followed by the interim adoption of Organisational Models B and C. There was much less support for the adoption of Organisational Model B or C as the basis for organising its operations. There was very little support for the adoption of Organisational Model A, which most closely resembled the existing organisational arrangements.

The final section in the second questionnaire explored a number of issues of detail raised by the responses to the first questionnaire, including the structure and content of training courses for DSS staff, possible strategies to reduce waiting times in local offices, the relocation of benefit administration from central to local offices, and the integration of specialist functions with the processing of claims.

Training in human relationships was regarded as the most important means of ensuring that staff treat claimants with courtesy and understanding (although the selection and deployment of staff were also regarded as important). Full-time courses and part-time day-release courses for social security staff were preferred to correspondence courses. Among the subjects which training courses ought to cover, greatest priority was attached to the following (in descending order): interviewing techniques, the administration of social security, social security law, and human relations. By contrast, lowest priority was attached to social policy and the social services, and computing in social security.

Assigning more staff to deal with callers and introducing more fast-stream reception points were regarded as the most effective means of ensuring that callers at local offices are dealt with promptly. The strength of support for the local assessment of centrally-administered benefits was less than for most other proposals. Support was greatest for the local assessment of family credit. Among the specialist functions there was greatest support for the inclusion of visiting and the Social Fund into the integrated working groups. There was some backing for the inclusion of appeals and liable relatives staff, but the inclusion of fraud staff was regarded as undesirable.

The responses of the four sub-groups were surprisingly similar. Average rankings of the overall importance of the policy options were calculated for respondents in each group. Few of the differences in the average rankings was statistically significant (even at the 10 per cent level).[16] The only statistically significant differences were found in the section on 'Organisational Issues' and in some of the follow-up proposals in the final section of the second questionnaire. For example, DSS personnel and people from other large organisations were much more in favour of the proposal that the DSS should organise its local office staff in integrated working groups than were welfare rights workers or academics and researchers. In contrast, on the proposal that the DSS should provide an expanded home visiting service for claimants who cannot easily visit the local office, welfare rights workers rated its overall importance significantly higher than DSS staff, though both groups considered the proposal to be desirable. In interpreting the data it must be borne in mind that the numbers involved were small and, on the whole, significance levels were low. The variations in these two sections were, in our view, far less striking than the degree of consensus in the rest of the questionnaire where the rankings of overall importance indicated that some issues were very strongly supported while others received comparatively little support.

CONCLUSIONS FROM THE CONSULTATIVE EXERCISE

Our conclusions from the consultative exercise[17] are structured around the four terms of reference of the research project, i.e. giving substance to the notion of quality of service, interpreting the whole person concept, suggesting a number of organisational innovations that could be assessed experimentally, and devising a package of evaluation criteria by which the performance of the DSS can be judged.

The consultative exercise suggests that the public would most welcome from the DSS a service which offers the highest standards of speed and accuracy in the processing of claims. In addition they would want to be provided with the fullest information about benefits in order to be able to claim all that they are entitled to, and to have confidence that an approach to the DSS would trigger off claims for other benefits for which there is a potential entitlement. They would wish to be able to understand clearly how decisions are reached. There was overwhelming support for the notion that staff should deal with claimants with courtesy and understanding, and assess claims with impartiality. In the local office claimants should be dealt with promptly and, on request, have their business conducted in private. Being *of* service also entailed the provision of clean and comfortable public waiting areas. These findings support the conclusions of the National Audit Office in their scrutiny of DSS local offices (NAO, 1988).

Our respondents attached lower priority to an extension of the DSS's activities beyond the processing of claims. Although many considered the offer of money advice or wider welfare advice to be desirable, there were strong doubts expressed about the appropriateness of the DSS engaging in this sort of activity. Such advice and help should be provided but preferably by bodies that can offer a totally independent assessment. From our reading of the Delphi questionnaires we conclude that our respondents' approach to the notion of the 'whole person' concept can best be captured by the rather narrower notion of the 'whole claimant'. In other words the primary concern of the DSS should be to ensure that all the social security needs of claimants are met, and not to devote resources to expanding into other related areas. The most favoured means of realising the 'whole claimant' concept was an expanded network of local offices serving smaller communities, staffed by 'professionally-trained' officers organised into integrated working groups which can deal with the whole range of social security benefits, including some (such as unemployment benefit and family credit) for which they do not currently have responsibility. There was little support for the assumption in *A Framework for the Future* (DHSS, 1982) that UBOs should remain the normal point of contact for unemployed claimants, but considerable support for the view that the DSS should itself assess claims from unemployed claimants in its local offices.[18] A single accessible point of contact, and the assignment of claimants to a team of staff who would, if necessary, visit claimants in their own homes and with whom claimants could more easily be in telephone contact comprised the model that most respondents endorsed. The immediate introduction of the Organisational Model which represented the highest level of integration within the local office accordingly received the most support.

In reaching this point we have in effect listed a number of experimental conditions that can be implemented and evaluated in a small number of DSS local offices. In practice it is inevitable that problems with implementation will be encountered and that unforeseen consequences will arise. This is why experimentation on a small scale is essential before decisions are taken which would apply to the whole social security system. It is far better to identify and deal with problems at an early stage than suffer the consequences of large-scale difficulties.

CONCLUSION – THE IMPACT OF COMPUTERISATION

> Technologies can be designed ... to open certain social options and close others (MacKenzie and Wajcman, 1985, p. 7).

The Operational Strategy has provided the DSS with the opportunity to restructure its own organisation, and if desired to adopt radical new forms of organisation. It raises the question of whether the traditional Weberian bureaucracy is best suited to the computerised delivery of social security. Thirty years ago, Burns and Stalker (1961) showed that 'mechanistic' systems of management, based on a well-defined division of labour and a clear ascription of responsibility, were less appropriate for micro-electronics firms seeking to exploit rapidly changing market conditions than 'organic' systems of management, in which employees have greater scope to use their own initiative. In an analogous way, computerisation of the social security system holds out the prospect that a unitary form of organisation, based on a cross-benefit division of labour, might be more appropriate than a highly segmented benefit-by-benefit structure such as currently exists.

Advocates of computerisation usually hold out the twin prospects of greater operational efficiency and improved quality of service. However, the costs of computerisation are often, as in the case of the Operational Strategy, so high as to make the pursuit of administrative savings rather doubtful. In these circumstances, the viability of the Operational Strategy is made to rest on its ability to enhance quality of service. The problem here is that the term 'quality of service' is a contested concept (Dworkin, 1986), i.e. a term which can be given a wide variety of meanings. Thus, whether or not computerisation enhances quality of service cannot be assumed *a priori* and depends on which of the several competing conceptions of quality of service is preferred. In addition it depends on the level of resources that are made available for administration. If, as has been suggested, the Treasury were to demand further cuts in staffing levels over and above those which are expected to result from the Operational Strategy to compensate for a projected increase in the cost of social security benefits (Hencke, 1990) this would clearly have a detrimental effect on quality of service whatever conception was adopted. Considerations such as these point to the desirability of specifying what is meant by quality of service in advance of designing a computer system and deciding on the level to which it should be resourced.

Information technology greatly extends the range of organisational possibilities but does not require any one particular form of organisational design. Computerisation allows for a move away from a compartmentalised benefit-by-benefit form of administration towards a more unitary cross-benefit approach without prescribing the type of organisation to implement it. However, if we start with the technology and not the wider objectives such as quality of service, then we succumb to technological determinism and are left merely assessing the impact of the Operational Strategy after the event.

Information technology also carries with it far-reaching implications for adjudication (Schartum, 1987). O'Higgins (1984) warned of the danger that computerisation would allow the complexity of existing social security provisions to be replicated in the computer software and would therefore undermine the need to simplify the statutory framework. However, he failed to note that computer software can cope much more easily with relatively crude rules which permit a 'yes/no' response than with more open-textured rules which call for the exercise of judgement.[19] Thus the replacement in 1988 of supplementary benefit by the simpler income support scheme can, to a large extent be explained by the government's commitment to the Operational Strategy and the difficulty of designing computer software which could have dealt effectively with the complexities of the supplementary benefit scheme. The Operational Strategy may therefore have been largely responsible for the loss of administrative flexibility associated with the assessment of individual cases which, until recently, has been a characteristic of the British social security system, and its replacement by a 'rougher justice' in which all members of a given category are treated alike.[20]

In addressing MacKenzie and Wajcman's question 'what has shaped the technology ...?' we have concluded that the organisational imperatives of the DSS have been the prime forces behind the overall strategy and the detailed implementation of computerisation. Thus, it has been argued that the Operational Strategy promotes the bureaucratic model of administrative justice described by Mashaw (1983). Some of the ideals of this model, e.g. speed and accuracy, were among the most strongly supported by the respondents to our consultative exercise. However, the exercise suggests that the Operational Strategy's potential for promoting the professional treatment and moral judgment models has not been exploited. For example, smaller and more accessible offices, an expanded home visiting service, and the provision of independent courses of training for social security staff, all of which would entail a more professional service, have not featured prominently on the DSS's policy agenda. Similarly, the provision of comprehensive information on benefits and how to claim them, the importance of explaining how decisions are made, and the development of multi-purpose claim procedures, all of which would promote the rights of claimants, have likewise not been emphasised.[21] At the same time the progress made through the Alvey Demonstrator project towards a comprehensive advice package appears to have been lost. As a result the Operational Strategy is likely to emphasise further the bureaucratic features of social security administration. However, the views of the cross-section of informed respondents we consulted give strong support for the argument that bureaucratic improvements should be balanced by an enhancement of the professional and juridical aspects of social security administration. At present the role of the claimant is largely a passive one – the claimant is a provider of information and a receiver of decisions. By enabling claimants to check their own entitlement through advice packages, by providing them routinely with breakdowns of benefit calculations, and with clear explanations of why decisions have been reached, they would have increased knowledge of their own social security status and of the relationship between their circumstances and their benefit entitlement, and would thus have an increased ability to identify errors and to challenge decisions. Computerisation thus provides an opportunity to restructure the power relationship between the claimant and the DSS.

The implementation of the Operational Strategy is well-advanced; whether or not it is still possible to change direction must be an open question. The unstated premise which underlay the consultative exercise was that some options were still open, and the invitation to suggest a small number of organisational experiments which would be carefully evaluated seemed to confirm this. However, there is little evidence that the Department is planning to act on our general conclusions or our specific recommendations.[22] According to the Minister for Social Security, Mr Peter Lloyd, there have been improvements in the speed and accuracy of processing income support claims in recent years,

> ... the average time taken to clear income support claims in 1988-89 has been five days compared with six days the previous year, and there have been a substantial fall in average error rates from 11.6 per cent in 1987-88 to 9.6 per cent in the year to date. (Hansard, 6 February 1989, col. 486).

However, he linked these improvements directly to the social security reforms introduced in April 1988, and not to the implementation of the Operational Strategy. Nevertheless, our respondents were clearly of the view that 'quality of service' entails more than speed and accuracy and should encompass the professional and juridical dimensions of service which the Department appears to have placed little emphasis on so far. In addition, we recommended a number of organisational innovations which could be run on an experimental basis, but there is now little time for the DSS to take up such suggestions as those which emerge from our study. Although we are not able to offer a truly bottom-up approach as we explained earlier, it is still clear that had the views of the consumer been taken more into account by the DSS a different looking service from the one which is emerging might have resulted, a situation reflecting the 'top-down' approach of the DSS in relation to policy-making in general and to the Operational Strategy in particular.[23] Nevertheless, the prospects for change are not necessarily gloomy. In April 1991, the delivery of social security benefits will be devolved from the DSS to a Benefits Agency operating outside the confines of the civil service.[24] It is to be hoped that the new agency is prepared to learn the lessons of the painful development of social security computerisation and give greater prominence to the legitimate demands of claimants than has been the case so far.

NOTES

1. The scale of the Operational Strategy reflects the size and scope of the DSS's responsibilities. In most countries, several government departments are responsible for policy-making, trade unions and other non-governmental bodies are responsible for administration, while public assistance is left to local authorities. In Britain, on the other hand, the DSS has sole responsibility for policy-making and is largely responsible for the administration of public assistance as well as social insurance benefits.
2. In spite of its scale and importance, there has been little social research on the Operational Strategy. Two recent exceptions are Wyatt, 1989, and Dyerson and Roper, 1989.
3. The models are offered as 'ideal types' in the sense that they are abstract yet coherent formulations that contain an internal logic to their structural features. They do not purport to describe reality but to provide models which can be used to analyse and understand observable patterns of behaviour (Weber, 1964).
4. Operational Strategy was not the DHSS's first venture into computerisation. In the mid 1970s computer centres at Reading, Newcastle and Livingston were established for recording information on unemployment benefit, supplementary benefits, pensions, child benefit and national insurance contributions. The CAMELOT project, which ran from 1977 to 1981, was an ambitious attempt to computerise local office tasks, but was abandoned due to poor control and planning and a shortage of programming staff (Dyerson and Roper, 1989, p. 4).
5. The terms 'top-down' and 'bottom-up' have previously been used to describe two contrasting approaches to the study of policy implementation (see, for example, Sabatier, 1986) but are also useful in the analysis of policy-making. In this chapter we are primarily interested in the relationship between computerisation and the social security claimant. We therefore concentrate on the second objective of the Operational Strategy (service to the public) and focus on the extent to which a bottom-up approach has been taken in its development, i.e. by taking into account the views and experiences of claimants. A bottom-up approach could also be applied to the design of systems which seek to enhance the job satisfaction of DSS staff (the third objective of the Operational Strategy), but here again the DSS appears to have acted in a top-down manner. According to Dyerson and Roper (1989, p. 18) the management consultants Arthur Andersen reported in July 1987 that 'the DSS had failed to gauge user requirements or consult local office staff over implementation'.
6. Epstein's conclusions on the public's assessment of the computer are as follows (1984, p. 1):

    Virtually everybody who used the computer – whatever their age, sex, or socioeconomic class – liked it and preferred it to any other way of getting information about welfare benefits. People experienced little difficulty using the computer, and most operated it on their own, without any help from staff.

7. Expert systems are programmes which are driven by a set of rules, usually in the form

    IF <conditions> THEN <conclusion>

    Ultimately, 'ground level' rules would involve facts which only the user would have knowledge of. The programme would ask the user to enter the appropriate values and would then calculate the claimant's eligibility. Programmes using expert systems have considerable advantages over more conventional ones. For example, the fact that the programme's knowledge of benefit regulations is specified entirely in the rules themselves and that these rules are intelligible to people who are not experts greatly strengthens the position of the claimant vis-à-vis the Department. It is possible to display a simplified version of the rules and, in particular, the rules which led to a conclusion so as to convey the reasons behind the programme's recommendations and to tell claimants the implications of their answers so that they can see the purpose of the question and respond with that in mind (Dawson, Buckland and Gilbert, 1990).

8. The first two short reports covering 1987 and 1988/89 respectively were placed in the House of Commons library (DHSS, 1987a; DSS, 1989a). They revealed a generally high level of satisfaction from social security claimants, although there was little difference between the two reports. The latest customer survey generated over 200,000 responses but at the time of writing had yet to be fully analysed by the DSS.

9. There were, however, one or two exceptions. The Operational Strategy assumed that Unemployment Benefit Offices (UBOs) would remain the normal contact point for unemployed claimants but argued that their role should expand 'in accordance with the whole person concept and the one office approach' (sic) to enable unemployed claimants to make initial claims for supplementary benefit at UBOs without having to visit two separate offices. The Operational Strategy also argued for the standardisation of payments and left open the possibility of decentralising decision-making to local offices of those benefits (in particular child benefit and retirement pensions) which were centrally administered.

10. The experience of actual costs bearing little relation to projected costs is not uncommon in large technological programmes (Freeman, 1982). As MacKenzie and Wajcman (1985) write:
    ... economic calculations about technological innovation are open to challenge. They often seem primarily to be used to legitimate decisions already taken, rather than as a rational basis for decision. It is notorious that large technological projects ... almost always end up costing enormously more than initially estimated, in part, at least, because an optimistic initial estimate helps gain support for the project. (p. 18)

11. The NAO found that the estimate of 20,000 staff savings by 1998–99 envisaged by the Department was subject to considerable uncertainty and that a shortfall of 3,400 staff would put the Operational Strategy in danger of not breaking even (NAO, 1989).

12. Because we are primarily concerned in this chapter with the social shaping of the Operational Strategy and not with the impact of computerisation, we do not intend to discuss how we addressed this particular research objective. For a full treatment, however, see Adler and Sainsbury, 1990.

13. In the second questionnaire we asked respondents to indicate the general perspective which they adopted in their assessment of the policy options. Seven of the 43 respondents either did not answer or said they had adopted no particular perspective. Of the remain-

ing 36, 10 said that they had replied from a claimant perspective.
14. Complete lists of the policy options used in the two questionnaires can be found in Part I of Adler and Sainsbury, 1990.
15. These are also two of the conclusions reached in the Moodie Report (DSS, 1988c).
16. A complete list of statistically significant differences can be found Part II of Adler and Sainsbury, 1990.
17. See Part I of Adler and Sainsbury, 1990, p. 12.
18. It has been suggested that this outcome could have resulted from our panels being selected for their expertise of social security rather than the employment services which have traditionally been responsible for unemployment benefit.
19. We are indebted to Martin Partington for drawing this to our attention.
20. The shift to 'rough justice' is usually explained in terms of increases in the size and changes in the composition of the claimant population, the loss of dignity experienced by claimants and the inequitable outcome which resulted from individual assessment.
21. We acknowledge that the DSS has sought to improve and give wider publicity to the leaflets which are available to the public, and that it has sought to promote the take-up of means-tested benefits, particularly Family Credit. However, in doing so it has continued to adopt traditional methods and has eschewed the more imaginative proposals suggested by our respondents.
22. See Adler and Sainsbury (1990, pp. 13–16) for a full list of the recommendations presented to the DSS following the consultative exercise.
23. See also Dyerson and Roper, 1989, pp. 37–38.
24. The government's proposals for the establishment of agencies can be found in *The Next Steps* (DSS, 1989b).

The social shaping of information technology

APPENDIX 1: FOUR ORGANISATIONAL MODELS

In each of the four organisational models 'specialist sections' refer to the following:

(i) Social Fund
(ii) Fraud
(iii) Appeals
(iv) Visiting
(v) Liable relatives

ORGANISATIONAL MODEL 'A'

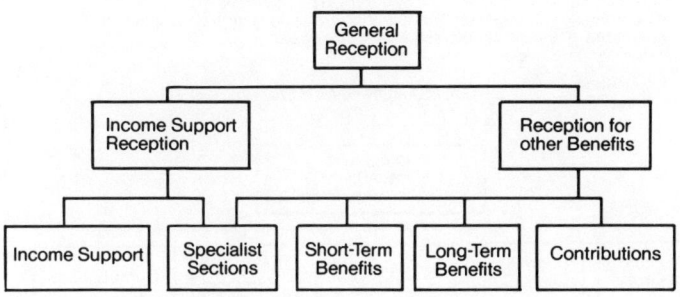

Notes:

(a) Reception: This model retains the current practice in DHSS local offices where there are separate public counters for Income Support claimants and claimants for other benefits. The 'General Reception' point is used to direct claimants to the correct counter, to receive completed claims, and to give out social security information material.
(b) Income Support: This section at present also processes applications for rent and fuel direct payments.
(c) Short-term benefits e.g. sickness benefit
(d) Long-term benefits e.g. retirement pensions, disablement benefit

ORGANISATIONAL MODEL 'B'

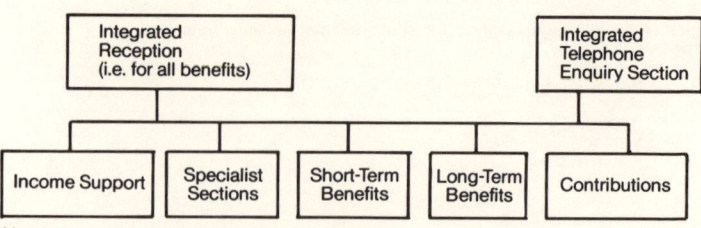

Notes:

(a) This model dispenses with distinct reception points for Income Support and other benefits, such that claimants would no longer be required occasionally to attend different counters in the same office
(b) A comparable arrangement for telephone enquiries would cut down the time 'claimants' calls are transferred within the office.

ORGANISATIONAL MODEL 'C'

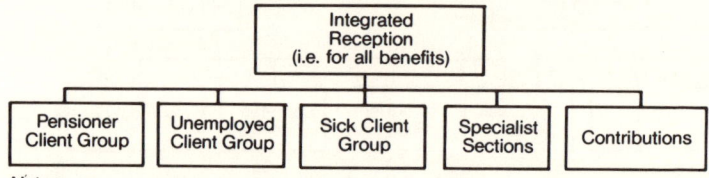

Notes:

(a) This model retains an integrated reception point
(b) Each working group would be specialised in dealing with the benefits associated with a particular client group, but would also be able to process other claims (such as Income Support)

ORGANISATIONAL MODEL 'D'

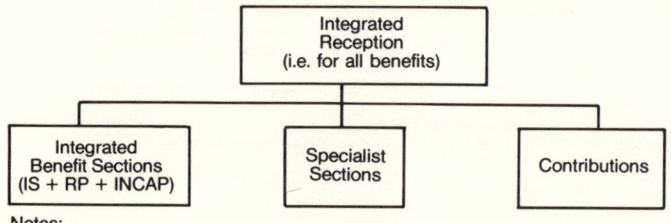

Notes:

(a) An integrated benefit section would be able to deal with the range of benefits which are processed within the local office

14
INTERORGANISATIONAL RELATIONS IN THE PURSUIT OF SOCIAL SECURITY*

BJØRN HVINDEN

Do official policies stressing the importance of collaboration between agencies necessarily mean that these relationships are close in practice? In this chapter it will be argued that the answer is no; there is often a striking contrast between the official emphasis on liaison, and the daily realities of the welfare sector. This situation is brought about by a relative scarcity of resources and the ways in which this is perceived and dealt with by lower-level staff interacting with the public in need. The first part of the chapter presents a general perspective on relationships between agencies in the welfare sector. In the second part of the paper the relations between state income maintenance and other welfare agencies in Norway and Britain are compared.

APPROACHES TO INTERORGANISATIONAL RELATIONS

Within organisational theory one may distinguish between three different approaches to interorganisational relations (Galaskiewicz, 1985):
1. *Resource acquisition and allocation*
    One approach stresses how organisations manage problems related to the acquisition and allocation of relevant resources. Emphasis has been given to (a) the dependence patterns this may create for organisations and (b) how boundary persons manage environmental uncertainty.
2. *Interorganisational coalitions and advocacy*
    Another set of approaches focuses on the formation of coalitions between organisations, for instance to improve the positions of some organisations *vis-à-vis* more dominant organisations or engage in advocacy *vis-à-vis* regulatory bodies.
3. *Legitimation and organisational symbolism*
    A third set of approaches pays special attention to processes of organisational legitimation, e.g. how organisations seek to get identified with highly legitimate symbols and values in society.

---

* I am grateful for encouraging and helpful comments from Michael Adler, Helen Bolderson, Egil Fivelsdal, Axsel Hatland, Michael Hill, Michael Lipsky and Natalie Rogoff Ramsøy.

All in all, models emphasising the acquisition and disposal of relevant resources appear to be the most fundamental. The other models tend to focus on phenomena derived from or determined by resource procurement problems, as perceived by members of organisations. I will take a resource dependence approach as my starting point, and then later integrate some elements from the other approaches.

RESOURCE DEPENDENCE

One early contribution to the development of a resource dependence perspective in interorganisational theory was the seminal work of Levine and White (1961), but unfortunately they restricted their work to voluntary transactions between organisations and excluded relations of dominance. Another important source of inspiration has been the general work on power and dependence by Richard M. Emerson. According to Emerson (1961, p 32):

> The dependence of actor A upon actor B is (1) directly proportional to A's *motivational investment* in goals mediated by B, and (2) inversely proportional to the *availability* of those goals outside the A-B relation (emphasis in original).

Some adjustments were called for when this specification of dependence was to be applied in the context of organisations. In Thompson's (1967, p. 30) reformulation the reference to motivational processes was abandoned altogether:

> an organisation is dependent on some element of its task environment (1) in proportion to the organisation's need for resources or performances which that element can provide and (2) in inverse proportion to the ability of other elements to provide the same resource or performance.

Interorganisational relationships in the welfare sector are largely established through negotiations between individuals, acting on behalf on their agency (Strauss, 1982). If these representatives enjoy *de facto* autonomy in work, their commitment to goals enhanced or hampered by interagency liaison is of considerable interest.

WHAT KIND OF RESOURCES?

Mobilisation of adequate amounts of relevant resources from other organisations is a major challenge for most organisations. What are 'relevant resources' in the context of the welfare sector? In the literature on interorganisational relations most attention is given to resources associated with the maintenance of organisations as identifiable units (e.g. Pfeffer and Salancik, 1978; Aldrich, 1979). In our context, examples of *maintenance resources* would be the funds allocated to agencies through decisions by higher-level regulatory bodies, i.e. central or local government. The political processes determining the size of budgets, programmes of restructuring and even discontinuation of particular agencies, are all

Interorganisational relations

important in their own right. However, in this context I concentrate on resources required in the daily, routine operation of agencies. *Task resources* are conceived as the elements determining how well the agency performs its tasks, rather than just deciding whether it will have any function at all. Agencies are delegated control over some task resources through their mandates, the size and qualifications of their staff, and the financial and technical means they have at their disposal. Other task resources have to be acquired through transactions with other agencies, more or less at the same level. These horizontal transactions will be at the centre of attention in the following discussion.

Task resources which are externally controlled and exchanged through horizontal transactions may, for instance, include the following:

Information

Other agencies frequently control information about clients and their circumstances. Moreover, other agencies can provide information about their regulations and priorities, guidelines for procedure and treatment of clients, expected time of decision in cases, expected or actual outcome of cases, reasons for decisions, or what might otherwise have been done in relation to particular clients.

Staff's service and expertise

The capacity of staff in other agencies and the way in which it is expended, determine how the public in need will be treated; for instance, how well informed people will be about their entitlements and prospects, or how closely clients are followed up and given support at different stages of their dependency. The capacity, efficiency and priorities of other agencies determine how quickly requests for expert opinion are answered.

Possibilities for making referrals

By pursuing restrictive intake policies for new clients, but actively referring registered clients to other organisations, agencies may buffer themselves from environmental pressures (Thompson, 1967, pp. 9-23). In this way agencies may to some extent limit demand and conserve their own task resources (Lipsky, 1980, pp. 132). Through their policies of intake other agencies determine the possibilities for making referrals *from* the focal organisation.

Material resources

Other agencies may control access to financial resources or scarce goods that can easily be translated into financial resources (e.g. housing, residential care or childcare facilities).

As indicated by these examples, the interaction between a given pair of organisations is likely to have several dimensions. For instance, two agencies may have a reciprocal relationship regarding the exchange of information, but a non-reciprocal one when it comes to the appropriation of material resources. Yet, in principle it is possible to summarise this matrix of relationships, that is to assess the overall relationship between the two organisations. On the basis of this assessment, the organisations may be judged to be equally affected by task resources controlled by the other, or one of them may be seen as the more dependent of the two.

But even if we take into consideration the Emerson/Thompson specification quoted previously, it is not completely clear what it means to be 'dependent' on other agencies. In many instances task resources controlled by other agencies are primarily relevant by virtue of their potential effect on the life and well-being of clients, rather than because they are indispensable for the focal organisation in itself. If these resources are not appropriated, the practical consequences may be substantial for clients, but slight for staff. Admittedly, one of the distinctive features of agencies in the welfare sector is that staff often act both on behalf of their agency and their clients, e.g. when staff members approach other agencies to mobilise resources. Some groups of staff have professional training and codes of conduct stating ideals of 'advocacy', i.e. that practitioners should 'use their knowledge, skill, and position to secure for clients the best treatment or position consistent with the constraints of service' (Lipsky, 1980, p. 72). Still, there is some ambiguity in the resource dependence between welfare sector agencies; to some extent it is indirect, being contingent on staff's commitment to norms of service and care.

REACTIONS TO UNILATERAL DEPENDENCE

An organisation may be more or less dependent on other agencies for the acquisition of task resources, and these other agencies will in their turn be more or less dependent on the focal organisation. To simplify, we can imagine an organisational pair where the parties are either dependent on or independent of each other. This will give us the fourfold table in Figure 14.1.

In general, one would expect the degree of symmetry in the relations between the organisations to have substantial consequences for the amount of contact between them, the way in which their decisions-makers perceive the relationship and what kind of strategies they will choose. Obviously transactions between organisations are less likely when neither of them requires resources from the other (I), than if one or both of them need resources controlled by the other (II, III or IV). When there is a reciprocal dependence between organisations (IV), one would expect the two parties to initiate contact to roughly the same extent. If we have a situation of unilateral dependence (II or III), the dependent organisation will probably initiate interaction more frequently than *vice versa* (Cook, 1977, p. 67).

In unilateral dependence relations the organisation controlling the resources will be in a position to determine the terms of transaction. It will have less impetus to accommodate wishes or needs from the other organi-

		Organisation A is dependant on task resources from B	
		No	Yes
Organisation B is dependant on task resources from A	No	I No interdependence	II Unilateral dependence
	Yes	III Unilateral dependence	IV Reciprocal dependence

FIGURE 14.1 Dependence relations in an organisational pair in terms of the flow of task resources

sation than it would if there was a reciprocal interdependence. Unbalanced situations increase the likelihood of a negative outcome from the more dependent organisation's point of view. For instance, decision-makers in the dependent organisation may find it difficult to plan future activities when access to essential resources is controlled by another organisation: this will create a significant element of environmental uncertainty. There may be a fear in the dependent organisation that interagency cooperation will undermine its autonomy. In other words, staff in the dependent organisation are charged with higher transaction costs. Williamson (1981, pp. 552-3) defines transaction costs as 'the comparative costs of planning, adapting and monitoring' in a transaction. Transaction costs may for instance be expressed in 'misunderstandings and conflicts that lead to delays, breakdown, and other malfunctions'. One would expect interorganisational conflicts to be more frequent and sharper in unilateral relations than in reciprocal ones. At the same time disagreements will probably be perceived as more prominent and consequential by staff in the dependent organisation than they will in the dominant organisation.

Staff are likely to seek strategies which may lessen the impact of unilateral dependence. According to the literature on dependence relationships they have three main options (Blau, 1964, p. 124; Aldrich, 1979, p. 270):

A. *Substitution:* They might try to obtain the resources from other channels or find an alternative resource serving more or less the same function.
B. *Force:* They might try to force the organisation controlling the resources to be more cooperative or obliging, and/or create a balance of power.
C. *Avoidance:* They might try to do without the task resource, that is, give less emphasis to the particular goals or tasks involving the utilisation of this resource.

Staff may try to combine these courses of action or pursue them in a sequence, for instance a sequence where option C is chosen if options A and/or B have proved unsuccessful. The conditions for pursuing the three options may be more or less favourable. For example, staff may try to obtain a task resource by establishing a more reciprocal relationship with another organisation, but in many cases it will be difficult to find other organisations that can provide the relevant resource. Sometimes an option might be to convert other resources under the organisation's own control to achieve the objective or task in question. This presupposes that convertible resources are available, and that regulatory agencies will not intervene and stop this alternative use of resources.

Action following from the force option (B) could seek to establish alliances with other corporate actors or bodies. One possibility for the dependent organisation could be to make appeals to higher-level bodies, for instance central government departments. These higher-level bodies may use authoritative or indirect strategies to stimulate interagency cooperation or make the dependent agency more self-sufficient. Moreover, the dependent organisation might expose the practices of the dominant organisation in the mass media, and in this manner mobilise a critical public opinion against it. These two courses of action will be more successful if the clientele of the dependent organisation enjoy general sympathy and legitimacy, and more difficult to pursue if clients are stigmatised in public opinion. A third possibility might be to establish horizontal alliances with other organisations, and by more or less disruptive strategies coerce the dominant organisation to alter its operational policy, for instance by initiating activities which strongly interfere with its effectiveness (Benson, 1975, p. 242). Favourable conditions for this option will be situations where several organisations are dependent on the same dominant unit, where linkages between them may easily be set up, and they have close contact with the public in need.

The avoidance option (C) is not feasible if the resource is required to accomplish a vital objective or primary task of the dependent organisation. But if there is some slack in the working of the organisation, or the goal mediated by this resource is marginal (or can be defined as marginal), the scope for this course of action will be greater. This means that the interorganisational consequences of internal goal-setting in organisations may be very significant indeed.

OPERATIONALISATION OF GOALS

The official goals of organisations in the welfare sector tend to be vague, ambiguous and sometimes in conflict. Before the actual implementation of welfare programmes can take place, goals have to be operationalised, i.e. translated into tasks or priorities of time and effort for the personnel concerned. The results of this process are operational goals, i.e. those aims that are embedded in actual operating policies, and in the ends sought through the daily decisions and activities of staff (Perrow, 1961). Even in income maintenance organisations some areas of work are less tightly controlled than others, and local units have at least some latitude: high priority may be given to some aims and practice while others can potentially be renounced or abandoned altogether.

Sometimes it is implied in the formal remit of agencies that staff should engage in interagency cooperation to activate resources. Frequently cooperation is mandated: instructions, regulations and procedures are imposed on relationships by legislative or administrative rulings (Hudson, 1987, p. 179). In other instances the relevant actors in the organisation decide in which circumstances interagency cooperation might be helpful and what kind of links would be appropriate.

But who are the relevant actors? In the literature on interorganisational relations it is often more or less taken for granted that they are managers or higher-level administrators in agencies; *their* views and perceptions are thought to determine what interaction will take place with other organisations. But one of the salient features of agencies in the welfare sector is that even lower-level staff have considerable contact with outside bodies. For instance, when income maintenance agencies are establishing eligibility for cash benefits, staff may interact extensively with employees of other organisations, either because information controlled by these organisations is required in the assessment or because officers are approached by other agencies with queries about outcomes of claims.

Still it could be argued that it is the opinions and decisions of senior personnel of agencies that matter, and that the activities of lower-level staff largely reflect agency policies as decided by managers. However, although these decisions certainly are important constraints on the decisions of lower-level staff, there is rarely a direct or simple one-to one relationship between the two. At least in some areas or subsectors of work, lower-level staff enjoy some *de facto* latitude or autonomy from their superiors. The main reason for this lies in the character of the tasks in question: conditions of work are shaped by the differences in the circumstances and behaviour of human beings. These widely differing conditions are difficult to predict and anticipate in rules and instructions. It is impractical that all problems and ambiguities that employees encounter in the course of their work should be presented to superiors. A considerable part of their work is carried out in direct interaction, either face-to-face or by telephone, with the public or with representatives of other organisations. It would neither be possible nor appropriate that superiors should control and monitor all these transactions. Apart from this, various situational factors will generate and sustain an element of autonomy: inconsistencies in the instructions and guidance that staff are expected to follow and insufficient time and other resources to carry out tasks as prescribed. Administrators may be engaged or difficult to get in touch with at short notice. As a result, lower-level staff have to make a large number of decisions on their own in the course of their work. Although many of these individual decisions may seem small and inconsequential, the aggregate effect may be substantial. From this point of view the 'motivational investment' of lower-level staff are of great interest.

What factors determine which operational goals and tasks are given priority by lower-level staff members? These goals and tasks are to some extent influenced by official aims and decisions made by senior staff. In addition, staff have usually internalised norms of service and care in that they are dedicated to helping people. This kind of general commitment to service and care may have been reinforced through occupational training or subsequent organisational socialisation. Experience of dealing with the public and other agencies, and the pressures staff are exposed to in the course of their work are also important. Lipsky (1980) suggests that when 'street-level bureaucrats' are confronted with shortage of resources, they may obtain a better fit between capabilities and objectives if they modify their conceptions of their tasks, and their clientele. If some operational goals are consistently difficult to achieve, they may be abandoned or redefined so that they become easier to accomplish. Considerations such as these result in a continuous process of defining and redefining operational goals.

COOPERATION BY MANDATE OR RESOURCE CONTROL?

To the extent that existing links between lower-level agencies are weak or non-existent and decision-makers in regulatory bodies want liaison and coordination to be strengthened, they have at least two strategic options[1]:

Authoritative strategies

Regulatory bodies may instruct agencies to cooperate more closely by specifying relations (e.g. regulation of contact, referrals, resource sharing etc.), or by establishing strict routines for securing accountability (e.g. frequent monitoring and evaluation exercises) (Benson, 1975, p. 244). These strategies are aimed at developing mandated liaison and coordination between agencies.

Indirect strategies

Regulatory bodies may restructure the arenas of interaction between lower-level agencies by altering resource channels (Benson, 1975, p. 243). If interagency problems or lack of cooperation have been caused by imbalanced resource flows, regulatory bodies may give the dependent party control over task resources needed by the dominant organisation. This kind of change is likely to make the dominant organisation somewhat more responsive to requests from the dependent organisation.

Both kinds of strategies may have some influence on actual interorganisational relations at local level. However, in light of the theoretical framework presented here, indirect strategies will probably be more effective than authoritative ones. Frequent monitoring represents a substantial cost since it requires the expenditure of time and money. More specifically, the impact of mandated liaison is likely to be limited unless three conditions are satisfied: (1) There must be a potential for some kind of reciprocal exchange of resources between the agencies in question. (2) Staff in these agencies must feel that interorganisational relations contribute to the accomplishment of high priority operational goals. (3) The value of the resources that can be mobilised through interagency contacts must be seen by staff to outweigh the transaction costs. In other words, if one or both of the agencies are relatively self-sufficient or have access to other resource channels, or if the goals mediated by these resources are defined as marginal by staff, or if interagency liaison has been experienced as threatening agency autonomy, cumbersome or too time-consuming, stable interagency relationships are less likely to materialise. Consequently, regulatory bodies' power to change the distribution of control over task resources among agencies is probably more significant than their control over the official policies and objectives of agencies.

MAIN CASE: RELATIONS BETWEEN INCOME MAINTENANCE AND SOCIAL SERVICES IN NORWAY AND SCOTLAND

Institutional and organisational arrangements

There are substantial similarities as well as significant differences between the institutional structures of state income maintenance and local social services in Norway and Britain. In both countries national insurance schemes, supplemented by non-contributory non-means-tested benefits, play central roles in governmental income maintenance programmes, while personal social services are the responsibilities of local authorities. The major differences in institutional arrangements are the following:

- In Britain, social assistance (means-tested, non-contributory cash benefits known first as national assistance, then as supplementary benefit and currently as income support) has since 1948 been provided by central government and administered alongside national insurance and other social security benefits while in Norway social assistance is provided by local authorities and administered through social services departments (Parry, 1986; Kuhnle, 1986).
- Unlike their British counterparts, Norwegian social services have a statutory, although marginal role in the assessment of claims for state benefits. According to the National Insurance Act 1966, social services departments may be requested to provide information about the social circumstances of claimants. This information, in the form of 'social reports' produced by social workers, is mainly required for the assessment of disability-related benefits. Consequently there is a small, but significant difference in organisational arrangements: in Norway local offices of the national insurance administration do not have any home visiting staff while, at least until recently, there have been a number of

visiting posts within local offices of the Department of Social Security in Britain.
- Within the Norwegian national insurance scheme there are particular means-tested 'transitional allowances' aimed at lone parents (Hatland, 1986, p. 38). After its introduction in the early 1970s the benefit for separated and divorced mothers was administered and partly financed by local authorities for an interim period. When this benefit was finally incorporated into the national insurance scheme in 1981, it was stated explicitly by the Norwegian central government that there should be close liaison between local offices of the national insurance administration and local social services departments regarding this group of recipients. The idea was that lone parents in receipt of transitional allowances ought to be encouraged to prepare themselves for the day when this allowance would no longer be payable, for instance by taking part in vocational training, and that it would be helpful if the two separate agencies were to collaborate closely with each other.

MANDATED COOPERATION?

In two specific areas, the assessment of disability-related claims and the preparation of lone parents in receipt of transitional allowance for financial independence, cooperation between the state income maintenance agency and local authority social service departments in Norway has been mandatory. There has been no equivalent to this mandated cooperation between local offices of the Department of Social Security and local authority social services in Britain, although general guidance, issued from time to time by the (then) Department of Health and Social Security and other bodies, has encouraged liaison and cooperation between the two kinds of agencies. In one particular area, the operation of the Social Fund, which was introduced in April 1988, consultation and liaison have been given special emphasis (DHSS, 1987b, paras 1038-1050). All in all, however, mandated cooperation between the two agencies in Britain seems to have been considerably weaker than in Norway.[2]

INTERAGENCY RELATIONS IN NORWAY AND SCOTLAND COMPARED

Through an exploratory case study carried out in Norway and Scotland I attempted to ascertain how the differences in interagency relationships described above worked out in practice (Hvinden, 1988b). The main results were as follows:
- In both countries social workers in local authority social services departments acted as go-betweens on behalf of clients *vis-à-vis* state income maintenance agencies. However, this advocacy role was considerably more developed in Scotland and figured more prominently in the work of the Scottish social workers. In Norway the possibility of paying out social assistance seemed to function as an alternative to pursuing an advocacy role in relation to the national insurance admin-

istration. This tendency was found most clearly in social services departments in the larger cities.
- There was a striking difference in the degree of symmetry in the relationships between the agencies. In Norway a large majority of staff in both agencies had regular contact with representatives of the other agency, and the two groups of staff apparently initiated contact to more or less the same extent. Apart from routine exchange of information and contacts resulting from the advocacy role of social workers, requests by national insurance staff for social reports and, to a lesser extent, regarding single parents, necessitated a degree of contact between the two agencies. In Scotland the relationship was clearly more asymmetrical: most of the contact was initiated by social workers and related to advocacy efforts of social workers. Occasionally social security staff initiated contact with social workers, for instance when they came across children or elderly people whom they felt might be at risk, but such contacts were clearly exceptional.
- In both countries, staff in each agency had a number of grievances regarding the other agency, and to a great extent the contents of specific complaints were similar. There were parallels between the criticisms expressed by Norwegian and Scottish social workers. Similarly, the comments made by staff in Norwegian national insurance offices and by staff in Department of Social Security offices in Scotland had much in common. However, while the two Norwegian groups gave the impression of being dissatisfied to nearly the same degree, Scottish social workers tended to find their relations with social security staff much more difficult than vice versa. Scottish social workers seemed to be considerably more displeased with the quality of interagency relationships that their Norwegian colleagues. Typically Scottish social workers were sharper and more emotional in their criticisms than the other three groups of staff. Confrontation appeared to characterise interagency relationships more frequently in Scotland than in Norway.

STAFF'S REACTIONS TO INTERAGENCY PROBLEMS

In both countries one could observe examples of how staff reacted to problems of acquiring needed resources:
- As noted above, one option might be to attempt to find substitutes (option A). For instance, Norwegian social workers found that national insurance staff tended to be rather inflexible in their interpretation of the rules for rehabilitation allowance. There seemed to be a tendency to let clients become long-term recipients of social assistance instead of pursuing an advocacy role *vis-à-vis* the national insurance office. Scottish social workers did not have this option: the Section 12 payments they might be involved in, were tightly controlled and the amounts of money that were payable very limited indeed.
- Another option might be to build alliances with other agencies to

influence the agency controlling needed resources (option B). Examples of this were most clearly evident in Scotland. At least until the social security reforms implemented in 1988, there had been effective alliances between social work departments and a large number of voluntary welfare rights groups. These alliances had supported benefit take-up campaigns with considerable success. Through their scale and timing these campaigns disrupted the normal functioning of the Department of Social Security offices, and this meant that control over the access to cash benefits (e.g. single payments) became temporarily less tight and strict.
- Staff could also give less emphasis to tasks or operational goals mediated by the resources controlled by other agencies (option C). I have already indicated that some Norwegian social workers found it so difficult to get a positive response from the national insurance offices that they relinquished attempts to realise rehabilitation plans. Some Scottish social workers defined the task of assisting people in sorting out social security problems as being outside their function, and referred people with such problems to welfare rights agencies or the Department of Social Security. Apart from situational factors, for instance pressures of work and lack of up-to-date knowledge of the benefit system, this was justified by reference to professional ideology. Finally staff members in Norwegian national insurance offices expressed concern that because of delays in the submission of social reports, they requested such reports less frequently although this meant that the circumstances of the claimant was less thoroughly elucidated. Some staff members felt that the lack of cooperation with social workers concerning single parents in receipt of transitional allowance meant that it was difficult to achieve very much in terms for motivating them to prepare for the termination of the benefit.

While the resource dependence between the two agencies was reciprocal in Norway, it was unilateral in Britain. As expected on the basis of the theoretical framework outlined above, the interaction between the two agencies was more symmetrical, while interagency relations appeared to be more harmonious in Norway than in Britain (Scotland). In both countries but particularly in Scotland staff developed several different ways of handling interagency dependence and domination through (A) substitution, (B) alliances, and (C) avoidance strategies.

RESTRUCTURING OF INTERAGENCY RELATIONS?

Recent changes in both countries illustrate how the opportunity structure of staff may be seriously affected by the intervention of regulatory bodies:
- In Norway a continuous growth in expenditure on social assistance in the late 1980s has become a matter of increasing concern (Hvinden, 1988a). One consequence of this is that councillors in local authorities have intervened to regain some of the decision-making power they

delegated to staff in social services departments in the late 1970s and early 1980s. Rules of eligibility have been tightened, and instructions and guidance regarding assessment and levels of payments have been made more stringent. Social workers have been put under heavy pressure to become more effective in referring clients to other agencies. In particular, there is considerable pressure to refer young unemployed people claiming social assistance to employment exchange offices (job centres) and to encourage middle-aged and elderly long-term recipients of social assistance to claim national insurance benefits, particularly rehabilitation allowance and invalidity pension. This means that Norwegian social workers will be less able to use social assistance as an alternative to the financial support clients might obtain from the national insurance scheme (option A), and consequently, that is has become more difficult to pursue avoidance strategies (option C).

- In Britain the introduction of the income support scheme in April 1988 has probably meant that there is less scope for the take-up campaigns of the welfare rights movement. The activity of welfare rights agencies was, to a large extent, based on encouraging people to claim 'extras', that is variable elements like additional requirements and single payments under the supplementary benefit scheme. As a consequence of the changes introduced in April 1988, the British scheme for means-tested assistance was made somewhat simpler and coherent in structure, and the variable elements became smaller, more automatic or more tightly controlled (Dilnot and Webb, 1989). There appears to have been substantial misgivings in welfare rights agencies about whether they should help people to claim the community care grants, budgeting loans and crisis loans which replaced single payments. To the extent that welfare rights agencies have been put on the defensive, there will be less scope for formal or informal alliances between these agencies and social workers in social services departments (option B).

These examples illustrate how policies implemented by regulatory bodies may restructure the field of interagency relations by altering the distribution of control over resources and the opportunity structure of the agencies concerned.

REFERENCE CASE: INCAPACITY BENEFITS AND VOCATIONAL REHABILITATION

The main income maintenance agency of Britain appears to be more self-contained and self-sufficient than its Norwegian counterparts. This difference in institutional design emerges even more clearly if we compare the particular programmes aimed at people whose capacity to work have been diminished. In both countries there is a division of labour between agencies providing income replacement and agencies offering services: while incapacity benefits are granted by state income maintenance agencies, labour market authorities are the major agencies for information, advice and expert opinion related to vocational rehabilitation. Moreover, employment agencies also provide a substantial part of the actual rehabilitation services, for instance in the form of centres offering assessment of residual functional capacity and suitable work, help to restoring working fitness, sheltered work and vocational training courses.

However, the two kinds of agencies are designed to operate much more separately in Britain than in Norway. When Norwegian national insurance offices are assessing claims for incapacity benefits, they are expected to maintain close contact with rehabilitation officers in employment exchange offices, and the latter have a statutory duty to provide the information or expert opinion requested from national insurance staff. By contrast, staff in the British Department of Social Security can hardly be said to have a mandated role in identifying those claimants who could benefit from vocational rehabilitation (Brown, 1984, pp. 333-7). Attention appears to be directed primarily towards the question of whether claimants may be considered fit for some kind of work or not. These judgments are made by doctors (the claimant's general practitioner or Department of Social Security doctors) and by lay staff in the department, whereas vocational rehabilitation staff, e.g. disablement resettlement officers, do not have any statutory role in the assessment (Mitchell, 1985). If a claimant is considered capable of some kind of work, it is largely up to him or her to decide whether to approach a disablement resettlement officer to get help with employment.

To summarise, the elements of mandated cooperation between the administration of incapacity benefits and vocational rehabilitation services are considerably stronger in Norway than in Britain. There appear to be almost no formal links between incapacity benefits and vocational rehabilitation in Britain. To what extent there are informal links is difficult to judge on account of the lack of research in this field in Britain. In Norway, the results of a few studies and reviews suggest that there is a substantial flow of resources between national insurance offices and vocational rehabilitation services (Grandaunet and Johnsen, 1984; Statskonsult, 1988; Arbeidsdirektoratet, 1989). On the other hand, the actual amount of contact and the actual number of referrals may be less than indicated by the formal mandates (SSB, 1983; TL, 1987; Noreik 1983, 1988). Currently attempts are being made by the Norwegian Government to ensure more effective liaison and coordination at local level, and this will probably improve interagency relations to some extent. However, dramatic changes are improbable unless the basic pattern of resource control between the agencies is altered. Thus in both countries more detailed examinations of interagency relations in practice are called for.

SUMMARY AND CONCLUDING REMARKS

We have discussed the relationship between state income maintenance and other welfare agencies (local authority social services and vocational rehabilitation) in Norway and Britain. The mandates to liaise and cooperate were stronger and more explicit in the Norwegian case. Officers in the Norwegian state income maintenance agency were more dependent on social and vocational services than their British counterparts. In both countries, local social services had numerous clients who required financial support from the state income maintenance agency. However, it was not evident that vocational rehabilitation services in either country experienced a similar need for contact with the state income maintenance agency.

According to the analytical framework presented in the first part of the chapter, unilateral resource dependence of one agency on another will produce more tense or defective relationships between them than reciprocal resource dependance between two agencies. The results of the main case-study suggested that there were indeed more antagonistic relationships and more confrontations between social workers and officials of the state income maintenance agency in Britain than in Norway. The study also demonstrated how lower-level staff in both countries reacted to relations of unilateral dependence through substitution, force and avoidance strategies. However, recent policy changes were about to restructure interagency relations by altering the distribution of control over resources, and this was likely to limit the opportunity for pursuing such strategies.

The analytical framework presented in the chapter provided a good basis for comparative research on relations between social security and other welfare agencies. Cross-national comparative research is generally defined as research that systematically studies similar phenomena in different national settings (Antal, Dierkes and Weiler, 1987, p. 22). Moreover, it is often specified that factors at more than one level should be included in the analysis and that the relationships between the phenomena in focus and their national context should be spelled out (Przeworski and Teune, 1970, p. 50; Lammers and Hickson, 1979, p. 5; Nowak, 1989). In the second part of this chapter we have linked institutional structures (i.e. the mandates of income maintenance, social services and vocational rehabilitation agencies) to organisation processes (i.e. to patterns of resource dependence and of interaction between staff in the agencies). In so doing, we have succeeded in meeting one of the fundamental challenges of comparative research; translating observed differences between phenomena in different countries into analytical variables. By focusing on patterns of resource dependence, we have been able to develop a unitary framework for comparing relations between social security and other welfare agencies in widely different socio-economic and political settings. However, in order to establish the generality of our findings and our interpretations of them, more research is called for. The analysis presented in this chapter could be taken further by studying the relationship between social security and other welfare agencies in other countries. Research of this kind could even point the way towards a more general analysis of social security as a social institution.

NOTES

1. Sometimes a third option may be to merge two or more agencies into one. This kind of reorganisation means that *inter*-agency relations are substituted for *intra*-agency relations.
2. I carried out a small follow-up study in November 1988, seven months after the introduction of the Social Fund, to see to what extent this had resulted in more contact between the agencies being initiated by social security staff. The results suggested that there was no unequivocal tendency in this direction.

15
SOCIAL INJUSTICE: THE DIFFERENTIAL ENFORCEMENT OF TAX AND SOCIAL SECURITY REGULATIONS

DEE COOK

INTRODUCTION

This chapter is primarily concerned with the social injustices which are perpetuated and reproduced through the enforcement practices of two crucial government departments – the Department of Social Security (DSS) and the Inland Revenue – whose activities symbolise the alleged redistributive functions of the modern British welfare state. Although empirical evidence does *not* support the view that the post-war British welfare state has effected any fundamental redistribution of income and wealth (Byrne, 1987), there is nonetheless a powerful mythology, pervading both political and popular discourse, which sustains the notion of the state as a latter-day equivalent to the folk-hero Robin Hood who took from the rich to give to the poor (Cook, 1989a). As will be argued more fully below, such ideologies inevitably constitute taxpayers as 'givers' to the state and social security claimants as 'takers' from it. This chapter examines what happens when these givers and takers engage in fiddling at the state's expense.

The research upon which the paper is based was conducted between 1984 and 1988.[1] However, 1988 saw dramatic changes in both taxation and social security policy in Britain, the former through a 'giveaway' Budget for the rich in March 1988, the latter through the implementation of the Social Security Act 1986 in April 1988. In addition, the vocabulary of social security changed: means-tested supplementary benefit was replaced by income support and later that year the health and social security functions of the Department of Health and Social Security (DHSS) were split into two. For the purposes of this chapter, the main analysis refers to the pre-1988 situation and hence uses the appropriate terms – supplementary benefit, administered by the DHSS. However, where current issues are under discussion, income support and the DSS will be referred to. But despite the semantics, the fundamental problem addressed here persists: the political, departmental and popular responses to the rich who fiddle their taxes and the poor who fiddle social security benefits remain inconsistent and unequal. The 1988 Budget and social security reforms have only accentuated this disparity by making the poor yet poorer and the rich richer still.

Those who defraud the state by fiddling welfare benefits and by fiddling personal taxes commit essentially similar economic crimes – making false statements to government departments in order to gain illegal financial advantage from the state. The outcome is identical – loss of state revenue – though the costs for the state of the two forms of fraud do differ: all available evidence supports the view that losses from tax evasion far outweigh those arising from benefit fraud. For example, the DSS recently indicated that for 1988/9 it had exceeded its target of 'saving' £240 million in benefits as a result of investigatory efforts. These 'savings' are calculated on a highly dubious, notional basis and probably reflect ministerial targets rather than verifiable amounts defrauded, but even if such figures were to be accepted, the £240 million allegedly saved by DSS investigations is clearly dwarfed by the £877 million that was actually recouped as a result of the Inland Revenue's counter-evasion work in 1988 (Cook 1989a; Board of Inland Revenue, 1988).

Despite these differences in the relative scale of social security and tax fraud, far more resources are directed towards the investigation of the former than the latter. In the 1980s the manpower directed to DHSS (and now DSS) anti-fraud work increased dramatically despite massive overall cutbacks in civil service staffing (Smith, 1985). But, at the same time, the highly successful counter-evasion work of the Inland Revenue has been jeopardised by lack of trained staff and, arguably, also by lack of political commitment (Cook, 1989b; Board of Inland Revenue, 1987 and 1988).

What follows will attempt to analyse how such disparities are produced and justified. The following themes will be used to structure this analysis:

1. The historical (and ideological) construction of taxpayers as *givers to* and welfare claimants as *takers from* the state.
2. The official policies and effective practices adopted to regulate those who are perceived as the economic 'successes' and the 'failures' of our society. Ultimately, enforcement policies stress seeking the *compliance* of the former, but involve *coercion* of the latter.
3. Current political emphases on the alleged values of the *enterprise culture* and the parallel denunciation of the evils of the *benefit culture*, effectively justifies different investigation techniques and different punishments for the 'enterprising' taxpayers and 'idle benefit scroungers' who fiddle the public purse.

GIVE AND TAKE

In order to analyse contemporary discourses about social security and taxation it is first necessary to identify the historical roots of our conceptions of 'givers' to and 'takers' from the state. For instance, the vocabulary associated with the 'takers' (the poor) in the 1980s echoes that of the 1834 Poor Law which asserted that:

> every penny bestowed that tends to render the condition of the pauper more eligible than that of the independent worker, is a bounty on indolence and vice. (quoted in Fraser, 1973, p. 35)

This argument and its imagery was still evident over a century later when, for example, Conservative MP Rhodes Boyson (later to become Minister for Social Security), wrote that

> The moral fibre of our people has been weakened. The state which does for its citizens what they can do for themselves is an evil state: and the state which removes all choice and responsibility from its people and makes them like broiler hens will create an irresponsible society. No one cares, no one bothers – why should they when the state spends all its energies taking money from the energetic, successful and thrifty to give to the idle, the failures and the feckless? (Boyson, 1971)

The moral hazard which the very claiming of welfare benefits poses is a recurrent theme in New Right commentaries:

> We are breeding a race which will regard dependence on the taxpayer as a normal state of affairs. Already the young claim social security without hesitation, as a matter of right. (Parker, 1982)

At the 1988 Conservative Party Conference, Social Security Secretary John Moore combined and emphasised these traditional concerns about morality, idleness, incentives and the 'undeserving poor':

> Is it right that an able-bodied adult can draw unemployment benefit simply by signing on once a fortnight without making any real effort to find work? ... Is the hope of a council flat and a guaranteed income a factor in unmarried teenage pregnancy? (*The Guardian*, 13.10.88)

Moreover, in relation to lone parents he later commented that the government should be 'wary of providing particular benefits which can erode the sense of personal responsibility and adversely distort behaviour' (*The Guardian*, 18.1.89). Margaret Thatcher has, more recently, relaunched this moral crusade against 'fatherless families', arguing that they represented a legacy of the 1960s permissive society which denied children 'the fundamental right to be brought up in a *real* family' - and also cost the state over £1 billion in 1989 (*The Guardian*, 18.1.90, my emphasis added).

It is significant that this 'new' undeserving poor - lone mothers and the able-bodied unemployed – has been the primary focus for the most intrusive forms of state regulation in recent years, notably through randomised surveillance by Special Claims Control Units (SCCUs) from 1981 to 1986 and, more recently, through the well-publicised activities of DSS and Department of Employment 'Dolebusters'. This disciplinary regulation has been accomplished under the guise of combating 'fraud and abuse' (Smith, 1985: Cook, 1989a; BBC 40 Minutes, *Dolebusters*, 20.10.88). (The techniques used to this end will be discussed later).

Important distinctions between fraud (illegality) and abuse (an essentially subjective term) have become blurred (NACRO, 1986) in popular and political discourses - perhaps deliberately so. For example, Minford argues that 'avoidable need' should not be relieved by the state, in order that 'self-inflicted suffering' will be deterred. Consequently, 'those who have illegitimate children will suffer: illegitimacy is therefore discouraged' (Minford, 1987, p. 81). Illegitimacy and able-bodied unemployment are both currently 'discouraged' through the formal and informal targeting of individuals who are, allegedly, 'fraud-prone' because they belong to an 'undeserving' claimant category. Groups of claimants are, therefore, regarded as 'scroungers' simply because of certain imputed personal characteristics that are seen to render them 'undeserving'. Significantly, these are the same characteristics that concerned nineteenth century moralists – idleness, promiscuity, lack of responsibility!

The twentieth century version of the scrounger mythology thus conflates 'fraud' and 'abuse', confuses issues of criminality and personal pathology, and replaces the notion that individuals are entitled to benefit as of *right* with the notion that they must prove they are deserving of state support.

However, the philosophy of discouragement (or deterrence) advocated by Minford clearly does work in practice: many claimants fail to claim the means-tested benefits to which they are entitled, perhaps in part because they fear coercive departmental policing and/or public disapproval. It is not surprising, then, that the DSS expected claims for income support in 1988/9 to be 26 per cent lower than claims for (the comparable) supplementary benefit in the previous year (*The Guardian*, 31.10.88 and 31.1.89). But this is not necessarily regarded as 'a problem' at all, as a spokesman for the influential Institute of Directors indicated:

> Some think these low take-up rates a weakness of the present system: we consider them a strength. First, a low take-up rate saves large amounts of government spending. Second, it is in substantial measure the result of self-selection amongst potential users of the welfare system. Some people are reluctant to accept such payments... for reasons of self-respect. We see nothing wrong in this sentiment and many would consider it admirable. (quoted in NCASSC, 1985, p. 2.)

If 'takers' (the undeserving poor) have in recent years increasingly become the object of state regulation and sanction, then the 'givers' (enterprising taxpayers) have increasingly been relieved of the 'burden' of 'red tape' and the state's allegedly stifling regulations. The traditional British hatred of state intrusion and of paying personal taxes is well exemplified in Disraeli's maxim that there are only two inevitabilities in life – death and taxation! Moreover, according to one commentator from the Institute of Economic Affairs (who was formerly the Secretary of the Inland Revenue Staff Federation and later a Labour Cabinet Minister) 'There are *no* ethics in taxation. There is no moral law in taxation' (Houghton, 1977). (However, ethics and morality are apparently upper-

Social injustice

most when judging who is deserving of poor relief!). In a similar vein it has been argued that 'Taxation has no merit in itself. It is but a necessary evil and should be limited to the lowest level possible.' (Boyson, 1978)

Acting firmly within the logic of this tradition, successive Thatcher governments have sought to ease the 'burden' (for high income-earners), of paying progressive personal taxes in order to give greater incentives for the release of their entrepreneurial spirit. This was certainly the rationale behind the 1988 Budget which reduced the highest rate of income tax from 60 per cent to 40 per cent. Mrs Thatcher announced that Chancellor Nigel Lawson's Budget was 'the obituary for the doctrine of high taxation ... the epitaph for socialism', and *The Times* (16.3.88) asserted that it put 'incentives and opportunity in place of old fashioned egalitarianism'. But one 'Tory entrepreneur', supposedly freed from the burden of high taxation to follow opportunity and incentive, commented

'I think Nigel's taking the piss now ... I don't think anyone will work any harder. I certainly won't work any harder. I'll just spend more ... People will have three skiing holidays instead of one. *(New Statesman and Society,* 25.3.88)

When taxpayers who are regarded as 'givers' to the state fiddle their taxes, they often invoke general criticisms of the role of progressive taxation in order to justify their actions and, in so doing, link the twin issues of taxation and welfare provision. Taking this argument a stage further, some commentators may seek to justify illegal evasion of taxes as a form of 'backdoor' tax revolt against the (mis)use of taxpayers money for subsidising 'tax consumers' (Burton, 1985). Similarly tax avoidance and evasion can be represented as 'heartening' evidence that the rich can save their wealth from their 'rapacious fellow citizens' (Shenfield, 1968, p. 26). The hard-pressed taxpayer is not only represented as a 'giver' to the state, but as a victim, of both the bureaucracy of taxation, and the idle poor who are subsidised at the taxpayer's expense.

The images of the idle poor and the hard-pressed taxpayer are crucial in understanding differential social, political and judicial responses to tax and benefit fraud. But beneath these images lie fundamental contradictions between the ideals of collectivism (realised through citizens willingly paying taxes to finance state welfare), and *individualism* (realised through the entrepreneurial spirit and the accumulation of personal wealth). According to the latter perspective, tax revenues evaded can be seen as belonging to the citizen, who merely fails to pass them on to the over-regulating state. According to the collectivist approach, taxpayers who fiddle are seen as failing to keep their side of the citizenship bargain with the state, although they still retain the economic status of 'givers'. But whichever perspective is adopted, the benefit claimant must always be constituted as a 'taker' from the state and, ultimately, from the taxpayer. The regulation and punishment of benefit fraudsters is rooted in this essentially negative economic and social status of 'taker'.

I have argued, then, that differential responses to tax and social security fraud are produced as a result of contradictory discourses concerning the status of tax and benefit fraudsters: they may be regarded as givers to or takers from the state, they may be perceived as enterprising wealthy creators or idle scroungers and they may consequently be regarded as fiddling their *own* or someone else's money. Attention will now shift to the consequences which these different conceptions have for the enforcement of tax and social security regulations, and for the investigation and punishment of those who defraud the two departments.

COMPLIANCE AND COERCION

Both the Inland Revenue and DSS are concerned to safeguard public funds. However, there are differences in emphasis on the relative importance of this function, and the manner in which it is best achieved. When it comes to Revenue enforcement policy, one tax official summarised a popular view that 'The first responsibility of the Revenue is to get money in and not to lock people up and prosecute them'. Enforcement policy and investigatory practices are thus geared to securing the compliance of the taxpayer to the tax laws, and the Revenue regards this as best achieved through negotiation, bargaining and private financial settlement where tax is found to be owed (*Cmnd 8822*, 1983).

All but a tiny minority of tax fraudsters 'pay' for their crimes through financial settlement with the Revenue and without recourse to the courts. If there is evidence of 'fraud, wilful default or neglect' on the part of a taxpayer, the Revenue may impose financial penalties in addition to recovering back taxes found to be due (with appropriate interest). Such penalties are calculated as a percentage of tax unpaid and in practice could be up to 100 per cent, though the percentage is reduced in accordance with the extent of the taxpayer's co-operation, the gravity of the offence involved and the fullness of voluntary disclosure s/he makes. Such compounded financial penalties are officially (and popularly) regarded as a pragmatic means of achieving Revenue goals – namely collecting taxes, ensuring compliance and deterring tax fraud. But financial penalties can only be imposed because tax fraudsters can literally 'pay' for their crimes: benefit fraudsters cannot afford to pay negotiated financial penalties and con-sequently 'while social security offenders who are prosecuted are publicly identified in the courts and in the media, most tax offenders remain unknown in the community.' (NACRO, 1986, p. 89).

It is worth stressing that prosecution is, in any case, reserved only for a selection of the most 'heinous' cases of tax fraud. Moreover we are asked to believe that the exemplary prosecution of the very few (322 convictions in 1987/8) serves as an effective deterrent against fraud, even when the majority of fraudsters enjoy negotiated private justice.

An additional problem is that the vast majority of Revenue prosecutions do not in fact relate to what is popularly regarded as 'tax fraud' at all:

of the 322 convictions secured by the Revenue in 1987/8, 170 referred to frauds involving sub-contractors exemption certificates (which are a form of identity card used to combat fiddles in the construction industry) and 119 prosecutions related to the theft of Revenue cheques (Board of Inland Revenue, 1988). Only 24 convictions related to the submission of false returns of income and accounts – that is, to income tax fraud as it is widely understood! This disparity arises partly because of difficulties in proving 'dishonesty or intent to defraud' in tax cases (though this element of *'mens rea'* or intent does *not* have to be proved in social security fraud cases) (Uglow, 1984, p. 30). The Revenue offences which *are* prosecuted are thus not only those which are easier to prove, but are also the ones which usually equate with what is popularly perceived as 'real crime' (that is, crimes akin to theft or forgery) and so can be more easily represented as criminal and as taking from the state. Tax frauds involving the understatement of profits or 'common law cheat' are not so readily perceived as 'real crime'. This popular view of the essentially 'non-criminal' status of tax fraud is apparent in the largely sympathetic media coverage (and apparent popular support) afforded to the celebrity defendants in the recent tax fraud trials of champion jockey Lester Piggott and comedian Ken Dodd.

Most of the offences which *are* prosecuted by the Revenue, therefore, involve traditional crime in the sense of 'taking' (not merely failing to pay to the state), and are investigated by the police or the Board's Investigation Office, which approximates to the Revenue's 'police'. Prosecution policy is not, therefore, determined solely by the pragmatic goal of ensuring taxpayers' compliance and the effective collection of taxes: it is shaped, in general, by stereotypes of crime and criminals and, in particular, by the ideological construction of taxpayers as entrepreneurial individuals who are the victims of state over-regulation (because of the compulsion to pay allegedly penal personal taxes). In this way the relatively lenient treatment of tax fraudsters is often justified, as one former Revenue Enquiry Branch official commented, as 'The only sensible way to carry on' because 'After all, we have all sinned!'

The theme of compliance is central to an understanding of Revenue investigatory practice and provides a striking contrast with DSS investigation methods which are, as will be argued below, geared to the deterrence of fraud and abuse through stigmatisation and punishment.

Much local Revenue investigation work involves the task of 'making connections' between the information routinely supplied to District Tax Offices by individual taxpayers, traders, companies and financial institutions, to ensure that all the earnings, investment income, fees, commission, expenses etc. paid to individuals are fully declared. If they are not, the taxpayer will be invited for interview and (tactfully) asked to make a voluntary and full disclosure, and repay back taxes due: if s/he does this, no further action will usually be taken. By contrast, if there is alleged 'evidence' of a benefit claimant working on the side, (or fiddling by any other means), benefit payments are very often stopped. Clearly compliance involves giving the taxpayer the benefit of the doubt, a concession not accorded to claimants in a similar position. Moreover, the rights of taxpayers to 'information, courtesy and consideration, fairness, privacy and confidentiality ... rights of independent review and appeal' are formally acknowledged in the *Taxpayers Charter* (Board of Inland Revenue Customs and Excise, 1986). No similar document exists to guarantee the rights of social security claimants who do not, in any event, have the taxpayer's economic and social power to insist upon those rights. Disparities in treatment are yet more pronounced when the activities and attitudes of Revenue and DSS specialist investigators are compared.

But first it is necessary to locate DSS investigatory practice within the framework of an enforcement policy which has long sought to perform two (sometimes contradictory) functions, namely

> prompt payment of benefit and relief of need with due consideration for people's dignity and welfare - and the highly important but secondary function of combating fraud and abuse (NACRO, 1986, p. 16).

I would argue that, in the 1980s, the former function has been subverted by the latter: important policy changes have taken place which apparently reflect the stated aim of departmental efficiency, yet fulfil very different political objectives. For example, the 1980s saw reductions in the home visiting of claimants, administrative changes in the handling of claims, tighter regulations governing availability for work and 'voluntary unemployment' and a growing emphasis on the pro-active approach to anti-fraud work, all of which were justified in the name of greater cost-effectiveness and the safeguarding of public funds. But implicit in the rhetoric of government ministers (and particularly evident in their rationales for the 1988 Social Security reforms), was the desire to target benefits for the really deserving poor, whilst discouraging/deterring claims from the less deserving. One crucial element in this welfare rationing strategy (as argued earlier), has been a continual emphasis on the alleged problem of 'fraud and abuse' and the prioritising of investigation work over the last decade.

Special Claims Control (SCC) units, set up on a nationwide basis in 1981, spearheaded this political prioritising of supplementary benefit fraud, but immediately attracted intense criticism (Moore, 1981; CPSA, 1984; NACRO, 1986). In signalling a departure from earlier policies (to 'prosecute where appropriate'), their primary objective was instead to achieve 'benefit savings' as a result of 'the cessation of a claim' (Moore, 1981). Benefit savings were calculated by 'multiplying' the weekly benefit of claimants whose claims ceased as a result of SCC efforts. But according to DHSS staff, the targets of 'benefit savings' set by government ministers effectively gave rise to 'unofficial league tables' amongst SCC officers, and to 'bullying tactics' to 'chase people off the books'. For example, methods used by SCC units to persuade one 'targeted' group of claimants (lone mothers) to relinquish their claims allegedly included intimidation, inducements, pretending to have evidence of fraud after lengthy surveillance ('telephone directories in manila folders') threats to mothers that children would be taken into care and 'threats to prosecute if benefit order books not handed over or if claimants do not sign off' A Departmental circular subsequently issued to investigators (in 1983) warned them against unacceptable tactics such as 'trying to gain the claimant's confidence by claiming to be a single parent'!

Non-prosecution policies which prevent claimants coming before the courts for crimes of poverty would, on the surface seem to merit praise. Certainly prosecutions have fallen from over 20,000 in 1980/81 to 8,090 five years later (Cook, 1989b). But any approval must be tempered by concerns that claimants may well have been coerced into withdrawing claims (often by threats of 'or else, prosecution'), without having the opportunity to seek legal advice and without the standards of evidence and proof required in the courts. In these respects the non-prosecution policy still espoused by the DSS represents a cheap and effective means of deterring 'undeserving' individuals. The disproportionate publicity given to fraud drives amplifies the threat which fraud allegedly poses whilst exaggerating investigators' effectiveness through the use of 'multipliers' and dubious estimates of benefit savings.

SCC units were officially wound up in 1986 but their objectives and the legacy they left, in terms of coercive investigation methods, persist because the political imperatives which produced them remain, notably:
1. To (be seen to) take the initiative against 'fraud and abuse'.
2. To avoid prosecution because this involves no added 'cash return'.
3. To favour the achievement of 'benefit savings' through non-prosecution interviews in an effort to deter fraud while appearing to be cost effective.

Key elements which were seen as so crucial for the 'success of antifraud squads still remain – the targeting of claimant groups, locations or fraud-prone occupations; the proactive approach to tackling the problem of fraud; and high profile publicity to aid the deterrent function. All three elements were amply demonstrated in television coverage showing examples of a non-prosecution strategy in action against unemployed claimants suspected of fraud (BBC '40 Minutes' *Dolebusters* 20.10.88). The investigations screened were either based on anonymous tip-offs from members of the public, or on targeting fraud-prone jobs (in, for instance, the building trade and taxi firms). This often involved the covert inspection of claimants' vehicles for signs of work (e.g. tools, a bucket, a ladder) or the scrutiny of the claimants themselves for 'dirty hands'. It is impossible to imagine British taxpayers being physically scrutinised and accused of fraud on the basis of being too well-dressed for their declared salary, yet this is the kind of intrusive regulation which is apparently justified where the suspect is seen as a taker from the public purse.

Revenue investigators do use some of the same techniques as their DSS counterparts – targeting occupations and locations, for example – although with differing results. Compliance Units (first set up on an experimental basis in 1981) use these methods to focus on 'moonlighters' and 'ghosts' (the former are workers who are known to the Revenue in one area of economic activity, but have other concealed earnings; the latter are workers who are entirely unknown for tax purposes): 'We'll do a purge ... concentrating on a single area ... or we might decide to look specifically at particular trades or occupations' (Compliance officer, quoted in *Network*, July 1985).

But a key difference is in the standard of evidence required: unlike DSS investigators this officer will not 'just go on hearsay', 'it's only when we are pretty sure of our facts that we confront people'.

On the face of it there are similarities in some of the 'cloak and dagger' aspects of the work of both sets of investigators – such as the use of two-way radios, surveillance etc. But Revenue staff are aware of the rights of the taxpayers they investigate, and that most taxpayers (because of their own social knowledge, or their capacity to 'buy' professional advice) are able to insist on those rights. Relations between Revenue investigators and taxpayers may be rather cool but are characterised by some degree of mutual respect. Relations between DSS investigators and claimants are characterised by a sense of mistrust on the one hand and a feeling of stigma and degradation on the other (Cook, 1989a).

This nexus of mistrust and degradation is generated by a variety of factors, some of which are institutional: staff cuts have put extreme pressure on routine staff (while anti-fraud staffing levels are increasing) generating desperation and violence in some local office caller areas (Mandla, 1987). But other factors emanate from the historical conceptions of the idle and undeserving poor already described: for example, Cooper (1985) quotes one manager of a local DHSS office who reflected with nostalgia on the NAB (National Assistance Board) days, but felt that

> Now it's easy for claimants; too easy ... it takes a lot of pride out of the job when you know that nine out of ten of your customers are fiddling you. What's more, welfare rights egg them on so you begin to feel you're anyone's mug. In this office we've a reputation for being a bit shrewd, a bit harder; that's deliberate... There's just too much abuse. (ibid: 13)

These views are not necessarily typical of all DSS staff, but relations between claimants and departmental staff are bound to be influenced by broader social stereotypes which are shaped by racism and sexism as well as 'scrounger' imagery. In addition, their views are influenced by political agendas which affect their own day-to-day work by determining levels of staffing and work priorities which over-stretch and antagonise the routine staff who deal with benefit claims (Beltram, 1984;

Cooper, 1985; Smith, 1985).

Judicial responses to benefit fraudsters invoke similarly negative 'scrounger' imagery: for example, magistrates sentencing supplementary benefit fraudsters made comments such as: 'The country's fed-up to the teeth with people like you scrounging from fellow citizens'; one of the worst forms of stealing there is' and 'deceiving society'. There was a common view amongst many sentencers that these scroungers needed 'to be taught a lesson', yet this justification for punishment is not equally invoked for the (very few) taxpayers who reach the courts. Rather, their status as upstanding citizens counts in mitigation even if, as in one case, they are former magistrates who have defrauded the Revenue! (Cook, 1989b). Lawyers and judges speak of men 'of high reputation' who have 'lost everything ... his professional career has been shattered' (ibid). Obviously it is felt that the poor have no reputation to lose, and cannot therefore 'pay' for their crimes through loss of status, stigma and publicity. They are also likely to pay in fines, despite the fact that their offences are motivated by poverty and need (not greed).

It is often argued that, in any event, tax fraudsters have already 'paid' for their offences, by repayment of taxes due (with interest) and sometimes by additional financial penalties, and that prosecution would be both gratuitous and counter-productive. The taxpayer's ability to pay is thus offered as a justification for an enforcement policy which 'spares the taxpayer's feelings' (*Cmnd 8822*, 1983). But it should be remembered that benefit fraudsters pay too: wherever benefits are overpaid (for reasons other than 'official error' claimants are required to repay the DSS, by deductions from benefit if they are still in receipt (NACRO, 1986). Current regulations state that where a claimant admits fraud, up to £7 per week may be deducted from income support payments until the debt to the DSS has been repaid (CPAG, 1989). It is difficult to see the practicality or justice of enforcement policies which may reduce a claimant's income to £7 below the poverty line and, if criminal proceedings are then taken, may possibly reduce that income still further through a fine. Ironically, in such circumstances fraud may become the only means of economic survival.

To summarise, there are several paradoxes within official discourses on Revenue and DSS enforcement policy. Both departments stress cost effectiveness, the importance of safeguarding public funds and officially espouse 'non-prosecution' policies. Yet in 1987/8 these policies resulted in only 322 Revenue prosecutions compared with over 9000 for supplementary benefit fraud. More manpower and resources are directed against benefit 'scroungers' than against tax evaders (and this despite the fact that tax fraud is estimated to be far greater in magnitude (NACRO, 1986; H.C., 1983/4; *Cmnd 8822* 1983, p. 772). For example, the Inland Revenue Staff Federation recently indicated that in some district offices the backlog of routine work (due to staff cuts), was in part being tackled by taking compliance officers away from their investigatory duties. In addition, although a further 850 compliance officers had been promised in 1984, by 1987 only 380 of these extra staff were in post (Board of Inland Revenue, 1987).

Yet when Norman Fowler announced the proposed deployment of 500 extra investigators by march 1989 on the grounds that '...we are not prepared to see taxpayers' money being used to finance the fraudulent' he was referring to 'dole' fraud and not to the far more costly fiddles of taxpayers (*The Times*, 13.10.88). The official rhetoric of 'cost-effectiveness' and 'benefit savings' is therefore put into practice very selectively. As a result the majority of taxpayers pay for defrauding the public purse through private financial settlement, yet thousands of benefit claimants each year pay twice - through reparation to the DSS and through sentences imposed by the courts.

THE ENTERPRISE AND BENEFIT CULTURES

In attacking anti-poverty groups for defining poverty in relation to the level of income support, social security Minister John Moore asserted that

> Their purpose in calling poverty what is in reality simply inequality is so they can call western capitalism a failure... It is hard to believe that poverty stalks the land when even the poorest fifth of families with children spend nearly a tenth of their income on alcohol and tobacco. (*The Guardian*, 12.5.89)

The views encapsulated here not only redefine the poor as merely 'less equal' but indicate current political thinking on the twin themes of the enterprise and benefit cultures. Clearly Western capitalism is presented as successful in creating, in the words of Moore, 'affluence beyond the wildest dreams' of the Victorians (ibid), but the idle poor (without the values of thrift or enterprise) fritter away their money on drink and cigarettes within the dependency-inducing benefits culture. Unfortunately we cannot merely laugh off gross stereotypes such as these because they are ideologically so powerful, tapping into a deep reservoir of imagery, dating back to the nineteenth century, about the 'undeserving poor'. Furthermore, if the 'ends' of wealth and enterprise are inevitably prized (whatever the 'means' used to achieve them), it then becomes possible to justify any excesses by the 'energetic, successful and thrifty' who allegedly make our 'affluence' possible. These excesses (including tax evasion) can be repackaged as wealth-creating enterprise. For instance, speaking about the 'black economy' in 1985, Margaret Thatcher said

> Where people find a direct relationship between the money they get in their hands and the work they do, they not only do that work but they go out and find it and seek it. The enterprise is still there.

But presumably this admiration for 'enterprise' does not extend to social security claimants who work 'on the side' in the hidden economy.

CONCLUSION

Whilst enterprise, at any cost, is rewarded and economic failure (defined by financial dependence on the state) is condemned, the injustices described here will be reproduced and justified. One way to begin to tackle them is to demonstrate that the DSS and Revenue enforcement policies which generate and sustain this disparity are, in any event, counterproductive in economic terms. Campaigners are currently exposing such issues. For example, the political sleight of hand which underpins the DSS's current assessments of 'benefit savings' is being revealed: recent changes in the guidelines governing the use of 'multipliers' (to calculate benefit savings) have led to dramatic increases in DSS figures of the savings they allegedly make from investigation work. The use of these 'notional' figures, which are then used to amplify both the scale of the fraud problem and the success of the enforcers, represents 'deceit on the part of the department' according to Tess Gill (the National Union of Civil and Public Servants' officer for social security, *The Guardian* 6.6.89). On the Revenue side, the Inland Revenue Staff Federation has long drawn attention to the undue emphasis on social security scroungers, while routine investigation work and compliance initiatives remain under-staffed. Moreover, the economic productivity of Revenue investigation staff is staggering: Special Office staff yield 32 times their salary in taxes recouped, investigators in local offices yield 15 times their salary (Board of Inland Revenue, 1988). Clearly there are far richer pickings available in investigating the rich than the poor: even with 'cooked' figures, the DSS is unlikely to be able to match this yield!

But unequal political, judicial and social responses to rich and poor who engage in similar economic crimes is not an issue which should have to be addressed primarily in economic terms (such as poor cost-effectiveness). Although such arguments do help to focus on fundamental inconsistencies in enforcement policies, it is the existence of glaring social injustice which must be the principle focus of resistance and challenge.

NOTES

1. My research involved interviews with departmental staff (from both the Inland Revenue and DHSS), benefit claimants, taxpayers, accountants, businessmen, advice workers, solicitors, magistrates, representatives of trades unions and campaigning groups with an interest in issues of poverty and social justice. For the purposes of this chapter where quotations are not attributed to another author, they derive from my own research sources who, for reasons of confidentiality, are unnamed (for a fuller discussion of the methodology used, see Cook, 1988). The research focussed on the frauds of individual taxpayers (Pay-As-You-Earn taxpayers, traders and the self-employed) and excluded larger corporate tax evaders so that a more direct comparison remained possible with the frauds of individual benefit claimants.

BIBLIOGRAPHY

Aaron, H. J., Bosworth, B. P. and Burtless, G. (1989) *Can America Afford to Grow Old? Paying for Social Security*, Washington, D.C.: The Brookings Institution.
Abel-Smith, B. and Titmuss, K. (eds.) (1974) *Social Policy: an Introduction*, London: Allen and Unwin.
Abel-Smith, B. and Townsend, P. (1965) *The Poor and the Poorest*, London: Bell.
Abel-Smith, B. and Titmuss, K. (eds.) (1987) *The Philosophy of Welfare: Selected Writings of Richard M. Titmuss*, London: Allen and Unwin.
Abrams, P., Deem, R., Finch, J. and Rock, P. (1981) *Practice and Progress: British Sociology 1950–1980*, London: Allen and Unwin.
ABS (Australian Bureau of Statistics) (1986) *Income Distribution Survey*, Sample File.
Adler, M. (1985) Administrative Decision Making in Social Security: an important topic for research on which little research has so far been undertaken. Paper presented at ERSC Social Security Workshop, London School of Economics, March (revised version of a paper presented at the first International Seminar on the Sociology of Social Security, held at the University of Bergen in June 1984).
Adler, M. (1988) Lending a Deaf Ear: the Government's Response to Consultation on the Reform of Social Security. In Davidson, R. and White, P. (eds.) *Information and Government*, Edinburgh: Edinburgh University Press.
Adler, M. and Sainsbury, R. (1990) *Putting the Whole Person Concept into Practice: Final Report* (Parts I and II), Department of Social Policy and Social Work, University of Edinburgh.
Alber, J. (1985) *How the West German Welfare State Passed Through the Recent Years of Economic Crisis*, Paper presented at the IV Nordic Social Policy Seminar, Stockholm.
Alber, J. (1987) *Vom Armenhaus zum Wohlfahrtsstaat. Analysen zur Entwicklung der Sozialversicherung in Westeuropa*, 2nd edition, Frankfurt a. M.: Campus.
Alber, J. (1988a) *Der Sozialstaat in der Bundesrepublik Deutschland*, Köln, unpublished manuscript (published with Campus, Frankfurt a. M. 1989).
Alber, J. (1988b) Die Gesundheitssysteme der OECD-Länder im Vergleich. In Schmidt, G. (ed.) *Staatstätigkeit. International und historisch vergleichende Analysen*, Opladen usf.: Westdeutscher Verlag, pp. 116–150 (Special Issue No. 19 of Politische Vierteljahresschrift).
Alber, J. (1988c) Is there a Crisis of the Welfare State? Cross-National Evidence from Europe, North America and Japan, *European Sociological Review*, 4, 3, pp. 181–207.
Aldendenter, M. S. and Blashfield, R. K. (1984) *Cluster Analysis*, Sage University Paper No. 44, Beverly Hills, London, New Delhi: Sage Publications Inc.
Aldrich, H. E. (1979) *Organisations and Environments*, Englewood Cliffs, N.J.: Prentice-Hall.
Allbeson, J. and Smith, R. (1984) *We Don't Give Clothing Grants Anymore*, Poverty Pamphlet No. 62, London: CPAG.

Altman, R. A. (1981) *Take up of Supplementary Benefit by Male Pensioners*, Discussion Paper 25, London School of Economics, SSRC Programme on Taxation, Incentives and the Distribution of Income.
Alvey, J. (1982) *Report of the Alvey Committee*, London: Department of Trade and Industry.
Anderson, B. (1983) *Imagined Communities: Reflections on the Origins and Spread of Nationalism*, London: Verso.
Antal, A. B., Dierkes, M. and Weiler, H. N. (1987) Cross-National Policy Research: Traditions, Achievements and Challenges. In Dierkes, M., Weiler, H. N. and Antal, A. B. (eds.) *Comparative Policy Research*, Aldershot: Gower.
Arbeidsdirektoratet (1989), *Attføringsstatistikken-årsstatistikken for 1987*, Oslo: Arbeidsdirektoratet.
Ashenfelter, O. (1983) Determining Participation in Income-tested Social Programmes, *Journal of the American Statistical Association*, 78, pp. 517–525.
Atkinson, A. B. (1984) *Take up of Social Security Benefits*, Discussion Paper 65, London School of Economics, ESRC Programme on Taxation, Incentives and the Distribution of Income.
Atkinson, A. B. (1985a) *How Should we Measure Poverty? Some Conceptual Issues*, Discusson Paper No. 82, ESRC Programme on Taxation, Incentives and the Distribution of Income, London School of Economics.
Atkinson, A. B. (1985b) *On the Measurement of Poverty*, Discussion Paper No. 90, ESRC Programme on Taxation, Incentives and the Distribution of Income, London School of Economics.
Atkinson, A. B. (1987) Income Maintenance and Social Insurance. In Auerbach, A. J. and Feldstein, M. (eds.) *A Handbook of Public Economics*, Elsevier: North Holland.
Atkinson, A. B. (1989) *Measuring Inequality and Differing Social Judgements*, Discussion Paper No. 129, ESRC Programme on Taxation, Incentives and the Distribution of Income, London School of Economics.
Atkinson, A. B. and Micklewright, J. (1983) On the Reliability of Income Data in the Family Expenditure Survey 1970–1977, *Journal of the Royal Statistical Society*, 146, 33–61.
Australian Bureau of Statistics (1988) *Superannuation, Australia, Summary*, Cat.6318.0.
Bach, H. U. and Brinkman C. (1986) Erwerbsbeteiligung von Frauen im internationalen Vergleich, Mitteilungen aus der Arbeitsmarkt- und Berufsforschung 3 i, pp. 356–361.
Bäcker, G. (1988) Normalarbeitsverhältnis und Soziale Sicherung: Sozial-versicherung und/oder Grundsicherung?, *Zeitschrift für Sozialreform*, 34, pp. 595–629.
Bäcker, G. and Steffen, J. (1990) Sozialunion: Was soll wie vereinigt werden? - Sozialpolitische Probleme des ökonomischen und politischen Umbruchs in der DDR und Anforderungen des Einigungsprozesses, *WSI-Mitteilungen*, 5, May, pp. 265–354.
Bakker, I. (1988) Women's Employment in Comparative Perspective. In Jenson, J., Hagen, E. and Reddy, C. (eds.) *Feminization of the Labour Forces. Paradoxes and Promises*, New York: Oxford University Press.
Baldock, C. and Cass, B. (eds.) (1988) *Women, Social Welfare and the State*, Sydney: Allen and Unwin.
Baldock, C. and Cass, B. (eds.) (1988) *Women, Social Welfare and the State*, revised edtion, Sydney: Allen and Unwin.
Banks, O. (1971) *The Sociology of Education*, 2nd edition, London: Batsford.
Barker, D. and Allen, S. (eds.) (1976) *Sexual Divisions and Society: Process and Change*, London: Tavistock.
Barkin, S. (1987) The Flexibility Debate in Western Europe. The Current Drive to Restore Managements' Rights over Personnel and Wages, *Relations Industrielles*, 42, 1, pp. 12–34.

Basic Income Research Group (1989) *Bulletin No. 9*.
Bauer, R. and Leibfried, S. (eds) (1986) *Sozialpolitische Bilanz II*, Tagung der Deutschen Gesellschaft für Soziologie in Bielefeld, 2 and 3 May, (Arbeitspapiere des Forschungsschwerpunktes Reproduktionsrisiken, soziale Bewegungen und Sozialpolitik, Nr. 56), University of Bremen.
Bayne, C.K., Beauchamp, J. J. Begovich, C. L. and Kane, V. E. (1980) Monte Carlo Comparisons of Selected Clustering Procedures, *Pattern Recognition*, 12, pp. 51–62.
Becker, U. (1989) Frauenerwerbstätigkeit - eine vergleichende Bestandsaufnahme, *Aus Politik und Zeitgeschichte. Beilage zur Wochenzeitung Das Parlament*, B 28/29, 7 July, pp. 22–33.
Beckerman, W. (1980) The Impact of Income Maintenance Programmes on Poverty in Britain. In Atkinson, A. B. (ed.) *Wealth, Income and Inequality*, 2nd edn, Oxford: Oxford Univertisy Press.
Beckett, J. (1987) *Torres Strait Islanders, Custom and Colonialism*, Cambridge: Cambridge University Press.
Beenstock, M. (1987) *Work, Welfare and Taxation: a Study of Labour Supply Incentives in the UK*, London: Allen and Unwin.
Behn, R. (1987) *Managing Innovation in Welfare, Training and Work: some Lessons from ET Choices in Masachusetts*, Paper presented at the Annual Meeting of the American Political Science Association, Chicage, IL., 4 Sept, 1987.
Beltram, G. (1984) *Testing the Safety Net*, London: Bedford Square Press.
Bendick, M. (1986) Targeting Benefit Payments in the British Welfare State. In McKinney, J. B. and Johnston, M. *Fraud, Waste and Abuse in Government – Causes, Consequences and Cures*, Philadelphia: Insititute for the Study of Human Issues.
Benson, K. (1975) The Interorganizational Network as a Political Economy, *Administrative Science Quarterly*, 20, pp. 229–249.
Bentley, P., Collins, D.J. and Drane, N.J. (1974) The Incidence of Australian Taxation, *The Economic Record*, 50.
Berghman, J. (1991) Defining Social Security. In Pieters, D. (ed) *Social Security in Europe*, Brussels: Bruylant.
Berghman J. and Muffels, R. (1988) Armoede en armoede-onderzoek in de EG: eerste en voorlopige resultaten voor Nederland. In Van Oorschot, W. (ed.) *De Maatschappelijke verdeling van Armoede. Verslag van de Oldendorff-lezingen 1987*, Tilburg University, the Netherlands.
Berthoud, R. (1984) *The Reform of Supplementary Benefit - Working Papers*, London: Policy Studies Institute (especially Working paper A).
Berthoud, R. Brown, J. C. and Cooper, S. (1981) *Poverty and the Development of Anti-Poverty Policy in the UK*., London: Heinemann Educational Books.
Best, L. (1989) *The Politics of Bureaucratic Disentitlement*, unpublished paper.
Besters, H. (ed.) (1988) *Auflösung des Normalarbeitsverhältnisses?* Gespräche der List Gesellschaft e.V., N.F. Bd. 11, Baden-Baden: Nomos Verlagsgesellschaft.
Beveridge, W. H. (1944) *Full Employment in a Free Society*, London: George Allen and Unwin.
Beveridge Report (1942) *Social Insurance and Allied Services*, Cmd 6404, London: HMSO.
Bieback, K-J. (1985) Das Sozialleistungssystem in der Krise. Bestandsaufnahme der Sparaktionen, ihre strukturellen Auswirkungen und ihre verfassungsrechtlichen Probleme, *Zeitschrift für Sozialreform*, 31, 10, pp. 557–590 (part I), no. 11, pp. 641–655, (part II), no. 12, pp. 705–722 (part III).
Bielenski, H. and Strümpel, B. (1988) *Eingeschränkte Erwerbsarbeit bei Frauen und Männern: Fakten - Wünsche - Realisierungschancen*, Berlin: Edition Sigma.
Bijsterveldt, Q. M., Van (1975) *Een Sociale voorziening en haar clienten: een onderzoek naar de bijstandsverlening aan vrouwelijke gezinshoofden*, Proefschrift, Catholic University Tilburg.
Birch, A. (1984) Overload Ungovernability and Delegitimation: The Theories and the British Case, *British Journal of Political Science*, 14, pp. 135–160.

Birch, S. (1986) Increasing Patient Charges in the National Health Service: a Method of Privatizing Primary Care, *Journal of Social Policy*, 15, 2, pp. 163–184.
Birmingham City Council (1989) *Poverty in Birmingham*, Birmingham.
Blashfield, R. K. (1976) Mixture Model Tests of Cluster Analysis, Accuracy of Four Agglomerative Hierarchical Methods, *Psychological Bulletin*, 83, pp. 377–388.
Blashfield, R. K. (1977) The Equivalence of Three Statistical Packages for Performing Hierarchical Cluster Analysis, *Psychometrika* 42, pp. 429–431.
Blashfield, R. K. (1980) The Growth of Cluster Analysis: Tyrone, Ward and Johnson, *Multivariate Behavioural Research* 15, pp. 439–458.
Blashfield, R. K. and Aldenderfer, M. S. (1978) The Literature on Cluster Analysis, *Multivariate Behavioural Research* 13, pp. 271–295.
Blashfield, R. K. and Morey, L. C. (1980) A Comparison of Four Clustering Methods Using MMPI Monte Carlo Data, *Applied Psychological Measurement* 4, pp. 57–64.
Blau, P. (1964) *Exchange and Power in Social Life*, New York: Wiley.
Block, F. et al. (1987) *The Mean Season, The Attack on the Welfare State*, N.Y.: Pantheon.
Blume, O. (1970) Die Position älterer Menschen in der Leistungsgesellschaft. Deutscher Verein für öffentliche und private Fürsorge (ed.) *Die Fürsorge im Sozialen Rechtsstaat*, Frankfurt, pp. 537–546.
Blundell, R., Fry, V. and Walker, I. (1987) *Modelling the Take Up of Means-tested Benefits: the Case of Housing Benefits in the UK*, London: Institute for Fiscal Studies.
Board of Inland Revenue (1987) *129th Annual Report*, London: HMSO.
Board of Inland Revenue (1988) *130th Annual Report*, London: HMSO.
Board of Inland Revenue/Customs and Excise (1986) *Taxpayers' Charter*, London: HMSO.
Bögenhold, D. (1987) *Der Gründerboom. Realität und Mythos der neuen Selbständigkeit*, Frankfurt/New York: Campus.
Bokor, A. (1984) Deprivation: Dimensions and Indices. In Andork, R. and Kolosi, T. (eds.) *Stratification and Inequality*, Budapest: Institute for Social Sciences.
Boos, C. (1987) *Single Parent Families in the Netherlands*, Department of Social Security Studies, Tilburg University, Tilburg.
Borchorst, A. and Siim, B. (1987) Women and the Advanced Welfare State - a New Kind of Patriarchal Power? In Showstack Sassoon, A. (ed.) *Women and the State*, London: Hutchinson.
Bosch, G. (1986) Hat das Normalarbeitsverhältnis eine Zukunft? *WSI-Mitteilungen*, 39, pp. 163–176.
Boulding, K. E. (1967) The Boundaries of Social Policy, *Social Work*, 12, 1, p. 7.
Bowles, S. and Gintis, H. (1986) *Democracy and Capitalism*, New York: Basic Books.
Boyson, R. (1971) *Down With the Poor*, London: Churchill Press.
Boyson, R. (1978) *Centre Forward*, London: Maurice Temple-Smith.
Bradshaw, J. and Beadham, R. (1987) *The Take Up of Housing Rebates by Families with Children*, York: Social Policy Research Unit.
Bradshaw, J. and Davies, R. (1986) *Not a penny to call my own. Poverty among Residents in Mental Illness and Mental Handicap Hospitals*, London: Disability Alliance/King's Fund.
Bradshaw, J. and Holmes, H. (1989) *Living on the Edge*, London: Tyneside Child Poverty Action Group.
Brennan, T. and Pateman, C. (1979) 'Mere Auxiliaries to the Commonwealth': Women and the Origins of Liberalism, *Political Studies*, 18, 2.
Brinkmann, C. (1989a) Arbeitszeitpräferenzen und Partnerarbeitsvolumen. In Peters, W. (ed.) *Frauenerwerbstätigkeit – Berichte aus der laufenden Forschung*, Arbeitskreis Sozialwissenschaftliche Arbeitsmarktforschung (SAMF), Arbeitspapier 1989–7, Paderborn, pp. 113–141.
Brinkmann, C. (1989b) *Neue arbeitsmarktpolitische Hilfen für den 'harten Kern' von Langzeitarbeitslosen*, Arbeitskreis Sozialwissenschaftliche Arbeitsmarktforschung (SAMF), Arbeitspapier 1989 – 8, Paderborn.

Brittan, S. (1975) The Economic contradictions of Democrary, *British Journal of Political Science*, 5, pp. 130–131.
Broad, P. (1977) *Pensioners and their Needs*, London: OPCS.
Brodkin, E. (1986) *The False Promise of Administrative Reform*, Philadelphia: Temple University Press.
Brose, H-G., Meyer, W. and Schulze-Böing, M. (1989) Zeitarbeit und Berufsverlauf. Ergebnis einer Untersuchung über den Verbleib ehemaliger Zeitarbeitnehmer, Arbeitskreis Sozialwissenschaftliche Arbeitsmarktforschung (SAMF), Arbeitspapier 1989 – 12, Paderborn.
Brown, C. (1981) Mothers, Fathers and Children: From Private to Public Patriarchy. In Sargent, L. (ed.) *Women and Revolution*, Boston: South End Press.
Brown, J. (1987) *The Future of Family Income Support*, Studies of the Social Security System No. 15, London: PSI.
Brown, J. (1988) *Child Benefit. Investing in the Future*, London: CPAG.
Brown, J. C. (1984) *The Disability Income System*, London: Policy Studies Institute.
Brown, R. (1985) *Money Matters for People with a Mental Handicap*, London: Disablement Income Group.
Büchtemann, C. F. (1989) Geringe Beschäftigungswirkung - erhöhte Beschäftigungsrisiken, *Die Mitbestimmung*, 35, pp. 548–553.
Büchtemann, C. F. and Höland, A. (1989) Die Erfahrungen mit der Befristungsregelung, *Wirtschaftsdienst*, 69, pp. 503–511.
Büchtemann, C. F. and Quack, S. (1989) 'Bridges' or 'traps'? Non-Standard Employment in the Federal Republic of Germany. In Rodgers, G. and Rodgers, J. (eds.) *Precarious Jobs in Labour Market Regulation: The Growth of Atypical Employment in Western Europe*, Geneva: International Labour Office.
Buckland, S. and Dawson, P. (1989) Household Claiming Behaviour, *Social Policy and Administration*, 23, pp. 60–71.
Buhmann, B., Rainwater, L. Schmaus, G. and Smeeding, T. (1989) Equivalence Scales, Well-Being, Inequality and Poverty: Sensitivity Estimates Across Ten Countries Using the Luxembourg Income Study (LIS) Database, *Review of Income and Wealth*, pp. 115–142.
Bull, D. (ed.) (1971) *Family Poverty, Programme for the Seventies*, London: CPAG/Duckworth.
Bull, D. (1984) The 1978 Review: Insights, Oversights and Hindsight', *Poverty*, 59, Winter 1984–85, pp. 16–24.
Burgbacher, H. G., Hartwig, M. and Liebau, E. (1989) Zur Empirie befristeter Arbeitsverträge. Eine Untersuchung in kleinen und mittleren Unternehmen, *Sozialer Fortschritt*, 38, pp. 101–104.
Burns, T. and Stalker, G. M. (1961) *The Management of Innovation*, London: Social Science Paperbacks.
Burton, J. (1985) *Why No Cuts?*, London: IEA.
Buttler, F. (1986) Regulierung und Deregulierung der Arbeitsbeziehungen. In Winterstein, H. (ed.) *Sozialpolitik in der Beschäftigungskrise II*, Schriften des Vereins für Socialpolitik, N. F. Bd. 152/II, Berlikn: Duncker and Humblot.
Byrne, D. (1987) Rich and Poor: the Growing Divide. In Walker, A. and Walker, C. (eds.) *The Growing Divide: A Social Audit 1979–1987*, London: CPAG.
Cameron, D. R. (1984) Social Democracy, Corporatism, Labour Quiescence and the Representation of Economic Interest in Advanced Capitalist Society. In Goldthorpe, J. H. (ed.) *Order and Conflict in Contemporary Capitalism*, Oxford: Clarendon Press.
Campbell, T. (1988) *Justice*, London: Macmillan.
Cantillon, B., Peeters, J. and De Ridder, E. (1987) *Atlas van de sociale zekerheid in Belgie: Kostprijs, Financierung, Doelmatigheid*, Acco, Leuven/Amersfoort.
Casey, B., Dragendorf, R. Heering, W. and John, G. (1989) Temporary Employment in Great Britain and the Federal Republic of Germany, *International Labour Re-*

view, 128, pp. 449–466.
Cass, B. (1985) The Changing Face of Poverty in Australia, *Australian Feminist Studies*, 2, Summer.
Cass, B. (1986) *Income Support for Families with Children*, Issues Paper No. 1, Social Security Review, Department of Social Security, Canberra: Australian Government Publishing Service.
Cass, B. and Whiteford, P. (1989) Income Support, the Labour Market and the Household. In Ironmonger, D. (ed.) *Households Work*, Sydney: Allen and Unwin.
Castles, F. G. (1987) Thirty Wasted Years: Australian Social Security Developments 1950–1980 in Comparative Perspective, *Canberra Bulletin of Public Administration*, 51 (May), pp. 47–56.
Castles, F. and Mitchell, D. (1990) Three Worlds of Welfare Capitalism or Four? *Discussion Paper 21*, Australian National University, Canberra.
Cates, J. (1983) *Insuring Inequality: Administrative Leadership in Social Security, 1935–54*, Ann Arbor: Michigan University Press.
Catrice-Lorey, A. (1980) The Acquisition of Service Values in a Predominantly Administrative Social Organisation and the Structuring of Staff Functions. In Grunow, D. and Hegner, F. (eds) *Welfare or Bureaucracy: Problems of Matching Social Services to Clients' Needs*, Cambridge Mass: Oegeschlager, Gunn and Hain.
Central Statistical Office (1988) The Effects of Taxes and Benefits on Household Income, 1986, *Economic Trends*, 422, December, pp. 89–117.
Chombart de Lauwe, P. (1977) *La Vie Quotidienne des Familles Ouvreires*, 3rd ed., Paris: Centre National de la Recherce Scientifique.
Chow, N. W. S. (1981) *Poverty in an Affluent City: A Report on a Survey on Low Income Families*, Department of Social Work, Chinese University of Hong Kong.
Clarke, S., Henning, R. and Ulph, D. (1981) On Indices for the Measurement of Poverty, *Economic Journal*, 91, pp. 515–526.
Clemenz, G. (1987) Kredit- und Arbeitsmärkte aus informationsökonomischer Sicht. In Keynessche Fragen im Lichte der Neoklassik, *Ökonomie und Gesellschaft*, Jahrbuch 5, Frankfurt a. M.: Campus.
Cmnd 8822 (1983) *Keith Committee Report on the Enforcement Powers of the Revenue Departments*, London: HMSO.
Cm 1014, (1990) *Government's Expenditure Plans 1990–91 to 1991–92*, London: HMSO.
Cole, D. and Utting, J. (1962) *The Economic Circumstances of Old People*, Occasional Papers in Social Administration, Welwyn: Codicote Press.
Commission of the European Communities (1977) *The Perception of Poverty in Europe*, Brussels.
Commission of the European Communites (1981) *Final Report from the First Programme of Pilot Schemes and Studies to Combat Poverty*, Brussels.
Cook, D. (1988) *Rich Law Poor Law: Different Responses to Tax and Supplementary Benefit Fraud*, unpublished PhD thesis, University of Keele.
Cook, D. (1989a) *Rich Law Poor Law: Different Responses to Tax and Supplementary Benefit Fraud*, Milton Keynes: Open University Press.
Cook, D. (1989b) Fiddling Tax and Benefits: Inculpating the Poor and Exculpating the Rich. In Carlen, P. and Cooke, D. (eds.) *Paying for Crime*, Milton Keynes: Open University Press.
Cook, K. (1977) Exchange and Power in Networks of Interorganizational Relations, *Sociological Quarterly*, 18, pp. 62–82
Cooke, K. R. and Baldwin, S. (1984) *How Much is Enough? A Review of Supplementary Benefit Scale Rates*, London: Family Policy Studies Centre.
Cooke, K., Bradshaw, J. and Lawton, D. (1983) Take Up of Benefits by Families with Dependent Children, *Child Care, Health and Development*, 9, pp. 145–156.
Coombs, H. C. (1982) *Trail Balance*, Melbourne, Macmillan.
Cooper, S. (1985) *Observations in Supplementary Benefit Offices, The Reform of Supplementary Benefit*, PSI Working Paper C, London: Policy Studies Institute.

Corden, A. (1981a) *The Process of Claiming Family Income Supplement: Background Paper I*, York: Social Policy Research Unit.
Corden, A. (1981b) *The Process of Claiming Family Income Supplement: Background Paper II*, York: Social Policy Research Unit.
Cordon, A. (1983) *Taking up a Means tested benefit. The Process of Claiming Family Income Supplement*, London: HMSO.
Cordon, A. (1985a) *The Process of Claiming Family Income Supplement, Study 3: Increasing Take up in Cumbria*, York: Social Policy Research Unit.
Corden, A. (1985b) *Operational Aspects of the Family Credit Scheme*, York: Social Policy Research Unit.
Corden, A. (1985c) *The Process of Claiming Family Income Supplement. Proposals for Further Research*, York: Social Policy Research Unit.
Corden, A. (1987a) *Disappointed Applicants. A Study of Unsuccessful Claims for Family Income Supplement*, Aldershot: Avebury.
Corden, A. (1987b) Claiming Behaviour and Take up: a Model for People with Mental Handicap, *British Journal of Mental Handicap*, 3, pp. 57–65.
Coughlin, R. M. (1980) *Ideology, Public Opinion and Welfare Policy: Attitudes towards Taxes and Spending in Industrial Societies*, Institute of International Studies, Research Series no. 42, University of California, Berkeley.
Cowell, F. A. (1986) *Welfare Benefits and the Economics of Take up*, Discussion Paper 89, London School of Economics, ESRC Programme on Taxation, Incentives and the Distribution of Income.
CPAG (Child Poverty Action Group) (1989) *National Welfare Benefits Handbook*, London.
CPD (Commonwealth Parliamentary Debates) House of Representatives, various dates.
CPSA (Civic and Public Services Association) (1984) Report of Special Conference, University College of Wales, Cardiff.
Craig, G. (ed.) (1989) *Your Flexible Friend? Voluntary Organisations, Claimants and the Social Fund*, London: Social Security Consortium.
Craig, P. (1991) Recent Research on the Take up of Income Related Benefits, *Journal of Social Policy* (forthcoming).
Cramer, U. (1987) Zur Entwicklung der Lohnersatzleistungen für Arbeitslose, *Mitteilungen aus der Arbeitsmarkt - und Berufsforschung*, 20, pp. 274–276.
Danziger, S. (1989) Fighting Poverty and Reducing Welfare Dependency: A Challenge for the 1990s. In Ellwood, D. and Cottingham, P. (eds.) *Welfare Reform*, Cambridge, Mass.: Harvard University Press.
Däubler, W. (1988) Deregulierung und Flexibilisierung im Arbeitsrecht, *WSI-Mitteilungen*, 41, pp. 449–457.
Davies, B. and Reddin, M. (1978) *Universality, Selectivity and Effectiveness in Social Policy*, London: Heinemann.
Davies, C. and Ritchie, J. (1988) *Tipping the Balance. A Study of Non-take up of Benefits in an Inner City Area*, London: HMSO.
Davis, K. (1984) Wives and Work: The Sex Role Revolution and its Consequences, *Population and Development Review*, 10, pp. 397–417.
Dawson, P., Buckland, S.and Gilbert, G. N. (1990) Expert Systems and the Public Provisions of Welfare Benefits Advice, *Policy and Politics*, 18, 1, pp. 43–54.
Deacon, A. and Bradshaw, J. (1983) *Reserved for the Poor. The Means Test in British Social Policy*, Oxford: Basil Blackwell / Martin Robertson.
Deininger, D. (1989) Sozialhilfeempfänger 1987, *Wirtschaft und Statistik*, pp. 537–543.
Delbecq, A. L., Van de Ven, A. H. and Gustafson, D. H. (1974) *Group Techniques for Program Planning: A Guide to Nominal Group and Delphi Processes*, Glenview, Illinois: Foreman and Co.
Deleeck, H. (1989) The Adequacy of the Social Security System in Belgium, 1976–1985, *Journal of Social Policy*, 18, 1, pp. 91–117.

Bibliography

Department of National Health and Welfare, Canada (1970) *The Measurement of Poverty*, Social Security Series Memorandum 19, Social Security Research Division, Research and Statistics Directorate, Toronto, Canada.
Department of the Environment (1975a) *Housing Act 1974: Renewal Strategies*, Circular, 13/75, London: HMSO.
Department of the Environment (1975b) *Housing Act 1974: Parts IV, V, and VI. Housing Action Areas, Priority Neighbourhoods and General Improvement Areas*, Circular 14/75, London: HMSO.
Department of Public Welfare (1986) *An Evaluation of the Massachusetts Employment and Training Choices Program: Interim Findings on Participation and Outcomes*, Boston: Commonwealth of Massachusetts Executive Office of Human Services.
Desai, M. (1986) Drawing the Line: On Defining the Poverty Threshold. In Golding, P. (ed.) *Excluding the Poor*, London: CPAG.
Desai, M. and Shah, A. (1988) An Econometric Approach to the Measurement of Poverty, *Oxford Economic Papers* 40, pp. 505–552.
De Vos, K. and Hagenaars, A. (1988) *A Comparison Between the Poverty Concepts of Sen and Townsend*, Erasmus University, Rotterdam.
DHSS (1979) *Relations with Social Services*, London.
DHSS (1980a) *A Strategy for Social Security Operations*, London.
DHSS (1980b) *Liaison in Practice*, London: Department of Health and Social Security, Association of Country Councils, Associaton of Metropolitan Authorities, Convention of Scottish Local Authorities, London Boroughs Association, and Welsh Office.
DHSS (1982) *Social Security Operational Strategy: A Framework for the Future*, London.
DHSS (1983) *Service to the Public. A handbook of good practice*, 1st ed., London.
DHSS (1984) *Supplementary Benefits Handbook*, London.
DHSS (1985) Reform of Social Security: Programme for Change, Cmnd 9517, London.
DHSS (1987a) *Quality Assessment Package, The Results*, London.
DHSS (1987b) *Social Fund Manual*, London.
DHSS (1988a) *Low Income Statistics, Report of a Technical Review*, London.
DHSS (1988b) *New Technology, Job Design and Organisation*, London.
Department of Social Security (1984) *The Economic and Social Circumstances of the Aged*, Research Paper No. 25, Canberra.
Dickes, P., Gailly, B., Hausman, P. and Schaber, G. (1984) Les Desadvantages de la Pauvrete: Definitions, Mesure et Realities en Europe, *Mondes en Developpement* 12, 45, pp. 131–190.
Dickes, P. (1987) *Un Indicateur Pour Mesurer la Pauvrete Objective: Theorie et Application dans la Premiere Vague du Panel Socio-Economique Luxembourgeois*, Luxembourg: Centre d'Etudes de Populations, de Pauvrete et de Politiques Socio-Economiques.
Dickes, P. (1989) *Pauvrete et Conditions d'Existence: Theories, Modeles et Mesures*, Luxembourg: Centre d'Etudes de Populations, de Pauvrete et de Politiques.
Dickey, B. (1980) *No Charity There*, Melbourne: Nelson.
Dilnot, A. W., Kay, J. A. and Morris, C. N. (1984) *The Reform of Social Security*, Oxford: Clarendon Press.
Dilnot, A. and Webb, S. (1989) The 1988 Social Security Reforms. In Dilnot, A. and Walker, I. (eds.) *The Economics of Social Security*, Oxford: Oxford University Press.
Donnison, D. (1985) The Cohabitation Rule. In Ungerson, C. (ed.) *Women and Social Policy*, London: Macmillan.
Donnison, D. (1988a) Defining and Measuring Poverty: A Reply to Stein Ringen, *Journal of Social Policy*, 17, 3, pp. 367–374.
Donnison, D. (1988b) *Rethinking the Relative Definition of Poverty*. Paper presented at the Workshop on Comparative Research in Social Policy, Stockholm, August 25–28.
Dorow, F. *et al*. (1989) Volkswirtschaftliche Gesamtrechnungen 1988, *Wirtschaft und*

Statistik, 3, pp. 123–148.
Dostal, W. (1985) Telearbeit. Anmerkungen zur Arbeitsmarktrelevanz dezentraler Informationstätigkeit, *Mitteilungen aus der Arbeitsmarkt- und Berufsforschung*, 18, pp. 467–480.
Drucker, P. (1969) The Sickness of Government, *The Public Interest*, 14, pp. 3–23.
DSS (Department of Social Security, Australia) (1988) *Annual Report*.
DSS (Department of Social Security, Australia) *Ten Year Statistical Summary*, various years.
DSS (1988a) *Social Services Select Committee: Benefit Levels and a Minimum Income*, London: Department of Social Security.
DSS (1988b) *The Measurement of Living Standards for Households Below Average Income, Reply by the Government to the Fourth Report from the Select Committee on Social Services*, Cmd 523, London: HMSO.
DSS (1988c) *The Business of Service* (the 'Moodie Report'), London.
DSS (1988d) *Service to the Public. A Handbook of Good Practice*, 2nd ed., London.
DSS (1989a) *Quality Assessment Exercise 1988/89. Customer Opinion in Local Offices, Synopsis of Findings*, London.
DSS (1989b) *The Next Steps*, London: HMSO.
Duncan, G. J. and Hoffman, S. D. (1988) The Use and Effects of Welfare: a Survey of Recent Evidence, *Social Service Review*, June.
Dunn, G. and Everitt, B. S. (1982) *An Introducion to Mathematical Taxonomy: Cambridge Studies in Mathematical Biology 5*, Cambridge: Cambridge University Press.
Dworkin, R. (1986) *Law's Empire*, London: Fontana Press.
Dyerson R. and Roper, M. (1989) *Computerisation at the DSS 1977–89: The Operational Strategy*, (Technology Project Papers No. 4), London: London Business School.
Edwards, M. and Whiteford, P. (1988) *The Development of Government Policies on Poverty and Income Distribution*, Social Policy Division, Department of Social Security, Canberra.
Edelbrock, C. (1979) Comparing the Accuracy of Hierarchical Clustering Algorithms: The Problem of Classifying Everybody, *Multivariate Behavioural Research*, 14, pp. 367–384.
Edelbrock, C. and McLaughlin, B. (1980) Hierarchical Cluster Analysis Using Intraclass Correlations: A Mixture Model Study, *Multivariate Behavioural Research*, 15, pp. 299–318.
Eldridge, J. (1980) *Recent British Sociology*, London and Basingstoke: Macmillan.
Ellwood, D. (1988) *Poor Support*, New York: Basic Books.
Elmore, R. (1979) Backward Mapping: Implementation Research and Policy Design, *Political Science Quarterly*, 94, 4.
Emerson, R. E. (1961) Power-Dependence Relations, *American Sociological Review*, 27, pp. 31–40.
EPAC (Economic Planning Advisory Council) (1988) *Economic Effects of an Aging Population*, EPAC Council Paper No. 29, Canberra: AGPS.
Epstein, J. (1984) *New Technology, New Entitlement*, London: Research Institute for Consumer Affairs.
ESCEC (1983) *Youth Employment*, Brussels: Economic and Social Committee of the European Communities.
Esping-Andersen, G. (1985) *Politics Against Markets: The Social Democratic Road to Power*, Princeton, N.J.: Princeton University Press.
Esping-Andersen, G. (1987) Citizenship and Socialism: Decommodification and Solidarity in the Welfare State. In Rein, M., Esping-Andersen, G. and Rainwater, L. (eds.) *Stagnation and Renewal in Social Policy*, Armonk, NY: M. E. Sharpe, Inc.
Esping-Andersen, G. (1988) *Dimensions of Stratifiction in Post-Industrial Employment*, Florence: European University Institute.
Esping-Andersen, G. (1989) The Three Political Economies of the Welfare State, *Canadian Review of Sociology and Anthropology*, 26, 1, pp. 10–36.

Esping-Andersen, G. (1990) *The Three Worlds of Welfare Capitalism*, Cambridge: Polity Press.
Eurostat (1984) *Sociale indicatoren voor de Europese Gemeenschap; geselecteerde reeksen*. Luxembourg: Office des Publications officielles des Communautés Européenes.
Eurostat (1983 and 1988) *Employment and Unemployment*. Luxembourg: Office des Publications officielles des Communautés Européennes.
Everitt, B. (1979) Unresolved Problems in Cluster Analysis, *Biometrics*, 35, pp. 169–181.
Everitt, B. (1980) *Cluster Analysis*, 2nd ed., London: Gower.
Fairbairns, Z. (1985) The Cohabitation Rule – Why it Makes Sense. In Ungerson, C. (ed.) op. cit.
Falkingham, F. (1985) *Take up of Benefits: a Literature Review*, Benefits Research Unit Review Paper 1:85, Department of Social Administration, Nottingham University.
Ferber, C.v. and Kaufmann, F.-X. (eds) (1977) *Soziologie und Sozialpolitik*, Opladen (Sonderheft 19 of the Kölner Zeitschrift für Soziologie und Sozialpsychologie).
Ferge, Z. and Miller, S. M. (eds.) (1987) *The Dynamics of Deprivation*, London: Gower.
Ferguson, D. G. (1985) *Take up of Family Income Supplement*, MSc Thesis, Ulster University.
Ferguson, D. G. (1986) *Take up of Family Income Supplement*, Stormont: DHSS.
Ferrand-Bechmann, D. (1990) *Pauvre et Mal Loge: Comparisons Internationales*, Paris: Editions L'Harmatan.
Ferrand-Bechmann, G. and Kouchner, B. (1989) *Les Assises des Nouvelles Solidarites: Synthese et Presentation des Debats*, Paris: Presses Universitaires de France.
Filet, B. C. (1974) *Kortsluiting met de Bureaucratie*, Samson, Alphen a.d. Rijn.
Finance (Department of..., Australia) (1988) *Report on the Forward Estimates of Budget Outlays, 1989–90 to 1991–92*.
Flesch, K. (1901) Sociale Ausgestaltung der Armenpflege, *Schriften des Deutschen Vereins fur öffenliche und private Füsorge*, 54, pp. 1–30, Leipzig: Deutscher Verein.
Flora, P. (1985) On the History and Current Problems of the Welfare State. In Eisenstadt, S. and Ahimeir, O. (eds.) *The Welfare State and its Aftermath*, London: Croom Helm.
Flora, P. (1986/87) *Growth to Limits: the Western European Welfare States since World War II*, volumes 1, 2 and 4, Berlin: de Gruyter.
Ford Foundation, The (1989) *The Common Good: Social Welfare and the American Future*, New York.
Foster, C. (1988) *Towards a National Retirement Incomes Policy*, Issues Paper No. 6, Social Security Review, Department of Social Security, Canberra: Government Publishing Service..
Foster, J. (1984) On Economic Poverty: A Survey of Aggregate Measures, *Advances in Econometrics*, 3, pp. 215–251.
Foster, P. (1983) *Access to Welfare: an Introduction to Welfare Rationing*, London: Macmillan Press.
Franz, W. (1989) Beschäftigungsprobleme auf Grund von Inflexibilitäten auf Arbeitsmärkten. In Scherf, H. (ed.) *Beschäftigungsprobleme hochentwickelter Volkswirtschaften*, Schriften des Vereins fur Socialpolitik, N.F. Bd. 178, Berlin: Duncker and Humblot.
Fraser, D. (1973) *The Evolution of the British Welfare State*, London: Macmillan.
Fraser, C. (1987) Women, Welfare and the Politics of Need Interpretation, *Thesis 11*, 17, pp. 88–106.
Freeman, C. (1982) *The Economics of Industrial Innovation*, 2nd ed., London: Frances Pinter.
Fry, V. and Stark, G. (1987) The Take up of Supplementary Benefit: Gaps in the Safety Net, *Fiscal Studies* 8, pp. 1–14.
Fukuyama, F. (1989) The End of History, *The National Interest*, 16.

Galaskiewicz, J. (1985) Interorganizational Relations, *Annual Review of Sociology*, 11, pp. 281–304.
Ganssmann, H. (1988) Der Sozialstaat als Regulationsinstanz. In Mahnkopf, B. (ed) *Der gewendete Kapitalismus*, Münster: Westfälisches Dampfboot.
Ganssmann, H. and Weggler, R. (1989) Interests in the welfare state. In Väth, W. (ed) *Political Regulation in the 'Great Crisis'*, Berlin: Sigma.
George, V. (1968) *Social Security: Beveridge and After*. London: Routledge and Kegan Paul.
George, V. (1988) *Wealth, Poverty and Starvation: An International Perspective*, Hemel Hempstead, Herts.: Wheatsheaf.
Gerhard-Teuschner, U. (1989) 'Die Armut im Alter ist die Armut von Frauen'. Über die steckengebliebene Gleichberechtigung im Rentenrecht und die Begünstigung der Hausfrauenehe. In *Frankfurter Rundschau*, 26, 144, p. 10.
Gerhard, U. Schwarzer, A. and Slupik, V. (eds.) (1988) *Auf Kosten der Frauen. Frauenrechte im Sozialstaat*, Weinham and Basel: Beltz.
Gerlach, K. and Hübler, O. (1985) Lohnstruktur, Arbeitsmarktprozesse und Leistungsintensität in Effizienzlohnmodellen. In Buttler, F., Kühl, J. and Rahmann, B. (eds) Staat und Beschäftigung, *Beiträge zur Arbeitsmarkt- und Berufsforschung*, 88, pp. 249–290.
Geyer, M. (1983) Ein Vorbote des Wohlfahrtsstaates. Die Kriegsopferversorgung in Frankreich, Deutschland und Grossbritannien nach dem Ersten Weltkrieg, *Geschichte und Gesellschaft*, 2, pp. 230–277.
Giddens A. (1982) *Sociology: a Brief but Critical Introduction*, London: Macmillan.
Giddens, A. (1986) *Sociology: a Brief but Critical Introduction*, 2nd ed., Basingstoke: Macmillan.
Gilbert, G. N. (1990a) Knowledge-based Systems for the Public. In Bench-Capon, T. (ed.) *Knowledge-based Systems and Legal Applications*, London: Academic Press.
Gilbert, G. N. (1990b) The Claimant Information Systems. In Bench-Capon, T. (ed.) *Knowledge-based Systems and Legal Applications*, London: Academic Press.
Gill, F. (1989) *Labour Market Flexibility and the Trade Cycle: Who Benefits?* Paper presented at National Social Policy Conference, July, University of New South Wales.
Glennerster, H., Power, A. and Travers, T. (1989) *A New Era for Social Policy: a New Enlightenment or a New Leviathan?* Welfare State Programme Paper 39, Suntory Toyota International Centre for Economics and Related Disciplines, London School of Economics.
Godfrey, N. (1986) *Merseyside County Council 1983 'Claim it Now' Campaign, Final Report*, Liverpool: Merseyside County Council.
Goffman, E. (1974) *Stigma; Notes on the Management of Spoiled Identity*, New York: J. Aronson.
Golding, P. and Middleton, S. (1982) *Images of Welfare. Press and Public Attitudes to Poverty*, Oxford: Martin Robertson.
Goodin, R. E. (1985) *Protecting the Vulnerable: a Reanalysis of Our Social Responsibilities*, Chicago: University of Chicago Press.
Goodin, R. E. (1988) *Reasons for Welfare*, Princeton: Princeton University Press.
Goodin, R. E. and LeGrand, J. (1987) Creeping Universalism in the Australian Welfare State. In Goodin, R. E. and LeGrand, J. *Not Only the Poor*, London: Allen and Unwin.
Gordon, L. (1976) *Women's Body, Women's Right*, New York: Penguin.
Gordon, M. (1988) *Social Security Policies in Industrial Countries: A Comparative Analysis*, Cambridge: Cambridge University Press.
Gorz, A. (1985) *Paths to Paradise*, London: Pluto.
Gough, I. (1979) *The Political Economy of the Welfare State*, London: Macmillan.
Government Statistical Service (1988) *Households Below Average Income: A Statistical Analysis 1981–1985*, London: Department of Health and Social Security.

Graham, J. (1984) *Take up of FIS. Knowledge, Attitudes and Experience – Claimants and Non-Claimants*, PPRU Occasional Paper 2, Social Research Division, Belfast: Department of Finance and Personnel, Stormont.
Grahl, J. and Teague, P.(1989) Labour Market Flexibility in West Germany, Britain and France, *West European Politics*, 12, pp. 91–111.
Grandaunet, A. and Johnsen, J. K. (1984) *Attføringsapparat – bedriftsmiljø. Lokalsamfunnsundersøkelse ave yrkeshemmedes forhold til arbeidsmarkedet*, Oslo: Statens Institutt for Alkoholforskning.
Groupe d'Etude Pour Les Problemes de La Pauvrete (1982a) *From Relative Disadvantages to an Objective Measurement of Poverty*, 9th Clark-Luxembourg Conference, Clark University Massachusetts, United States.
Groupe d'Etude Pour Les Problemes de la Pauvrete (1982b) *The Measurement of Poverty According to the 'Rasch' Model: Principles and Applications*, 9th Clark-Luxembourg conference, Clark University Massachusetts, United States.
Gruen, F. H. (1985) *The Federal Budget: How Much Difference do Elections Make*, Discussion Paper 120A, Canberra: Centre for Economic Policy Research, Australian National University.
Gueron, J. (1986) *Work Initiatives for Welfare Recipients*, New York: Manpower Demonstration Research Corporation.
Habermas, J. (1975) *Legitimation Crisis*, Boston: Beacon Press.
Hagenaars, A. J. M. (1985) *The Perception of Poverty*, Alblasserdam, The Netherlands: Offsetdrukkerij Kanters B. V.
Hagenaars, A. J. M. and DeVos, K. (1988) The Definition and Measurement of Poverty, *Journal of Human Resources*, 23, pp. 211–222.
Hakim, C. (1989) Workforce Restructuring, Social Insurance Coverage and the Black Economy, *Journal of Social Policy*, 18, 4, pp. 471–504.
Hall, S. (1979) The Great Moving Right Show, *Marxism Today*, January, pp. 14–20.
Hancock, K. J. (1976) *A National Superannuation Scheme for Australia*, Final Report of the National Superannuation Committee of Inquiry, Canberra:AGPS.
Handler, J. (1987) Consensus on Redirection – Which Direction? *Focus: Journal of the Wisconsin-Madison Institute for Research on Poverty*, 11, 1, Spring.
Hansen, E. J. (ed.) (1986) *Vor tids Fattigdom*, Copenhagen, Denkmark: Hans Reitzels Forlag.
Hansot, E. and Tyack, D. (1988) Gender in American Public Schools: Thinking Institutionally, *Signs*, 13, 4, Summer.
Harding, S. and Hintikka, M. (eds.) (1983) *Discovering Reality: Feminist Perspectives on Epistemology, Metaphysics and Philosophy of Science*, Dordrecht: Reidel.
Harris, A. I., Smith, C. R. W. and Head, E. (1972) *Income and Entitlement to Supplementary Benefit of Impaired People in Great Britain*, London: HMSO.
Hartmann, H. (1981a) *Sozialhilfebedürftigkeit und 'Dunkelziffer der Armut'*, Stuttgart: Kohlhammer.
Hartmann, H. (1981b) The Unhappy Marriage of Marxism and Feminism: Towards a More Progressive Union. In Sargent, L. (ed.) op. cit.
Hatland, A. (1986) *The Future of Norwegian Social Insurance*, Oslo: Institute of Applied Social Research.
H. C. (House of Commons) (1983/84) *Committee of Public Accounts: Second Report, DHSS*, London: HMSO.
Heclo, H. (1974) *Modern Social Politics in Britain and Sweden*, New Haven: Yale University Press.
Heclo, H. (1981) Towards a New Welfare State. In Flora, P. and Heidenheimer, A. J. (eds.) *The Development of Welfare States in Europe and America*, New Brunswick, N.J.: Transaction Books.
Hegner, F. (1987) Dezentrale Erwerbsarbeit und Familie. In Hoff, A. (ed.) *Vereinbarkeit von Familie und Beruf – Neue Forschungsergebnisse im Dialog zwischen Wissenschaft und Praxis*, Bd. 230 der Schriftenreihe des Bundesministers für Jugend, Familie,

Frauen und Gesundheit, Stuttgart; Berlin; Köln; Mainz: W. Kohlhammer.
Heidenheimer, A. J. (1981) Education and Social Security Entitlements in Europe and America. In Heidenheimer, A. J. and Flora, P. (eds.) *The Development of Welfare States in Europe and America*, New Brunswick, N.J.: Transaction Books.
Heidenreich, H-J. (1989) Erwerbstätigkeit im April 1988. Ergebnis des Mikrozensus, *Wirtschaft und Statistik*, pp. 327–339.
Heinelt, H. (1989) Die 'Niedersachsen-Initiative' und das 'Strukturhilfegesetz' vor dem Hintergrund gestiegener kommunaler Sozialhilfeausgaben fur Arbeitslose, *WSI-Mitteilungen*, 42, pp. 182–188.
Hencke, D. (1990) £2bn Saving Sought in Benefit Costs, *The Guardian*, 10 July.
Hennessy, P. (1990) Priorities in Social Research. In Department of Health, *DH Yearbook of Research and Development 1989 incorporating the Report for 1989 of Research supported by the Department of Social Security*, London: HMSO.
Henwood, M and Wicks, M. (1986) *Benefit or Burden? The Objectives and Impact of Child Support*, Occasional Paper 3, London: Family Policy Studies Centre.
Herder-Dorneich, P. (1982) *Der Sozialstaat in der Rationalitätenfalle*, Stuttgart: Kohlhammer.
Hill, M. (1969) The Exercise of Discretion in the National Assistance Board, *Public Administration*, 47, pp. 75–90.
Himmelreich, F-H. (1988) Arbeitsmarkt und Lohn. In Reyher, L. and Kühl, J. (eds.) *Resonanzen, Arbeitsmarkt und Beruf – Forschung und Politik. Festschrift für Dieter, Mertens*, Beiträge zur Arbeitsmarkt und Berufsforschung, Bd. 111, Nürnberg.
Hinrichs, K. (1989) Irreguläre Beschäftigungsverhältnisse und soziale Sicherheit. Facetten der 'Erosion' des Normalarbeitsverhältnisses, *PROKLA*, 19, 4, pp. 7–32.
Hinrichs, K. (1990) Working Time Development in West Germany: Departure to a New Stage. In Hinrichs, K., Roche, W. K. and Sirianni, C. J. (eds.) *Working Time in Transition. The Political Economy of Working Hours in Industrial Nations*, Philadelphia: Temple University Press.
HMSO (1988) *The Government's Expenditure Plans 1988–9 to 1990–1, Vol II*, Cmnd 288–II, London: HMSO.
Holtermann, S. (1975) Areas of Deprivation in Great Britain: An Analysis of 1971 Census Data, *Social Trends*, 6, pp. 43–48
Houghton, Lord (1977) Administration, Politics and Equity. In Prest, A. R. *The State of Taxation*, London: Institute of Economic Affairs.
Howe, B. (1987) *A Fair Go for Australia's Children*, Canberra: Ministerial News Release, 15 September.
Howe, L. E. A. (1985) The 'Deserving' and the 'Undeserving': Practice in an Urban Local Security Office, *Journal of Social Policy*, 14, 1, pp. 49–72.
Hubert, L. (1972) Some Extensions of Johnson's Hierarchical Clustering Algorithms, *Psychometrika*, 37, pp. 261–274.
Hubert, L. (1974) Aproximate Evaluation Techniques for the Single-Link and Complete-Link Hierarchical Clustering Procedures, *Journal of the American Statistical Association*, 69, pp. 698–704.
Huberty C. J. (1975) Discriminant Analysis, *Review of Educational Research*, 45, pp. 543–598.
Huberty, C. J. (1984) Issues in the Use and Interpretation of Discriminant Analysis, *Psychological Bulletin*, 95, pp. 156–171.
Huberty, C. J., Wisenbaker, J. M. and Smith, J. C. (1987) Assessing Predictive Accuracy in Discriminant Analysis, *Multivariate Behavioural Research*, 22, pp. 307–329.
Hudson, B. (1987) Collaboration in Social Welfare: a Framework for Analysis, *Policy and Politics*, 15, pp. 175–182.
Hvinden, B. (1988a) *Tilbake til fattighjelpen? Utviklingen i sosialhjelpen pa 1980-tallet*, (Back to the Poor Law? The development in social assistance in the 1980s) Rapport No. 4, Oslo: Institute of Applied Social Research.

Hvinden, B. (1988b) *Collaboration between Social Work and Social Security: Who wants it?*, Preliminary Report, Oslo: Institute of Applied Social Research.
Inland Revenue (1987) *How Settlements are Negotiated*, Leaflet No. 73, London: HMSO.
IAB (Institut für Arbeitsmarkt- und Berufsforschung) (1988) *Zur Einkommenssituation von Arbeitslosen*, IAB-Kurzbericht VII/2 - Bri/Spi vom 31.05.1988, Nürnberg (mimeo).
International Labour Office (1984) *Into the Twenty-First Century: The Development of Social Security*, Report of a Working Group to the Director-General of the International Labour Office on the Response of the Social Security System in Iindustrialised Countries to Economic and Social Change, Geneva: ILO.
International Labour Office (1987) *Employment Promotion and Social Security*, Report IV (1) of the International Labour Conference, 73rd Session, Geneva: ILO.
International Sociology (1986) Volume 3 of this journal contained five papers (by Gretschmann, Land, Øyen, Sigg and Watanuki) which were originally given at the first International Seminar on the Sociology of Social Security held at the University of Bergen, Norway in June 1984).
Jagenas, B. (1985) *The Swedish Approach to Labour Market Policy*, Uppsala: The Swedish Institute.
Jansen, L. et al. (1988) *Bijstand als Bodem*, The Hague: Vuga.
Jardine, N. and Sibson, R. (1968) The Construction of Hierarchic and Non-Hierarchic Classifications, *Computer Journal*, 11, pp. 117–184.
Jardine, N. and Sibson, R. (1971) *Mathematical Taxonomy*, New York: John Wiley.
Jenkins, S. P. (1989) *Recent Trends in UK Income Inequality*, Centre for Fiscal Studies, University of Bath.
Johnson, S. C. (1967) Hierarchical Clustering Schemes, *Psychometrika*, 32, pp. 241–254.
Jones, C. (1985) Types of Welfare Capitalism. In *Government and Opposition*, 20, 3, pp. 328–342.
Jones, K. B. and Jonasdottir, A. G. (1988) *The Political Interests of Gender*, London: Sage.
Jordan, A. (1981) *As His Wife, Social Security Law and Policy on De Facto Marriage*, Canberra: Development Division, Department of Social Security, Research Paper No. 16.
Jordan, B. (1988) The Prospects for Basic Income, *Social Policy and Administration*, 22, 2, pp. 115–123.
Judge, K. (ed.) (1980) *Pricing the Social Services*, London: Macmillan.
Kalecki, M. (1943) Political aspects of full employment. Reprinted in Hunt, E. K. and Schwartz, J. G. (1972) *A Critique of Economic Theory*, Harmondsworth: Penguin.
Kamerman, S. B. and Kahn, A. J. (eds) (1978) *Family Policy, Government and Families in Fourteen Countries*, New York: Columbia University Press.
Kamerman, S. B. and Kahn, A. J. (1981) *Child Care, Family Benefits and Working Parents: A Study in Comparative Policy*, New York: Columbia University Press.
Karr, W. and John, K. (1989) Mehrfacharbeitslosigkeit und Kumulative Arbeitslosigkeit, *Mitteilungen aus der Arbeitsmarkt- und Berufsforschung*, 22, pp. 1–16.
Kaufman, F-X. (1970) *Sicherheit als soziologisches und sozialpolitisches Problem: von Untersuchungen zur einer Wertidee hochdifferenzierter Gesellschaften*, Stuttgart: Enke.
Kean, J. (1984) *Public Life and Late Capitalism*, Cambridge: Cambridge University Press.
Kean, J. and Owens, J. (1986) *After Full Employment*, London: Hutchinson.
Kerr, S. (1982a) *Differential Take up of Supplementary Pensions. Final Report*, Department of Psychology, Edinburgh University.
Kerr, S. (1982b) Deciding about Supplementary Pensions: a Provisional Model, *Journal of Social Policy*, 11, pp. 505–517.
Kerr, S. (1983) *Making Ends Meet: an Investigation into the Non-claiming of Supplementary Pensions*, London: Bedford Square Press.
Kewley, T. H. (1973) *Social Security in Australia 1900–72*, 2nd Edition, Sydney: Sydney University Press.

King, A. (1975) Overload: Problems of Governing in the 1970s, *Political Studies*, 23, pp. 290–293.
King, A. (1983) The Political Consequences of the Welfare State. In Spiro, S. and Yuchtman-Yaar, E. (eds) *Evaluating the Welfare State: Social and Political Perspectives*, N.Y.: Academic Press.
King, D. (1987) The State and the Social Structure of Welfare in Advanced Industrial Democracies, *Theory and Society*, 16, pp. 841–868.
Klau, F. and Mittelstädt, A. (1986) Labour Market Flexibility, *OECD Economic Studies*, 6, pp. 7–45.
Klecka, W. R. (1980) *Discriminant Analysis*, Beverley Hills and London: Sage Publications.
Klein, R. and O'Higgins, M. (1988) Defusing the Crisis of the Welfare State. In Marmor, T. R. and Mashaw, J. L. (eds) *Social Security: Beyond the Rhetoric of Crisis*, Princeton: Princeton University Press.
Klein, T. (1987) Verarmung durch Arbeitslosigkeit im Haushaltszusammenhang, *WSI-Mitteilungen*, 40, pp. 621–627.
Knechtel, E. (1960) Die Zahl der einkommensschwachen kinderreichen Familien in der Bundesrepublik, *Soziale Welt*, pp. 330–339.
Knegt, R. (1986) *Regels en Redelijkheid in de Bijstandsverlening: Participerende observatie bij een Sociale Dienst*, Proefschrift, University of Amsterdam, the Netherlands.
Knight, I. (1981) *Family Finances*, OPCS Occasional Paper 26, London: OPCS.
Kock, K. (1989) Entwicklungstendenzen der zugelassenen Leiharbeit - Zum 6. Bericht der Bundesregierung über Erfahrungen bei der Anwendung des Arbeitnehmerüberlassungsgesetzes, *WSI-Mitteilungen*, 42, pp. 24–32.
Köditz, V. (1981) *Youth Unemployment and Vocational Training: the Material and Social Standing of Young People During Transition from School to Working Life*, Synthesis Report, CEDEFOP, Berlin.
Kohl, J. (1986) Krisentendenzen und Strukturprobleme im Bereich der Sozialtransfers. In Bauer, R. and Leibfried, S. (eds), op cit.
Kohl, J. (1987) Alterssicherung im internationalen Vergleich. Zur Einkommensstruktur und Versorgungssituation älterer Haushalte, *Zeitschrift für Sozialreform*, 33, 11/12, pp. 698–719.
Kohl, J. (1988) Alterssicherung in Westeuropa: Strukturen und Wirkungen. In Schmidt, M. G. (ed) *Staatstätigkeit. International und Historisch Vergleichende Analysen*, Opladen: Westdeutscher Verlag (special issue of *Politische Vierteljahresschrift*, 29, 19).
Kohler, P. A. and Zacher, H. F. (eds) (1982) *The Evolution of Social Insurance 1881–1981*, London: Frances Pinter.
Konings, M. and in't Groen (1989) *Niet-gebruik van Soziale Zekerheid onder Tilburgse Bijstandclienten*, Department of Social Security Studies, Tilburg University, the Netherlands.
Korpi, W. (1980) Social Policy and Distributional Conflict in Capitalist Democracies, *West European Politics*, 3, pp. 296–316.
Korpi, W. (1989) Can we Afford to Work? in Bulmer, M., Lewis, J., Piachaud, D. (eds.) *The Goals of Social Policy*, London: Unwin Hyman.
Korpi, W. (1991) The Political Economy of Post-War Unemployment; a Comparative Study of 18 OECD Countries, *British Journal of Political Science* (forthcoming).
Krätke, M. (1985) Klassen und Sozialstaat, *Prokla*, 58, March, pp. 89–108.
Krätke, M. (1987) Steuern der Reichen - Steuern der Armen. Für eine 'sociale Steuerpolitik' im grünen Geist. In Opielka, M. and Ostner, I. (eds) op cit.
Krüger, M. (1987) Leiharbeit - Zur Entwicklung eines personalpolitischen Flexibilisierungsinstruments, *WSI-Mitteilungen*, 40, pp. 423–432.
Kühl, J. (1989) Arbeitsmarkt ohne Vollbeschäftigung – Reaktionsweisen und Strategieoptionen öffentlicher Arbeitsmarktpolitik. In Peters, W. (ed) *Massenarbeitslosigkeit und Politik. Reaktionsweisen und Strategieoptionen in verschiedenen*

Politikarenen, Arbeitskreis Sozialwissenschaftliche Arbeitsmarktforschung (SAMF), Arbeitspapier 1989–1, Paderborn.
Kuhn, A. and Wolpe, A. M. (eds) (1978) *Feminism and Materialism*, London: Routledge and Kegan Paul.
Kuhnle, S. (1986) Norway. In Flora, P. (ed) *Growth to Limits*, Vol. 1, Berlin: Walter de Gruyter.
Kurz-Scherf, I. (1989) Teilzeitarbeit: Individuelle Notlösung und/oder Vorbote in einer neuen Zeitordnung? In. Müller, U. and Schmidt-Waldherr, H. (eds) *FrauenSozialKunde*, Bielefeld: AJZ.
Kuttner, R. (1980) *Revolt of the Haves*, New York: Simon and Schuster.
Lammers, C. J. and Hickson, D. J. (1979) Towards a Comparative Sociology of Organizations. In Lammers, C. J. and Hickson, D. J. (eds) *Organizations Alike and Unlike*, London: Routledge and Kegan Paul.
Lachenbruch, P. A. (1975) *Discriminant Analysis*, New York: Hafner.
Land, H. (1976) *Women: Supporters or Supported?* In Barker, D. and Allen, S. (eds) op cit.
Land, H. (1983) Who still cares for the family? In Lewis, J. (ed) *Women's Welfare, Women's Rights*, London: Croom Helm.
Land, H. and Parker, R. (1978) *United Kingdom*. In Kamerman, S. B. and Kahn, A. J. (eds) op cit.
Landt, J. and Foreman, H. (1989) *The Circumstances of Families in Receipt of Family Allowance Supplement*, Paper presented at Third Australian Family Research Conference, Ballarat, Victoria, 26–27 November.
Larsson, A. (1988) Flexibility in Production and Security for Individuals, National Labour Market Board Reprint, Stockholm.
Lash, S and Urry, J. (1987) *The End of Organised Capitalism*, Cambridge: Polity Press
Laurence, J. (1987) Avoidance Tactics?, *New Society*, 29th May.
Lawson, R. (1986) *Unemployment, Social Security and Poverty: European Comparisons*, European Programme to Combat Poverty Working Paper no. 21, Centre for the Analysis of Social Policy, University of Bath.
Lederer, E. and Marschak, J. (1927) Die Klassen auf dem Arbeitsmarkt und ihre Organisationen. In *Grundriss der Sozialökonomik*, Bd. 11/2, Tübingen: J. C. B. Mohr.
LeGrand, J. and Robinson, R. (eds) (1985) *Privatisation and the Welfare State*, Introductory Chapter, London: George Allen and Unwin.
Leibfried, S. (1976) Armutspotential und Sozialhilfe in der Bundesrepublik: zum Prozess des Filterns von Ansprüchen auf Sozialhilfe, *Kritische Justiz*, 9, 4 pp. 376–393.
Leibfried, S. (1982) Existenzminimum and Försorge-Richsätze in der Weimarer Republik, *Jahrbuch der Sozialareit*, 4.
Leibfried, S. (1990) *Income Transfers and Poverty Policy in EC Perspective: On Europe's Slipping into Anglo-American Welfare Models*, Alghero/Bremen: European Anti-Poverty Program, Centre for Social Policy Research.
Leibfried, S. and Tennstedt, F. (eds) (1985a) *Politik der Armut und die Spaltung des Sozialstaats*, Frankfurt a.M.: Suhrkamp.
Leibfried, S. and Tennstedt, F. (1985b) Armenpolitik und Arbeiterpolitik. Zur Entwicklung und Krise der traditionellen Sozialpolitik der Verteilungsformen. In Leibfried, S. and Tennstedt, F. (eds) op cit.
Leibman, L. and Stewart, R. (1983) Bureaucratic Vision (Review of Jerry Mashaw's *Bureaucratic Justice), Harvard Law Journal*, 96.
Lepsius, M. R. (1979) Soziale Ungleichheiten und Klassenstrukturen in der Bundesrepublik Deutschland. In Wehler, H. U. (ed) *Klassen in der europäischen Sozialgeschichte*, Göttingen: Vandenhoek und Ruprecht.
Levine, S. and White, P. E. (1961) Exchange as a Conceptual Framework for the Study of Interorganizational Relationships, *Administrative Science Quarterly*, 5, pp. 583–601.

Lewis, G. W. and Ulph, D. T. (1988) Poverty, Inequality and Welfare, *Economic Journal*, 98 (conference 1988), pp. 117–131.
Linne, G. and Voswinkel, S. (1989) *Befristete Arbeitsverträge: Aspekte eines Arbeitsverhältnisses ohne Bestandsschutz*, Arbeitskreis Sozialwissenschaftliche Arbeitsmarktforschung (SAMF), Arbeitspapier 1989–5, Paderborn.
Linstone, H. A. and Turoff, M. (eds) (1975) *The Delphi Method: Techniques and Applications*, Reading, Mass.: Addison Wesley Publishing Co.
Lipsky, M. (1980) *Street-Level Bureaucracy*, New York: Russell Sage.
Lipsky, M. (1984) Bureaucratic Disentitlement in Social Welfare Programs, *Social Service Review*, 58, 1.
Lister, R. (1974) *Take up of Means Tested Benefits*, Poverty Pamphlet 18, London: CPAG.
Lister, R. (1976) Take up: Same Old Story, *Poverty*, 34, pp. 3–8.
Lompe, K. and Pollmann, B (1986) Abstieg der Arbeitslosen in die Sozialhilfe: Rekrutierungsmuster neuer Armut – Analyse empirischer Untersuchungen, *Soziale Sicherheit*, 35, pp. 198–207.
Lukes, S. (1977) *Essays in Social Theory*, London: Macmillan.
Luttgens, A. and Perelman, S. (1988) *Comparing Measures of Poverty and Relative Deprivation: An Example for Belgium*, Paper presented at the annual meeting of the European Society for Population Economics held at the University of Mannheim, Federal Republic of Germany, University of Liege, Belgium.
Lutz, B. (1988) Notwendigkeit und Ansatzpunkte einer angebotsbezogenen Vollbeschäftigungspolitik. In Reyher, L. and Kühl, J. (eds) *Resonanzen. Arbeitsmarkt und Beruf – Forschung und Politik. Festschrift für Dieter Mertens*, Beiträge zur Arbeitsmarkt- und Berufsforschung, Bd. III, Nürnberg.
Lynes, A. (1979) The Cost of Justice for Lone Parents, *New Society*, 25 October, 189–190.
McClements, L. (1978) *The Economics of Social Security*, London: Heinemann.
McIntosh, M. C. (1978) The State and the Oppression of Women. In Kuhn, A. and Wolpe, A. M. (eds) op cit.
McLanahan, S. and Sørensen, A. (1987) Married Women's Economic Dependency, 1940–1980, *American Journal for Sociology*, 93, pp. 659–687.
Mack, J. and Lansley, S. (1985) *Poor Britain*, London: Allen and Unwin.
Mackenzie, D. and Wajcman, J. (eds) (1985) *The Social Shaping of Technology*, Milton Keynes: Open University Press.
Mackinnon, C. A. (1983) Feminism, Marxism, Method, and the State: Towards Feminist Jurisprudence, *Signs*, 8, 4.
Macintyre, S. (1985) *Winners and Losers*, Sydney: Allen and Unwin.
Mackie, T. and Rose, R. (1982) *The International Almanac of Electoral History*, 2nd Ed., London: Macmillan.
Maine, H. S. (1959) *Ancient Law. Its Connection with the Early History of Society and Its Relation to Modern Ideas*, London: Oxford University Press (original pub: 1861)
Manchester City Council (1989) *Poverty in Manchester: the Third Investigation*, Manchester: Campaign and Public Information Unit.
Manchester City Council Welfare Rights Service (1985) *Claim it Now. Take up Campaigns in Manchester 1982-4*. Manchester City Council.
Mandla, D. (1987) War on the Dole, *New Society*, 26 June.
Marklund, S. (1988) *Paradise Lost? – The Nordic Welfare States and the Recession 1975–1985*, Lund: Arkiv.
Marklund, S. and Svallfors, S. (1987) *Dual Welfare: Segmentation and Work Enforcement in the Swedish Welfare System*, Research Report No. 94, Department of Sociology, University of Umeå, Sweden.
Markovits, A. S. and Halfmann, J. (1988) The Unravelling of West German Social Democracy? In Brown, M. K. (ed.) *Remaking the Welfare State. Retrenchment and Social Policy in America and Europe*, Philadelphia: Temple University Press.
Marmor, T. R. (1989) Review of Goodwin and LeGrand, *Ethics*, 99, pp. 442–443.

Marmot, M. G. (1989) Social Class and Mortality: Trends and Explanations. In Gunning-Schepers, Spruit, I. P. and Krijnen, J. H. (eds.) *Socio-Economic Inequalities in Health: Questions on Trends and Explanations*, The Hague, the Netherlands: Ministry of Welfare, Health and Cultural Affairs.
Marsden, D. (1973) *Mothers Alone: Poverty and the Fatherless Family*, Harmondswoth: Penguin.
Marshall, T. H. (1963) Citizenship and Social Class. In *Sociology at the Crossroads and other Essays*, London: Heinemann.
Marx, K (1867) *Capital*, vol. 1, New York: International Publishers, 1967.
Mashaw, J. L. (1983) *Bureaucratic Justice*, New Haven and London: Yale University Press.
Matthews, A. and McDonagh, T. (nd) *Take up of Rent Allowances: Further Research*, London: Department of the Environment.
Mayer, H-L (1988) Erwerbslosigkeit 1987 – auch im Internationalen Vergleich. Ergebnisse des Mikrozensus und der EG-Arbeitskräftestichprobne, *Wirtschaft und Statistik*, pp. 849–863.
Mayer, S. E. and Jencks, C. (1989) Poverty and the Distribution of Material Hardship, *Journal of Human Resources*, 24, 1.
Mayer, U. and Paasch, U. (1987) Deregulierung von Arbeitsbedingungen durch selbständige Beschäftigung – Das Beispiel des Versicherungsaussendienstes –, *WSI-Mitteilungen*, 40, pp. 581–589.
Mendeloff, J. (1977) Welfare Procedures and Error Rates: An Alternative Perspective, *Policy Analysis*, 3.
Mezey, S. G. (1988) *No Longer Disabled: The Federal Courts and the Politics of Social Security Disability*, New York: Greenwood Press.
Midgley, J. (1984) *Social Security, Inequality and the Third World*, Chichester: Wiley.
Millar, J. (1983) *Take up of Means-Tested Benefits in Work*, Cohort Study of Unemployed Men, Working Paper 3, London: DHSS.
Millar, J. (1988) Barriers to Equal Treatment and Equal Outcome: Means Testing and Unemployment. In ISSA, *Equal Treatment in Social Security*, Studies and Research no. 27, International Social Security Association, Geneva.
Millar, J. and Cooke, K. (1984) *A Study of the Take up of One Parent Benefit in Hackney*, York: Social Policy Research Unit.
Millar, J. Cooke, K. and McLaughlin, E. (1988) *The Employment Lottery, Risk and Social Security Benefits*, Paper presented to Employment and Unemployment Workshop, Department of Employment, 20 May.
Millar, J., Cooke, K. and McLaughlin, E. (1989) *Determinants of the Labour Supply Behaviour of Long-Term Unemployed Families*, Aldershot: Avebury.
Milligan, G. W (1980) An Examination of the Effects of Six Types of Error Perturbation on Fifteen Clustering Algorithms, *Psychometrika*, 45, pp. 325–342.
Milligan, G. W. (1981) A Review of Monte Carlo Tests of Cluster Analysis, *Multivariate Behavioural Research*, 16, pp. 379–407.
Mills, C. W. (1959) *The Sociological Imagination*, New York: Oxford University Press.
Minford, P. (1987) The Role of the Social Services: a View from the New Right. In Loney, M. (ed.) *The State or the Market*, Milton Keynes: Open University Press.
Ministry of Social Affairs and Employment (1985) *Financiele Nota Sociale Zekerheid 1985*, The Hague.
Ministry of Social Affairs and Employment (1986) *Inkomensbeleid 1986*, The Hague.
Mishra, R. (1984a) *The Welfare State in Crisis*, Brighton: Harvester Wheatsheaf.
Mishra, R. (1984b) *The Welfare State in Crisis, Social Thought and Social Change*, New York: St. Martin's Press.
Mitchell, P. (1985) *Rehabilitation, International Study of Social Security Benefits for Disabled People: United Kingdom Monograph* London: Royal Association for Disability and Rehabilitation.
Mjöset, L. (ed.) (1986) Norden Dagen Derpa: De Nordiske Oekonomisk-Politiske

Modellene og deres Problemer pa 70- og 80-tallet, Oslo: Universitetsforlaget.
Moffitt, R. (1980) Participation in the AFDC Programme and the Stigma of Welfare Receipt, *Southern Economic Journal*, 47, pp. 753–762.
Moffitt, R. (1983) An Economic Model of Welfare Stigma, *American Economic Review*, 73, pp. 1023–35.
Mojena, R. (1977) Hierarchical Grouping Methods and Stopping Rules – An Evaluation, *Computer Journal*, 20, pp. 359–363.
Moore, J. (1989) *The End of the Line for Poverty*, London, Conservative Political Centre.
Moore, P. (1981) Scroungermania again at the DHSS, *New Society*, 22 January.
Moran, M. (1988) Review Article: Crises of the Welfare State, *British Journal of Political Science*, 18, pp. 397–414.
Moray, L. C., Blashfield, R. K. and Skinner, H. A. (1983) A Comparison of Cluster Analysis Techniques Within a Sequential Validation Framework, *Multivariate Behavioural Research*, 18, pp. 309–329.
MORI (Market Opinion Research International) (1988) Gosschalk, B., Lancaster, H. and Townsend, P., *Service Provision and Living Standards in Islington*, Research Study conducted for the London Borough of Islington, London.
Mosse, E. (1983) *Les Riches et Les Pauvres*, Paris: Editions du Seuil.
Mückenberger, U. (1985) Die Krise des Normalarbeitsverhältnisses – Hat das Arbeitsrecht noch Zukunft? – , *Zeitschrift für Sozialreform*, 31, pp. 415–434 and 457–475.
Mückenberger, U. (1986) Zur Rolle des Normalarbeitsverhältnisses bei der sozialstaatlichen Umverteilung von Risiken, *Prokla*, 16, 3, pp. 31–45.
Mückenberger, U. (1989a) Der Wandel des Normalarbeitsverhältnisses unter Bedingungen einer 'Krise der Normalität', *Gewerkschaftliche Monatshefte*, 40, pp. 211–222.
Mückenberger, U. (1989b) Non-Standard Forms of Work and the Role of Changes in Labor and Social Security Regulations, *International Journal of the Sociology of Law*, 17.
Muffels, R. *et al* (1988) *Resultaten Analyses Woonlasten en Nietgebruik van Huursubsidie op basis van SEP, Oktober 1985, CBS*. Bewerking door KUB-Tilburg, 29 Juni 1988. Voorlopige analyse t.b.v. Inkomensnota Ministerie van Sociale Zaken en Werkgelegenheid, Vakgroep Sociale Zeker heidswetenschap, KUB, Tilburg.
Münch, R. (1984) *Die Struktur der Moderne (II Gemeinschaft)*, Frankfurt: Suhrkamp.
Munday, B. (ed.) (1989) *The Crisis in Welfare*, Hemel Hempstead: Harvester Wheatsheaf.
Murray, C. (1984) *Losing Ground: American Social Policy, 1950–1980*, New York: Basic Books.
Murray, C. *et al.* (1990) *The Emerging British Underclass*, London: Institute of Economic Affairs.
NACRO (National Association For The Care & Resettlement of Offenders (1986) *Enforcement of the Law Relating to Social Security*, London.
National Audit Office (1985) *DHSS: Arrangements for Delivering Social Security Benefits*, London: HMSO.
National Audit Office (1988) *DHSS: Quality of Service to the Public at Local Offices*, London: HMSO.
National Audit Office (1989) *Department of Social Security: Operational Strategy*, London: HMSO.
National Consumer Council (1976) *Means-Tested Benefits. A Discussion Paper*, London: National Consumer Council.
National Economic Summit Conference (1983) *Documents and Proceedings, Vol. 1, Government Documents*, Canberra: AGPS, pp. 407-26.
NCASSC (National Campaign Against Social Security Cuts) (1985) Bulletin 3.
Nelson, B. J. (1984) Women's Poverty and Women's Citizenship: Some Political Consequences of Economic Marginality, *Signs*, 10, 2.

Netherlands Scientific Council for Government Policy (1985) Report No. 23, Safeguarding Social Security, The Hague.
Network: the Quarterly Magazine of the Inland Revenue (1985), July, Burnham, Bucks., pp. 10–11.
Newman, B. A. and Thomson, R. J. (1989) *Economic Growth and Social Development: A Longitudinal Analysis of Causal Priority*, World Development.
Noreik, K. (1983) Vedtak om uførepensjon i tre fylkesnemnder. In Kjønstad, A. (ed.) *Stønad ved uførhet*, Oslo: Universitetsforlaget
Noreik, K. (1988) Vedtak om uførepensjon i tre fylkesnemnder. In Kjønstad, A. (ed.) *I uførepensjonens og sosialhjelpens gråsone*, Oslo: Universitetsforlaget.
Nowak, Stefan (1989) Comparative Studies and Social Theory. In Kohn, M. (ed.) *Cross-National Research in Sociology*, Newbury Park: Sage Publications.
NSWPD (New South Wales Parliamentary Debates) Legislative Assembly, 14 November 1900.
O'Connor, J. (1974) *The Fiscal Crisis of the State*, New York: St. Martin's Press.
OECD (1976) *Public Expenditure on Income Maintenance and Programmes, Studies in Resources Allocation No. 3*, Paris.
OECD (1981) *The Welfare State in Crisis*, Paris.
OECD (1985) *Social Expenditure: 1960–1990: Problems of Growth and Control*, Paris.
OECD (1986) *Employment Outlook*, Paris.
OECD (1988a) *Poverty and Low Incomes*, Paris.
OECD (1988b) *Employment Outlook*, Paris.
OECD (1988c) *Reforming Public Pensions*, Paris.
OECD (1988d) *Labour Force Statistics 1966–1986*, Paris.
OECD (1989a) *Employment Outlook*, Paris.
OECD (1989b) *Public Benefits and Private Poverty: The International Evidence from Household Income Surveys*, Paris.
Offe, C. (1984) *Contradictions of the Welfare State*, London: Hutchinson.
Offe, C. (1988) Democracy Against the Welfare State? Structural Foundations of Neoconservative Political Opportunities. In Moon, J. D. (ed) *Responsibility, Rights and Welfare: the Theory of the Welfare State*, London: Westview Press.
Offe, C. and Hinrichs, K. (1985) The Political Economy of the Labour Market. In Offe, C. *Disorganized Capitalism, Contemporary Transformations of Work and Politics*, ed. by Keane J., Cambridge: Polity Press.
Ogus, A. I. (1982) *Great Britain*. In Kohler, P. A. and Zachar, H. F. (eds.) op cit.
O'Higgins, M. (1984) Computerising the Social Security System: An Operational Strategy in Lieu of a Policy Strategy, *Public Administration*, 62, pp. 201–210.
O'Higgins, M. (1987) *Les Familles Monoparentales dans les pays de l'OCDE: Effectifs et Caracteristiques Socio-economiques*, Document 3, Paris: OECD.
Oi, W. Y. (1962) Labor as a Quasi-Fixed Factor of Production, *Journal of Political Economy*, 70, pp. 538–555.
Okin, S. M. (1989) *Justice, Gender and the Family*, New York: Basic Books.
Oorschot, W. van and Kolkhuis Tancke, P. (1989) *Niet-Bebruik van Sociale Zekerheid: Feiten, Theorieen en Onderzoeksmethoden*, COSZ-reeks no. 16, The Hague.
Oorschot, W. van (1990) *Non Take-up of Social Security Benefits in Europe*, Paper presented at the Annual Conference of the Social Policy Association, University of Bath, 10–12 July.
Opielka, M. and Ostner, I. (eds) (1987) *Umbau des Sozialstaats*, Essen: Klartext.
Ostner, I. (1986) Prekäre Subsidiarität und partielle Individualisierung – Zukünfte von Haushalt und Familie. In Berger, J. (ed.) *Die Moderne – Kontinuitäten und Zäsuren*, Göttingen: Otto Schwartz and Co.
Ostner, I. (1990) Der Partikularistische Sozialstaat – das Beispiel der Frauen. In Dressel, W., Heinz, W. R., Peters, G. and Schober, K. (eds.) *Lebenslauf, Arbeitsmarkt und Sozialpolitik*, Nürnberg: Institut fur Arbeitsmarkt – und Berufsforschung der Bundesanstalt für Arbeit. (Beiträge zur Arbeitsmarkt und

Berufsforschung No. 133).
Otton, G. (1984) Managing Social Security: Government as Big Business, *International Social Security Review*, 2, pp. 158–170.
Oude Engerberink, G. (1984) *Minima Zonder Marge*, Rotterdam: Gemeentelijke Sociale Dienst Rotterdam.
Owen, J. (1987) *Survey of Living Standards in London: Fieldwork Reports*, London: Research Centre, Survey Services and Methodology Group. London Residuary Body.
Øyen, E. (1986a) The Sociology of Social Security – Editorial Introduction: The Bergen Conference, *International Sociology*, 1, 3, pp. 219–21.
Øyen, E. (1986b) Identifying the Future of the Welfare State. In Øyen, E. (ed.) *Comparing Welfare States and Their Futures*, Aldershot: Gower.
Page, D. and Weinberger, B. (1975) *Birmingham Rent Rebate and Allowances Study*, Centre for Urban and Regional Studies Research Memorandum 44, Birmingham University.
Pahl, J. (1980) Patterns of Money Management within Marriage, *Journal of Social Policy*, 9, 3, pp. 313–315.
Pahl, J. (1983) The Allocation of Money in the Structuring of Inequality within Marriage, *Sociological Review*, 31, pp. 237–262.
Pahl, R. (1988) Some Remarks on Informal Work, Social Polarisation and the Social Structure, *International Journal of Urban and Regional Research*, 12, 2, pp. 247–267.
Paloheimo, H. (1984) *Governments in Democratic Capitalist States 1950–1983: A Data Handbook*, Studies in Political Science No. 8, Turku, Finland: University of Turku.
Papadakis, E. and Taylor-Gooby, P. (1987) *The Private Provision of Public Welfare*, Brighton, Sussex: Wheatsheaf Books.
Parker, H. (1982) *The Moral Hazards of Social Benefits: a Study of the Impact of Social Benefits and Income Tax on Incentives to Work*, Research Monographs 37, London: Institute of Economic Affairs.
Parker, J. (1975) *Social Policy and Citizenship*, London: Macmillan Press.
Parker, R. A. (1976) Charging for the Social Services, *Journal of Social Policy*, 5, 4.
Parry, R. (1986) United Kingdom. In Flora, P. (ed.) *Growth to Limits*, Vol. II., Berlin: Walter de Gruyter.
Pateman, C. (1988a) The Patriarchal Welfare State. In Gutman, A. (ed.) *Democracy and the Welfare State*, Princeton: Princeton University Press.
Pateman, C. (1988b) *The Sexual Contract*, Cambridge: Polity Press.
Perrow, C. (1961) The Analysis of Goals in Complex Organizations, *American Sociological Review*, 26, pp. 854–866.
Pfeffer J. and Salancik, G. R. (1978) *The External Control of Organizations*, New York: Harper and Row.
Phillips, A. (1987) *Divided Loyalties*, London: Virago Press.
Piachaud, D. (1979) *The Cost of a Child*, London: Child Poverty Action Group.
Piachaud, D. (1981) *Children and Poverty*, London: Child Poverty Action Group.
Piachaud, D. (1988) Poverty in Britain 1899–1983, *Journal of Social Policy*, 17, 3, pp. 335–349.
Pierson, P. (1988) *Cutting Against the Grain: The Politics of Welfare State Retrenchment in Britain and the United States*, Cambridge, MA (unpublished manuscript).
Pinker, R. (1971) *Social Theory and Social Policy*, London: Heinemann.
Piven, F. F. and Cloward, R. A. (1971) *Regulating the Poor, the Functions of Public Welfare*, New York: Vintage.
Piven, F. F. and Cloward, R. (1982) *The New Class War*, New York: Phanteon.
Piven, F. F. and Cloward, R. (1988) Popular Power and the Welfare State. In Brown, M. K. (ed.) *Remaking the Welfare State, Retrenchment and Social Policy in America and Europe*, Philadelphia: Temple University Press.
Plant, M. W. (1984) An Empirical Analysis of Welfare Dependence, *American Economic Review*, 74, pp. 673–83.

Podder, N. and Kakwani, N. C. (1975) Distribution and Redistribution of Household Income in Australia. In *Taxation Review Committee*, op. cit.
Polanyi, K. (1957) *The Great Transformation*, Boston: Beacon Press. (originally published 1944).
Przeworski, A (1985) *Capitalism and Social Democracy*, Cambridge: Cambridge University Press.
Przeworski, A. and Teune, H. (1970) *The Logic of Comparative Social Inquiry*, New York: Wiley.
PSI (1984) *The Reform of Supplementary Benefit: Working Papers*, London.
Rainwater, L. (1988) *Inequalities in the Economic Well-Being of Children and Adults in Ten Nations*, Paper presented at the Workshop on Comparative Research in Social Policy, Labour Markets, Inequality and Distributive Conflict, ISA Research Committee 19, Stockholm, August 25–28, (LIS Working Paper 19).
Rainwater, L., Rein, M. and Schwartz, J. (1986) *Income Packaging and the Welfare State. A Comparative Study of Family Income*, Oxford: Clarendon Press.
Rawls, J. (1972) *A Theory of Justice*, Oxford: Oxford University Press.
Reich, R. (1989) As the World Turns: U.S. Income Inequality Keeps on Rising, *New Republic*, May 1.
Reichsbund (der Kriegsopfer, Behinderten, Sozialrentner und Hinterbliebenen E. V.) (1986) *Einschränkungen im sozialen Bereich 1975–1985*, Bonn, mimeo.
Rein, M. Esping-Andersen, G. and Rainwater, L. (eds.) (1987) *Stagnation and Renewal in Social Policy, The Rise and Fall of Policy Regimes*, Armonk, New York: M. E. Sharpe, Inc.
Rein, M. and Rainwater, L. (1987) From Welfare State to Welfare Society. In Rein, M. Esping-Andersen, G. and Rainwater, L. (eds) op cit.
Rentoul, J. (1988) The New Idle Rich, *New Statesman and Society*, 25 March.
Richardson, A. and Naidoo, J. (1978) *The Take up of Supplementary Benefits: a Report on a Survey of Claimants*, London: DHSS/London University.
Riede, T., Schott-Winterer, A. and Woller, A. (1988) Soziale Dienstleistungen und Wohlfahrtsstaat. Vergleichende Analysen zur Beschäftigung im Arbeitsmarktsegment 'Soziale Dienstleistungen' in der Bundesrepublik Deutschland und den USA, *Soziale Welt*, 39, 3, pp. 292–314.
Riedmüller, B. and Kickbusch, I. (eds) (1982) *Die armen Frauen. Frauen und Sozialpolitik*, Frankfurt: Suhrkamp.
Ringeling, A. (1981) The Passivity of the Administration, *Policy and Politics*, 9, 3, pp. 295–309.
Ringen, S. (1988) Direct and Indirect Measures of Poverty, *Journal of Social Policy*, 17, 3, pp. 351–365.
Ritchie, J. and Davies, C. (1986) Tipping the Balance: a Study of Non Take-up of Benefits in an Inner City Area, Social Community Planning Research, London.
Ritter, G. A. (1989) *Der Sozialstaat. Entstehung und Entwicklung im internationalen Vergleich*, München: Oldenbourg, IX.
Roberts, K. (1985) A New Deal for All, *Basic Income Research Group Bulletin*. No. 3, Spring, pp. 2–3.
Rodgers, G. and Rodgers, J. (eds.) (1989) *Precarious Jobs in Labour Market Regulation: the Growth of Atypical Employment in Western Europe*, Geneva: International Labour Office.
Roebroek, J. and Berben, T. (1988) *The 'Incrementalist' Paradox: Securing a Subsistence Minimum and the Introduction of a Basic Income in the Netherlands*, Social Security Studies Series, Tilburg University, the Netherlands.
Room, G. (1987) *'New Poverty' in the European Community*, Centre for the Analysis of Social Policy, University of Bath.
Room, G., Lawson, R. and Laczko, F. (1989) 'New Poverty' in the European Community, *Policy and Politics* 17, pp. 165–176.
Root, L. S. (1981) Employee Benefits and Income Security, Private Social Policy and

the Public Interest. In Tropman, J. E. *et al* (eds.) *New Strategic Perspectives on Social Policy*, 2nd Ed., New York: Pergamon Press.

Rowthorn, R. (1989) Corporatism, Wage Dispersion and Equality. In Pekarinnen, J. and Pohjola, M. (eds.) *Coping with the Crisis: Lessons from the Corporatist Experience* (in press).

Royal Commission on the Distribution of Income and Wealth (The Diamond Commission) (1978) Report No. 6, Lower Incomes, Cmnd 7175, London: HMSO.

Rudolph, H. (1987) Befristete Beschäftigung – Ein Überblick, *Mitteilungen aus der Arbeitsmarkt- und Berufsforschung*, 20, pp. 288–304.

Ruggles, P. and O'Higgins, M. (1987) Retrenchment and the New Right: A Comparative Analysis of the Thatcher and Reagan Administrations. In Rein, M., *et al* (eds.) op cit.

Rys, V. (1964) The Sociology of Social Security, *Bulletin of the International Social Security Association*, 1–2, pp. 3–34.

Sabatier, P. A. (1986) Top-down and Bottom-up Approaches to Implementation Research: A Critical Analysis and Suggested Synthesis, *Journal of Public Policy*, 6, 1, pp. 21–48.

Sachsse, C. and Tennstedt, F. (1988) *Geschichte der Armenfürsorge in Deutschland*, vol. 2: Fürsorge und Wohlfahrtsplege 1871 bis 1929, Stuttgart: Kohlhammer.

Sainsbury, R. (1989) The Social Security Chief Adjudication Officer: The First Four Years, *Public Law*, Summer, pp. 323–341.

Sargent, L. (ed.) (1981) *Women and Revolution*, Boston: South End Press.

Sarpellon, G. (1983) *La Poverta in Italia*, Milan: Franco Angeli.

Saunders, P. (1987a) *Growth in Australian Social Security Expenditures, 1959–60 to 1985–86*, Social Security Review, Background Paper No. 19, Canberra: AGPS.

Saunders, P. (1987b) *Redistribution and the Welfare State*, Social Welfare Research Centre, Reports and Proceedings, No. 67.

Saunders, P. (1987c) An Agenda for Social Security in the Years Ahead, *Australian Journal of Social Issues*, 22, 2.

Saunders, P. (1987d) The Changing Nature and Effects of the Australian Social Security System, *Canberra Bulletin of Public Administration*, No. 51 (May), pp. 57–67.

Saunders, P. (1989) *Towards an Understanding of Commonwealth Social Expenditure Trends*, Discussion Paper No. 11, Social Welfare Research Centre.

Sawyer, M. (1976) *Income Distribution in OECD Countries*, Occasional Study, Paris: OECD.

Schaber, G. (1984) Introduction, *Mondes en Developpement*, 12, 45, pp. 15–27.

Scharpf, F. (1986) Strukturen der post-industriellen Gesellschaft oder: Verschwindet die Massenarbeitslosigkeit in der Diensleistungs- und Informationsökonomie?, *Soziale Welt*, 37, 1, pp. 3–24.

Schartum, D. W. (1987) *The Introduction of Computers in Norwegian Local Insurance Offices*, Oslo: Norwegian University Press.

Scheibler, D. and Schneider, W. (1985) Monte Carlo Tests of the Accuracy of Cluster Analysis Algorithms: A Comparsion of Hierarchical and Non-Hierarchical Methods, *Multivariate Behavioural Research*, 20, pp. 283–304.

Schell, J. and Pieters, D. (1989) *De Middelentoets in Rechtsvergelijkend Perspectief*, COSZ, The Hague.

Schupp, J. (1988) Trotz Anstiegs der Beschäftigung wurde Wiedereingliederung Erwerbsloser schwieriger. Ergebnisse einer Längsschnittstudie für die Jahre 1984 bis 1987, *DIW-Wochenbericht*, 55, pp. 409–416.

Schupp, J. (1989) Teilzeitbeschäftigte in der Bundesrepublik Deutschland. Opfer oder Gewinner der Arbeitszeitflexibilisierung, *Sozialer Fortschritt*, 38, pp. 245–252.

Schmidt, M. (1983) The Welfare State and the Economy in Periods of Economic Crisis: A Comparative Study of twenty three OECD Nations, *European Journal of*

Political Research, 11, pp. 1–25.
Schütte, W. and Süss, W. (1986) *Armut in Hamburg*, Eigenverlag, Fachhochschule Hamburg.
Schütte, W. and Süss, W. (1988) *Armut in Hamburg*, Hamburg: VSA-Verlag.
Schwartze, J., Gornig, M. and Steinhöfel, M. (1990) Die Bedeutung der Frauenerwerbstätigkeit fur die Einkommenssituation in beiden deutschen Staaten, *Wirtschaftsdienst*, 5.
Segal, L. (1987) *Is the Future Female?* London: Virago.
Sen, A. K. (1981) *Poverty and Famines: An Essay on Entitlement and Deprivation*, Oxford: Clarendon Press.
Sen, A. K. (1983) Poor, Relatively Speaking, *Oxford Economic Papers*, 35, pp. 135–169.
Sen, A. K. (1985a) A Sociological Approach to the Measurement of Poverty: A Reply to Professor Peter Townsend, *Oxford Economic Papers*, 37, pp. 669–676.
Sen, A. K. (1985b) *Commodities and Capabilities*, Amsterdam: North Holland.
Sen, A. K. (1985c) Well-being, Agency and Freedom, *Journal of Philosophy*, 82, 22, pp. 169–221.
Shaver, S. (1983) *Sex and Money in the Welfare State*. In Baldock, C. and Cass, B. (eds.) op cit.
Shaver, S. (1984) The Assets Test and the Politics of Means Testing, *Australian Journal of Social Issues*, 22, 2.
Shaver, S. (1987) Design for a Welfare State: the Joint Parliamentary Committee on Social Security, *Historical Studies*, 22, 88.
Shenfield, A. A. (1968) The Political Economy of Tax Avoidance, *Occasional Paper 24*, London: Institute of Economic Affairs.
Sigg, R. (1985) Sociology and Social Security: a Fresh Approach, *International Social Security Review*, 1/85, pp. 3–19.
Sigg, R. (1986) The Contribution of Sociology to Social Security, *International Sociology*, 1, 3, pp. 282–295.
Silva, M., and DaCosta, A. B. (1989) *Pobreza Urbana em Portugal*, Centro de Refexao Crista, Departamento de Pesquisa Social, Caritas Portuguesa.
Simmel, G. (1908) *Soziologie: Untersuchungen über die Formen der Vergesellschaftung*, (Siebentes Kapitel: Der Arme), Leipzig: Duncker and Humblot.
Sinfield, A. (1978) Analyses in the Social Division of Welfare, *Journal of Social Policy*, 7, 2, pp. 129–156.
Sinfield, A. (1983) The Necesssity for Full Employment. In Glennerster, H. (ed) *The Future of the Welfare State, Remarking Social Policy* Aldershot: Gower.
Sinfield, A. (1989) Social Security and its Social Division: A Challenge for Sociological Analysis, *New Waverly Papers: Social Policy Series No. 2* University of Edinburgh (revised version of a paper presented at the first International Seminar on the Sociology of Social Security held at the University of Bergen in June 1984).
Smeeding, I. S., O'Higgins, M., Rainwater, L. and Atkinson, A. B. (1989) *Poverty, Inequality and Income Distribution in Comparative Perspective*, Hemel Hempstead: Simon and Schuster.
Smeeding, I. M. and Torrey, B. B. (1988) Poor Children in Rich Countries, *Science*, pp. 873–877, 11 November.
Smith, D. E. (1983) Women, Class and Family, *The Socialist Register* 1983, London: Merlin Press.
Smith, R. (1985) Who's Fiddling? In Ward, S. (ed) *DHSS in Crisis* London: CPAG.
Social Security Advisory Committee (1988) *Sixth Report of the Social Security Advisory Committee*, London: HMSO.
Social Security Review, Department of Social Security (1987) *Bringing Up Children Alone: Policies for Sole Parents*. Issues Paper No. 3, Canberra: Australian Government Publishing Service.
Social Services Committee (1988) *Families on Low Income: Low Income Statistics, Fourth Report, Session 1987–88*, House of Commons 565, London: HMSO.

Social Welfare Policy Secretariat, Australia (1981) *Report on Poverty Measurement*, Canberra: Australian Government Publishing Service.
Spicker, P. (1984) *Stigma and Social Welfare*. London: Croom Helm.
SSB (1983) Arbeid og helse 1982, rapport 83/3, Oslo: Statistisk Sentralbrå.
Stark, M. (1988) *An A to Z of Income and Wealth*, London: Fabian Society.
Starr, P. (1985) The Meaning of Privatization, National Conference on Social Welfare, Project on the Federal Social Role, Working Paper No. 6, Washington, D.C.
Statistical Reports of the Nordic Countries *(1989) Social Security in the Nordic Countries 1987*, Copenhagen 1989.
Statistisches Bundesamt (1987) *Volkswirtschaftliche Gesamtrechnungen*, Fachserie 18, Reihe S 1, Wiesbaden.
Statistisches Bundesamt (1987) *Der Staat in den Volkswirtschaftlichen Gesamtrechnungen*, Fachserie 18, Reihe S 10, Wiesbaden.
Statskonsult (1988) *Rapport om samarbeid ved yrkesmessig attføring*, Oslo: Direktoratet for Forvaltningsutvikling.
Stone, D. (1984) *The Disabled State*, Philadelphia: Temple University Press.
Strauss, R. P. (1977) Information and Participation in a Public Transfer Programme, *Journal of Public Economics*, 8, pp. 385–96.
Strauss, A. (1982) *Interorganizational Negotiation*, Urban Life, 11, 3, pp. 350–367.
Supplementary Benefits Commission (1976) Annual Report. London: HMSO.
Supplementary Benefits Commission (1978) Take-up of Supplementary Benefits, *Supplementary Benefits Administration Paper, 7*, London: HMSO.
Taylor-Gooby, P. (1976) Rent Benefits and Tenants' Attitudes. The Batley Rent Rebate and Allowance Study, *Journal of Social Policy*, 5, 1, pp. 33–48.
Taylor-Gooby, P. (1988) The Future of the British Welfare State: Public Attitudes, Citizenship and Social Policy under the Conservative Government of the 1980s, *European Sociological Review*, 24, 1, pp. 1–19.
Taxation Review Committee (1975) Commissioned Studies, Canberra: Australian Government Publishing Service.
Tennstedt, F. (1983) *Vom Proleten zum Industriearbeiter. Arbeiterbewegung und Sozialpolitik in Deutschland 1800–1914*, Cologne: Bund Verlag.
Tessaring, M. (1988) Arbeitslosigkeit, Beschäftigung und Qualifikation,*Mitteilungen aus der Arbeitsmarkt- und Berufsforschung*, 21, 2, pp. 177–193.
Therborn, G. and Roebroeck, J. (1986) The Irreversible Welfare State: Its Recent Maturation, Its Encounter with the Economic Crisis, and Its Future Prospects, *International Journal of Health Services*, 16, 3, pp. 319–338.
Thompson, J. D. (1967) *Organizations in Action*, New York: McGraw-Hill.
Titmuss, R. M. (1958) The Social Division of Welfare. In *Essays on 'The Welfare State'*, London: Unwin University Books.
Titmuss, R. M. (1968) *Commitment to Welfare*. London: Allen and Unwin.
Titmuss, R. M. (1970) *The Gift Relationship: from Human Blood to Social Policy*, London: Allen and Unwin.
Titmuss, R. M. (1987) Developing Social Policy in Conditions of Rapid Change: the Role of Social Welfare. In Abel-Smith, B. and Titmuss, K. (eds), op cit.
TL (1987) *Undersøkelse av 943 uførepensjonssaker*, Oslo: Trygdekontorenes Landsforening.
Townsend, P. (1957) *The Family Life of Old People. An Inquiry in East London*, London: Routledge.
Townsend, P. (1979) *Poverty in the United Kingdom. A Survey of Household Resources and Standards of Living*, Harmondsworth, Middlesex: Allen Lane and Penguin Books.
Townsend, P. (1985) A Sociological Approach to the Measurement of Poverty: A Rejoinder to Professor Amartya Sen, *Oxford Economic Papers*, 37, pp. 659–668.
Townsend, P. (1986) Why are the Many Poor? *International Journal of Health Services*, 16, 1, pp. 1–32.

Townsend, P. (1987a) 'Conceptualizing Poverty' and 'Poverty in Europe'. In Ferge, Z. and Miller, S. M. (1986) *The Dynamics of Deprivation*, London: Gower.
Townsend, P. (1987b) Deprivation, *Journal of Social Policy*, 16, pp. 125–146.
Townsend, P. (1989) 'The Price of Poverty: Retreat from Meaning' and 'Our Greater Divide', *Community Care*, 27 April and 4 May.
Townsend, P. (1990a) Poverty. In Outhwaite, W. and Bottomore, T. *The Blackwell Dictionary of Social Thought*, Oxford: Blackwell.
Townsend, P. (1990b forthcoming) *Poverty and Planning in India*.
Townsend P., Davidson, N. and Whitehead, M. (1988) *Inequalities in Health: The Black Report and the Health Divide*, 2nd ed., Harmondsworth: Penguin Books.
Treasury (Department of..., Australia) (1988) *Treasury Economic Roundup*, monthly.
Triest, M. and Doorne-Huiskes, J. van (1988) Flexibiliserung en emancipatie: een ambivalente relatie. In Flap, H. D. and Arts, W. A. (eds) *De Flexibele Arbeidsmarkt. Theorie en Praktijk*, Deventer: Van Loghum Slaterus.
Uglow, S. (1984) Defrauding the Public Purse, *Criminal Law Review*, March, pp.128–141.
Ungerson, C. (ed) (1985) *Women and Social Policy* London: Macmillan.
United States Department of Health Education and Welfare (1976) *The Measure of Poverty: A Report to Congress as Mandated by the Education Amendments of 1974*, Washington D.C.
Van Praag, B. M. S., Hagenaars, A. J. M. and van Weeren, J. (1982) Poverty in Europe, *Review of Income and Wealth*, 28, pp. 345–359.
Van Slooten, R. and Coverdale, A. G. (1978) The Characteristics of Low Income Households, *Social Trends 1977*, pp. 26–39.
Vaubel, R. (1989) Möglichkeiten einen erfolgreichen Beschäftigungspolitik. In Scherf, H. (ed) *Beschäftigungsprobleme hochentwickelter Volkswirtschaften*, Schriften des Vereins für Socialpolitik, N.F. Bd. 178, Berlin: Duncker and Humblot.
Vaughan, D. R. (1985) Using Subjective Assessments of Income to Estimate Family Equivalence Scales, a Report of Work in Progress in Surveys of Income and Program Participation and Related Longitudinal Surveys, 1984, Population Division, Bureau of the Census, Washington D.C.
Vaughan, D. and Lancaster, C. (1980) Applying a Cardinal Measurement Model to Normative Assessments of Income: A Preliminary Look, paper presented at the 1980 meetings of the American Statistical Association, Office of Research and Statistics, Social Security Administration, Washington D.C.
Veit-Wilson, J. (1987) Consensual Approaches to Poverty Lines and Social Security, *Journal of Social Policy*, 16, 2, pp. 183–212.
Villeneuve, A. (1984) Construire un Indicateur de Précarité: Les Etapes d'une Dé Marche Empirique, *Sociology et Statistique*.
Vobruba, G. (1983) *Politik mit dem Wohlfahrtsstaat*, Frankfurt a. M.: edition Suhrkamp.
Vobruba, G. (1990) Lohnarbeitszentrierte Sozialpolitik in der Krise der Lohnarbeit. In Vobruba, G. (ed) *Strukturwandel der Sozialpolitik*, Frankfurt a. M.: edition Suhrkamp.
Vogel, J., Andersson, L-G, Davidsson, U. and Hall, L. (1988) Living Conditions, Report No. 58, *Inequality in Sweden: Trends and Current Situation*, Stockholm: Statistics Sweden.
Vogt, W. (1986) *Theorie der kapitalistischen und einer laboristischen Ökonomie*, Frankfurt a. M.: Campus.
Wadensjo, E. (1987) Labour Market Policy and Employment Growth in Sweden, *Review of Labour Economics and Industrial Relations*, 1, 3, Winter.
Walinsky, A. (1965) Keeping the Poor in Their Place: Notes on the Importance of Being One-Up. In Shostak, A. B. and Gomberg, W. (eds) *New Perspectives on Poverty*, Englewood Cliffs, N.J.: Prentice Hall.
Walker, A. (1980) The Social Creation of Poverty and Dependency in Old Age, *Journal of Social Policy*, 9, 1, pp. 49–76.

Walker, A. and Walker, C. (1987) *The Growing Divide*, London: Child Poverty Action Group.
Walker, R. (1980) Temporal Aspects of Claiming Behaviour: Renewal of Rent Allowances, *Journal of Social Policy*, 9, 2, pp. 207–22.
Walker, R., Lawson, R. and Townsend, P. (1984) *Responses to Poverty in Europe*, London: Heinemann.
Walsh, K. (1982) Duration of Unemployment: Methods and Measurement in the European Community, *Eurostat*.
Walzer, M. (1983) *Spheres of Justice*, Oxford: Martin Robertson.
Ward, S. (ed) (1983) *DHSS in Crisis* London: CPAG.
Watts, H. W. (1968) An Economic Definition of Poverty, In Moynihan, D.P. (ed) *On Understanding Poverty*, New York: Basic Books.
Watts, R. (1980) Origins of the Australian Welfare State, *Historical Studies*, 19, 75.
Watts, R. (1987) *The Foundations of the National Welfare State*, Sydney: Allen and Unwin.
Waxman, C. (1983) *The Stigma of Poverty: a Critique of Poverty Theories and Policies*, Oxford: Pergamon Press
Weale, A. (1983) *Political Theory and Social Policy*, London: Macmillan.
Weatherley, R. (1979) *Reforming Special Education*, Cambridge, Mass: MIT Press.
Weber, M. (1964) *The Theory of Social and Economic Organisation*, (trans. Henderson, A. R. and Parsons, T.) London: Collier-Macmillan.
Weber, M. (1972) *Wirtschaft und Gesellschaft*, Tübingen: Mohr Verlag.
Weir, M., Orloff, A. S. and Skocpol. T. (1988) *The Politics of Social Policy in the United States*, Princeton, N.J.: Princeton University Press.
Weisbrod, B. A. (1970) On the Stigma Effect and the Demand for Welfare Programmes – a Theoretical Note, Institute for Research on Poverty Discussion Paper 82–70, University of Wisconsin, Madison.
Welzmüller, R. (1986) Niedrige Arbeitseinkommen: Einkommensrisiko bei Erwerbstätigkeit, *WSI-Mitteilungen*, 39, pp. 745–755.
Whiteford, P. (1981) The Concept of Poverty, *Social Security Journal*, Department of Social Security, Canberra.
Whiteford, P. (1985) A Family's Needs: Equivalence Scales, Poverty and Social Security, Research Paper No. 27, Development Division, Department of Social Security, Canberra.
Whiteford, P. (1987) How Should We Measure the Standard of Living of Low Income Families?, presented to a Workshop on 'Family Well-Being' organised by the Australian Institute of Family Studies, Melbourne, 3 June (publication forthcoming).
Whyte, G. (1989) Council Directive 79/7/EEC in Ireland. In Whyte, G. (ed.) *Sex-Equality, Community Rights and Irish Social Welfare Law, The Impact of the Third Equality Directive*, Irish Centre for European Law, Trinity College, Dublin.
Wichert, A. (1988) Die Systematik der Diskriminierung im Rentenrecht. In Gerhard, U., Schwarzer, A. and Slupik, V. (eds) *Auf Kosten der Frauen. Frauenrechte im Sozialstaat*, Weinheim and Basel: Beltz.
Wilensky, H. L., Luebbert, L. M. and Reed Hahn, S. (1987) Comparative Social Policy: Theories, Methods, Findings. In Dierkes, M., Weiler, H. N. and Antal, A. B. (eds) *Comparative Policy Research: learning from experience*, Adershot: Gower.
Wilkinson, R. G. (ed) (1986) *Class and Health: Research and Longitudinal Data*, London: Tavistock.
Wilkinson, R. G. (ed) (1990) *Occupational Incomes and Mortality Rates*, Medical Research Department, University of Sussex.
Williamson, O. E. (1981) The Economics of Organization: The Transaction Cost Approach, *American Journal of Sociology*, 87, pp. 548–557.
Wilson, E. (1977) *Women and the Welfare State*, London: Tavistock.
WISTA (1981) Erwerbslosigkeit im Haushaltszusammenhang. Ergebnis des

Bibliography

Mikrozensus, *Wirtschaft und Statisktik*, pp. 657–663.
Working for Patients (1989) *The Health Service, Caring for the 1990s*, London: HMSO.
Wyatt, S. (1989) Social Security and Information Technology in the UK. Paper presented to the Conference on Comparative Research on Social Security and Information Technology, Stockholm.
Yearbook of Nordic Statistics 1988, vol 27, Stockholm: Nordstedts.
Zachert, U. (1988) Entwicklung und Perspektiven des Normalarbeitsverhältnisses, *WSI-Mitteilungen*, 41, pp. 457–466.
Zapf, W. et al. (1987) *Individualisierung und Sicherheit. Untersuchungen zur Lebensqualität in der Bundesrepublik Deutschland*, München: Beck.
Zaretsky, E. (1982) The Place of the Family in the Origins of the Welfare State. In Thorne, B. and Yalom, M. (eds) *Rethinking the Family: Some Feminist Issues*, New York: Longman.

INDEX

Note: Page numbers in *italics* are figure or table references.

Accord (Australia), 25–6, 101–2, 103
Administration, Departments of, 3, 4
administration, social security, 10–11, 14–15, 230–1
Administrative Law Judges (ALJs), 219–20
aged, resister to change in social security, 72
Aid to Families with Dependent Children (AFDC), 212
    error reduction, 217–18
    generosity reduction, 216–17
    increasing responsiveness, 221
Anglo–American social policy model, 176–7
assets tests, 102, 108
attrition, privatisation strategy, 75–6
Australia
    Accord, 25–6, 101–2, 103
    contributory systems, 155–6
    decommodification, 151–5
    ethnicity, 150, 152
    equivalence scales, 44
    full employment, 159, 160
    income security system, 149–51, 158–63
    income supplementation, 153
    Invalid and Old Age Pensions Act (1908), 95, 97
    invalid pension, 96, 106, 155
    Marxist/feminist paradigm, 146–7
    maternity allowance, 152, 153, 155
    means–testing, 155–8
    poverty, 36–7
    recession, 160
    subsistence, 153
    unemployment benefit, 152–3, 156
    universalism, 95–7, 159, 160
    wage fixation, 24
    welfare state, 22: models of reform, 28, 30–1
    women's movement, 160
    see also old–age pension; salami tactics; widows' pension
Austria, Bismarck social policy model, 175–6
autonomy, 17–18, 23

basic income guarantee/labour market linkages model, 33–4
    full employment, 31–2
    Swedish active labour market policy, 32
    weaknesses, 32–3
basic income model, 33
    citizenship rights, 26–7
    strengths, 27, 28
    weaknesses, 27–8
Belgium
    means–tested benefits, 196, 202, 206–7: single parent families, 200–1; unemployment, 198–200
Bismarck social policy model, 175–6

capitalism
    and future of social security, 74–7
    and unemployment, 138–40
    in the United States, 170–1
caring work
    in West Germany, 171
    and women, 165–6
    work/welfare contract model, 30
child endowment (Australia), 152
child support allowance (Australia), 104, 158
citizenship
    and means–testing, 193–4, 208
    rights, 39–40, 148
    and social justice, 17, 18
civil servants, administrators, 4
claimants
    and fraud, 266–8: investigation, 272–3, 276; penalties, 271–2, 274–5
    and politics, 148
    treatment, 234, 237, 240
class and gender, 13, 145–51, 161–3
    and decommodification, 151–5
    and income security system, 158–61

Index

and means-testing, 155–8
cluster analysis, 53, 54–6
Commonwealth pension (Australia), 152, 155
computerisation, 14–15, 229–30, 241–3
 policy-making, 232–3
 quality of service, 233–4
 solutions to organisational problems, 231–2
Conservatives, privatisation, 71, 74, 79
 creeping privatisation, 75
 economic motivation, 74–5
 ideological motivation, 74
 wealthy groups, motivation, 75
contributory systems, 155–6
 for old-age pensions: in Australia, 98–9; in West Germany, 183
corporatism, 23–4, 25–6

decommodification of labour power, 149, 151–5, 158
Delphi Method, 234–9
demography, resister to change in social security, 73
Denmark
 expenditure on social security, 183
 labour market participation of women, 167
 recession: economic situation, 86–8; expenditure on social security, 81, *82*; political importance, *88*, 89–90; welfare cutbacks, 83, *84*; welfare stability, 90–4
Department of (Health and) Social Security, *see* United Kingdom
Departments of Social Administration, 3, 4
deprivation, 9
 operational measure, 56–7: material deprivation, 58–60; multiple deprivation, 57–8; social deprivation, 58, 60–1
 underclass, 42
DHSS, *see* United Kingdom
Disability Insurance, *see* Social Security Disability Insurance
discretion, 14, 213–16, 227–8
 Aid to Families with Dependent Children, error reduction, 217–18
 and bureaucracy, 220–1, 225–7
 disability insurance, controlling appeals in, 218–20
 generosity reduction, 216–17
 and programme responsiveness, 221–5

discriminant analysis of poverty, 52–3
 assumptions, 53–4
 data validity, 53
 optimal number of groups, 53
 wealth problem, 53
disposable income
 changes, *65*
 and poverty avoidance: in Greater London, *66*; in Islington, *67*
 public opinion, 46–7
 and unemployment, 124
distributive justice, *see* justice, social
DSS, *see* United Kingdom

East Germany, women's status, 178–9
education, 4, 5
 in West Germany, 169–70
egalitarianism
 and corporatist institutions, 25–6
 and social justice, 24
 and universalism, 96
eligibility, Australian welfare state, 151–5
employment
 distribution through service sectors, *172*
 in West Germany, 169–70: growth, 181; and women, 179–82
 women's aspirations, 31
 see also full employment; unemployment
Employment and Training (ET), 222–5
equivalence scales, 43–5
ethnicity, 150, 152
European Commission, poverty definition, 37
European Community, extent of poverty, 35–6
expenditure, *see* welfare state, expenditure

Fabian socialism, 3, 4
family allowance (Australia)
 family income supplement, 153
 income test, 103, 104
 means–tests, 156–7, 158
Family Credit Scheme (UK), 206
Family Income Supplement Scheme (Ireland), 206
Family Support Act (1988) (US), 212–13
feminism
 conception of family, 165
 and corporatism, 25
 and Marxism, 146–7

redistributive model of social
    justice critique, 20–1
  welfare state critique, 148
Finland, recession
  economic situation, 86–8
  expenditure on social security, 81, 82
  political importance, *88*, 89–90
  welfare cutbacks, *84*, 85
  welfare stability, 90–4
fixed–term contracts, and Standard Employment Relationship, 117–18
France, means–testing
  single parent families, 200–1
  unemployment, 198–200
fraud, 15, 265–6, 276–7
  benefit claimants, 266–8: investigation, 272–3, 276; penalties, 271–2, 274–5; stigmatisation, 193
  enterprise and benefit cultures, 276
  taxpayers, 268–9: investigation, 273–4; penalties, 270–2, 275
full employment, 136–7
  Australian welfare state, 159, 160
  autonomy, 23
  capitalism, 138–40
  labour market reform, 24, 31–2
  Marx's 'industrial reserve army', 129–30
  politics, 140–2
  pull–down effects of unemployment, 135–6
futures of social security, 11–12, 70–1
  little or no change, 71, 73–4, 79: ageing of population, 72; demographic factors, 73; single parent families, 73; unemployment growth, 72–3
  Neo–Conservative dream, 71, 74–7, 79
  private welfare states, 72, 77–78, 79

GAIN (Greater Avenues for Independence), 29
gender
  caring work, 165–6
  and class, 13, 145–51, 161–3: and decommodification, 151–5, and income security system, 158–61; and means–testing, 155–8
  dependencies, 9, 149
  division of labour, *178*
  equality and inequality (Sweden), 33

  and irregular employment, 116–17
  and Standard Employment Relationship, 114–15, 121–2
  see also women
Germany, East, women's status, 178–9
Germany, West, 6, 170–1, 183–5
  Bismarck social policy model, 175–6
  education, 169–70
  employment, 169–70, *172*
  expenditure, 169, 170, 183–4
  irregular employment patterns, 110–11: changing labour market, 115–22; future of the SER, 125–6; impoverishment, 122–5; Standard Employment Relationship (SER), 111–15
  means–testing: earnings-replacement ratio, 203; entitlement conditions, 204; introduction, 205; single parent families, 200–1; unemployment, 198–200
  non-take-up, 194
  pension scheme, contributory, 98
  poverty, 164–7
  social policy, 167, 169
  unemployment, 130–3, 141–2, 184–5
  universalism, 184
  wages, 171, *173*
  welfare mix, 13–14, 166
  women: employment, 179–82; old-age poverty, 182–3; status, 177–9
government intervention in labour market, 23–4
Great Britain, *see* United Kingdom
GAIN (Greater Avenues for Independence), 29
Greece, labour market participation of women, 167
Grey Power Movement (Australia), 105

handicapped child's allowance (Australia), 153
higher education, 4, 5
human needs
  narrowing definition, 23
  social democratic views, 20

impoverishment, and unemployment, 122–5
income, disposable, *see* disposable income
income distribution, equivalence scale, 43–5

Index

income inequality, 41
  and trade unions, 24
income inequality standard, 37–8
income security system (Australia), 149–51, 161–3
  and redistribution, 158–61
income supplementation (Australia), 153
income support scheme (UK)
  and interorganisational relations, 261
  and transitional protection, 47
income test (Australia), 102–4
individualism
  and privatisation, 74
  in social contract models, 17
  and women, 166–7
'industrial reserve army', Marx's, 129–30
information, as task resource, 251
information technology, *see* computerisation
Inland Revenue, *see* tax
institutional arrangements
  resister to change in social security, 73–4
  for social justice, 18
interorganisational relations, 15, 249, 257–9, 262–3
  approaches, 249–50
  cooperation, 256–7, 258
  dependence: resources, 250; unilateral, 252–4
  income maintenance agencies, 261–2
  operationalisation of goals, 254–6
  resources, 250, 252: maintenance resources, 250–1; task resources, 251–2
  restructuring, 260–1
  staff reactions, 259–60
Invalid and Old–Age Pensions Act (1908) (Australia) 95, 97
invalid pension (Australia)
  and means–testing, 155
  policy intervention, 106
  and universalism, 96
Ireland, means–testing
  earnings–related supplements, 203–4
  introduction, 205–6
  single parent families, 200–1
  unemployment, 198–200
  see also United Kingdom
irregular employment patterns, 110–11, 115–16

fixed–term contracts, 117–18
part–time work, 116–117
self–employment, 119
teleworking, 119–20
temporary work, 118–19

Japan, private welfare states, 77
justice, social, 11, 16–18, 230–31
  conception, 21–2
  labour market reform, 23–6
  principles, 22–3
  redistributive model, 19: feminist critique, 20–1; social democratic critique, 19–20
  welfare state reform, models, 26: basic income, 26–8, 33; basic income guarantee/labour market linkages, 31–3, 34; work/welfare contract, 28–31, 33–4

Keynes, *see* full employment

labour market
  and class, 147–8
  decommodification, *see* decommodification of labour power
  and gender, 147–8, *178*
  inequalities, 9, 12
  participation of women, 167, *168*, *175*, *179*
  redistributive justice, 22–3
  reform: dual strategy, 24–5; egalitarian corporatist institutions, 25–6; intervention, by government and trade unions, 23–4
  trade unions, 30
labour market linkages/basic income guarantee model, 33–4
  full employment, 31–2
  Swedish active labour market policy, 32
  weaknesses, 32–3
liberal model of old–age pensions (Australia), 108–9
long–term unemployment, *199*
  see also unemployment
Luxembourg Income Study, 36, 43

marginalisation, social, 9, 13
  of the unemployed, 128
  of women, 164–5
Marx
  and feminism, 146–7

'industrial reserve army', 129–30
material deprivation, 58–60
material resources, and
    interorganisational relations,
    251
maternity allowance (Australia), 152,
    155
    abolition, 153
means–testing, 14, 155–8, 188, 207–8
    and citizenship, 193–4, 208
    clientele, 196–7: political effects,
      189, 202–7; single parent
      families, 200–1; unemployment,
      197–200
    and deprivation, 9
    dysfunctions: non–take–up, 194–6;
      poverty trap, 189–91; social
      division, 191–4
    functions, 188–9
    old–age pensions (Australia), 97,
      108: abolition, 99–101; re–
      imposition, 102–3
minimal definition of income, 41–2
minimum income
    and poverty, 40: public opinion,
      45–51
    in West Germany, 125–6
minimum rights to resources, 39–40
modern welfare state model, 174–5
modernisation
    of social security, 187
    and women, 167
multiple deprivation
    measurement, 49–51, 57–8: material
      deprivation, 49, 58–60;
      social deprivation, 49, 58, 60–1
    poverty threshold, 49, 50–1
    weekly income for avoidance, *68,
      69*
needs, human
    narrowing definition, 23
    social democratic views, 20
Neo–Conservatives, *see* Conservatives,
    privatisation
Netherlands, 6
    income inequality, decrease, 41
    means–testing: earnings–replace-
      ment ratio, 203; entitlement
      conditions, 204; introduction,
      204–5; single parent families,
      200–1; unemployment, 198–200
    non-take-up of benefits, 194
    poverty trap, 190–1
    social assistance beneficiaries, *203*
non–take–up of benefits, 194–6, 268

Norway
    egalitarianism, 24
    interorganisational relations, 258–9,
      262–3: income maintenance
      agencies, 261–2; mandatory
      cooperation, 258; restructuring,
      260–1; staff reactions, 260; social
      assistance, 257–8
    recession: economic situation, 86–8;
      expenditure on social security,
      81, *82*; political importance, *88,
      89*–90; welfare cutbacks, 83, *84,
      85*; welfare stability, 90–4
oil prices, effect on recession, 80, 83
old–age pension
    in Australia: contributory schemes,
      99–101; decommodification,
      151–2, 154, 155; future, 106–8
    Grey Power movement, 105;
      history, 97–9, 151–2; liberal
      model, 108–9; means–testing,
      102–4; universalism, 96–7
    and women, 165: in West Ger-
      many, 182–3
one–parent families, *see* single parent
    families
Operational Strategy, 229–30, 241–3
    policy–making, 232–3
    quality of service, 233–4
    solutions to organisational
      problems, 231–2
outworking, and Standard Employ-
    ment Relationship, 119–20

part–time work
    and Standard Employment
      Relationship, 116–17
    and women, *180*
pension, *see* invalid pension; old–age
    pension; widows' pension
politics
    and claimants, 148
    and means–testing, 189, 202–7
    as resister to change in social
      security, 73
    and unemployment, 140–2
poverty
    adequacy of disposable incomes,
      46–8
    alleviation, 104–5
    analysis: cluster, 54–6; discrimi-
      nant, 52–4
    avoidance, 11
    deprivation, 56–8: material, 58–60;
      social, 60–1

Index

economic perspectives: absolute and relative poverty, 39–40; income and social needs, 38–9; poverty definition, 37–8
equivalence scales, 43–5
extent (UK), 41, *64*
income inequality, 41
London survey, 61–3
means-testing: non-take-up, 194–6; poverty trap, 189–91; stigmatisation, 192–3
measurement, 35–7
minimalist definition, 41–2
in old-age, 182–3
participation standard of income: objective evidence, 48–51; subjective evidence, 45–6
social needs of people, 40–1
subsistence, 40, 42–43
underclass, 42
universalism, 96
and women, 165, 182–183
private welfare states, 72, 79
description, 77
supporters, 78
privatisation strategies, 74
attrition, 75–6
tax relief, 76
user charges, 76
professional training for social security, 5–7
protection, and social justice, 17, 23
pull–down effects, 13, 136–7
of unemployment, 128–9, 133–6: Marx's 'industrial reserve army', 129–30; in West Germany, 130–3, 141–2; trade unions, 132

Quality Assessment Package (QAP), 233

race, in Australia, 150, 152
Rawls, John, social justice, 16, 18, 19
feminist critique, 20–1
social democratic critique, 19–20
recession
in Australia, 160
reduction of social expenditure, 23
in Scandinavia, 12, 80–1: economic situation, 85–8; expenditure on social security, 81, *82*; political importance, *88*, 89–90; welfare cutbacks, 81, 83–5; welfare stability, 90–4

redistributive justice, *see* justice, social
referrals, as task resource, 251
research funding, 4–5
residual social policy model, 177
residualism, 23
resources
and interorganisational relations, 250–2
minimum rights, 39–40
retrenchment of welfare state, 183–5

salami tactics, 12
economic context, 101
future, 108
modifications to selectivity, 99–100: contributory schemes, 100–1
political context, 101–2
poverty alleviation, 104–5
social security, purposes of, 105
universalism, 95–7, 102–4
Scandinavia
corporatism, 23–4
modern welfare state model, 174–5
recession, 12, 80–81: economic situation, 85–8; expenditure on social security, 81, *82*; political importance, *88*, 89–90; welfare cutbacks, 81, 83–5; welfare stability, 90–4
Scotland, interorganisational relations, 258–9, 262–3
income maintenance agencies, 261–2
mandatory cooperation, 258
restructuring, 261
social assistance, 257
staff reactions, 259–60
see also United Kingdom
selectivity, in Australia, 99–101
self–employment, and Standard Employment Relationship, 119
SER, *see* Standard Employment Relationship
service sectors, distribution of employment, *172*
single parent families
and means–tests, 157, 200–1
as resisters to change in social security, 73
Social Administration, Departments of, 3, 4
social contract models, 17
social democratic welfare state, 71
redistributive model of social justice, critique, 19–20

social deprivation, 58, 60–1
social division, and means–testing, 191–4
social justice, *see* justice, social
social obligations of people, 40–1
social security, 1, 8–9
    administration, 10–11, 14–15, 230–1
    fraud, 265–6, 276–7: claimants, 266–8; investigation, 272–3, 276; penalties, 271–2, 274–5
    future, *see* futures of social security
    history (Australia), 97–9
    purposes (Australia), 105
    reform (Australia), 22
    training, 5–7
    see also welfare state
Social Security Disability Insurance (SSDI) (US), 214, 216
    administration study, 10
    controlling appeals, 218–20
sociology, 1, 7–11
sociology of social security, 3–7, 187–8
Soviet Union, extent of poverty, 37
Special Claims Control units (SCCs), 267, 272–3
stability of welfare state, in Scandinavia
    contributory factors, 93–4
    finance, 91–2
    labour market orientation, 92
    selectivity, 90–1
staff, as task resource, 251
Standard Employment Relationship (SER), 12–13
    development, 111–12
    employer reaction, 115
    functions, 113–14
    future, 125–6
    gender imbalance, 114–15
    irregular employment, 115–22
    limitations, 112–13
standards of living, and poverty, 39–40
stigmatisation, and means–testing, 192–93
stratification, *see* marginalisation
subsistence, 40
    abolishment, 42
    Australian welfare state, 153
superannuation (Australia), 103–4
supplementary benefits (UK), 157
supporting parent's allowance (Australia), 153, 157
Sweden, 6
    active labour market policy, 32–3
    egalitarianism, 24

    employment principle, 30
    expenditure on social security, 183
    poverty measurement, 38
    recession: economic situation, 86–8; expenditure on social security, 81, 82; political importance, *88*, 89–90; welfare cutbacks, *84*, 85; welfare stability, 90–4
    social policy, 169
    solidaristic wages policy, 24

tax, *173*
    frauds, 265–6, 276–7: investigation, 273–4; penalties, 270–2; tax-payers, 268–9
    public opinion, 48
tax/benefit system, 24
tax relief, as privatisation strategy, 76
tax/transfer system, 159–60, 161
teleworking, and Standard Employment Relationship, 119–20
temporary work, and Standard Employment Relationship, 118–19
trade unions
    and income inequality, 24
    and labour market, 30
    and unemployment, 132, 134
    training, 4, 6

underclass, effect of deprivation, 42
unemployment, 12–13, 136–7
    benefit: Australia, 152–3, 156; West Germany, 184–5
    and capitalism, 138–40
    and disposable income, 124
    European levels, *197*
    and impoverishment, 31, 122–5
    insurance, 135, 140
    and irregular employment patterns, 120–1
    and means–tests, 197–200
    and politics, 140–2
    pull–down effects, 128–9, 133–5: Marx's 'industrial reserve army', 129–30; in West Germany, 130–3
    as resister to change in social security, 72–3
    youth unemployment, *198*
unions, *see* trade unions
United Kingdom, 3–7
    administrative justice, 230–1
    consultation, 234–40
    employment, in service sectors,

Index

168, 171
expenditure on social security, 161, 183
Family Credit Scheme, 206
full employment, 31
income security system, 150, 154, 161
income support scheme, 261: and phasing out of transitional protection, 47
means–testing: earnings–related supplements, 203; entitlement conditions, 204; introduction, 206; non–take–up, 194; poverty trap, 190–1; single parent families, 200–1; social assistance beneficiaries, *202;* unemployment, 198–200
poverty measurement: equivalence scales, 43–5; extent of poverty, 41; income inequality, 41; minimalist definition, 41–2; social needs of people, 40–1; subsistence, 40, 42–3; underclass, 42
social policy, 169: residual model, 177
'whole person' concept, 234, 240
see also computerisation; interorganisational relations; fraud
United States
Anglo–American social policy model, 176–7
capitalism, 170 –1
and discretion, 212–13, 227–8: Aid to Families with Dependent Children, 216–18; bureaucracy, 220–221, 225–7; programme responsiveness, 221–2; Social Security Disability Insurance, 214, 216, 218–20
employment, distribution through service sectors, *172*
Employment and Training (ET), 222–5
expenditure, social security, 161
Family Support Act (1988), 212–13
income security system, 150, 154, 161
poverty extent, 36
social policy, 167, 169
wages, 173
work/welfare contract model, 28–9: criticisms, 30

universalism
in Australia, 95–7, 159, 160: pensions, 98; salami tactics, 102–4
in Scandinavia, 174–5
in West Germany , 184
user charges, as privatisation strategy, 76

wage fixation (Australia), 24
in West Germany, 171, 173
in the United States, 173
welfare mix, 13–14, 166
welfare state, 22, 71
cutbacks, in Scandinavia, 81, 83–5
expenditure: in recession, 23, 161, 183; in Scandinavia, 81, *82*; in West Germany, 169, 170, 183–4
and feminism, 148
future (Australia), 105–9
justice, 19
models: Anglo-American, 176–7; Bismarck, 175–6; modern, 174–5; residual, 177
models of reform, 26: basic income, 26–8; basic income guarantee/ labour market linkages, 31–3; work/welfare contract, 28–31
private, 72, 77–9
recession, 80
retrenchment , 183–5
stability, in Scandinavia: contributory factors, 93–4; finance, 91–2; labour market orientation, 92; selectivity, 90–1
see also social security
West Germany, *see* Germany, West
'whole person' concept, 234, 240
widows' pension (Australia), 152
means–testing, 157
phasing out, 103, 153
universalism, 96
women, 14
caring services, 171
education, 170
employment, 31, 170, 179–182
labour market participation, 167, *168, 175, 179*
old–age poverty, 182–3
poverty and marginality, 164–7
status, 177–9
and welfare state models, 174–7
and welfare state retrenchment, 183–5
see also gender

women's movement, 25–6, 160
work/welfare contract model, 33–4
   caring work, 30–1
   compulsion to work, 28–9

trade unions, 30

youth unemployment, *198*